Business
Plans
Handbook

Business Plans

A COMPILATION OF BUSINESS PLANS DEVELOPED BY INDIVIDUALS THROUGHOUT NORTH AMERICA

Handbook

VOLUME

17

**Lynn M. Pearce,
Project Editor**

GALE
CENGAGE Learning

Detroit • New York • San Francisco • New Haven, Conn • Waterville, Maine • London

Business Plans Handbook, Volume 17

Project Editor: Lynn M. Pearce

Product Manager: Jenai Drouillard

Product Design: Jennifer Wahi

Composition and Electronic Prepress: Evi Seoud

Manufacturing: Rita Wimberley

For product information and technology assistance, contact us at
Gale Customer Support, 1-800-877-4253.
For permission to use material from this text or product,
submit all requests online at **www.cengage.com/permissions.**
Further permissions questions can be emailed to
permissionrequest@cengage.com

While every effort has been made to ensure the reliability of the information presented in this publication, Gale, a part of Cengage Learning, does not guarantee the accuracy of the data contained herein. Gale accepts no payment for listing; and inclusion in the publication of any organization, agency, institution, publication, service, or individual does not imply endorsement of the editors or publisher. Errors brought to the attention of the publisher and verified to the satisfaction of the publisher will be corrected in future editions.

Gale
27500 Drake Rd.
Farmington Hills, MI, 48331-3535

ISBN-13: 978-14144-4571-7
1084-4473

Printed in the United States of America
1 2 3 4 5 6 7 12 11 10

Contents

CONTENTS

Highlights

Business Plans Handbook, Volume 17 (BPH-17) is a collection of business plans compiled by entrepreneurs seeking funding for small businesses throughout North America. For those looking for examples of how to approach, structure, and compose their own business plans, *BPH-17* presents 20 sample plans, including plans for the following businesses:

- Apparel Manufacturer
- Architecture Firm
- Bed and Breakfast
- Bookkeeping Practice
- Children's Bookstore
- Currency Trading
- Dog Training Business
- Health Advocacy Business
- Healthcare Translation & Interpretation Business
- Home Repair and Improvement Contractor
- Microbrewery
- Mobile Veterinary Practice
- Mortgage Banking Firm
- Oil and Gas Manufacturing and Services Company
- Organic Lawn Care Services
- Pipeline Fracture Testing Service
- Safety Consulting Firm
- Self-Service Laundry Business
- Solar Energy Farm
- Utilities Reclamation Services

FEATURES AND BENEFITS

BPH-17 offers many features not provided by other business planning references including:

- Twenty business plans, each of which represent an attempt at clarifying (for themselves and others) the reasons that the business should exist or expand and why a lender should fund the enterprise.
- Two fictional plans that are used by business counselors at a prominent small business development organization as examples for their clients. (You will find these in the Business Plan Template Appendix.)
- A directory section that includes: listings for venture capital and finance companies, which specialize in funding start-up and second-stage small business ventures, and a comprehensive

listing of Service Corps of Retired Executives (SCORE) offices. In addition, the Appendix also contains updated listings of all Small Business Development Centers (SBDCs); associations of interest to entrepreneurs; Small Business Administration (SBA) Regional Offices; and consultants specializing in small business planning and advice. It is strongly advised that you consult supporting organizations while planning your business, as they can provide a wealth of useful information.

- A Small Business Term Glossary to help you decipher the sometimes confusing terminology used by lenders and others in the financial and small business communities.

- A cumulative index, outlining each plan profiled in the complete Business Plans Handbook series.

- A Business Plan Template which serves as a model to help you construct your own business plan. This generic outline lists all the essential elements of a complete business plan and their components, including the Summary, Business History and Industry Outlook, Market Examination, Competition, Marketing, Administration and Management, Financial Information, and other key sections. Use this guide as a starting point for compiling your plan.

- Extensive financial documentation required to solicit funding from small business lenders. You will find examples of: Cash Flows, Balance Sheets, Income Projections, and other financial information included with the textual portions of the plan.

Introduction

Perhaps the most important aspect of business planning is simply doing it. More and more business owners are beginning to compile business plans even if they don't need a bank loan. Others discover the value of planning when they must provide a business plan for the bank. The sheer act of putting thoughts on paper seems to clarify priorities and provide focus. Sometimes business owners completely change strategies when compiling their plan, deciding on a different product mix or advertising scheme after finding that their assumptions were incorrect. This kind of healthy thinking and re-thinking via business planning is becoming the norm. The editors of *Business Plans Handbook, Volume 17 (BPH-17)* sincerely hope that this latest addition to the series is a helpful tool in the successful completion of your business plan, no matter what the reason for creating it.

This seventeenth volume, like each volume in the series, offers business plans used and created by real people. *BPH-17* provides 20 business plans. The business and personal names and addresses and general locations have been changed to protect the privacy of the plan authors.

NEW BUSINESS OPPORTUNITIES

As in other volumes in the series, *BPH-17* finds entrepreneurs engaged in a wide variety of creative endeavors. Examples include a proposal for an apparel manufacturing firm, an architectural firm, and a bed and breakfast. In addition, several other plans are provided, including a health advocacy business, a mobile veterinary practice, an organic lawn care service, and a safety consulting firm, among others.

Comprehensive financial documentation has become increasingly important as today's entrepreneurs compete for the finite resources of business lenders. Our plans illustrate the financial data generally required of loan applicants, including Income Statements, Financial Projections, Cash Flows, and Balance Sheets.

ENHANCED APPENDIXES

In an effort to provide the most relevant and valuable information for our readers, we have updated the coverage of small business resources. For instance, you will find: a directory section, which includes listings of all of the Service Corps of Retired Executives (SCORE) offices; an informative glossary, which includes small business terms; and a cumulative index, outlining each plan profiled in the complete Business Plans Handbook series. In addition we have updated the list of Small Business Development Centers (SBDCs); Small Business Administration Regional Offices; venture capital and finance companies, which specialize in funding start-up and second-stage small business enterprises; associations of interest to entrepreneurs; and consultants, specializing in small business advice and planning. For your reference, we have also reprinted the business plan template, which provides a comprehensive overview of the essential components of a business plan and two fictional plans used by small business counselors.

SERIES INFORMATION

If you already have the first sixteen volumes of *BPH*, with this seventeenth volume, you will now have a collection of over 360 business plans (not including the one updated plan in the second volume, whose original appeared in the first, or the two fictional plans in the Business Plan Template Appendix section of the second, third, fourth, fifth, sixth, and seventh volumes); contact information for hundreds of organizations and agencies offering business expertise; a helpful business plan template; more than 1,500 citations to valuable small business development material; and a comprehensive glossary of terms to help the business planner navigate the sometimes confusing language of entrepreneurship.

ACKNOWLEDGEMENTS

The Editors wish to sincerely thank the contributors to *BPH-17*, including:

- Laura Becker
- BizPlanDB.com
- Paul Greenland
- Kari Lucke
- Gerald Rekve and Elisha Violet Rekve, Corporate Management Consultants

COMMENTS WELCOME

Your comments on *Business Plans Handbook* are appreciated. Please direct all correspondence, suggestions for future volumes of *BPH*, and other recommendations to the following:

Managing Editor, Business Product
Business Plans Handbook
Gale, a part of Cengage Learning
27500 Drake Rd.
Farmington Hills, MI 48331-3535
Phone: (248)699-4253
Fax: (248)699-8052
Toll-Free: 800-347-GALE
E-mail: BusinessProducts@gale.com

Apparel Manufacturer

TTK Outdoor Apparel Company

789 Pine Grove
Port Huron, Michigan 48060

Gerald Rekve

TTK Outdoor Apparel's mission is to lead our market category in green clothing, made in USA Clothing for our clients. We will not be the low price product, however our mission to own the medium market we will operate in.

EXECUTIVE SUMMARY

What is old is new again; we will be opening a business that existed profitably in the past but failed because a large USA retailer went broke leaving us with large loss. This loss knocked us down but not out. Our new company is well funded with a $200,000 investment from an angel investor. With this funding we will be rolling our name banded clothing lines for next season. Already we have $600,000 in sales commitments from past clients and we have yet to attend any trade show clothing shows.

We will be selling the same branded products we did in the past, with a few sublet changes to meet current trends to the market. Also we will be adding some product lines that we see the value in. The only major change we have decided upon was to have all our products manufactured in the USA, more specifically in New York.

There will be an ownership change, with the angel investor taking 51% of the ownership and David Smith owning the rest. David Smith will manage all day-to-day activities of the business. Along with this, there will be two new positions added to the managing and running of the company. There will be a Marketing Manager and an Online Content Manager; these both will be there to boost the sales focus of the business.

MISSION

It will be our mission to lead our market category in clothing made in USA for our clients. We will not be the low price product; however our mission is to own the medium market we will operate in. We will measure this by watching our competitors to see if they adopt any of our manufacturing traits; this will tell us we are in the lead.

COMPANY OVERVIEW

TTK Outdoor Apparel Company LLC is an old company that went bankrupt in the mid 2000's. However in 2009 the former founder of the company decided to reopen after he was given a reprieve by an angel investor. The investor gave Sam Brown $200,000 for 51% of the company's trademark sportswear. When the company was operating the year before closing, the revenues were $2.5 million dollars. The main reason the company closed in the 2006 was due to a supplier agreement it had with a large American retailer that went bankrupt and left the holding company for TTK Outdoor Apparel Company LLC being owed close to $1.3 million dollars after everything was said and done. This resulted in the holding company having to close because the loss from the one major department store resulted in a loss for the year of $2.3 million dollars.

The revamped company now has new contracts in place with retailers requiring a 35% cash payment in advance of shipment of goods to store and the balance to be paid a week prior to confirmed shipment of order to that store. While the clothing business can be difficult, considering what happened in the past, TTK Outdoor Apparel Company LLC did not adopt the industry standard of 100% payment of order 6 months in advance of season. It was felt that this may be too hard on small retailers. The major focus of TTK Outdoor Apparel Company LLC is to target small retailers and only supply large retailer chains if they meet 100% prepayment requirements.

The old company never had a single write–off from medium to small retailers; this is the major reason why TTK Outdoor Apparel Company LLC has adopted the new policy.

The angle investor will stay with the company for as long as it exists. This means the $200,000 will be paid back at 11% interest per year over a 5 year period. Once all paid back, the angel investor will remain 51% shareholder. While the angel investor will be the major shareholder, the partner will take the CEO role and run all the day-to-day operations of the firm.

INVESTMENT & OWNERSHIP

TTK Outdoor Apparel Company LLC will be owned jointly by David Smith and an angel investor. The investor will invest $200,000 in the firm and David Smith will, in turn, give all his trade markets for the clothing line to the company and the angel investor.

*   David Smith—49%

*   Angel investor—51%

START–UP COSTS

Start-up expenses

Clothes manufacturing	$50,000
Sales & marketing	$20,000
Tradeshows	$ 5,000
Travel	$20,000
Hotel	$15,000
Samples	$10,000
Shipping/Courier	$ 2,000
Telephone	$ 1,000
Legal	$12,000
Accounting	$ 4,000
Business licence	$ 250
Insurance	$ 1,200
Meals	$ 2,000
Copies/flyers/etc	$ 1,500
Office expense	$10,000
Staffing for first 3 months, then cash flows cover this expense	$65,000
Misc other	$ 1,000
Advertising	$ 5,000
Business plan writing by management consulting firm	$ 4,500

The balance of the funds will be used where needed.

Both David Smith and the angle investor will sign off on all expenses and checks written for the company.

PRODUCT MANUFACTURING

All the products will be produced by a New York-based company. You may ask why we are not going off shore to get the clothes made. It is simple—the price we are getting it produced for in New York is only 12% higher than overseas. We know our price points will be higher than competitors' similar products, however our brand is well known and accepted by our target group.

The quality factor we know will be top notch by this company because they are sourced by some very well known brands in the USA.

We will start off with the roll out of the 2010 spring line of coats and jerseys. This will get the cash flows running and put our name out to the public again.

We will be making some changes to our line up of product design and colors; this will be to meet current trends in the market.

We also will be introducing a new hoodie with layered pocket design that allows for storage of various types of smart phones.

All the original design patents are still in place; David Smith still has them under lock and key. Once the company is signed off on by all parties, these design patents will be given to the production company in New York to start tooling up.

MARKETING & SALES

Once the investment is in place, David Smith will hire the sales and marketing manager to oversee the roll out of the product lines. The research has shown that there is enough time to get ready for the major clothing shows that all the retailers attend each season. The spec lines will be produced and the models hired to attend the shows. Normally about 70% of a company's first season sales revenue can be attributed to the attendance of the shows.

Addition to the clothing shows, TTK Outdoor Apparel Company LLC will also set up an online presence that was not available back in 2005 to the extent it is in 2009. The online store will have full shopping cart functions that will also for people throughout the world to buy the clothes we offer. With the online store we will make sure we are always 15% higher that what our retailers sell our products for. This way we will try not to compete with our clients stores. We know this may be hard to manage because our clients might be getting higher margins based on where they are located. We will make sure to tell our clients to check our website and if our prices are lower than theirs, to tell us as quickly as possible. If we do get hits from that client's region, we will adjust our pricing to meet this new requirement.

ADVERTISING & MARKETING

TTK Outdoor Apparel Company LLC will focus its advertising on the following areas:

- Direct mail
- Billboard
- Magazine

- Internet search
- Newspaper
- TV specialty channels
- Sports events
- Special events
- Free product give–aways to non profits

All of the advertising will focus on the product style as well function of the clothing lines. The function of the clothing will play an important part of the advertising in that each advertisement will carry a theme showing the reader or viewer of the ad the variety of functions of the clothing. The end user of the clothing will see the advantage of the advertised product and how it will relate to their daily life.

STAFFING

- Brian Smith—CEO
- Sue McMaster—Marketing Manager
- Harry Quiton—Distribution Manager
- Guy Lebank—Online Content Manager/Developer
- Gerade PonseyvTheme Sales Manager/Tradeshow Manager

PAYROLL

- Brian Smith, CEO—$65,000 plus 5% of gross sales and 49% share of the net profit
- Sue McMaster, Marketing Manager—$45,000 plus 1% gross sales, plus a $5,000 bonus if sales quota is met
- Harry Quiton, Distribution Manager—$45,000 plus 1% of gross sales plus a $5,000 bonus if sales quota is met
- Guy Lebank, Online Content Manager/Developer—$45,000 plus 1% of gross sales and a $5,000 bonus if sales quota is met
- Gerade Ponsey, Theme Sales Manager/Tradeshow Manager—$33,000 plus 1% of gross sales and a $5,000 bonus if sales quota is met

Angel Investor—Paid back his original investment with monthly payments over 48 months, and then 51% of the net profit. However it was agreed based on the companies' success that half of this would be reinvested into the company in order to grow it.

All bonuses are paid on a quarterly basis or annually for the $5,000 bonus.

PRODUCTS

We will carry a few different products, some of which we used to carry with the old company and new ones we have just developed, and products that we will create in the future to meet our market's requirements.

Here is a list of products, keeping in mind that they will increase as we move forward.

Hoodie—This product is one of those we used for the old company. We will carry all sizes of this product and all current colors the market generally uses. The Hoodie will have new features and features that will vary between models we carry. For example we have put together a list of the models below with some of the features that each model will have.

Standard Hoodie—This hoodie will be simple in design; it will have our small logo on the front left chest and two small logos on the cuffs on the outer edge of the wrist. The logo will be 3/8 inch x 5/8 inch. It will have V-neck with a hood that lies on the back of the person wearing it.

Teen's Hoodie—This hoodie will be an outgoing design and will have a large abstract image on the front and back. This image will be tested to meet the requirements of the teen market. Also, the hoodie will have our small logo on the front left chest and two small logos on the cuffs on the outer edge of the wrist. The logo will be 3/8 inch x 5/8 inch. The hoodie will also have a full length zipper with a hood that lies on the back of the person wearing it. In addition, it will have two arm pockets, a front pocket and an inside pocket.

Adult Hoodie—This hoodie will be designed to attract the adult wearer; will have our small logo on the front left chest and two small logos on the cuffs on the outer edge of the wrist. The logo will be 3/8 inch x 5/8 inch. A zipper will be full length with a hood that zips into a small pocket around the neck. There will be no images on these units. There will be a number of fabrics used to build this Hoodie to meet the adult market for both men and women.

Rain Coat—This product will be made out of water resistant material, be light weight and offered in a variety of colors. The design will focus on both the teen market and the adult market, with each having design attributes that will attract both markets.

Pants—This product will also be built to attract both markets of the teen and the adult market.

Hats—This is a growing market with more people wearing hats.

COMPETITION

There is considerable competition in this market; we fully understand this. Our market is driven mostly on style, image, branding and so on. Our brand is in a good position because we were in the market in the past and have a solid track record of sales success. A large USA retailer went out of business owing our former company a substantial amount of money, forcing us to close our business—if it was not for that, we would still be in business. From our understanding the large retailer sales of our product was in their top five sellers. This meant there was little inventory left for us to collect when they went out of business.

In this area there are a number of major suppliers for these product types. All of these sellers have their products produced in Asia; the quality completely depends on which plant is manufacturing the products. We have seen a slip in quality for example with some of the new products rolled out by Nike in the past year. We know this is a result of Nike trying to stay profitable while continuing to supply North America's largest retailer (without giving a name we will use the letter W to tell you who this retailer is).

We will not be selling to this retailer so, therefore, we can maintain product quality.

Entering this market after being out of it for two years, we will start with a market share of 0%. Our goal by the end of year one is to have 1% of the market. We know this may not seem like a lot, but with close to one billion dollars in sales of these products in USA, this will mean we will end up with $1 million dollars in gross sales. Front contact with old clients, we have already gotten commitments of $600,000 in sales. This is not bad with 12 months left in the year for us to get the balance of $400,000 to meet out sales goal for year one.

PROFIT AND LOSS

Pro forma profit and loss	2008	2009	2010
Sales	$1,000,000	$ 5,000,000	$ 7,000,000
Direct cost of sales	$ 400,000	$ 4,000,000	$ 5,000,000
Other	$ 53,000	$ 58,000	$ 59,000
Total cost of sales			
Gross margin	$3,550,000	$35,950,000	$107,950,000
Gross margin %	71.00%	71.90%	71.97%
Expenses			
Payroll	$ 522,000	$ 300,000	$ 700,000
Sales and marketing and other expenses	$ 230,000	$ 340,000	$ 430,000
Depreciation			
Communications	$ 26,400	$ 90,000	$ 150,000
Client relations	$ 24,000	$ 120,000	$ 200,000
Rent	$ 9,600	$ 30,000	$ 30,000
Payroll taxes	$ 84,783	$ 120,000	$ 150,000

Architecture Firm

Smith Architecture Firm, Inc.

123 5th Ave.
New York, NY 10002

BizPlanDB.com

The purpose of this business plan is to raise $125,000 for the development of an architectural design firm while showcasing the expected financials and operations over the next three years.

EXECUTIVE SUMMARY

The purpose of this business plan is to raise $125,000 for the development of an architectural design firm while showcasing the expected financials and operations over the next three years. Smith Architecture Firm, Inc. ("the Company") is a New York-based corporation that will provide design of new facilities, design services for renovating existing facilities, and project management to customers in its targeted market. The Company was founded in 2009 by John Smith.

The Services

As stated above, the primary function of the Company will be to provide architectural design and drafting services for new and existing structures undergoing renovation. At the onset of operations, the Company intends to have a staff of three licensed architects (including the owner) as well as a three member drafting staff. The Company will earn substantial gross margins on the services provided by Smith Architecture Firm.

To a limited extent, the Company will also provide project management services as it relates to the development and renovation of properties and buildings. This will be an important source of secondary revenue for the firm.

The third section of the business plan will further describe the services offered by Smith Architecture Firm.

Financing

Mr. Smith is seeking to raise $125,000 from as a bank loan. The interest rate and loan agreement are to be further discussed during negotiation. This business plan assumes that the business will receive a 10 year loan with a 9% fixed interest rate. The financing will be used for the following:

- Development of the Company's office location.

- Financing for the first six months of operation.

- Capital to purchase computers and CAD software.

Mr. Smith will contribute $10,000 to the venture.

Mission Statement

Smith Architecture Firm's mission is to become the recognized leader in its targeted market for architectural design and project management services.

Management Team

The Company was founded by John Smith. Mr. Smith has more than 10 years of experience as an architect. Through his expertise, he will be able to bring the operations of the business to profitability within its first year of operations.

Sales Forecasts

Mr. Smith expects a strong rate of growth at the start of operations. Below are the expected financials over the next three years.

Proforma profit and loss (yearly)

Year	2009	2010	2011
Sales	$726,978	$799,676	$863,650
Operating costs	$432,886	$447,846	$463,149
EBITDA	$185,319	$232,179	$271,278
Taxes, interest, and depreciation	$ 87,736	$100,923	$115,266
Net profit	**$ 97,583**	**$131,256**	**$156,012**

Sales, operating costs, and profit forecast

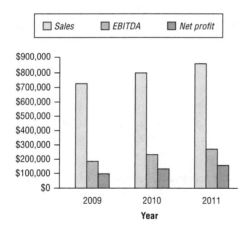

Expansion Plan

The Founder expects that the business will aggressively expand during the first three years of operation. Mr. Smith intends to implement marketing campaigns that will effectively target individuals, contractors, and real estate developers within the target market.

COMPANY AND FINANCING SUMMARY

Registered Name and Corporate Structure

Smith Architecture Firm, Inc. is registered as a corporation in the State of New York.

Required Funds

At this time, Smith Architecture Firm requires $125,000 of debt funds in addition to the $10,000 contributed by John Smith. Below is a breakdown of how these funds will be used:

Projected startup costs

Initial lease payments and deposits	$ 20,000
Working capital	$ 28,000
FF&E	$ 27,000
Leasehold improvements	$ 5,000
Security deposits	$ 5,000
Insurance	$ 2,500
Computers and CAD software	$ 35,000
Marketing budget	$ 7,500
Miscellaneous and unforeseen costs	$ 5,000
Total startup costs	**$135,000**

Use of funds

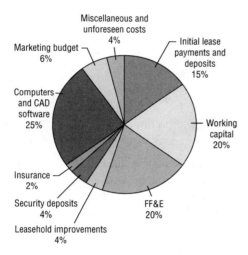

Investor Equity

Mr. Smith is not seeking an investment from a third party at this time.

Management Equity

John Smith owns 100% of Smith Architecture Firm, Inc.

Exit Strategy

If the business is very successful, Mr. Smith may seek to sell the business to a third party for a significant earnings multiple. Most likely, the Company will hire a qualified business broker to sell the business on behalf of Smith Architecture Firm. Based on historical numbers, the business could fetch a sales premium of up to 5 to 7 times earnings.

PRODUCTS AND SERVICES

Below is a description of the architectural and project management services offered by the Company.

Architectural Design Services

The primary focus of the Company's services is to provide design and development of architectural plans for new constructions and buildings/properties that are undergoing renovation. Smith Architecture Firm will work closely with both individual clients and real estate developers to ensure that they have the proper plans (with aesthetic appeal) for their properties and developments. The business will also work closely with structural engineering firms to ensure that all blueprints and design plans developed by the Company are feasible and structurally sound. Smith Architecture Firm will generate significant gross margins from the fees charged to clients for these services.

Project Management Services

On a limited basis, the Company will also act in a project management capacity during the development of properties and renovations. The business will charge a flat set fee for these services, which will primarily consist of design and implementation oversight in conjunction with general contractors and real estate developers.

STRATEGIC AND MARKET ANALYSIS

Economic Outlook

This section of the analysis will detail the economic climate, the architecture industry, the customer profile, and the competition that the business will face as it progresses through its business operations.

Currently, the economic market condition in the United States is in recession. This slowdown in the economy has also greatly impacted real estate sales, which has halted to historical lows. Many economists expect that this recession will continue until the end of 2009, at which point the economy will begin a prolonged recovery period. This may contribute to the business having some difficulty with obtaining new business at the onset of operations as the demand for new housing and housing renovations has slowed. However, the Company will earn substantial gross margins on its services, and as such, the Architectural Firm will be able to maintain profitability despite the current drawbacks in the aggregate economy.

Industry Analysis

The architectural industry has gone through a major change over the last ten years. With the advent and prevalence of online communications, more architects have developed their own private practices in lieu of working directly for a business. With the increased communication reach, small architectural firms can quickly and easily gain national and international level clientele through Internet advertising and communications. This trend is expected to continue as advancements in the telecommunications industry allow businesses and engineers to communicate quicker and more effectively.

Aggregately, the 23,000 architectural firms in the Untied States generate in excess of $25 billion dollars in gross receipts and provide jobs for more than 200,000 people. Average annual payrolls have exceeded $10 billion dollars for each of the last five years. The growth rate of this industry has greatly exceeded the growth of the general economy. The average annual growth rate in the number of establishments doing business in an architectural design capacity has been in excess of 6% per year, while a receipt generated by these businesses has increased 8% per year.

One of the most common trends within this industry is to develop structures that are environmentally friendly and have minimal impact on the surrounding ecology.

Customer Profile

The Architectural Firm will have two primary client bases: individuals and real state developers. Here is an overview of the demographics of each of these market groups.

Common traits among individual clients will include:

- Annual household income exceeding $150,000
- Will spend $5,000 with the Architectural Firm
- Is seeking to develop a home with a value in excess of $800,000

Among real estate developers and contractors, Management has identified the following common characteristics:

- Annual revenues in excess of $1,000,000
- Will spend $15,000 to $30,000 per year with the firm
- Develops properties with a value in excess of $2,000,000

Competition

Within the New York metropolitan area, there are 780 firms that provide architectural services. Major architectural firms in the New York metropolitan area include, but are not limited to:

- 5-H Design
- Alan Gaynor & Co.
- Lee Harris Pomeroy Associates
- RA German Architects, PC

Management intends to maintain a competitive niche within the industry by focusing on moderate sized home developments while concurrently working with middle market real estate developers and construction firms.

MARKETING PLAN

Smith Architecture Firm intends to maintain an extensive marketing campaign that will ensure that the business becomes well known among real estate developers, contractors, and the general public. Below is an overview of the marketing strategies and objectives of Smith Architecture Firm.

Marketing Objectives

- Implement a regional marketing campaign that will brand the Company as a premium architectural firm.
- Develop an online presence by developing a website and placing the Company's name and contact information with online directories.
- Establish relationships with real estate developers and general contractors within the target market.

Marketing Strategies

Foremost, the Company intends to develop relationships with general contractors and real estate developers that will call on the firm for drafting, design, and limited project management services. Mr. Smith anticipates that 75% of the Company's revenues will come directly from this group, and as such, it is imperative that Smith Architecture Firm develop these relationships from the onset of operations.

In addition to maintaining close relationships with companies that frequently need architectural services, the business will also develop an online platform that will allow potential clients to see previous developments by Mr. Smith, contact information, and preliminary pricing information regarding the Company's services. One of the most important aspects to internet-based marketing is that the website should showcase general pricing information for the business' services.

The Company will also maintain a sizable amount of print and traditional advertising methods among local real estate publications to promote the architectural services and brand name of the Architectural Firm.

Pricing

On a per hour basis, the Architectural Firm will charge $150 to $200 per hour depending on the complexity of the design and drafting work. Project management fees will be negotiated on an individual basis with each client.

ORGANIZATIONAL PLAN AND PERSONNEL SUMMARY

Corporate Organization

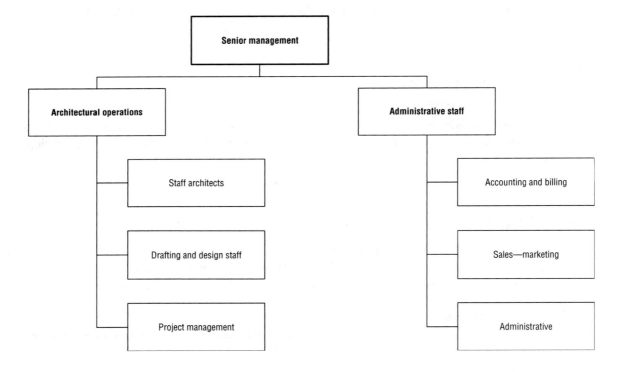

Organizational Budget

Personnel plan—yearly

Year	2009	2010	2011
Owner	$ 70,000	$ 72,100	$ 74,263
Architects	$110,000	$113,300	$116,699
Drafting staff	$ 97,500	$100,425	$103,438
Bookkeeper (P/T)	$ 19,000	$ 19,570	$ 20,157
Administrative	$ 22,000	$ 22,660	$ 23,340
Total	**$318,500**	**$328,055**	**$337,897**
Numbers of personnel			
Owner	1	1	1
Architects	2	2	2
Drafting staff	3	3	3
Bookkeeper (P/T)	1	1	1
Administrative	1	1	1
Totals	**8**	**8**	**8**

Personnel expense breakdown

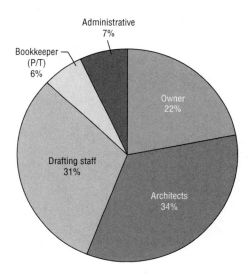

Management Biographies

Mr. John Smith is a highly experienced architect with more than 10 years in the industry. Mr. Smith's skill set includes, but is not limited to:

- A complete understanding of accounting of the complex marketing, service related, and accounting issues that the business will face on a day to day basis.

- Licensure to operate as an architect in the State of New York.

- Membership in the American Architectural Foundation.

- Membership in the AIA.

FINANCIAL PLAN

Underlying Assumptions

The Company has based its proforma financial statements on the following:

- Smith Architecture Firm will have an annual revenue growth rate of 9% per year.

- The Owner will acquire $125,000 of debt funds to develop the business.

- The loan will have a 10 year term with a 9% interest rate.

Sensitivity Analysis

In the event of an economic downturn, the business may have a decline in its revenues. As the demand for housing has waned over the last two years, the demand for related design, drafting, project management, and other architectural services has also decreased. However, the high margin income derived from the Company's revenues will ensure that the business maintains profitability and is able to service the debt sought in this loan despite the current deleterious housing market.

Source of Funds

Financing

Equity contributions	
Management investment	$ 10,000.00
Total equity financing	**$ 10,000.00**
Banks and lenders	
Banks and lenders	$ 125,000.00
Total debt financing	**$125,000.00**
Total financing	**$135,000.00**

General Assumptions

General assumptions

Year	2009	2010	2011
Short term interest rate	9.5%	9.5%	9.5%
Long term interest rate	10.0%	10.0%	10.0%
Federal tax rate	33.0%	33.0%	33.0%
State tax rate	5.0%	5.0%	5.0%
Personnel taxes	15.0%	15.0%	15.0%

Profit and Loss Statements

Proforma profit and loss (yearly)

Year	2009	2010	2011
Sales	$726,978	$799,676	$863,650
Cost of goods sold	$108,773	$119,651	$129,223
Gross margin	85.04%	85.04%	85.04%
Operating income	$618,205	$680,025	$734,427
Expenses			
Payroll	$318,500	$328,055	$337,897
General and administrative	$ 25,200	$ 26,208	$ 27,256
Marketing expenses	$ 3,635	$ 3,998	$ 4,318
Professional fees and licensure	$ 5,219	$ 5,376	$ 5,537
Insurance costs	$ 1,987	$ 2,086	$ 2,191
Travel and vehicle costs	$ 7,596	$ 8,356	$ 9,191
Rent and utilities	$ 14,250	$ 14,963	$ 15,711
Miscellaneous costs	$ 8,724	$ 9,596	$ 10,364
Payroll taxes	$ 47,775	$ 49,208	$ 50,684
Total operating costs	**$432,886**	**$447,846**	**$463,149**
EBITDA	**$185,319**	**$232,179**	**$271,278**
Federal income tax	$ 61,155	$ 73,265	$ 86,441
State income tax	$ 9,266	$ 11,101	$ 13,097
Interest expense	$ 10,922	$ 10,164	$ 9,335
Depreciation expenses	$ 6,393	$ 6,393	$ 6,393
Net profit	**$ 97,583**	**$131,256**	**$156,012**
Profit margin	**13.42%**	**16.41%**	**18.06%**

Sales, operating costs, and profit forecast

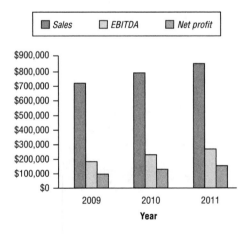

Cash Flow Analysis

Proforma cash flow analysis—yearly

Year	2009	2010	2011
Cash from operations	$103,976	$137,649	$162,405
Cash from receivables	$ 0	$ 0	$ 0
Operating cash inflow	**$103,976**	**$137,649**	**$162,405**
Other cash inflows			
Equity investment	$ 10,000	$ 0	$ 0
Increased borrowings	$125,000	$ 0	$ 0
Sales of business assets	$ 0	$ 0	$ 0
A/P increases	$ 37,902	$ 43,587	$ 50,125
Total other cash inflows	**$172,902**	**$ 43,587**	**$ 50,125**
Total cash inflow	**$276,878**	**$181,237**	**$212,530**
Cash outflows			
Repayment of principal	$ 8,079	$ 8,837	$ 9,666
A/P decreases	$ 24,897	$ 29,876	$ 35,852
A/R increases	$ 0	$ 0	$ 0
Asset purchases	$ 57,500	$ 34,412	$ 40,601
Dividends	$ 72,783	$ 96,355	$113,683
Total cash outflows	**$163,259**	**$169,480**	**$199,802**
Net cash flow	**$113,618**	**$ 11,756**	**$ 12,728**
Cash balance	**$113,618**	**$125,375**	**$138,103**

Proforma cash flow (yearly)

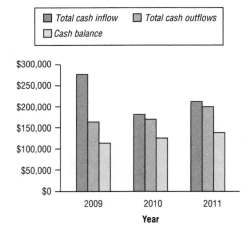

Balance Sheet

Proforma balance sheet—yearly

Year	2009	2010	2011
Assets			
Cash	$113,618	$125,375	$138,103
Amortized expansion costs	$ 27,500	$ 42,986	$ 61,256
Computers and CAD software	$ 35,000	$ 48,765	$ 65,005
FF&E	$ 27,000	$ 32,162	$ 38,252
Accumulated depreciation	($ 6,393)	($ 12,786)	($ 19,179)
Total assets	**$196,726**	**$236,501**	**$283,437**
Liabilities and equity			
Accounts payable	$ 13,005	$ 26,716	$ 40,990
Long term liabilities	$116,921	$108,084	$ 99,247
Other liabilities	$ 0	$ 0	$ 0
Total liabilities	**$129,926**	**$134,800**	**$140,236**
Net worth	**$ 66,800**	**$101,702**	**$143,201**
Total liabilities and equity	**$196,726**	**$236,501**	**$283,437**

Proforma balance sheet

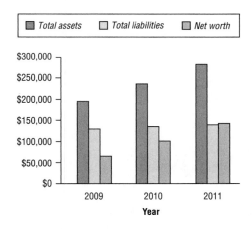

Breakeven Analysis

Monthly break even analysis

Year	2009	2010	2011
Monthly revenue	$ 42,421	$ 43,887	$ 45,387
Yearly revenue	$509,052	$526,644	$544,640

Break even analysis

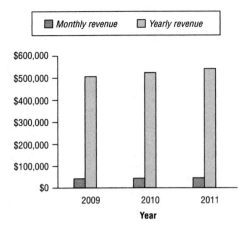

Business Ratios

Business ratios—yearly

Year	2009	2010	2011
Sales			
Sales growth	0.0%	10.0%	8.0%
Gross margin	85.0%	85.0%	85.0%
Financials			
Profit margin	13.42%	16.41%	18.06%
Assets to liabilities	1.51%	1.75%	2.02%
Equity to liabilities	0.51%	0.75%	1.02%
Assets to equity	2.95%	2.33%	1.98%
Liquidity			
Acid test	0.87%	0.93%	0.98%
Cash to assets	0.58%	0.53%	0.49%

Bed and Breakfast

Home Again Bed & Breakfast

200 Route 100
Katonah, New York 10536

BizPlanDB.com

The purpose of this business plan is to raise $750,000 for the development of a bed and breakfast while showcasing the expected financials and operations over the next three years. The Home Again Bed & Breakfast is a New York-based corporation that will provide nightly room lodgings and food/catering services to customers in its targeted market.

EXECUTIVE SUMMARY

The purpose of this business plan is to raise $750,000 for the development of a bed and breakfast while showcasing the expected financials and operations over the next three years. The Home Again Bed & Breakfast ("the Company") is a New York based corporation that will provide nightly room lodgings and food/catering services to customers in its targeted market. The Company was founded in 2009 by Jesse Osborne.

The Services

Home Again Bed & Breakfast will be a unique facility that will feature a number of amenities for clients staying with the Company. This old styled facility will feature 6 to 7 bed and breakfast style rooms. Within the facility, guests will experience state-of-the-art technology coupled with a staff that provides food/beverage service, as well as spa services to patrons. (The spa services will be outsourced to other providers.)

The business will also provide large parties with site rentals so that a number of guests can use the facility exclusively. This is an important revenue center for the business as it will provide a highly predictable stream of revenue, primarily from event and wedding planners that want to use an entire (but relatively smaller) facility.

Financing

Mr. Osborne is seeking to raise $750,000 from as a bank loan. The interest rate and loan agreement are to be further discussed during negotiation. This business plan assumes that the business will receive a 30 year loan with a 7% fixed interest rate. The financing will be used for the following:

- Acquisition of the Company's Home Again Bed & Breakfast location.

- Financing for the first six months of operation.

- Capital to purchase FF&E and kitchen equipment.

Mr. Osborne will contribute $250,000 to the venture.

Mission Statement

Home Again Bed & Breakfast's mission is to become the recognized leader in its targeted market for quality lodging, food service, and catering services.

Management Team

The Company was founded by Jesse Osborne. Mr. Osborne has more than 20 years of experience in the hotel management industry. He is focused on developing the bed and breakfast into a premier weekend vacation location in the State of New York.

Sales Forecasts

Mr. Osborne expects a strong rate of growth at the start of operations. Below are the expected financials over the next three years.

Proforma profit and loss (yearly)

Year	2009	2010	2011
Sales	$584,298	$642,728	$707,001
Operating costs	$269,391	$280,280	$291,740
EBITDA	$229,509	$268,510	$311,930
Taxes, interest, and depreciation	$163,908	$158,529	$174,662
Net profit	$ 65,601	$109,982	$137,268

Expansion Plan

The Founder expects that the business will aggressively expand during the first three years of operation. Mr. Osborne intends to implement marketing campaigns that will effectively target individuals and travelers within the target market.

COMPANY AND FINANCING SUMMARY

Registered Name and Corporate Structure

Home Again Bed & Breakfast is registered as a corporation in the State of New York.

Required Funds

At this time, Home Again Bed & Breakfast requires $750,000 of debt funds in addition to the $250,000 contributed by Jesse Osborne. Below is a breakdown of how these funds will be used:

Projected startup costs

Business startup year	2009
Facility acquisition	$ 750,000
Working capital	$ 50,000
FF&E	$ 75,000
Facility improvements	$ 50,000
Security deposits	$ 12,500
Insurance	$ 12,500
Kitchen equipment	$ 25,000
Marketing budget	$ 20,000
Miscellaneous and unforeseen costs	$ 5,000
Total startup costs	$1,000,000

Use of funds

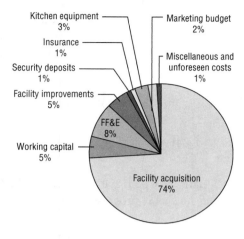

Kitchen equipment
3%

Insurance
1%

Security deposits
1%

Facility improvements
5%

Working capital
5%

FF&E
8%

Marketing budget
2%

Miscellaneous and
unforeseen costs
1%

Facility acquisition
74%

Investor Equity

Mr. Osborne is not seeking an investment from a third party at this time.

Management Equity

Jesse Osborne owns 100% of the Home Again Bed & Breakfast.

Exit Strategy

If the business is very successful, Mr. Osborne may seek to sell the business to a third party for a significant earnings multiple. Most likely, the Company will hire a qualified business broker to sell the business on behalf of the Home Again Bed & Breakfast. Based on historical numbers, the business could fetch a sales premium of up to 8 times earnings.

PRODUCTS AND SERVICES

Below is a description of the services offered by Home Alone Bed & Breakfast.

Hospitality Services

The facility itself will feature six to seven rooms that will have a number of modern amenities. Each room will have a flat screen TV and internet access so that customers can remain in touch with the world while they are on their vacation stay. Many travelers will only stay in places where internet access is available, and Management feels that is imperative that the Company maintain standards that are applicable to the rest of the bed and breakfast industry. Each room will feature a queen sized bed, a bathroom, desk, and two nightstands.

The Company will also contract with local massage therapists, cosmetologists, and other service providers to provide a small variety of massage and spa services onsite in an outsourced capacity.

Catering Services and Food/Beverage Services

Home Again Bed & Breakfast will make a full food and beverage service available to all of its customers. Management feels that by providing a number of food and drink amenities, clients will become loyal customers of the bed and breakfast, and as such, they will always return to the business when traveling in the area.

The Company is also developing an additional catering service that will be used for events that are hosted at Home Again Bed & Breakfast. Management feels that this business segment will make the Company extremely profitable as the sales of catering packages usually generate contribution margins in excess of 70%. Additionally, the catering services that are offered to guests may be expanded so that local events can use the Company's catering service as an outsourced vendor for their party and event planning needs.

STRATEGIC AND MARKET ANALYSIS

Economic Outlook

This section of the analysis will detail the economic climate, the bed and breakfast industry, the customer profile, and the competition that the business will face as it progresses through its business operations.

Currently, the economic market condition in the United States is in recession. This slowdown in the economy has also greatly impacted real estate sales, which has halted to historical lows. Many economists expect that this recession will continue until the end of 2009, at which point the economy will begin a prolonged recovery period. However, as many people are reducing the travel expenditures to major resort destinations, bed and breakfasts have become popular weekend getaways as an alternative to longer vacations. This, coupled with the Company's ability to provide a venue for moderate sized events, will ensure that the business is able to remain profitable and cash flow positive at all times.

Industry Analysis

There are over 12,900 bed and breakfast inns in the United States, which collectively generate more than $700 million dollars a year of revenue. A vast majority of these inns are owned by individuals or partners that are seeking a different way of life. The industry employs more than 16,000 people and generates gross annual payrolls in excess of $168 million dollars per year. The industry has grown at a healthy clip over the last five years. Each year the industry expands its capacity by 3%, which is on target with the growth of the general economy.

Customer Profile

Management anticipates that the Company will have a highly broad audience of customers that will want to experience a stay at Home Again Bed & Breakfast. As many people enjoy traveling, it is difficult to determine the exact demographics of this market as it is excessively large. However, Management has developed the following demographic table that it will use when developing its marketing campaigns:

- Male or Female

- Primarily from the continental United States

- Between the ages of 30 and 60

- Has an annual income exceeding $75,000 per year

Among people that will host events at Home Again Bed & Breakfast, Management expects similar demographics as the guests outlined above. The anticipated budget among this segment of the Company's operations is $5,000 to $25,000.

Competition

Home Again Bed & Breakfast will be located approximately 50 miles north of the New York metropolitan area. Within this market area (a 50 mile diameter), there are approximately 60 bed and breakfasts. Each bed and breakfast location is located approximately 10 miles apart. As such, competition is limited within the Company's local market.

The business will maintain a strong competitive advantage over other bed and breakfast locations within the area by having the ability to host moderate scale events at the Company's facilities.

MARKETING PLAN

Home Again Bed & Breakfast intends to maintain an extensive marketing campaign that will draw visitors from the Tri-State area to the Company's inn location. Below is an overview of the marketing strategies and objectives of the Home Again Bed & Breakfast.

Marketing Objectives

- Implement a regional marketing campaign with the Company's targeted market (50 miles north of New York City) via the use of flyers, local newspaper advertisements, and word of mouth advertising.

- Establish relationships with travel agents and online travel portals throughout the United States.

Marketing Strategies

Management intends to use a number of marketing strategies that will ensure that Home Again Bed & Breakfast operates at near 100% capacity on a year round basis. These strategies include working with event planners (for event hosting), maintaining a highly visible website, and registering with major online travel portals.

Mr. Osborne will also develop ongoing relationships with event planners within the New York metropolitan area (and within the Company's targeted market) that will schedule Home Again Bed & Breakfast's location for moderate sized events such as small weddings, corporate retreats, and anniversaries. In time, these relationships will become invaluable to the Company.

As with many hospitality businesses, it is also imperative that Mr. Osborne develop an online website that allows potential guests to see images of the location, obtain contact/pricing information, and book stays via an online reservation portal. This website will be developed immediately after Mr. Osborne acquires the Company's property.

The business will also register the location with major travel agencies and online portals such as Expedia, Travelocity.com, and Priceline.com so that the Company can gain nationwide exposure among people seeking to stay in Bed in Breakfasts within the Company's local target market.

Pricing

Management anticipates that individual rooms within Home Again Bed and Breakfast facility will generate revenues of $125 to $200 per night depending on the season. Catering and event hosting service pricing will range from $5,000 to $15,000 depending on the complexity and size of the event.

ORGANIZATIONAL PLAN AND PERSONNEL SUMMARY

Corporate Organization

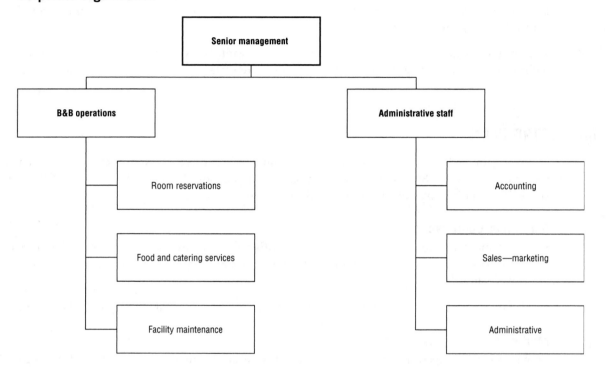

Organizational Budget

Personnel plan—yearly

Year	2009	2010	2011
Owner	$ 40,000	$ 41,200	$ 42,436
B&B manager	$ 35,000	$ 36,050	$ 37,132
B&B staff	$ 51,000	$ 52,530	$ 54,106
Bookkeeper	$ 12,500	$ 12,875	$ 13,261
Administrative	$ 22,000	$ 22,660	$ 23,340
Total	**$160,500**	**$165,315**	**$170,274**
Numbers of personnel			
Owner	1	1	1
B&B manager	1	1	1
B&B staff	3	3	3
Bookkeeper	1	1	1
Administrative	1	1	1
Totals	**7**	**7**	**7**

Personnel expense breakdown

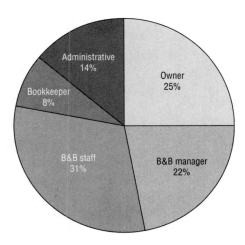

Management Biographies

Over the past ten years, Mr. Osborne has acted as a manager of bed and breakfast facilities throughout the State of New York. Additionally, he has already obtained all of the proper licensure so that the business can serve as an inn and a catered venue concurrently. Through his experience, he will be able to effectively manage and market Home Again Bed & Breakfast on a daily basis with a focus on bottom line income growth for each successive year of operation.

FINANCIAL PLAN

Underlying Assumptions

The Company has based its proforma financial statements on the following:

- Home Again Bed & Breakfast will have an annual revenue growth rate of 10% per year.

- The Owner will acquire $750,000 of debt funds to develop the business.

- The loan will have a 30 year term with a 7% interest rate.

- Management will contribute $250,000 towards the development of the business.

Sensitivity Analysis

The Company's revenues are somewhat sensitive to the overall condition of the economy. Since the bed and breakfast industry provides a leisure service, pullbacks in the general economic markets can affect Home Again Bed & Breakfast's ability to generate revenues. However, the Company will run its operations with a wide margin of safety, and the contribution margins generated from gross sales are large enough to allow the business to operate profitability even in times in economic recession.

Source of Funds

Financing

Equity contributions	
Management investment	$ 250,000.00
Total equity financing	**$ 250,000.00**
Banks and lenders	
Banks and lenders	$ 750,000.00
Total debt financing	**$ 750,000.00**
Total financing	**$1,000,000.00**

General Assumptions

General assumptions

Year	2009	2010	2011
Short term interest rate	9.5%	9.5%	9.5%
Long term interest rate	10.0%	10.0%	10.0%
Federal tax rate	33.0%	33.0%	33.0%
State tax rate	5.0%	5.0%	5.0%
Personnel taxes	15.0%	15.0%	15.0%

Profit and Loss Statements

Proforma profit and loss (yearly)

Year	2009	2010	2011
Sales	$584,298	$642,728	$707,001
Cost of goods sold	$ 85,397	$ 93,937	$103,331
Gross margin	85.38%	85.38%	85.38%
Operating income	**$498,901**	**$548,791**	**$603,670**
Expenses			
Payroll	$160,500	$165,315	$170,274
General and administrative	$ 13,200	$ 13,728	$ 14,277
Marketing expenses	$ 17,529	$ 19,282	$ 21,210
Professional fees and licensure	$ 12,500	$ 12,875	$ 13,261
Insurance costs	$ 15,000	$ 15,750	$ 16,538
Travel and vehicle costs	$ 10,000	$ 11,000	$ 12,100
Facility maintenance	$ 14,250	$ 14,963	$ 15,711
Miscellaneous costs	$ 2,337	$ 2,571	$ 2,828
Payroll taxes	$ 24,075	$ 24,797	$ 25,541
Total operating costs	**$269,391**	**$280,280**	**$291,740**
EBITDA	**$229,509**	**$268,510**	**$311,930**
Federal income tax	$ 75,738	$ 71,545	$ 86,068
State income tax	$ 11,475	$ 10,840	$ 13,041
Interest expense	$ 52,259	$ 51,708	$ 51,117
Depreciation expenses	$ 24,436	$ 24,436	$ 24,436
Net profit	**$ 65,601**	**$109,982**	**$137,268**
Profit margin	**11.23%**	**17.11%**	**19.42%**

Cash Flow Analysis

Proforma cash flow analysis—yearly

Year	2009	2010	2011
Cash from operations	$ 90,037	$134,417	$161,704
Cash from receivables	$ 0	$ 0	$ 0
Operating cash inflow	**$ 90,037**	**$134,417**	**$161,704**
Other cash inflows			
Equity investment	$ 250,000	$ 0	$ 0
Increased borrowings	$ 750,000	$ 0	$ 0
Sales of business assets	$ 0	$ 0	$ 0
A/P increases	$ 37,902	$ 43,587	$ 50,125
Total other cash inflows	**$1,037,902**	**$ 43,587**	**$ 50,125**
Total cash inflow	**$1,127,939**	**$178,005**	**$211,829**
Cash outflows			
Repayment of principal	$ 7,619	$ 8,169	$ 8,760
A/P decreases	$ 24,897	$ 29,876	$ 35,852
A/R increases	$ 0	$ 0	$ 0
Asset purchases	$ 930,000	$ 33,604	$ 40,426
Dividends	$ 63,026	$ 94,092	$113,193
Total cash outflows	**$1,025,542**	**$165,742**	**$198,230**
Net cash flow	**$ 102,398**	**$ 12,262**	**$ 13,599**
Cash balance	**$ 102,398**	**$114,660**	**$128,259**

Balance Sheet

Proforma balance sheet—yearly

Year	2009	2010	2011
Assets			
Cash	$ 102,398	$ 114,660	$ 128,259
Amortized development/expansion costs	$ 30,000	$ 41,762	$ 55,911
Kitchen equipment	$ 25,000	$ 33,401	$ 43,508
FF&E	$ 50,000	$ 63,442	$ 79,612
Property value	$ 848,000	$ 898,880	$ 952,813
Accumulated depreciation	($ 24,436)	($ 48,872)	($ 73,308)
Total assets	**$1,030,962**	**$1,103,273**	**$1,186,794**
Liabilities and equity			
Accounts payable	$ 13,005	$ 26,716	$ 40,990
Long term liabilities	$ 742,381	$ 734,212	$ 726,043
Other liabilities	$ 0	$ 0	$ 0
Total liabilities	**$ 755,386**	**$ 760,928**	**$ 767,032**
Net worth	**$ 275,575**	**$ 342,345**	**$ 419,762**
Total liabilities and equity	**$1,030,962**	**$1,103,273**	**$1,186,794**

Breakeven Analysis

Monthly break even analysis

Year	2009	2010	2011
Monthly revenue	$ 26,292	$ 27,355	$ 28,473
Yearly revenue	$315,503	$328,256	$341,678

Business Ratios

Business ratios—yearly

Year	2009	2010	2011
Sales			
Sales growth	0.0%	10.0%	10.0%
Gross margin	85.4%	85.4%	85.4%
Financials			
Profit margin	11.23%	17.11%	19.42%
Assets to liabilities	1.36%	1.45%	1.55%
Equity to liabilities	0.36%	0.45%	0.55%
Assets to equity	3.74%	3.22%	2.83%
Liquidity			
Acid test	0.14%	0.15%	0.17%
Cash to assets	0.10%	0.10%	0.11%

Bookkeeping Practice
Kohn Bookkeeping Practice

7500 Main St.
New York, NY 10012

BizPlanDB.com

The purpose of this business plan is to raise $100,000 for the development of a bookkeeping practice while showcasing the expected financials and operations over the next three years. Kohn Bookkeeping Practice, Inc. is a New York-based corporation that will provide business bookkeeping and tax preparation to customers in its targeted market.

EXECUTIVE SUMMARY

The purpose of this business plan is to raise $100,000 for the development of a bookkeeping practice while showcasing the expected financials and operations over the next three years. Kohn Bookkeeping Practice, Inc. ("the Company") is a New York-based corporation that will provide business bookkeeping and tax preparation to customers in its targeted market. The Company was founded in 2009 by Scott Kohn.

The Services

As stated above, the business's primary stream of revenue will come from the sale of business bookkeeping services to small- and medium-sized businesses within the target market. These services will primarily consist of accounts receivable, accounts payable, general ledger management, and cash flow management in conjunction with accounting software suites such as QuickBooks, Microsoft Money, and Peachtree Accounting.

The secondary streams of revenue will come from small business tax preparation services. During the primary tax season (February to April), the business will assist small business owners with preparing their yearly tax returns.

Financing

Mr. Kohn is seeking to raise $100,000 from as a bank loan. The interest rate and loan agreement are to be further discussed during negotiation. This business plan assumes that the business will receive a 10 year loan with a 9% fixed interest rate. The financing will be used for the following:

• Development of the Company's office location.

• Financing for the first six months of operation.

• Capital to purchase a company vehicle.

Mr. Kohn will contribute $10,000 to the venture.

Mission Statement

Kohn Bookkeeping Practice's mission is to become the recognized leader in its targeted market for business bookkeeping and tax preparation services.

Management Team

The Company was founded by Scott Kohn. Mr. Kohn has more than 10 years of experience in the accounting industry. Through his expertise, he will be able to bring the operations of the business to profitability within its first year of operations.

Sales Forecasts

Mr. Kohn expects a strong rate of growth at the start of operations. Below are the expected financials over the next three years.

Proforma profit and loss (yearly)

Year	2009	2010	2011
Sales	$487,578	$585,094	$684,560
Operating costs	$289,441	$334,792	$347,206
EBITDA	$173,758	$221,047	$303,125
Taxes, interest, and depreciation	$ 78,873	$ 93,146	$123,925
Net profit	**$ 94,885**	**$127,900**	**$179,200**

Sales, operating costs, and profit forecast

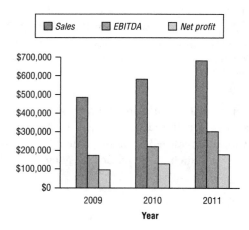

Expansion Plan

The Founder expects that the business will aggressively expand during the first three years of operation. Mr. Kohn intends to implement marketing campaigns that will effectively target individuals within the target market.

COMPANY AND FINANCING SUMMARY

Registered Name and Corporate Structure

Kohn Bookkeeping Practice, Inc. is registered as a corporation in the State of New York.

Required Funds

At this time, Kohn Bookkeeping Practice requires $100,000 of debt funds in addition to the $10,000 contributed by the owner. Below is a breakdown of how these funds will be used:

Projected startup costs

Business startup year	2009
Initial lease payments and deposits	$ 10,000
Working capital	$ 35,000
FF&E	$ 23,000
Leasehold improvements	$ 5,000
Security deposits	$ 5,000
Insurance	$ 2,500
Company vehicle	$ 17,000
Marketing budget	$ 7,500
Miscellaneous and unforeseen costs	$ 5,000
Total startup costs	**$110,000**

Investor Equity

Mr. Kohn is not seeking an investment from a third party at this time.

Management Equity

Scott Kohn owns 100% of Kohn Bookkeeping Practice, Inc.

Exit Strategy

If the business is very successful, Mr. Kohn may seek to sell the business to a third party for a significant earnings multiple. Most likely, the Company will hire a qualified business broker to sell the business on behalf of Kohn Bookkeeping Practice. Based on historical numbers, the business could fetch a sales premium of up to 4 times earnings.

PRODUCTS AND SERVICES

Below is a description of the bookkeeping and tax preparation services offered by Kohn Bookkeeping Practice.

Bookkeeping Services

The primary revenue source for the business will come from bookkeeping services for small- and medium-sized businesses. Primarily, Kohn Bookkeeping Practice's clientele will consist of business owners that are simply too busy to do their own accounting or own to small of a firm to hire someone on a full-time basis. The Company will provide full-charge bookkeeping services, which will consist of overseeing and managing a small/medium sized business's accounts receivable, accounts payable, invoicing, general ledger entries, payroll entries, basic inventory management, and other core accounting functions.

Kohn Bookkeeping Practice will bill its clients on a per hour basis. Pricing for these services will be further discussed later in this business plan.

Tax Preparation Services

Seasonally, Kohn Bookkeeping Practice will make a substantial amount of money for filing tax returns for businesses. Each tax return will generate $300 to $1,000 depending on the complexity and the amount of paperwork to file.

STRATEGIC AND MARKET ANALYSIS

Economic Outlook

This section of the analysis will detail the economic climate, the bookkeeping industry, the customer profile, and the competition that the business will face as it progresses through its business operations.

Currently, the economic market condition in the United States is in recession. This slowdown in the economy has also greatly impacted real estate sales, which has halted to historical lows. Many economists expect that this recession will continue until the end of 2009, at which point the economy will begin a prolonged recovery period. However, bookkeepers operate with great economic stability as small and medium sized business owners will continue to require bookkeeping services despite deleterious economic conditions.

Industry Analysis

The accounting and bookkeeping industry is a highly fragmented group of individual practitioners, small firms, and large auditing institution. There are over 621,000 accountants in the United States. The industry generates over $38 billion dollars a year, and employs over 390,000 Americans.

The demand for accounting/bookkeeping services is expected to increase as the number of businesses and the complication of tax issues increase.

One of the most common trends within the accounting industry is to develop ancillary investment management and small lending services (such as mortgage origination and loan rebate checks). In the future, Kohn Bookkeeping Practice may develop these services to greatly increase the revenues of the business.

Customer Profile

Kohn Bookkeeping Practice's average client will be a small- to medium-sized business within the Company's target market. Common traits among clients will include:

- Annual revenues exceeding $200,000.

- The client's operations are no more than 15 miles from the Company's location.

- Will spend $250 per month on bookkeeping services with Kohn Bookkeeping Practice.

- Will spend $300 to $1,000 for corporate tax return services.

Within the Company's targeted market of the New York Metropolitan area, there are approximately 500,000 businesses that fall into the above demographic profile.

Competition

Competition within the New York metropolitan area among bookkeepers is strong. Direct competition ranges from independent bookkeepers, bookkeeping practices, and accounting/CPA practices that provide bookkeeping services for their clients. Within the greater New York metropolitan area, there are more than 2,000 companies that render bookkeeping and tax preparation services to businesses (and individuals).

MARKETING PLAN

Kohn Bookkeeping Practice intends to maintain an extensive marketing and advertising campaign that will ensure that the Company can quickly enroll small/medium sized businesses into its bookkeeping service programs. Below is an overview of the marketing strategies and objectives of Kohn Bookkeeping Practice.

Marketing Objectives

- Develop an online presence by developing a website and placing the Company's name and contact information with online directories.

- Implement a local campaign with the Company's targeted market via the use of flyers, local newspaper advertisements, and word of mouth.

- Establish relationships with certified public accountants in Kohn Bookkeeping Practice's targeted market.

Marketing Strategies

Mr. Kohn intends on using a number of marketing strategies that will allow Kohn Bookkeeping Practice to easily target small and medium sized businesses within the targeted New York metropolitan area market. These strategies include traditional print advertisements and ads placed on search engines on the Internet. Below is a description of how the business intends to market its services to the general public.

Kohn Bookkeeping Practice will also use an internet-based strategy. This is very important as many people seeking local services, such as bookkeepers, now use the Internet to conduct their preliminary searches. Mr. Kohn will register Kohn Bookkeeping Practice with online portals so that potential clients can easily reach the business. The Company will also develop its own online website, which will showcase Mr. Kohn's experience in the accounting industry, contact information, and preliminary pricing information. The business will place advertisements on popular search engines as well as on classified sites such as Craigslist in order to generate traffic to the Company's website.

The Company will maintain a sizable amount of print and traditional advertising methods within targeted New York area markets to promote the bookkeeping and tax preparation that the Company is selling. Mr. Kohn will also develop relationships with certified public accounting firms that will generate substantial amounts of referral business for the Company.

Pricing

For bookkeeping services, the Company will charge approximately $250 per month for ongoing bookkeeping services.

Tax return preparation service fees will range from $300 to $1,000 depending on the complexity of the tax return.

ORGANIZATIONAL PLAN AND PERSONNEL SUMMARY

Corporate Organization

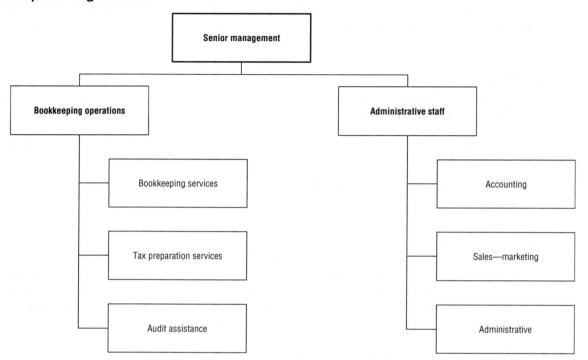

Organizational Budget

Personnel plan—yearly

Year	2009	2010	2011
Owner	$ 40,000	$ 41,200	$ 42,436
Office manager	$ 35,000	$ 36,050	$ 37,132
Bookkeepers—tax preparers	$ 87,000	$119,480	$123,064
Owner's assistant	$ 22,000	$ 22,660	$ 23,340
Administrative	$ 22,000	$ 22,660	$ 23,340
Total	**$206,000**	**$242,050**	**$249,312**
Numbers of personnel			
Owner	1	1	1
Office manager	1	1	1
Bookkeepers—tax preparers	3	4	4
Owner's assistant	1	1	1
Administrative	1	1	1
Totals	**7**	**8**	**8**

Management Biographies

Mr. Scott Kohn is a highly experienced bookkeeper with more than 10 years in the industry. Since beginning his career as a bookkeeper, Mr. Kohn has acquired his Enrolled Agent (for tax preparation services) license and he is now ready to launch his own firm. Scott's skill set includes:

- The ability to oversee agents and employees
- A complete understanding of accounting
- Licensure to operate as a tax preparer

FINANCIAL PLAN

Underlying Assumptions

The Company has based its proforma financial statements on the following:

- Kohn Bookkeeping Practice will have an annual revenue growth rate of 16% per year.
- The Owner will acquire $100,000 of debt funds to develop the business.
- The loan will have a 10 year term with a 9% interest rate.

Sensitivity Analysis

The Company's revenues are not sensitive to changes in the general economy. Despite deleterious economic changes, people and small businesses will require tax advice as well as regular accounting services. As such, only trained professionals, like those employed by Kohn Bookkeeping Practice, can render these services. Only a severe economic downturn could result in a decline in the Company's revenues.

Source of Funds

Financing

Equity contributions	
Management investment	$ 10,000.00
Total equity financing	**$ 10,000.00**
Banks and lenders	
Banks and lenders	$ 100,000.00
Total debt financing	**$100,000.00**
Total financing	**$110,000.00**

General Assumptions

General assumptions

Year	2009	2010	2011
Short term interest rate	9.5%	9.5%	9.5%
Long term interest rate	10.0%	10.0%	10.0%
Federal tax rate	33.0%	33.0%	33.0%
State tax rate	5.0%	5.0%	5.0%
Personnel taxes	15.0%	15.0%	15.0%

Profit and Loss Statements

Proforma profit and loss (yearly)

Year	2009	2010	2011
Sales	$487,578	$585,094	$684,560
Cost of goods sold	$ 24,379	$ 29,255	$ 34,228
Gross margin	95.00%	95.00%	95.00%
Operating income	$463,199	$555,839	$650,332
Expenses			
Payroll	$206,000	$242,050	$249,312
General and administrative	$ 25,200	$ 26,208	$ 27,256
Marketing expenses	$ 2,438	$ 2,925	$ 3,423
Professional fees and licensure	$ 5,219	$ 5,376	$ 5,537
Insurance costs	$ 1,987	$ 2,086	$ 2,191
Travel and vehicle costs	$ 7,596	$ 8,356	$ 9,191
Rent and utilities	$ 4,250	$ 4,463	$ 4,686
Miscellaneous costs	$ 5,851	$ 7,021	$ 8,215
Payroll taxes	$ 30,900	$ 36,308	$ 37,397
Total operating costs	**$289,441**	**$334,792**	**$347,206**
EBITDA	**$173,758**	**$221,047**	**$303,125**
Federal income tax	$ 57,340	$ 70,262	$ 97,567
State income tax	$ 8,688	$ 10,646	$ 14,783
Interest expense	$ 8,738	$ 8,131	$ 7,468
Depreciation expenses	$ 4,107	$ 4,107	$ 4,107
Net profit	**$ 94,885**	**$127,900**	**$179,200**
Profit margin	**19.46%**	**21.86%**	**26.18%**

Cash Flow Analysis

Proforma cash flow analysis—yearly

Year	2009	2010	2011
Cash from operations	$ 98,992	$132,008	$183,307
Cash from receivables	$ 0	$ 0	$ 0
Operating cash inflow	**$ 98,992**	**$132,008**	**$183,307**
Other cash inflows			
Equity investment	$ 10,000	$ 0	$ 0
Increased borrowings	$100,000	$ 0	$ 0
Sales of business assets	$ 0	$ 0	$ 0
A/P increases	$ 37,902	$ 43,587	$ 50,125
Total other cash inflows	**$147,902**	**$ 43,587**	**$ 50,125**
Total cash inflow	**$246,894**	**$175,595**	**$233,433**
Cash outflows			
Repayment of principal	$ 6,463	$ 7,070	$ 7,733
A/P decreases	$ 24,897	$ 29,876	$ 35,852
A/R increases	$ 0	$ 0	$ 0
Asset purchases	$ 57,500	$ 33,002	$ 45,827
Dividends	$ 69,295	$ 92,405	$128,315
Total cash outflows	**$158,155**	**$162,353**	**$217,727**
Net cash flow	**$ 88,739**	**$ 13,242**	**$ 15,706**
Cash balance	**$ 88,739**	**$101,981**	**$117,687**

Balance Sheet

Proforma balance sheet—yearly

Year	2009	2010	2011
Assets			
Cash	$ 88,739	$ 101,981	$117,687
Amortized expansion costs	$ 17,500	$ 20,800	$ 25,383
FF&E	$ 23,000	$ 47,751	$ 82,122
Vehicles	$ 17,000	$ 21,950	$ 28,824
Accumulated depreciation	($ 4,107)	($ 8,214)	($ 12,321)
Total assets	**$142,132**	**$184,269**	**$241,694**
Liabilities and equity			
Accounts payable	$ 13,005	$ 26,716	$ 40,990
Long term liabilities	$ 93,537	$ 86,467	$ 79,397
Other liabilities	$ 0	$ 0	$ 0
Total liabilities	**$106,542**	**$113,183**	**$120,387**
Net worth	**$ 35,591**	**$ 71,086**	**$121,308**
Total liabilities and equity	**$142,132**	**$184,269**	**$241,694**

Breakeven Analysis

Monthly break even analysis

Year	2009	2010	2011
Monthly revenue	$ 25,390	$ 29,368	$ 30,457
Yearly revenue	$304,675	$352,413	$365,480

Business Ratios

Business ratios—yearly

Year	2009	2010	2011
Sales			
Sales growth	0.0%	20.0%	17.0%
Gross margin	95.0%	95.0%	95.0%
Financials			
Profit margin	19.46%	21.86%	26.18%
Assets to liabilities	1.33%	1.63%	2.01%
Equity to liabilities	0.33%	0.63%	1.01%
Assets to equity	3.99%	2.59%	1.99%
Liquidity			
Acid test	0.83%	0.90%	0.98%
Cash to assets	0.62%	0.55%	0.49%

Children's Bookstore
Under the Shade Tree

4500 Peach Tree Drive
Columbia, Missouri 65202

Kari Lucke

Under the Shade Tree is a children's bookstore designed to offer a variety of children's books for ages 0 to 12. Our mission is to provide a comfortable, relaxed, low-pressure, and fun atmosphere (hence the "shade tree" logo) for both parents and children as they browse an array of printed and audio products that satisfy a wide range of children in terms of age, interests, and reading level.

INTRODUCTION

Mission Statement

Under the Shade Tree is a children's bookstore designed to offer a variety of children's books for ages 0 to 12. Our mission is to provide a comfortable, relaxed, low-pressure, and fun atmosphere (hence the "shade tree" logo) for both parents and children as they browse an array of printed and audio products that satisfy a wide range of children in terms of age, interests, and reading level.

Executive Summary

Under the Shade Tree is a new children's bookstore based in Columbia, Missouri, and founded by Renee Wilson. The store will offer books and related items for parents and children around the mid-Missouri area. Anticipated clients include middle-class to affluent families, mainly mothers, interested in engaging their children in educational and recreational reading activities.

Business Philosophy

Our business philosophy is that shopping for children's books should be fun, relaxing, and informed. As a former librarian at the Columbia Public Schools libraries, Renee Wilson has a wealth of knowledge about both books and children and will provide friendly and compassionate guidance as needed for parents who are striving to choose books that are appropriate and engaging for their children.

Goals and Objectives

The short-term goal of Under the Shade Tree is to realize a profit by year 2; the long-term goal is to become the premier children's bookseller in Columbia.

INDUSTRY AND MARKET

Industry Analysis

According to industry experts, the children's bookstore industry has remained fairly unaffected by the recent economic recession (http://www.underdown.org/the-economy.htm). Although several publishers initiated hiring freezes and cut back in other ways, overall book sales rose 5 percent in 2007, with the juvenile category registering a 6.2 increase. In 2008, despite the economy, total book sales rose 1 percent, according to Book Industry Study Group. The U.S. Census Bureau reported that book sales in September 2008 alone totaled almost $1.5 billion.

Market Analysis

Our market consists of residents of Columbia, Missouri, specifically those residing in the south part of the city. Columbia is a town of approximately 94,000, not including the student population (Columbia is home to two private four-year colleges and one major state university). The median household income of Columbia residents is $42,163, with a race distribution of 83 percent White, 9 percent Black, and 8 percent other. Our target market consists of middle- and upper-income families with children. Estimates show that this constitutes about 28 percent of the households in the city.

Columbia has grown significantly in the past decade and is expected to see continued growth. It is consistently rated one of the best places to live in America by such well-known entities as *Forbes*, *Money* magazine, and Kiplinger.com due to its excellent educational systems, access to health care, and quality of life. For example, in 2007 *Forbes* ranked Columbia "Third Best Metro for Business and Careers" in its study that factored in the cost of doing business, job growth, and educational attainment.

Due to these factors of demographics and growth trends as well as others, we see significant potential for a children's bookstore in this location. Unlike many small towns in Missouri which are losing population, Columbia's population is growing. In addition, the specific location within Columbia makes the bookstore especially accessible to the upper-class populace of the city.

Competition

There are no other bookstores in Columbia that are designed especially for children. The largest competitor for Under the Shade Tree will be Barnes & Noble Bookstore, located in the Columbia Mall. Although that store does have a children's section, it is located in the northwest part of town. There are no independent bookstores on the south side of town, where Under the Shade Tree will be located.

PERSONNEL

Management

Renee Wilson will be the owner and manager of Under the Shade Tree. Renee has a master's degree in library science from the University of Missouri and several years' experience working in Columbia Public Schools' libraries. Her background and experience will enable her to determine the best books to stock and help clients choose books, as well as to work with children and their parents. Renee is friendly, knowledgeable, and experienced with both books and children.

Staffing

Owner Renee Wilson will be onsite during most hours the bookstore is open. In addition, three part-time salespeople will be hired. One employee will work 10 a.m. to 3 p.m. Monday through Friday, one will work from 3 p.m. to 8 p.m. Monday through Friday, and the third will work from 9 a.m. to 5 p.m. on Saturdays and noon to 5 p.m. on Sundays. Salespeople will be required to assist customers, check out customers, stock books, and perform other related duties as required. Qualifications will include a high school diploma, the ability to work with people and perform the job duties, and an interest in books and reading. Part-time employees will earn $12 an hour with no benefits. Employees will be recruited via a classified ad in the local newspaper, the *Columbia Daily Tribune*. Renee will interview and hire employees based on their experience, background, and perceived suitability for the job. All employees will receive on-the-job training from Renee.

Professional and Advisory Support

Tina Green, an accountant with Accounting and More in Columbia, Missouri, will provide all bookkeeping services, including payroll and taxes.

Professional support will come from the American Booksellers Association (ABA), a national trade association for independent booksellers. The ABA provides education, services, and support for bookstore owners around the country. As a member, Renee has access to an annual conference, online training and support, newsletters and publications about the industry, and other tools that will help her keep up with industry trends and important events, as well as online forums and communities with other booksellers.

GROWTH STRATEGY

Growth of Under the Shade Tree will come in two forms. One is the services provided by the store. Although the store will be based on a retail model, it will also provide services to draw in customers. Examples include a monthly book club, a story hour, signings and readings by children's authors, and other services designed to foster community and loyalty in customers. Another area of growth will be in online sales. Although the store will have a website immediately upon opening, Renee plans to expand the types of services and products available on the site.

PRODUCTS AND SERVICES

Description
Under the Shade Tree Children's Bookstore will offer a variety of books for children ages zero to 12 in a fun and relaxed atmosphere.

Unique Features/Niche
Under the Shade Tree will be the only bookstore in Columbia geared specifically toward children and their parents and thus will be the premier bookstore choice for residents of Columbia and surrounding areas.

Pricing
Books sold at Under the Shade Tree will range in price from $0.99 to $35 and will be priced at approximately 30 percent above wholesale.

MARKETING AND SALES

Advertising and Promotion
Using the logo drawn by a local artist of a parent and child sitting on a blanket reading a book under a tree, Under the Shade Tree's initial advertising will consist of a quarter-page ad in the *Inside Columbia*

magazine, a monthly publication geared toward the upper-middle and upper class residents of Columbia; a smaller ad in the local newspaper, the *Columbia Daily Tribune*; and a website. The store will hold a Grand Opening celebration on opening day, which will include drawings for free books, refreshments, music, and other activities that appeal to children and parents. Flyers advertising the event will be printed and distributed to area businesses, particularly the new Hy-Vee grocery store and other high-traffic locations.

Cost

Cost of the ad in *Inside Columbia* will run $200 a month for three months and, for the *Columbia Daily Tribune*, $30 a week for one month. Decisions on future advertising will be based on response and activity generated by the ads. Flyers for the grand opening will cost around $100.

OPERATIONS

Customers

Our customers are middle- and upper-class parents and their children residing on the southern part of Columbia and outlying areas. Twenty-seven percent of Columbia households have incomes above $75,000, and 51 percent have children. As a town with a large population of young families, Columbia is an excellent location for a children's bookstore. Also, bookstore customers tend to have a higher level of education. According to the U.S. Census Bureau, more than half of Columbia residents have bachelor's degrees and more than a quarter hold master's degrees, making it the thirteenth most highly educated city in the United States. These demographics also make the city an ideal setting for a children's bookstore.

Suppliers

Books for inventory will be purchased from Baker & Taylor, a book wholesaler that has been in business for more than 100 years and is currently one of the largest book distributors in the country. The company has about 385,000 books in stock and more than 1.5 million available for order. Although headquartered in Charlotte, North Carolina, Baker & Taylor has several branches in the Midwest, including one at 501 South Gladiolus Street in Momence, Illinois. Baker & Taylor also offers a "First Call" program, whereby members can purchase books at a 40 percent discount. Shipping is only $1 per order for an unlimited number of boxes, and the minimum order if only 10 items.

Equipment

Equipment includes shelving and racks, cash wrap (checkout counter), computer, cash register, chairs, rugs, lighting, and other necessary fixtures. All equipment and installation will be provided by Retail Designs of Columbia. The initial cost is $10,000.

There will be six "sections" to the store, one containing parenting books and the others based on age group: baby (age 0-2), preschool (age 3-4), beginning reader (age 5-6), elementary (age 7-10), and "tweens" (age 11-12). Each section will contain approximately 200 books, for a total inventory of 1,200 books. The store provides about 1,200 square feet of space, so this level of inventory leaves plenty of room for wide aisles and browsing areas, as well as a few comfortable chairs. The format will be based somewhat on the Barnes & Noble model, in which customers are encouraged to take their time looking through the selection of books and even reading them before deciding on a purchase. Generally people like to have plenty of time to choose books to buy and do not want to feel pressured to "hurry up and make a decision." The layout and ambiance of Under the Shade Tree will provide a low-pressure and relaxed atmosphere for customers to make their selections.

The store will also purchase and use a computerized inventory control system provided by Anthology Inc. The Visual Anthology system is one of the leading inventory and POS systems for booksellers in the country and has been installed in more than 1,000 bookstores. Anthology provides all the hardware and software as well as online training for using the system and one year of free technical support. The cost of the system, including all hardware, is around $5,000.

Hours

The store will be open from 10 a.m. to 8 p.m. Monday through Friday, 10 a.m. to 5 p.m. Saturday, and noon to 5 p.m. Sunday.

Facility and Location

Renee will rent a storefront in the Peach Tree Plaza strip mall located at 4500 Peach Tree Drive on the south side of Columbia. Rent on the 1,200 square-foot space is $1,500 a month, and utilities average $200 a month. A large parking lot will serve Under the Shade Tree as well as the other businesses in the plaza.

FINANCIAL ANALYSIS

Start-up costs

Starting book inventory	$ 8,000
Fixtures, furniture, equipment	$10,000
Inventory control system	$ 5,000
Signs	$ 2,000
Advertising	$ 750
Grand opening costs	$ 1,000
Rent and deposit	$ 3,000
Business license/LLC	$ 500
Insurance	$ 100
Office supplies	$ 100
Total start-up costs	**$30,450**

Start-up costs will be financed by inheritance funds received by Renee Wilson.

Profit and Loss Statement

Most expenses are expected to increase at an approximate rate of 3 percent per year. Figures are rounded.

	Year 1	Year 2	Year 3
Net sales	$100,000	$115,000	$130,000
Cost of sales	$ 40,000	$ 46,000	$ 52,000
Gross profit margin	$ 60,000	$ 69,000	$ 78,000
Gross profit margin	60%	60%	60%
Operating expenses			
Rent	$ 18,000	$ 18,540	$ 19,100
Utilities and phone	$ 3,600	$ 3,710	$ 3,820
Part-time employee salaries	$ 36,000	$ 37,000	$ 38,000
Accounting services	$ 1,200	$ 1,240	$ 1,280
Insurance	$ 1,200	$ 1,240	$ 1,280
Advertising	$ 3,000	$ 3,100	$ 3,200
Office and other supplies	$ 1,200	$ 1,240	$ 1,280
Total expenses	**$ 64,200**	**$ 66,070**	**$ 67,960**
Profit (before taxes)	$ −4,200	$ 2,930	$ 10,040

Currency Trading

Fundex Currency Trading Co. Inc.

123 Main St.
Saskatoon, Saskatchewan Canada

Gerald Rekve
Eilsha Violet Rekve

Fundex Currency Trading Co. Inc. is a trading company that focuses on the market of currency trading. This is a very complicated market that requires great software, great people skills, and great customer acquisition skills.

EXECUTIVE SUMMARY

Fundex Currency Trading Co. Inc. is a trading company that focuses on the market of currency trading. This is a very complicated market that requires great software, great people skills, and great customer acquisition skills.

Opening in fall of 2009, Fundex Currency Trading Co. Inc. is going to be a one–owner business. Bob Brown will open the business after working with Firstdata International for over 10 years. Firstdata International is the world's largest credit card processing company.

Fundex Currency Trading Co. will be operating out of Saskatoon with affiliate offices around North America. All the services of the company will meet all regulatory requirements of all countries in which we operate.

To begin, the markets that Fundex Currency Trading Co. Inc. will be operating in include all twelve provinces of Canada, and six of the largest states in USA. To point out the size of the markets, California alone has more people than all of Canada. Therefore Canada will be considered a secondary market even though the head offices will be located in Canada.

PRODUCTS & SERVICES

Fundex Currency Trading Co. Inc. will be set up at the beginning to offer one product—to buy and sell currencies for clients as a hedge against a variety of markets such as stock exchange, gold, commodities, futures, and so on.

We will be using the largest bank network in Canada and the largest in the USA to hold all our trades as well as our funds. We will not have any money onsite at any of our locations across North America; all money payments will be taken electronically. This will help to ensure the safety of all of our staff.

Our business from 30,000 feet is simple—we buy and sell all of the currencies for our clients on a minute–by–minute basis, 365 days a year. From a close up view there is a lot of skill required and a great deal of computer and software power. We will earn our money from each buy and each sell regardless if the purchase makes any money for the client. This is because we will instruct all of our clients that there is no guarantee of success or profit with these trades.

Here is how our service works—we buy the $10,000 US dollar for a client at $1.02 Canadian, we charge the client 2 cents fee, and a 25% fee on any profit derived from the transaction. What this means if we sell the $10,000 US Dollars for $1.09 Canadian, the client will net profit out of this transaction $1.10 minus 1.02 = .08 cents less .02 cents (Our Fee) = .06 cents less 25 % or .06 x (–25) % = .015 cents our extra commission, therefore the client will net profit out of this for this transaction .045 cents.

THE MARKET

With the crash of 2008 and 2009, there are a lot of investors on the sidelines. These investors are everyone from large mutual funds to small investors. Our target market will be for institutional investors. These will be clients who on average will invest anywhere from $100,000 – $5,000,000 at a time.

There are a number of competitors now who operate in this market. Like any business model that is complicated there will be great operators and not-so-great operators. We will hire the best traders and use the best trading software.

Fundex Currency Trading Co. Inc. will focus all of its energies on the trade, knowing that success will breed success. With this being said, the market size right now for currency trading in the USA is approximately $250 billion gross. This means there is about $25 billion in potential revenue to be shared with all traders.

Fundex Currency Trading Co. Inc. will set a goal of $10,000,000 in sales in year one, a small number in comparison to the market size. However, we feel that growing small is a smart strategy. We will not over promise anything to clients; we will use our track record to show what we can accomplish while not guaranteeing future returns for clients.

OUR PRODUCTS & SERVICES

Fundex Currency Trading Co. Inc. works like this. We buy and sell all the currencies of the world on a daily basis to clients. Almost all of these trades will be performed electronically and we will never see the actual money. There will be situations where an office will get a request for a client to buy dollars in another currency for reasons like they are going on holidays or going to that country to buy materials or equipment and require this money to be in cash. This market is not a market we will try to sell into; there are too many risks, so we will be look at each transaction on an individual basis.

Here are some of the currencies we will be buying and selling:

- US dollar
- Canada dollar
- Euro
- Yen

OUR SOFTWARE

There are a number of suppliers of software that are used to trade currencies; we will take a trial use of each one and then use them in order to determine which one fits our needs and which one fits the needs of our clients.

Because all of our transactions will fall under the scrutiny of regulators, we will need to make sure the software functions for easy access and easy understanding for anyone viewing the past transactions.

HOW FUNDEX CURRENCY TRADING CO. INC. MAKES MONEY

Here is how our service works; we buy the $10,000 US dollar for a client at $1.02 Canadian, we then charge the client 2 cents fee, and a 25% fee on any profit derived from the transaction. What this means if we sell the $ 10,000 US Dollars for $ 1.09 Canadian , the client will net profit out of this transaction $ 1.10 minus 1.02 = .08 cents less .02 cents (Our Fee) = .06 cents less 25% or .06 x (−25) % = .015 cents our extra commission, therefore the client will net profit out of this for this transaction .045 cents.

In this transaction we made $150 (25% of profit) plus $200.00 for a grand total of $350.00. While this might not seem like a lot of money, this is one trade by one trader for a given day. Our goal is to be making hundreds of trades *per hour*.

We will open our head office in Saskatoon Saskatchewan, then from there open offices in Los Angeles, Seattle, New York, Chicago, Miami, Toronto, and Vancouver. All these offices will be owned by Fundex Currency Trading Co. Inc.

Affiliate offices will also be opened. An affiliate office is where someone else owns the office, such as an independent trader, etc. The affiliate office will have access to our traders. We will still do all the trades, but this affiliate office will acquire clients and electronically secure payments from the clients before we do the trades.

Both in Canada and the USA all funds are secured by federal agencies that oversee the client's investments. None of our offices will recommend any currency or investment to clients. Clients are required to tell us which transaction they would like to do. From that we will make the transaction.

We have determined the following—if we do 50 trades per day with a gross profit of $250 per trade, our daily revenue for one office will be $12,500 not including trader's commission and bonus and our operating expense. For one month the revenue will be $250,000 or $3 million for one office for one year.

We know we will never make profit for our clients on all the trades; however our goal will be to provide at least a 70% average with all our trades. The average is 47% for the industry. If we see the client may be putting their money into something that we are certain they will lose part or all of their money, we will not do the trade and tell the client the reasons. We feel this open and honest approach will secure clients for the long term.

OPENING BUDGET

This opening budget includes the Head Office only; all branch offices will open within the 3rd quarter of the 1st year.

Budget

Office rental	$ 6,000
Office equipment	$25,000
Office furniture	$15,000
Legal	$10,000
Accounting	$ 2,500
Supplies	$ 2,000
Travel	$ 5,000
Hire staff	$10,000
Advertising—short term (first month)	$15,000
Advertising—long term (first 12 months)	$50,000
Software testing	$25,000
Telephone	$ 1,500
Internet	$ 500
Cable TV	$ 200
Office renovation or setup	$10,000

STAFFING

- CEO/Owner— Bob Brown

- VP Client Manager—Jeff Smart

- VP Network Security—Ron Stettner

- VP Trading & Funding—Jim Ambrose

- VP Legal—Sara Parker

- VP Finance—Harry Walker

- Traders—There will be 20 traders in the Saskatoon office

In other company–owned offices, there will be just client support staff, such as sales staff that will acquire new clients and support staff. The number of these staff will be determined as we roll out the branch offices and these numbers will be based on the success of our head office.

INVESTMENT & START UP FUNDING

Bob Brown has invested $1 million into the business, and with this investment he has secured $700,000 in an operating line of credit secured with two notes. The first note is due in 24 months at 13% interest, and the 2nd note due in 36 months at 14% interest. This gives the business a total of $ 1.7 million start up to hire staff, open offices, gain clients, and so on.

Bob Brown is very frugal in nature. All the office furniture will be purchased via used venues, while making sure it does have a certain amount of quality, so clients coming into the office will feel comfortable with the setting.

Starting in year two, Bob Brown and the holder of the notes will start to take their equity out of the business. This should not impact the business, because at that stage the funds will be in place from company revenue to sustain the business from sales revenue.

In addition, the owner of the commercial office building where Fundex Currency Trading Co. Inc. will be leasing their office space has agreed to forgo the first six months lease payments if we sign a five year contract. Also, the supplier of the computers has agreed to void the first three months lease payments on the equipment.

These extra perks are not really required, but we will take advantage of the offers because we were going to sign this term anyway and a free offer is never turned down.

SOFTWARE PROVIDERS

We will test a number of software providers in order to determine which may give us the best trading platforms. Some of our requirements are listed below; we will adapt and change these requirements as we move forward in order to determine the best fit for the market in which we operate.

Here is a list of our current requirements:

- Must show by the second values of world currencies

- Must allow us to buy a spot price and open price where indicated

- Must allow us the ability to adjust commissions on each trade, so we know if we are making money on each trade and how much money we are making

- Needs to show our client name attached to each trade

- Must show value of trade

- The buy price must be shown

- The sell price must be shown

- Daily, weekly, monthly, and annually accumulated total must be shown

- There must be a level of customizability to the software allowing us to change features as we move along with our business.

- All of the above must be shown along with anything else as we see fit

STAFF TRAINING & EDUCATION

It is a misnomer that you require a high level of education do be a currency trader—this is not true. From past experience it has been shown that people that are good at this business come from all walks of life, with wide-ranging skills and education. For this reason we will look for more of an attitude when we hire traders, not ego-driven types for they prove to be all talk and no walk in this given profession.

We will train all our traders with our methodologies on trading currencies, and then from there let them loose. One of the keys to the success of our traders will be to understand the clients' needs. If a client tells us they do not want to lose any more than 5% on a trade, we will then put a stop loss on the trade for this client at 3.5%; we will never put our clients in a position where we lost exactly what their max was. This will not look good and our clients will start to wonder. On the other side we will always tell our clients to sell at a certain point, even if they are up 10% or 20%, because it is just as important to take your profits when you can, so you can reinvest those in other currencies that may be going up allowing the client to maximize their ROI for their investments.

MARKETING & ADVERTISING

Fundex Currency Trading Co. Inc. will spend their money on a wide variety of advertising methods to reach potential clients, including:

- Newspapers

- Magazines

- Internet

- TV shows & channels such as CNBC & CNN & BNN, Bloomberg etc.

- Website that is interactive to the currency market

All of the marketing for the company will focus on our company's ability to trade currencies of all countries while remaining impartial. We will advertise the fact that we do not guarantee the success of any trade or the ability for the investor to get guarantee of making profit or not losing money. We will be very honest with our clients and even tell our clients we will not do certain trades because we know the high risk of loss is too great for both the client and our reputation.

The demographics of our clients are mutual funds, private client services, individual clients who are in the high to medium high income brackets of $75,000 annual or more.

The newspaper and magazine advertisements will be soft sell, mostly telling about our service, how we can provide an income as well profit from trading in currencies.

All of the rest of the marketing and advertising will also focus on the soft sell, and not on the hard sell. We feel this is the best way for us to promote our business. Of course being a successful trader will also provide us with the ability to become known as traders who make money. This is no easy task, but it is the best way to gain clients, as success breeds success.

THE TRADING SYSTEM

In order to ensure all of our trades are managed for the benefit of our clients, we have embarked on the following quality control system.

In this the process, the client instructs us to buy $5,000 LBs at 2.50 USD. The support person to the trader then looks at the currencies to determine if it meets our requirements based on past performance and futures. Then if it meets those, the support person then sends the trader the buy order, and the trader again reviews the order to make sure it meets our requirements. Once complete, the trader then places the trade with the stop loss on it. We will hold the trade once successfully complete for as long as the client wants and as long as it does not start to lose money. It is given that all our trades are secured with real funds from the client.

This twofold system will allow us to monitor all the traders' trades. We have also added another form checking—we will have a Trading Manager who will on a daily basis check any 25 percent of trades for any warning signs. These signs are traders not following our protocol, or anything that might put our clients or us at risk. This manager will have full authority to pull a trader off the floor for any reason they feel needs attention.

The Trading Manager then reports to the Regional Trading Manager. The Regional Trading Manager will determine if the trader needs more training, or if there is another reason why the trader should be allowed to go back to the floor. For the first year we will let all our traders know that on a weekly basis we will pull them off the floor; this way when we do pull one off the floor it will not be a big thing and the traders will become used to seeing their trading buddies and them taken off the trading floor. It should be mentioned that the trading floor is just the trading system. The trader's password will be blocked; this is done privately so the trader being reviewed will not be made a public spectacle of.

OFFICE SET UP

Equipped with state of the art computers and software, this trading floor will be one to be outdone. All the computers will have multiple screens for each trader and the software will be chosen after the evaluation periods.

The security of the office will be the best in the business—all digital. Cameras will be placed strategically throughout the office space. The office will be connected to ADT security monitoring service. This way there will be 24/7 monitoring off the office space. Additionally the office location chosen will have an onsite security guard in place after hours. This will protect all the equipment, the client files, and so on. There will also be one of the most sophisticated online security systems in the market, similar to what banks use; this security system will protect all the online activity of the business.

GENERAL ASSUMPTIONS

General assumptions	Month 1	Month 2	Month 3	Month 4	Month 5	Month 6
Plan month	1	2	3	4	5	6
Current interest rate	10.00%	10.00%	10.00%	10.00%	10.00%	10.00%
Long-term interest rate	10.00%	10.00%	10.00%	10.00%	10.00%	10.00%
Tax rate	30.00%	30.00%	30.00%	30.00%	30.00%	30.00%

	Month 7	Month 8	Month 9	Month 10	Month 11	Month 12
Plan month	7	8	9	10	11	12
Current interest rate	10.00%	10.00%	10.00%	10.00%	10.00%	10.00%
Long-term interest rate	10.00%	10.00%	10.00%	10.00%	10.00%	10.00%
Tax rate	30.00%	30.00%	30.00%	30.00%	30.00%	30.00%

PROFIT AND LOSS

Pro forma profit and loss	Month 1	Month 2	Month 3	Month 4	Month 5	Month 6
Sales	$ 0	$ 0	$ 0	$222,500	$453,545	$456,681
Direct cost of sales	$ 0	$ 0	$ 0	$ 11,375	$211,532	$411,002
Other costs of sales	$ 0	$ 0	$ 0	$ 0	$ 0	$ 0
Total cost of sales						
Gross margin	$ 0	$ 0	$ 0	$ 2,125	$ 3,013	$ 5,679
Gross margin %	0.00%	0.00%	0.00%	85.00%	85.00%	85.00%
Expenses						
Payroll						
Sales and marketing and other expenses	$ 0	$ 0	$ 0	$ 0	$ 0	$ 0
Depreciation	$ 317	$ 317	$ 317	$ 317	$ 317	$ 317
Rent	$ 650	$ 650	$ 650	$ 650	$ 650	$ 650
Utilities	$ 150	$ 150	$ 150	$ 150	$ 150	$ 150
Insurance	$ 150	$ 150	$ 150	$ 150	$ 150	$ 150
Payroll taxes 15%	$ 750	$ 863	$ 1,463	$ 1,538	$ 1,613	$ 1,688
Other	$ 150	$ 150	$ 150	$ 150	$ 150	$ 150
Total operating expenses						
Profit before interest and taxes	($ 7,167)	($ 8,030)	($ 12,630)	($ 11,080)	($ 10,766)	($ 8,676)
EBITDA	($ 6,850)	($ 7,713)	($ 12,313)	($ 10,763)	($ 10,449)	($ 8,359)
Interest expense	$ 0	$ 0	$ 0	$ 0	$ 0	$ 0

	Month 7	Month 8	Month 9	Month 10	Month 11	Month 12
Sales	$458,641	$459,312	$104,987	$141,110	$155,585	$142,784
Direct cost of sales	$ 1,296	$521,397	$321,648	$211,667	$231,820	$251,909
Other costs of sales	$ 0	$ 0	$ 0	$ 0	$ 0	$ 0
Total cost of sales						
Gross margin	$ 7,345	$ 7,916	$ 9,339	$ 9,444	$ 10,315	$ 10,816
Gross margin %	85.00%	85.00%	85.00%	85.00%	85.00%	85.00%
Expenses						
Payroll						
Sales and marketing and other expenses	$ 0	$ 0	$ 0	$ 0	$ 0	$ 0
Depreciation	$ 317	$ 317	$ 317	$ 317	$ 317	$ 317
Rent	$ 650	$ 650	$ 650	$ 650	$ 650	$ 650
Utilities	$ 150	$ 150	$ 150	$ 150	$ 150	$ 150
Insurance	$ 150	$ 150	$ 150	$ 150	$ 150	$ 150
Payroll taxes	$ 1,688	$ 1,688	$ 1,688	$ 1,688	$ 1,688	$ 1,688
Other	$ 150	$ 150	$ 150	$ 150	$ 150	$ 150
Total operating expenses						
Profit before interest and taxes	($ 7,010)	($ 6,439)	($ 5,016)	($ 4,911)	($ 4,040)	($ 3,539)
EBITDA	($ 6,693)	($ 6,122)	($ 4,699)	($ 4,594)	($ 3,723)	($ 3,222)
Interest expense	$ 0	$ 55	$ 0	$ 25	$ 25	$ 23

CASH FLOW

Pro forma cash flow	Month 1	Month 2	Month 3	Month 4	Month 5	Month 6
Cash received						
Cash from operations						
Cash sales	$ 0	$ 0	$ 0	$ 2,500	$ 3,545	$ 6,681
Subtotal cash from operations	$ 0	$ 0	$ 0	$ 2,500	$ 3,545	$ 6,681
Additional cash received						
New current borrowing	$ 0	$ 0	$ 0	$ 0	$ 0	$ 0
Subtotal cash received	$ 0	$ 0	$ 0	$ 2,500	$ 3,545	$ 6,681
Expenditures						
Expenditures from operations						
Cash spending	$ 5,000	$ 5,750	$ 9,750	$10,250	$10,750	$11,250
Bill payments	$ 62	$ 1,854	$ 1,983	$ 2,578	$ 3,020	$ 3,262
Subtotal spent on operations	$ 5,062	$ 7,604	$11,733	$12,828	$13,770	$14,512

	Month 7	Month 8	Month 9	Month 10	Month 11	Month 12
Cash received						
Cash from operations						
Cash sales	$ 8,641	$ 9,312	$10,987	$11,110	$12,135	$12,724
Subtotal cash from operations	$ 8,641	$ 9,312	$10,987	$11,110	$12,135	$12,724
Additional cash received						
New current borrowing	$ 0	$ 0	$ 0	$ 3,000	$ 0	$ 0
Subtotal cash received	$ 8,641	$ 9,312	$10,987	$14,110	$12,135	$12,724
Expenditures						
Expenditures from operations						
Cash spending	$11,250	$11,250	$11,250	$11,250	$11,250	$11,250
Bill payments	$ 3,799	$ 4,087	$ 4,193	$ 4,437	$ 4,484	$ 4,636
Subtotal spent on operations	$15,049	$15,337	$15,443	$15,687	$15,734	$15,886

BALANCE SHEET

Pro forma balance sheet	Starting balances	Month 1	Month 2	Month 3	Month 4	Month 5	Month 6
Assets							
Current assets							
Cash	$1500,000	$223,938	$ 61,335	$ 43,602	$212,225	$341,019	$262,218
Other current assets	$ 7,000	$ 7,000	$ 7,000	$ 7,000	$ 7,000	$ 7,000	$ 7,000
Long-term assets							
Long-term assets	$ 239,000	$239,000	$239,000	$239,000	$239,000	$239,000	$239,000
Accumulated depreciation	$ 0	$317	$ 634	$ 951	$ 1,268	$ 1,585	$ 1,902
Total long-term assets	$ 19,000	$ 18,683	$ 18,366	$ 18,049	$ 17,732	$ 17,415	$ 17,098
Total assets	$ 105,000	$ 99,621	$ 91,701	$ 79,651	$ 69,007	$ 58,464	$ 50,316
Liabilities and capital							
Current liabilities							
Accounts payable	$ 0	$ 1,788	$ 1,897	$ 2,477	$ 2,912	$ 3,136	$ 3,663
Current borrowing	$ 0	$ 0	$ 0	$ 0	$ 0	$ 0	$ 0
Subtotal current liabilities	$ 0	$ 1,788	$ 1,897	$ 2,477	$ 2,912	$ 3,136	$ 3,663
Paid-in capital	$ 125,000	$125,000	$125,000	$125,000	$125,000	$125,000	$125,000
Retained earnings	($ 20,000)	($ 20,000)	($ 20,000)	($ 20,000)	($ 20,000)	($ 20,000)	($ 20,000)
Earnings	$ 0	($ 7,167)	($ 15,197)	($ 27,826)	($ 38,906)	($ 49,672)	($ 58,347)

	Starting balances	Month 7	Month 8	Month 9	Month 10	Month 11	Month 12
Assets							
Current assets							
Cash	$1500,000	$229,809	$163,715	$ 19,312	$ 17,732	$ 24,152	$ 692 12
Other current assets	$ 7,000	$ 7,000	$ 7,000	$ 7,000	$ 7,000	$ 7,000	$ 7,000
Long-term assets							
Long-term assets	$ 239,000	$239,000	$239,000	$239,000	$239,000	$239,000	$239,000
Accumulated depreciation	$ 0	$ 2,219	$ 2,536	$ 2,853	$ 3,170	$ 3,487	$ 3,804
Total long-term assets	$ 19,000	$ 16,781	$ 16,464	$ 16,147	$ 15,830	$ 15,513	$ 15,196
Total assets	$ 105,000	$ 43,590	$ 37,249	$ 32,476	$ 30,582	$ 26,666	$ 22,888
Liabilities and capital							
Current liabilities							
Accounts payable	$ 0	$ 3,947	$ 4,045	$ 4,288	$ 4,330	$ 4,478	$ 4,561
Current borrowing	$ 0	$ 0	$ 0	$ 0	$ 3,000	$ 3,000	$ 2,700
Subtotal current liabilities	$ 0	$ 3,947	$ 4,045	$ 4,288	$ 7,330	$ 7,478	$ 7,261
Paid-in capital	$ 125,000	$125,000	$125,000	$125,000	$125,000	$125,000	$125,000
Retained earnings	($ 20,000)	($ 20,000)	($ 20,000)	($ 20,000)	($ 20,000)	($ 20,000)	($ 20,000)
Earnings	$ 0	($ 65,357)	($ 71,796)	($ 76,812)	($ 81,748)	($ 85,813)	($ 89,374)

Dog Training Business

A-1 Dog Training & Behavior LLC

7158 Charles St.
Springburg, Illinois 62051

Paul Greenland

A-1 Dog Training & Behavior LLC provides in-home obedience training for dogs.

EXECUTIVE SUMMARY

Business Overview

According to data from the American Pet Products Manufacturers Association (APPMA), by the late 2000s there were nearly 45 million dogs in the United States. Information from different studies indicates that approximately 40 percent of North American homes include a dog. Given the many benefits associated with owning a pet, this may not come as a surprise. However, some surveys suggest that as many as 70 percent of dogs have some form of behavioral problem. These can range from simple issues, such as a lack of focus and attention or loose leash walking, to more serious problems, such as chewing, digging, and aggressive behavior.

When problems such as these present themselves, A-1 Dog Training & Behavior LLC is here to help frustrated dog owners identify a solution. We provide motivation-based (not punishment-based) training for all kinds of dogs. In addition to helping prospective dog owners choose the right breed prior to purchase, we provide them with new puppy training after they bring their new pet home. We also help existing pet owners address a wide variety of behavioral problems. Successful trainers must have a good understanding of both human and animal behavior, and in many ways, the training we provide pertains just as much to the owners as it does to the dogs.

In recent years, dog training has become big business. For example, one industry leader became successful by developing a relationship with a leading pet supplies retailer, and went on to handle dog training in approximately 750 stores throughout North America. Although the "big box" business model is one approach, ample opportunity still exists in most markets for smaller, independent dog training businesses. Those who develop a good reputation, work hard to build relationships with area veterinarians (a key referral source), and manage their business responsibly, will find success.

Company History

Lisa Butler has been surrounded by canines for as long as she can remember. Growing up, her family included two golden retrievers. Her love for dogs led to volunteer service at a local animal shelter at the age of 14. Two years later, she became a part-time employee of the shelter, where she cleaned kennels, walked dogs, assisted veterinary technicians and veterinarians, ordered and stocked supplies, and helped the office staff with paperwork.

During her employment at the shelter, Butler became familiar with several trainers who were occasionally brought in to help dogs with behavioral problems. While attending a local community college, she began shadowing one of these trainers, who inspired her to pursue dog training as a profession. Butler recently graduated with honors, earning an associate's degree in business management. She plans to continue working part-time at the shelter while building her new dog training business.

MARKET ANALYSIS

Overview

According to data from the American Pet Products Manufacturers Association (APPMA), roughly 63 percent of U.S. households contain a pet. By the late 2000s, the nation was home to an estimated 44.8 million dogs. After growing to $38.5 billion in 2006, consumer spending on pets was expected to reach $40.8 million in 2007 and $52.0 billion by 2009.

U.S. Census data indicates that the community of Springburg, Illinois, consists of approximately 56,756 households. Using formulas from the 2007 *U.S. Pet Ownership & Demographics Sourcebook*, the community includes an estimated 4,538 dog-owning households (7,715 dogs).

Competition

Springburg, Illinois, is home to SuperPet Universe, a big-box store with approximately 485 locations throughout the United States. In addition to selling dogs and pet supplies, SuperPet offers dog training within its store; it is a one-stop shop for pet owners. Although no research data exists, based on conversations with other local dog trainers, as well as news articles about SuperPet's typical market share, we estimate that the retailer has cornered 35 percent of the dog training market in Springburg.

GoodDawgz is another major player in our local market. This independently-owned dog training business employs eight full-time trainers and three part-time trainers. The business has been a part of the Springburg community for 12 years and has a good reputation among local veterinarians. Good-Dawgz has likely cornered about 20 percent of the dog training market in our community.

Various independent dog trainers and small dog training businesses control the remainder of the dog training market in Springburg. Conversations with many of these individuals indicates that the demand for dog training services in our area is very strong; there seems to be no shortage of potential customers.

INDUSTRY ANALYSIS

Dog training dates back thousands of years. In the United States, professional dog training is well-established. Humane, reward-based training was used before World War I. However, the need for dogs during the war ushered in methods focused on punishment and fear. During the 1970s, Ireland's Barbara Woodhouse became well known for her use of more humane training methods involving treats and other rewards. She authored the popular book *No Bad Dogs: The Woodhouse Way*. Animal behaviorists such as Gary Wilkes and Karen Pryor introduced so-called "click and treat" training during the late 1980s, which involves the use of a mechanical clicker during the training process.

The primary professional organization within our field is the Association of Pet Dog Trainers (APDT). As the association explains on its Web site, APDT "offers individual pet dog trainers a respected and concerted voice in the dog world." Its primary functions include the promotion of dog-friendly training techniques, as well as the promotion of professional dog trainers to veterinarians.

Established in 1993, the association had approximately 6,000 members throughout the world by 2009. Each year, APDT hosts an annual conference attended by 1,500 people. Like most large professional organizations, the association offers a newsletter, seminars, a membership directory, and opportunities to network with professionals within the field. Although APDT does not endorse specific trainers, it does serve as a referral source for pet owners seeking dog trainers.

PERSONNEL

Lisa Butler will be the sole employee of A-1 Dog Training & Behavior during its initial years of operation. In addition, she has secured professional and advisory support in a number of key areas. For example, she has established a business banking account with Springburg Community Bank, as well as a merchant account for accepting credit card payments. Legal services are provided by the firm of Holmstrom & Brooks, and tax advisory services are provided by ACME Accounting Services LLC.

GROWTH STRATEGY

Lisa Butler plans to grow A-1 Dog Training & Behavior at a steady, measured pace. She realizes that business will be slower during the business' first year, as she focuses on establishing her client base and generating awareness about her services. She anticipates operating the business full-time beginning in year two. During year three, her goal is to add one additional full-time trainer, followed by another full-time trainer in year four.

During year five, Butler plans to add a third full-time trainer and also begin leasing a small facility where she can offer cost-effective training to groups of five-to-seven dog owners at a time. This approach will allow her to compete more aggressively with SuperPet Universe and GoodDawgz. In addition, A-1 Dog Training & Behavior plans to begin operating a doggy day care service at this facility, which will be unique in the Springburg community.

SERVICES

A-1 Dog Training & Behavior offers all dog training services in the customer's home.

When working with clients, we follow a clearly defined process:

1. *Initial Consultation.* All new client relationships begin with a free telephone consultation. This allows us to learn about the caller's situation and determine whether or not our training services will be beneficial.

2. *Assessment.* If it appears that we can be of assistance, we provide a detailed intake form (via mail or our Web site) to the customer for completion. We then schedule an in-home assessment to meet the dog, the owners, and evaluate the home environment. This information is then combined with the intake form to provide the owners with our observations and recommendations. The process provides a framework/game plan for the actual training. Assessments are provided at a cost of $50, which must be paid in advance.

3. *Training.* Once the assessment process is complete, we proceed with training focused on obedience and dog behavior. When appropriate, basic training services (e.g. new puppy training) are provided in packages with one flat fee. In addition, we also offer ongoing services at a rate of $75 per hour. Our training approach is motivation-based (e.g., food and toys), as opposed to punishment-based.

Generally speaking, we require basic training packages to be completed within 10 weeks, while specialized/difficult behavior issues often require more time.

Examples of the services we provide include:

- Grooming
- Instruction
- Advice about puppy-/dog-proofing homes
- Breed selection (prior to purchase)
- Health & nutrition
- Socialization (with other dogs and people)
- Potty training
- Hand signal/voice command training
- Puppy obedience
- On/off-leash obedience
- Crate training

Examples of the dog behaviors our training programs address include:

- Focus & attention
- Loose leash walking
- Licking
- Chewing
- Digging
- Inappropriate jumping
- Aggressive/dominant behavior
- Barking
- Separation problems (anxiety/stress when owner is not present)
- Shy/fearful behavior

MARKETING & SALES

A-1 Dog Training & Behavior has developed a marketing plan that involves the following primary tactics:

1. A simple bi-fold brochure describing our business.
2. A basic Yellow Page listing under Pet Services.
3. The development of professional relationships with local veterinarians to secure training referrals.
4. A weekly appearance on the cable access program "You & Your Pet", which includes a local veterinarian answering frequently-asked questions about health. Owner Lisa Butler will accept questions about pet behavior problems and basic pet training.
5. A web site with complete details about our business and the services we offer.
6. A monthly pet training e-newsletter for area pet owners.

7. Flyers distributed via area veterinary offices, pet grooming businesses, and pet supply stores, in order to promote our training services.

8. A customer loyalty program that provides a 10 percent discount to those referring a friend or family member to our business.

OPERATIONS

Because A-1 Dog Training & Behavior provides all services directly in the customer's home, we have no facility costs. The owner has dedicated a small space within her apartment to be used exclusively for business purposes. Telephone calls for the business will be received on a dedicated cell phone, allowing the owner to accept calls while she is in the field.

Lisa Butler has purchased a computer, as well as a specialized software program developed specifically for dog training businesses. The application includes an online registration function that can be integrated easily with any Web site, a scheduling/calendar function, a training log feature that can be customized for each dog/owner, and more.

In addition, a basic arrangement of training equipment has been acquired, including leashes, collars, scratch pants, bite sleeves, jackets and vests, clickers, whistles, bite tugs, dog treats, and play toys.

Payment & Fees

We provide dog training assessments at a cost of $50, which must be paid in advance.

Basic training services are provided as packages, with one flat fee. For example, our most popular packages are:

- New Puppy ($300)—Includes one hour per week for five weeks. Suitable for dogs younger than six months of age.

- Basic Manners & Skills ($375)—A program for dogs more than six months old.

A 10 percent discount is offered for packages paid for in advance.

In addition, we also offer ongoing services at a rate of $75 per hour.

Cancellations for all services must be made 24 hours in advance. For last-minute cancellations, we assess a charge equal to one hour of regular service ($75). We require that all customers provide us with their credit card number, even if they do not choose to pay via credit card, so that we can bill for last-minute cancellations.

FINANCIAL ANALYSIS

Start-up Budget
- Advertising & Marketing—$950

- Equipment—$650

- Transportation/Fuel—$1,200

- Miscellaneous Items—$500

- Legal—$550

- Accounting—$825

- Office Supplies—$300

- Computers/Peripherals—$1,200

- Liability Insurance—$500

- Salary—$5,000

Based on an analysis of the local market and our aforementioned growth strategy, financial projections for the first five years of operations are as follows:

Revenue
- 2010—$15,000

- 2011—$35,000

- 2012—$62,500

- 2013—$95,300

- 2014—$153,500

Expenses
- 2010—$11,675

- 2011—$26,275

- 2012—$49,800

- 2013—$73,550

- 2014—$131,750

Net Profit
- 2010—$3,325

- 2011—$8,725

- 2012—$12,700

- 2013—$21,750

- 2014—$21,750

Lisa Butler is contributing first-year start-up costs of $11,675 from her personal savings.

Health Advocacy Business

Medical Navigation Services Inc.

115 E. Peters Ave.
Myersville, FL 01225

Paul Greenland

Medical Navigation Services LLC is an independent advocacy business that helps consumers navigate the complexities of the healthcare system, identify treatment options, and secure appropriate resources.

EXECUTIVE SUMMARY

Business Overview

During the late 21st century, healthcare had become an incredibly complex industry. Multiple inter-connected, yet independently operating entities—including doctors, clinics, hospitals, healthcare systems, pharmacies, insurance companies, state and federal agencies, employers, and more—were involved in providing care for individual patients. With so many elements involved, individual healthcare consumers were frequently frustrated, and sometimes jeopardized, by miscommunication, broken processes, medical errors, uncoordinated healthcare delivery, and billing mistakes.

Medical Navigation Services LLC is an independent advocacy business that helps consumers navigate the complexities of the healthcare system, identify treatment options, and secure appropriate resources. Our business helps patients and their families cut through the clutter, understand their rights, decode confusing information, and secure the very best, highest-quality healthcare possible. Staffed by two veteran registered nurses and an experienced medical social worker, our business has the knowledge to help others navigate the healthcare jungle. Equally important is that we genuinely care about the people we serve. They are the reason we established Medical Navigation Services in the first place.

Organizational Structure

Our company is a privately held corporation based in the state of Florida. The organization is owned by Penny Marshall, RN, BSN; Sharon McCarthy, RN, MSN; and Paul Webster, MSW.

Company History

Medical Navigation Services was born of first-hand experience. In 2007, Penny Marshall, a staff nurse at a Chicago-area hospital, celebrated the birth of her first child. Although she was looking forward to a 12-week maternity leave with her new baby, the experience turned out to be very unsettling. Only a few hours after giving birth, Marshall learned that her father had had been severely injured in a construction accident—in Florida. Penny's mother had died many years before, and she had no siblings. Because she had power of attorney for her father's healthcare, medical providers were soon contacting her to obtain answers to difficult questions about her father's care. The hospital billing department also wanted to speak with her, to determine who would be paying his medical bills.

In the weeks and months that followed, Marshall would temporarily relocate, with her new baby, to Florida. Living in her father's apartment, she divided her time visiting him in the hospital; making phone calls to insurance companies; making important decisions regarding his care; securing an attorney to deal with her father's employer, which was contesting workers compensation liability; researching area rehabilitation centers that would accept her father after his discharge from the hospital; trying to estimate his long-term prognosis, and whether or not he could live independently; and trying to bond with her baby.

For more than a year, the man who had raised Penny Marshall without a mother, and who had always been a source of strength for his daughter, depended on her completely. Ultimately, her tireless advocacy for her father played a critical role in his recovery. Inspired by this life-changing experience, and realizing the important role her medical knowledge had played, Marshall decided to devote her career to helping others navigate similar, seemingly overwhelming situations.

After relocating permanently to Florida, Marshall spent 2008 researching what it would take to establish her own medical advocacy business. During her father's long hospital stays, she met Sharon McCarthy, a former critical care nurse who no longer worked in direct patient care due to a back injury, and Paul Webster, a hospital social worker who had spent his entire career advocating for patients and their families. After learning about Marshall's business idea, McCarthy and Webster indicated a desire to partner with her in the new enterprise.

MARKET ANALYSIS

Medical Navigation Services is located in Fort Myers, Florida (Lee County). According to the Lee County Economic Development Office, the city of Fort Myers included 67,851 residents in 2008. Beyond Fort Myers, the county included 164,523 residents in Cape Coral; 45,148 residents in Bonita Springs; 7,037 residents in Fort Myers Beach; 6,297 residents in Sanibel; and 324,885 in unincorporated areas.

According to demographic data from SRC LLC, the larger Fort Myers-Naples DMA included an estimated 461,176 households in 2009. On average, household incomes totaled $74,017, and were expected to increase to $75,771 by 2014.

Each year, consumers in our market devote considerable financial resources to healthcare. On average, annual household expenditures on healthcare totaled $3,455 in 2009. Of this amount, a large percentage ($1,668) was attributed to health insurance. Healthcare supplies and equipment ($957) ranked second, followed by healthcare services ($830).

In addition to numerous primary care and specialty clinics, healthcare consumers in our local and regional markets are served by several large healthcare organizations. These include Lee Memorial Health System and Peace River Regional Medical Center. The patients of these two facilities alone provide us with ample opportunities for advocacy services.

Due to the nature of our business, providing services beyond our local and regional markets would be easy to do (e.g., via phone, fax, and e-mail. In addition, numerous other communities throughout Florida are within easy driving distance of Fort Myers, for clients requiring or desiring in-person meetings.

Significant opportunities exist as we expand our business to other areas of the state. According to the Florida Hospital Association (FHA), Florida is home to 294 hospitals, offering 65,887 beds. In 2009 patient discharges totaled 2.3 million. Some 1.4 million outpatient surgeries were performed that year, followed by 586,172 inpatient surgeries.

The FHA reports that Florida's population included in 19 million people in 2009. By 2030 this number is expected to reach 24 million. Those aged 65 and older represented 18 percent of the state's population, or 3.4 million people. Among the state's population, 7.74 million residents were covered by some form of commercial insurance, while 1.86 million were covered by a commercial HMO. Another 2.42 million residents were covered by Medicare, with 716,358 covered by a Medicare HMO. Approximately 1.52 million people were covered by Medicaid, while 844,453 individuals were covered by a Medicaid HMO. The Kid Care program covered 218,707 children. Finally, some 3.8 million individuals were uninsured.

Currently, we face competition from several national advocacy services, including TGS Health Advocacy Associates and Care Counselors. In addition, national associations such as the American Cancer Society also provide limited resources to consumers that overlap with the services we provide. We plan to differentiate ourselves from our competitors by leveraging our in-depth knowledge of the Florida healthcare market, and the relationships we have established with providers and community resources in our home state.

INDUSTRY ANALYSIS

Medical advocacy is not a new profession. In fact, advocates have been providing services to patients for several decades. Uniform statistics regarding the size and scope of the industry are not available. However, providers within our industry are growing numbers as the healthcare system becomes more complex and fragmented.

In addition to independent advocates, some of the players within our industry work on behalf of organizations and insurance companies. For example, Bertelsmann and Home Depot were among larger organizations that provided their employees with complimentary access to health advocates during the late 2000s. According to *Business Week*, in 2008 more than 3,000 employers were expected to offer services like ours to their workforces. One criticism of services sponsored by organizations and/or insurance companies is that, ultimately, they will side with options that are in the best interests of those who are funding the service. Although advocates who work for other organizations claim that they are not influenced by them, it is our belief that healthcare consumers benefit from independent advocates.

PERSONNEL

Medical Navigation Services is owned by Penny Marshall, RN, BSN; Sharon McCarthy, RN, MSN; and Paul Webster, MSW. Collectively, the owners have more than 65 years of combined experience in the healthcare industry.

Penny Marshall, RN BSN

Penny received her education in the state of Pennsylvania. She is a graduate of the Barnes Hospital School of Nursing and received her BSN from Penn State University. She began her career as a medical/surgical staff nurse at Peter Stanbury General Hospital in Chicago, Illinois, where she worked for many years. In 2002 Penny accepted a position as a charge nurse at Chicago Memorial Hospital. Two years later, she was promoted to nurse manager of ambulatory surgery. In addition to performing traditional management duties, Penny was responsible for implementing a nurse liaison program at Chicago Memorial. This program involved the assignment of staff nurses to surgical waiting areas, where they provided regular updates to families whose loved ones were having surgery.

Sharon McCarthy, RN, MSN

Sharon McCarthy, RN, MSN, attended Rogers County Community College in Dallas, Texas, and obtained her BSN and MSN degrees from the University of Arkansas. After devoting 10 years to the telemetry & ICU units at Good Shepherd Hospital near Orlando, Florida, Sharon began working as a home health nurse. In this role, she gained tremendous insight into the impact that health challenges, and importantly good healthcare, have on families. A management opportunity presented itself in 2004, and Sharon became a nursing supervisor at Good Shepherd. This allowed her to gain a broader perspective on hospital operations and familiarize herself with operational issues such as staffing challenges, nurse-to-patient ratios, media relations, and more.

Paul Webster, MSW

Paul Webster, MSW, received his undergraduate education at Smithfield College, in Petersburg, Florida, and earned his Masters in Social Work degree from Florida State University. Paul has been employed by several Florida-area hospitals. In this role, he worked in discharge planning, and consulted with about patients and families in a variety of areas. Specifically, he provided advisement regarding illnesses, diagnoses, treatments, hospitalization-related issues, as well as emotional, mental, and substance abuse disorders.

Professional & Advisory Support

Medical Navigation Services utilizes the Community Bank of Fort Myers for its business banking, including a merchant account for credit card payments. Legal services are provided by Cacciatore & Ferrone, a law firm that includes a healthcare law division. Tax advisory services are provided by Borough Marsh & Co. Finally, John J. Hamilton MD, a semi-retired Florida physician, has been retained as a consultant, serving in an advisory role on an as-needed basis. Occasionally, Dr. Hamilton consults with our clients' physicians in matters regarding their care.

GROWTH STRATEGY

Following is a five-year growth strategy for our new business.

Years 1-2: During our first two years of operations, we will focus on the implementation and maintenance of sound small business principles. Because we have no prior business ownership experience, we realize this is very important. In addition to a small business ownership class that the owners have already completed at a local community college, we will continue to pursue additional business-related continuing education. Considerable energy also will be devoted to generating awareness of the services we offer among local healthcare consumers, and building/strengthening relationships with area healthcare professionals.

Year 3-4: During our third year, we plan to begin expanding geographically. We will concentrate marketing activities on nearby regional markets during this time.

Year 5: If regional expansion is successful during our third and fourth years, medical navigation services will pursue state-wide expansion during year five.

SERVICES

All new relationships begin with a conference to discuss the client's situation and identify objectives/desired outcomes. Enough information is gathered to provide the client with a time and cost estimate. Once an estimate has been agreed upon, we complete paperwork that allows us to work on our client's behalf and begin gathering detailed information from them. This often includes medical records, as well as contact information for healthcare providers and insurance companies.

When working in an advocacy/advisory capacity, our services may include one or more of the following services:

- Understanding complex medical terminology/situations
- Making/expediting appointments with healthcare providers

- Accompanying patients to doctor visits

- Helping patients interpret or understand medical bills and health insurance statements

- Identifying and resolving billing errors

- Providing patient education

- Negotiating the settlement of insurance claims

- Identifying and securing community resources, including eldercare services

- Improving the continuity of healthcare services from one facility/provider to another

- Providing wellness coaching

- Helping patients and families choose the best hospital or most effective treatment options

- Performing research regarding specific medical treatments, conditions, and diagnoses

- Educating patients about their rights

In most cases, we charge $100 per hour for our services. However, we charge a flat fee for certain service packages.

Our physician referral service ($100) involves an interview with the patient to learn about their current medical situation or diagnosis, and the research required to provide them with the names of one to five medical specialists who are capable of treating their condition. When needed, we consult with nurses and physicians with whom we have established relationships to learn as much as possible about the physicians we are recommending.

We also offer a basic medical research ($350) package that provides consumers with foundational knowledge about a particular disease/disorder, as well as a summary of the latest research and treatment options. For this service, we rely on various online databases to which we subscribe, as well as medical librarians at medical schools and hospitals.

For families who need assistance with ongoing medical issues, including the parents of special needs children, as well as those with elderly parents suffering from chronic health conditions, we offer the Family Friend package, which provides 10 hours of services for only $750. Clients are required to pre-pay for this service.

Clients may pay us by cash, money order, check, credit card (Visa, MasterCard, Discover, and American Express) and PayPal (a popular online payment service).

MARKETING & SALES

We have developed a marketing plan that involves the following primary tactics:

1. Printed collateral describing our business.

2. A Yellow Page advertisement.

3. A Web site with complete details about our business and the services we offer.

4. Ongoing direct mail campaigns to households within a 75-mile radius of Fort Myers. Specifically, campaigns will target female consumers, ages 45 to 64, who are the primary healthcare decision-makers for their families, as well as aging parents. Mailing lists will target consumers with household incomes of $45,000 and above.

5. Free public events, advertised online, via direct mail, and in our local newspaper, where consumers can learn about the benefits of having a personal health advocate.

6. A public relations campaign that involves the submission of "success stories," in the form of press releases, to local news media.

7. Relationship-building efforts (e.g., lunch meetings, department meeting presentations, etc.) targeting counselors, social workers, nurses, and discharge planners at area hospitals and clinics.

OPERATIONS

Facility & Location

In order to keep our overhead low, the owners of Medical Navigation Services will maintain home offices for the first few years of operations. Because we will spend a considerable amount of time in the field, meeting with healthcare professionals and consumers, or performing research, we feel this model will work well for our business.

In addition, we will take advantage of virtual office space (VOS). For low monthly fee, a local VOS service provides us with:

- A receptionist who receives calls to our business and coordinates messages during business hours.

- An after-hours answering service.

- A "mailroom" service, which handles our incoming/outgoing U.S. mail and overnight packages.

- Access to limited conference/meeting room space, with basic refreshment service (e.g., coffee, water, etc.), when personal meetings are required.

Hours of Operation

Medical Navigation Services will maintain office hours of 8:00 a.m. to 5:00 p.m., Monday through Friday. However, because healthcare is a 24-hour business, one of our advocates will be available on an on-call basis, via an answering service, for existing clients who need our assistance in urgent or emergency situations. Each month, on-call time will be divided equally among our firm's owners.

LEGAL

Medical Navigation Services operates in full compliance with the Health Insurance Portability & Accountability Act of 1996 (HIPAA), a public law passed by Congress that protects the privacy of health information. Our business signs legal agreements with the healthcare consumers we work with, obligating us to maintain strict confidentiality standards. In addition, we provide medical release forms to their healthcare providers to secure access to all necessary medical records.

FINANCIAL ANALYSIS

Start-up Budget
- Advertising & Marketing—$2,500

- Virtual Office Services—$5,500

- Miscellaneous items—$1,000

- Legal—$2,750
- Health Insurance—$12,800
- Accounting—$825
- Office supplies—$500
- Laptop computers/peripherals—$3,400
- Liability Insurance—$6,500
- Salaries—$150,000

Projected Expenses

Based upon the above start-up budget, and considering cost increases, we are projecting the following expenses for years one through three:

- 2010—$185,775
- 2011—$191,494
- 2012—$201,068

Revenues

During our first year of operations, the owners of Medical Navigation Services anticipate that they will each bill four hours of regular services per day. We anticipate that average daily billable hours per employee will increase to five during our second year, and six during year three, at which time we will need to consider adding a fourth (and possibly a fifth) employee to support regional expansion.

In addition to regular billable hours (which includes charges for our Physician Referral service), we anticipate additional revenues from the sale of pre-paid Family Friend and Medical Research packages. Specifically, we anticipate the sale of 15 Family Friend packages in year one, 30 packages in year two, and 45 in year three. In addition, we expect to sell 50 Medical Research packages in year one, 100 in year two, and 150 in year three.

Based on the above expectations, our projected gross revenues for the first three years of operations are as follows:

- 2010—$316,750
- 2011—$417,500
- 2012—$518,250

Net Profits

Based on the above revenues and expenses, we anticipate strong profits during our first three years of operations:

- 2010—$130,975
- 2011—$226,006
- 2012—$317,182

We plan to use these profits to fund regional and state-wide expansion beginning in 2012.

Healthcare Translation & Interpretation Business

Cross–Cultural Communications Inc.

715 Miriam Way, Suite 25
Mason Ridge, Illinois 61099

Paul Greenland

Cross–Cultural Communications Inc. (CCC) provides interpretation and translation services to the healthcare industry, removing language barriers between English–speaking providers and Spanish–speaking patients.

EXECUTIVE SUMMARY

Mission Statement

CCC will provide timely, effective, confidential cross–cultural communication services that remove barriers for physicians, clinics, hospitals, and healthcare systems, allowing them to provide high-quality care to patients.

Business Overview

Receiving healthcare can be a stressful experience, especially in emergency situations or when a difficult or complex surgical procedure is involved. Communication barriers result in additional stress and confusion. CCC offers both interpretation (spoken words) and translation (written words) services to the healthcare industry so that English–speaking providers are able to communicate clearly with Spanish–speaking patients and their families.

Due to an influx of Hispanic residents in the Mason Ridge, Illinois, community, there is a strong demand for our company's services. Population projections and healthcare utilization forecasts suggest that this demand will increase at a strong pace for the foreseeable future. CCC is led by brothers Pablo and Hector Ramirez, who have both healthcare industry experience and specialized interpretation/ translation skills.

Organizational Structure

Our company is incorporated in the State of Illinois. Co–owner Pablo Ramirez manages the translation services component of our business. In addition to spending about half of his time providing actual translation services, he oversees one part–time translator, as well as two freelance translators who provide occasional assistance with larger projects.

Hector Ramirez is responsible for the interpretation side of the business. In addition to spending about half of his time providing interpretation services, he also manages three full–time interpreters, one part– time interpreter, and a pool of five freelance interpreters.

Specifically, we dedicate one full–time interpreter to each of the area hospitals with whom we work (Mason Ridge Medical Center and Community General Hospital). Another full–time interpreter spends about 75 percent of her time working with various area clinics, and the remaining 25 percent of her time providing back–up coverage at the two aforementioned hospitals.

Our structure is lean, ensuring that all of our regular employees always have a consistent flow of work. The utilization of freelancers allows us to scale up or down, based on fluctuations in demand.

Company History

CCC was established in 2002, when brothers Pablo and Hector Ramirez decided to establish their own company. At the time, Pablo was working as a file clerk in the medical records department of Community General Hospital. After working for eight years in that role, he became intimately familiar with the workings of a hospital. In addition, he received specialized training in medical terminology. Gifted with excellent written communication skills, Pablo also was a regular contributor to Mason Ridge's Spanish–language newspaper, where he moonlighted as a part–time editor.

Hector also has a healthcare background, having worked as a paramedic for the Mason Ridge Fire Department, and later as an emergency room technician at Mason Ridge Medical Center. As an experienced first responder with excellent oral communication skills, Hector has been accustomed to facilitating communication between healthcare providers and patients/families for many years.

MARKET ANALYSIS

Mason Ridge, Illinois, is approximately 135 miles from Chicago in Northern Illinois. The community has a strong industrial base, as well as a burgeoning agricultural industry. According to recent population data, the city of Mason Ridge had an estimated 151,283 residents in 2008. This marked a 17 percent increase from 2000. Persons of Hispanic or Latino origin constituted 31.8 percent of the population, compared to 15.2 percent for the state as a whole. Additionally, 18.4 percent of residents speak a language other than English at home. Foreign–born individuals account for 11.3 percent of the population. Contributing to high levels of healthcare utilization, those aged 65 years or older represent a sizable share of the population (23.1%), compared to state–wide levels of 12.2 percent.

The healthcare industry in Mason Ridge includes Community General Hospital, Mason Ridge Medical Center, and Franklin W. Peters Health System. CCC provides interpretation services at Community General and Mason Ridge, but not Franklin W. Peters. Collectively, the community's hospitals discharged approximately 57,000 inpatients in 2008, and registered more than 1 million outpatient visits. These figures reflect estimated annual growth of approximately 8 percent.

Like other hospitals and healthcare systems nationwide, each facility continues to invest in new technology and physical expansion. In particular, two of the hospitals have experienced dramatic growth in emergency care volumes, due to low–income residents utilizing these resources for primary medical care purposes. In response, separate urgent care facilities (located adjacent to the emergency rooms) have been constructed to provide more efficient, cost–effective care. The new urgent care facilities, as well as the adjacent emergency rooms, are heavy utilizers of our interpretation services.

Growth in the local healthcare market also has increased demand for translation services. All three area hospitals have began creating Spanish–language versions of their existing printed materials, including patient information guides and brochures. In addition, these organizations also have created Spanish–language versions of their Web sites. We are the exclusive translation service for Mason Ridge Medical Center, which provides the bulk of our translation–related revenues. Community General Hospital uses our translation services as well, while Franklin W. Peters Health System relies exclusively on one of our competitors.

We are the largest interpretation and translation business in Mason Ridge. Our primary competitor is Torrez Translation Service. The remainder of our competition comes from various independent contractors who work directly with area medical clinics and hospitals. However, several of these individuals have now aligned with our operation because we are able to provide them with a regular stream of work.

In addition to the three area hospitals, CCC is the exclusive interpretation and translation service for 25 medical clinics in our community, as well as the George County Health Department and a number of dental practices.

INDUSTRY ANALYSIS

According to data from the Bureau of Labor Statistics (BLS), 41,000 interpreters and translators were employed in 2006. By 2016 this number is projected to grow 24 percent, reaching 51,000. The BLS indicates that its figures are likely on the low side, because many practitioners within our industry work on a sporadic basis. In addition, approximately 22 percent of translators and interpreters are self–employed, many of whom work on a freelance or part–time basis. One of the leading drivers of growth in our industry is heightened demand for healthcare.

PERSONNEL

In addition to Pablo and Hector Ramirez, CCC's staff includes the following individuals:

- Maria Herrera (part–time translator)

- Carmen Vasquez (part–time interpreter)

- Gabriel Arellano (full–time interpreter)

- Luis Gonzalez (full–time interpreter)

- Rosa Ortega (full–time interpreter)

Professional & Advisory Support

CCC relies upon the firm of Santillan & Flores for legal services. Tax services are provided by Mason Ridge Accounting LLC. In addition, our firm has established checking accounts with the Mason Ridge Community Bank.

GROWTH STRATEGY

Because there is a strong demand for the services we provide, heavy marketing was not needed to build our business initially. We have experienced strong organic growth, and have benefited considerably from "word–of–mouth" referrals.

Currently, gaining additional market share has become difficult. One of the area hospitals mentioned above does not wish to work with our firm, because we currently provide services to their competitors. At the present time, our focus is to gain a larger share of Community General Hospital's business and add more area clinics and dental practices to our client roster.

SERVICES

Interpretation and translation are two distinct services, even though it is possible for both to be provided by the same person.

Interpretation: At CCC, this service involves the conversion of one spoken language (Spanish) into English. In addition to having a strong command of both languages, our interpreters have specialized healthcare knowledge. Prior to employment, our interpreters successfully complete a medical terminology course and spend 16 hours job shadowing co–owner Hector Ramirez in both clinic and hospital settings.

Translation: This service involves the conversion of written material from English to Spanish. Our translators have excellent writing and editing skills, and are accustomed to performing additional research when needed. They have completed formal medical terminology coursework.

MARKETING & SALES

Although heavy marketing has not been required to grow our business, CCC employs a number of marketing tactics, including:

- Printed collateral describing our practice for prospective clients and referral sources.

- Introductory letters to the managers of area clinics with whom we are not currently doing business.

- Occasional "drop–ins" at area clinics with whom we are not currently doing business, in order to build relationships and gain their business. For top prospects, we occasionally will bring lunch to a clinic for the office staff.

- A Yellow Page advertisement.

- A professional networking strategy that involves membership in the local chamber of commerce.

- A Web site with complete details about our business and the services we offer.

OPERATIONS

Facility & Location

Pablo and Hector Ramirez operate CCC from the first floor of a two–family apartment building owned by their family, which is zoned for both residential and commercial use. While the upstairs is used as a private residence, the downstairs portion of the building is devoted to CCC's operations. This arrangement allows the business to keep its overhead very low.

Our facility includes a combination reception/general office area. Of the apartment's three bedrooms, one is utilized as a conference/meeting room, while the other two service offices for Pablo and Hector Ramirez.

Fees

CCC's standard rate for interpretation services is $45 per hour. A two–hour minimum charge applies. In the case of Mason Ridge Medical Center, we have agreed to provide services at a lower rate, because we are their exclusive interpretation service. Translation services are provided at a rate of $60 per hour, with a minimum one–hour charge.

Hours of Operation

Our regular office hours are 9 am to 5 pm, Monday through Friday. The majority of our direct employees, as well as the independent contractors working on behalf of our company, work off–site (e.g., in clinics and hospitals). Because our largest customers are open 24 hours a day, 365 days a year, a member of our staff is available by phone at all times. An answering service forwards relevant after–hours calls received via our main number to the on–call staff member's cell phone.

LEGAL

CCC operates in full compliance with the Health Insurance Portability & Accountability Act of 1996 (HIPAA), a public law passed by Congress that protects the privacy of health information. Our business has signed legal agreements with the healthcare providers we work for, obligating us to maintain strict confidentiality standards.

In addition, we also adhere to a strict, written Code of Ethics specifying how our employees will carry themselves in the field. Our Code of Ethics addresses issues such as accuracy, cultural sensitivity, confidentiality, proficiency, non–discrimination, impartiality/conflict of interest, professional demeanor, ethical violations, and professional development.

FINANCIAL ANALYSIS

Following is CCC's balance sheet for 2008.

Income	
Interpretation	$464,400
Translation	$132,600
Total income	**$597,000**
Expenses	
Salaries	$455,900
Utilities	$ 2,950
Insurance	$ 21,540
Office supplies	$ 2,670
Marketing & advertising	$ 2,500
Telecommunications & internet	$ 3,076
Professional development	$ 4,500
Subscriptions & dues	$ 975
Taxes	$ 17,650
Total expenses	**$511,761**
Net income	85,239

Based on our analysis of the market, and taking current economic conditions into consideration, we are forecasting that net income for our business will grow at a compound annual rate of 6 percent for the next five years, as noted below.

Year	Net income
2009	$ 90,353
2010	$ 95,774
2011	$101,520
2012	$107,611
2013	$114,068

Home Repair and Improvement Contractor

HandyGals Inc.

147 S. Main St.
Edgarsville, Minnesota 56549

Paul Greenland

HandyGals Inc. is a female–owned home repair and improvement business.

EXECUTIVE SUMMARY

Business Overview

HandyGals Inc. is a female–owned home repair and improvement contractor business. Although we are a general remodeling contractor, a considerable portion of our business will fall within the kitchen/bath, painting/wallpapering, and closet organization categories.

Being a female–owned and operated business is a differential for us; there are no other contractors in our market that can make such a claim. Despite the fact that we are in a minority position within our industry, this has worked to our advantage while doing independent contract work. Specifically, we have become the contractor of choice for single female homeowners, as well as their parents.

Organizational Structure

Our company is incorporated in the State of Minnesota. Sheila Johnson and Penny Masters each own equal shares of the business. The co–owners will perform most work directly, but sometimes utilize sub–contractors.

Company History

HandyGals was established in November of 2009, when Sheila Johnson and Penny Masters lost their jobs at a local home–improvement retailer. Johnson worked in the building materials department for seven years, where she became very familiar with this aspect of the home–improvement business. Masters worked in a number of different departments over the course of 10 years, including hardware, tools, and paint. Johnson and Masters began doing home repair and improvement projects together (as independent contractors) to earn extra money in 2004. During their retail career, they both became familiar with local and regional contractors. This knowledge will benefit them as co–owners of HandyGals, when assistance is needed from reputable sub–contractors.

MARKET ANALYSIS

Even in the worst economic times, all homeowners must perform routine maintenance. In addition, those with limited budgets continue to invest in less expensive home improvement projects that promise a greater return on their investment. Finally, a more limited market for discretionary improvement projects exists among affluent consumers.

Edgarsville, Minnesota, is approximately 75 miles from the Twin Cities. According to recent population data, the city had an estimated 285,144 residents in 2008. This marked a 4 percent increase from 2000. Females constitute 53 percent of the population, above the national average of 51 percent. We also have an elderly population that is larger than the national average (16.4%, compared to 12.1% nationally).

Prior to the economic recession, a construction boom occurred in northern Edgarsville. Several large, upper–income subdivisions were developed, creating strong demand for basement remodeling projects and decks, as well as a steady stream of smaller projects, such as the installation of electric garage door openers, deadbolt locks, and garbage disposals. These market opportunities allowed the co–owners of HandyGals to establish new customer relationships while working as part–time independent contractors.

In addition, our market contains many older, established neighborhoods, providing ample opportunities for a wide range of repair and improvement projects. In particular, these areas of the community contain higher concentrations of elderly individuals. In addition to female customers, the elderly have become a unique market niche for us while working as independent contractors. Women have recommended us to their parents, who in turn have recommended us to their friends.

One notable trend in our market is an increase in multi–generational households. According to data from the U.S. Census Bureau, in 2007 approximately 3.6 million adults lived with adult children. This marked an increase of 67 percent from 2000. Remodeling projects involving bedroom additions, handicapped–accessible sinks, shower grab bars, and wider/wheelchair–friendly doorways are becoming more commonplace. Those aged 65 and older are expected to grow more than four times as fast as the general population, according to the AARP. Specifically, the association forecasts that this age group will experience 89 percent growth between 2007 and 2030.

Another notable trend in our market, mirroring conditions nationwide, is increased competition. As new home construction has decreased, in the wake of recessionary conditions, homebuilders have begun offering remodeling services as well. In addition, unemployment has caused an increase in independent contractors performing home improvement and repair services.

INDUSTRY ANALYSIS

As of late 2009, conditions were difficult within our industry. At that time challenges included low consumer confidence, more restrictive access to credit, and declining home values. Nevertheless, home improvement remains a sizable industry. Research from Harvard University's Joint Center for Housing Studies, issued in 2007, valued the industry at $280 billion in 2005. This figure was expected to increase 44 percent by 2015. Along with increasing revenues, employment has grown within our industry during the past decade. For example, according to the Harvard study, the number of contractors in the general and specialty trade remodeling category increased 32 percent between 1997 and 2002 alone, reaching 530,000. Of this total, many of the contractors are self–employed.

PERSONNEL

Co–owners Sheila Johnson and Penny Masters will oversee every project and perform the majority of all work. However, HandyGals will rely upon assistance from reputable subcontractors when needed (e.g., to complete larger projects, or when specialized expertise is needed). For example, our business will not directly handle complicated plumbing or electrical projects.

Professional & Advisory Support

HandyGals relies upon the firm of Johnson & Rogers for legal services. Tax advisement is provided by Reliable Accounting LLC. Our firm has established checking accounts with the Edgarsville Community Bank, which also has provided us with merchant accounts so that we may accept credit card payments.

GROWTH STRATEGY

HandyGals plans to devote its first three years of operations to becoming well established in our local market. During this time period, our objective will be to gain a reputation for quality, reliable work and build our brand name. While we recognize that this is a challenging time to establish a new home improvement and repair business, due to the current economic climate, we are confident in our ability to succeed. Several other women in our community have expressed an interest in working for us. This is an important consideration as we consider expanding beyond our third year of operations.

SERVICES

We will begin all home improvement projects with a discovery meeting, during which time we will discuss goals and objectives with the customer and learn what their expectations are. Following this, we will develop an estimate for all projects. No project work will begin until the customer has agreed to the estimate in writing.

As a general remodeling contractor, HandyGals will provide a wide range of typical home repair and improvement services, including:

- Cabinet installation
- Cabinet refacing
- Painting/wallpapering
- Closet organization
- Countertop installation
- Deck construction
- Green remodeling
- Insulation
- Kitchens and baths
- Basic lighting installation/repairs
- Simple plumbing installations/repairs
- Handicap accessibility
- Doors and windows

As independent contractors, the co–owners of HandyGals have generated a considerable portion of their business from the Kitchens and Baths, Painting/Wallpapering, and Closet Organization categories. In addition, recent energy conservation trends have generated many projects within the Insulation and Doors/Windows categories. In particular, we are currently benefiting from The American Recovery and Reinvestment Act, a $787 billion government initiative that provides consumers with up to $4,000 in rebates for energy–related improvements to their homes.

As independent contractors, the co–owners of HandyGals have developed specialized expertise in several niche areas. Capitalizing on the explosive growth of wine and related sales, we have begun constructing wine cellars for customers in our market. Despite difficult economic times, this particular type of remodeling project continues to prove popular with both medium– and upper–income consumers. According to the International Wine and Spirit Record, the United States is expected to become the largest consumer market for wine in the world by 2012, eclipsing Italy. The publication revealed that, in 2007 alone, Americans spent approximately $22 billion on wine–related purchases.

Another specialized area for us has been the construction of exercise rooms. We have found that it is relatively simple to convert unused space into an exercise room, making this an affordable option for cost–conscious consumers who have been forced to do away with expensive exercise club memberships. Oftentimes, individuals already have quality exercise equipment in their homes, which goes unused due to the lack of an ideal/appealing setting.

MARKETING & SALES

Because the female ownership aspect of our business is unique, we already have attracted considerable attention in our local market (as independent contractors). To capitalize on this, we developed a unique brand identity. To save on costs, we worked with students in the marketing and graphic design programs at Edgarsville Community College to develop our brand image.

HandyGals will utilize a number of traditional and innovative marketing techniques to grow our business:

- Printed collateral describing our business.
- A Yellow Page advertisement.
- A Web site with complete details about our business and the services we offer.
- A home repair and improvement advice column in our local newspaper, The Edgarsville Gazette.
- An ongoing series of home repair and improvement videos, which we will post on YouTube. These will provide information for do–it–yourselfers, and also showcase the quality of our work.
- Inclusion of the HandyGals brand identity on our trucks, trailers, and marketing materials.
- A monthly e–newsletter, which we will distribute to both former and prospective customers. This will allow us to showcase unique projects, answer DIY–related questions we receive via our Web site, and talk about home improvement trends.

OPERATIONS

Facility & Location

HandyGals plans to lease a small outbuilding from an area farmer. This will provide ample space to store our tools and equipment, two trucks, two storage trailers, and a limited supply of building materials. In addition, the building includes a workbench, as well as a small, climate–controlled room where we can complete paperwork.

Hours of Operation

HandyGals will perform most of its projects between 7:00 a.m. and 7:00 p.m., Monday through Saturday. However, we will work odd or expanded hours when required. Customers contact us via cell phone or e–mail. Sheila Johnson and Penny Masters both carry smart phones, allowing them to stay in constant contact with prospects, suppliers, other contractors, and each other.

LEGAL

HandyGals has secured all necessary licenses to work in our field. We are bonded and insured, and adhere to all local, state, and federal building codes and construction laws. Permits are secured from the local building department for all projects, and we work with building inspectors to obtain all necessary approvals.

FINANCIAL ANALYSIS

Start Up Costs

Start-up budget

Advertising	$ 4,500
Miscellaneous items	$ 2,000
Legal	$ 1,750
Accounting	$ 745
Office supplies	$ 500
Tools & equipment	$ 19,240
Office equipment	$ 400
Facility lease	$ 4,500
Insurance	$ 4,500
Auto	$ 13,250
Fuel	$ 4,500
Phone book ads	$ 550
Salaries	$ 60,000
Total	**$116,435**

The owners' investment is $45,000. We are seeking financing to cover remaining start–up costs.

Based on our knowledge of the market and current workload (as independent contractors, prior to establishing this business), we are forecasting that we will essentially break even during our first year of operations. Although current economic conditions make long–term projections challenging, we anticipate more substantial net profits during our second and third years.

Year	Net income
2009	$ 1,850
2010	$17,800
2011	$18,690

SWOT ANALYSIS

- *Strengths:* As a female–owned home repair and improvement business, we are unique in the marketplace, setting us apart from our competitors.

- *Weaknesses:* Because we are a small operation, very large projects can be difficult for us to take on without the involvement of sub–contractors.

- *Opportunities:* We are in a unique position to corner the project market pertaining to single female homeowners, as well as their older parents.

- *Threats:* We continue to face strong competition from homebuilders, unemployed individuals moonlighting in our field, and unpredictable economic conditions.

Microbrewery

Smith Microbrewery, Inc.

12345 Ridge St.
Glens Falls, New York 12801

BizPlanDB.com

The purpose of this business plan is to raise $400,000 for the development of a microbrewery while showcasing the expected financials and operations over the next three years.

EXECUTIVE SUMMARY

The purpose of this business plan is to raise $400,000 for the development of a microbrewery while showcasing the expected financials and operations over the next three years. Smith Microbrewery, Inc. ("the Company") is a New York-based corporation that will produce and distribute a number of specialized and seasonal beers for regional and national distribution. The Company was founded in 2009 by Ben Smith.

The Products

Mr. Smith intends to develop a highly specialized microbrewery that will produce a number of seasonal and specialized beers such as stouts, pale ales, porters, lagers, and a number of specialized ales/lagers with proprietary formulas developed by the Company's brew master. At this time, Mr. Smith is not only sourcing the required equipment for the business, but also a highly experienced brew master that will apply their years of experience and specialized beer recipes to the Company's microbrews. The business expects to distribute approximately 15,000 barrels of beer per year.

Financing

Mr. Smith is seeking to raise $400,000 from as a bank loan. The interest rate and loan agreement are to be further discussed during negotiation. This business plan assumes that the business will receive a 10 year loan with a 9% fixed interest rate. The financing will be used for the following:

- Development of the Company's Microbrewery location.

- Financing for the first six months of operation.

- Capital to purchase equipment related to brewing beer.

Mr. Smith will contribute $75,000 to the venture.

Mission Statement

Smith Microbrewery's mission is to become a recognized regional (and then national) brewery that provides an outstanding variety of specialized and seasonal beers.

Management Team

The Company was founded by Ben Smith. Mr. Smith has more than 20 years of experience in the beer production and distribution industry. Through his expertise, he will be able to bring the operations of the business to profitability within its first year of operations.

Sales Forecasts

Mr. Smith expects a strong rate of growth at the start of operations. Below are the expected financials over the next three years.

Proforma profit and loss (yearly)

Year	2009	2010	2011
Sales	$1,683,780	$2,104,725	$2,567,765
Operating costs	$ 765,992	$ 910,778	$1,031,358
EBITDA	$ 203,764	$ 301,417	$ 447,520
Taxes, interest, and depreciation	$ 140,953	$ 163,276	$ 217,150
Net profit	**$ 62,812**	**$ 138,141**	**$ 230,370**

Sales, operating costs, and profit forecast

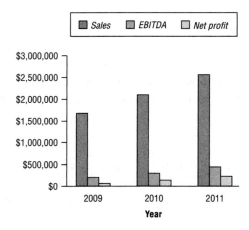

Expansion Plan

The Founder expects that the business will aggressively expand during the first three years of operation. Mr. Smith intends to implement marketing campaigns that will effectively target individuals within the target market. The Company will also regularly reinvest a substantial portion of its after–tax cash flow into expanding Smith Microbrewery's production and distribution infrastructure.

COMPANY AND FINANCING SUMMARY

Registered Name and Corporate Structure

Smith Microbrewery, Inc. is registered as a corporation in the State of New York.

Required Funds

At this time, Smith Microbrewery requires $400,000 of debt funds in addition to the $75,000 contribution by Mr. Smith. Below is a breakdown of how these funds will be used:

Projected startup costs

Business startup year	2009
Initial lease payments and deposits	$ 35,000
Working capital	$ 35,000
FF&E	$ 50,000
Leasehold improvements	$ 25,000
Security deposits	$ 15,000
Insurance	$ 10,000
Beer brewing equipment	$250,000
Marketing budget	$ 40,000
Miscellaneous and unforeseen costs	$ 15,000
Total startup costs	**$475,000**

Use of funds

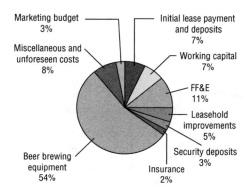

Investor Equity

Mr. Smith is not seeking an investment from a third party at this time.

Management Equity

Ben Smith owns 100% of Smith Microbrewery, Inc.

Exit Strategy

If the business is very successful, Mr. Smith may seek to sell the business to a third party for a significant earnings multiple. Most likely, the Company will hire a qualified business broker to sell the business on behalf of Smith Microbrewery. Based on historical numbers, the business could fetch a sales premium of up to 5 to 7 times earnings.

MICROBREWERY PRODUCTS

As stated in the executive summary, the business intends to hire a brew master that will provide the Company with an expansive number of beers that it will brew in its tanks. At any given time, Mr. Smith anticipates that the business will have three to four different types of beers in production. On an average yearly basis, the Company will produce and distribute 15,000 barrels of beer to distributors on a regional and national basis. As will be discussed in the fifth section of the business plan, Smith Microbrewery intends to develop an expansive marketing campaign that will effectively brand the Company's premium line of beers. Specialty and seasonal beers to be produced by the Company include, but are not limited to:

- Stouts

- Pale ales

- Porter beers

- Lagers

- Light beers

- Flavored beers

- Seasonal blends

In the Company's facility, the business will be able to produce, bottle, and distribute all beer products offered by Smith Microbrewery.

It should be noted that at all times, the business will comply with all local, state, and federal laws regarding the production, bottling, and distribution of alcohol based products. Mr. Smith is committed to operating the microbrewery with the highest professional standards in the industry.

STRATEGIC AND MARKET ANALYSIS

Economic Outlook

This section of the analysis will detail the economic climate, the microbrewery industry, the customer profile, and the competition that the business will face as it progresses through its business operations.

Currently, the economic market condition in the United States is in recession. This slowdown in the economy has also greatly impacted real estate sales, which has halted to historical lows. Many economists expect that this recession will continue until the end of 2009, at which point the economy will begin a prolonged recovery period. However, Smith Microbrewery will operate with moderately high profit margins that will ensure that the business can remain profitable despite the current economic climate.

Industry Analysis

Within the United States, there are approximately 700 microbreweries that provide a number of crafted and specialty beers. This industry is a sub–segment of the greater brewery industry. Aggregately breweries in the United States generate $19 billion of revenue while providing jobs to more than 40,000 people. Payrolls in each of the last five years have exceeded $1.8 billion. The microbrewery segment of this industry accounts for approximately 20% of the aggregate revenues and payrolls generated each year.

The growth of this industry has remained strong in recent years as the popularity of microbreweries has increased among the general public. As beers produced by microbreweries typically are more expensive, this growth has been primarily attributed to the fact that the average American has greater wealth. With the current economic situation at hand, the industry may experience sluggish growth over the next 2 to 3 years.

Customer Profile

As there are many microbreweries competing locally, regionally, and nationally, it is difficult to determine the average customer that will purchase the Company's brands of beer. However, among its targeted demographics (which will be used in conjunction with the marketing campaigns discussed in the next section of the business plan), Management has outlined the following characteristics that will be common among the Company's end user:

- Annual household income of $50,000+

- Lives within a 50 miles radius of a major metropolitan area

- Has an interest in beers and breweries that produce specialty beers

- Gender Demographic (75% Male, 25% Female)

- Between the ages of 27 and 65

Competition

The competition among breweries is intense. The Company will face competition from major beer producers such as Budweiser, Miller, Michelob, and Natural Light. These businesses are multi–billion dollar organizations that have substantial marketing infrastructures. However, the business will primarily face competition from other local breweries that specifically cater to individuals that have an interest in small batch produced beers.

As stated above, there are more than 700 licensed microbreweries in the United States that operate in a similar or identical capacity to that of Smith Microbrewery, Inc.

MARKETING PLAN

Smith Microbrewery, Inc. intends to maintain an extensive marketing campaign that will ensure maximum visibility for the business and its wide selection of produced beers. Below is an overview of the marketing strategies and objectives of the Company.

Marketing Objectives

- Develop an online presence by developing a website and placing the Company's name and contact information with online directories.

- Establish relationships with local and regional beer distributors within the targeted market.

- Regularly attend beer festivals and contests within the Company's regional market.

Marketing Strategies

As the microbrewery industry has grown significantly over the past ten years, Mr. Smith feels that it is imperative that the Company hire a public relations and marketing firm to assist the business in properly positioning its products regionally and then onto a national level. As such, Mr. Smith is currently sourcing a number of regional marketing firms that will act as both a developer of the Company's advertisements as well as a publicity agent.

Mr. Smith will regularly attend well known beer festivals, contents, and other events that focus on the products produced by microbreweries. If the Company can produce outstanding beers, then the business can easily penetrate the microbrew market by advertising awards, accolades, and other recognition generated from these events.

Mr. Smith, at the onset of operations, will work closely with regional and local beer distributors that sell microbrew beers to local bars and taverns. This will ensure that the business will be able to divest its initial batches of beer from the onset of operations while Mr. Smith and the Company's retained marketing firm generate substantial interest in the brand.

Finally, the business (once fully established) may begin to develop television and radio advertisements that showcase the premium quality and diversity of the Company's micro brewed beer selection.

Pricing

Each case of beer sold to a distributor will generate $15 to $20 of revenue for the business. The anticipated gross margins from each dollar of revenue will be approximately 57 cents.

ORGANIZATIONAL PLAN AND PERSONNEL SUMMARY

Corporate Organization

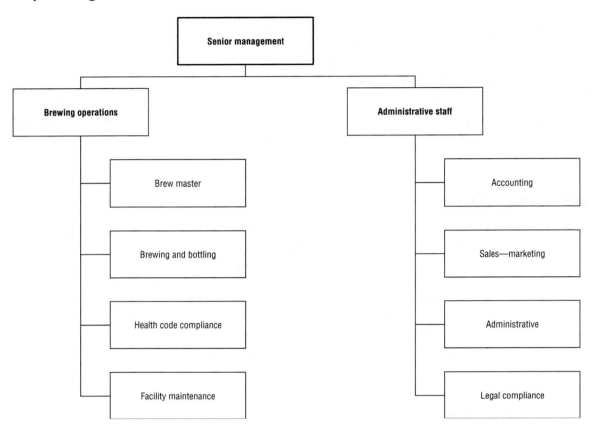

Organizational Budget

Personnel plan—yearly

Year	2009	2010	2011
Owner	$ 60,000	$ 61,800	$ 63,654
Facility manager	$ 50,000	$ 51,500	$ 53,045
Brew master	$ 45,000	$ 46,350	$ 47,741
Facility employees	$275,000	$339,900	$379,272
Administrative	$ 50,000	$ 77,250	$106,090
Total	**$480,000**	**$576,800**	**$649,801**
Numbers of personnel			
Owner	1	1	1
Facility manager	1	1	1
Brew master	1	1	1
Facility employees	10	12	13
Administrative	2	3	4
Totals	**15**	**18**	**20**

Management Biographies

Mr. Ben Smith is a highly experienced brew master with more than 20 years in the industry. Since beginning his career in the beer production industry, Mr. Smith has become a master of a number of different beer styles. Mr. Smith's skill set includes, but is not limited to:

- The ability to oversee agents and employees.

- A complete understanding of accounting of the complex inventory, accounting, and marketing issues that Smith Microbrewery will face on a day to day basis.

- A complete understanding of the science behind beer production.

FINANCIAL PLAN

Underlying Assumptions

The Company has based its proforma financial statements on the following:

- Smith Microbrewery will have an annual revenue growth rate of 20% per year.

- The Owner will acquire $400,000 of debt funds to develop the business.

- The loan will have a 10 year term with a 9% interest rate.

- Mr. Smith will contribute $75,000 towards the development of Smith Microbrewery, Inc.

Sensitivity Analysis

In the event of an economic downturn, the business may have a decline in its revenues. Microbrew beers are considered to be a luxury by most standards, and as such, during an economic recession the business may experience a drop in top line income. However, and as stated earlier, the business will generate significant revenues from each batch of completed beer sold, and the Company will be able to remain profitable and cash flow positive even in the event of moderate revenue declines.

Source of Funds

Financing

Equity contributions

Management investment	$ 75,000.00
Total equity financing	**$ 75,000.00**
Banks and lenders	
Banks and lenders	$ 400,000.00
Total debt financing	**$400,000.00**
Total financing	**$475,000.00**

General Assumptions

General assumptions

Year	2009	2010	2011
Short term interest rate	9.5%	9.5%	9.5%
Long term interest rate	10.0%	10.0%	10.0%
Federal tax rate	33.0%	33.0%	33.0%
State tax rate	5.0%	5.0%	5.0%
Personnel taxes	15.0%	15.0%	15.0%

Profit and Loss Statements

Proforma profit and loss (yearly)

Year	2009	2010	2011
Sales	**$1,683,780**	**$2,104,725**	**$2,567,765**
Cost of goods sold	$ 714,024	$ 892,530	$ 1,088,887
Gross margin	57.59%	57.59%	57.59%
Operating income	**$ 969,756**	**$1,212,195**	**$1,478,878**
Expenses			
Payroll	$ 480,000	$ 576,800	$ 649,801
General and administrative	$ 25,200	$ 26,208	$ 27,256
Marketing expenses	$ 101,027	$ 126,284	$ 154,066
Professional fees and licensure	$ 12,500	$ 12,875	$ 13,261
Insurance costs	$ 15,000	$ 15,750	$ 16,538
Facility maintenance expenses	$ 27,596	$ 30,356	$ 33,391
Rent and utilities	$ 24,250	$ 25,463	$ 26,736
Miscellaneous costs	$ 8,419	$ 10,524	$ 12,839
Payroll taxes	$ 72,000	$ 86,520	$ 97,470
Total operating costs	**$ 765,992**	**$ 910,778**	**$1,031,358**
EBITDA	**$ 203,764**	**$ 301,417**	**$ 447,520**
Federal income tax	$ 67,242	$ 88,734	$ 137,824
State income tax	$ 10,188	$ 13,445	$ 20,882
Interest expense	$ 34,951	$ 32,526	$ 29,873
Depreciation expenses	$ 28,571	$ 28,571	$ 28,571
Net profit	**$ 62,812**	**$ 138,141**	**$ 230,370**
Profit margin	**3.73%**	**6.56%**	**8.97%**

Sales, operating costs, and profit forecast

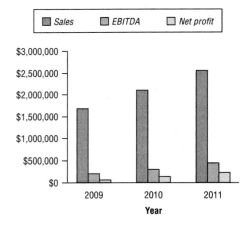

Cash Flow Analysis

Proforma cash flow analysis—yearly

Year	2009	2010	2011
Cash from operations	$ 91,383	$166,713	$258,941
Cash from receivables	$ 0	$ 0	$ 0
Operating cash inflow	**$ 91,383**	**$166,713**	**$258,941**
Other cash inflows			
Equity investment	$ 75,000	$ 0	$ 0
Increased borrowings	$400,000	$ 0	$ 0
Sales of business assets	$ 0	$ 0	$ 0
A/P increases	$ 37,902	$ 43,587	$ 50,125
Total other cash inflows	**$512,902**	**$ 43,587**	**$ 50,125**
Total cash inflow	**$604,285**	**$210,300**	**$309,067**
Cash outflows			
Repayment of principal	$ 25,854	$ 28,279	$ 30,932
A/P decreases	$ 24,897	$ 29,876	$ 35,852
A/R increases	$ 0	$ 0	$ 0
Asset purchases	$400,000	$ 25,007	$ 38,841
Dividends	$ 63,968	$116,699	$181,259
Total cash outflows	**$514,719**	**$199,861**	**$286,883**
Net cash flow	**$ 89,566**	**$ 10,439**	**$ 22,183**
Cash balance	**$ 89,566**	**$100,005**	**$122,189**

Proforma cash flow (yearly)

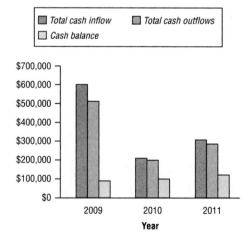

Balance Sheet

Proforma balance sheet—yearly

Year	2009	2010	2011
Assets			
Cash	$ 89,566	$100,005	$122,189
Amortized development/expansion costs	$ 100,000	$102,501	$106,385
Beer brewing equipment	$ 250,000	$262,503	$281,924
FF&E	$ 50,000	$ 60,003	$ 75,539
Accumulated depreciation	($ 28,571)	($ 57,143)	($ 85,714)
Total assets	**$ 460,995**	**$467,869**	**$500,322**
Liabilities and equity			
Accounts payable	$ 13,005	$ 26,716	$ 40,990
Long term liabilities	$ 374,146	$345,868	$317,589
Other liabilities	$ 0	$ 0	$ 0
Total liabilities	**$ 387,151**	**$372,584**	**$358,578**
Net worth	**$ 73,843**	**$ 95,286**	**$141,744**
Total liabilities and equity	**$ 460,995**	**$467,869**	**$500,322**

Proforma balance sheet

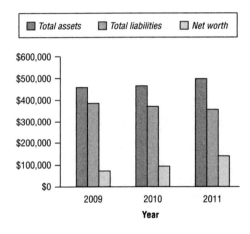

Breakeven Analysis

Monthly break even analysis

Year	2009	2010	2011
Monthly revenue	$ 110,832	$ 131,781	$ 149,228
Yearly revenue	$1,329,986	$1,581,377	$1,790,739

Break even analysis

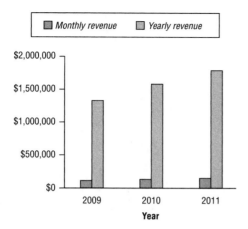

Business Ratios

Business ratios—yearly

Year	2009	2010	2011
Sales			
Sales growth	0.0%	25.0%	22.0%
Gross margin	57.6%	57.6%	57.6%
Financials			
Profit margin	3.73%	6.56%	8.97%
Assets to liabilities	1.19%	1.26%	1.40%
Equity to liabilities	0.19%	0.26%	0.40%
Assets to equity	6.24%	4.91%	3.53%
Liquidity			
Acid test	0.23%	0.27%	0.34%
Cash to assets	0.19%	0.21%	0.24%

Mobile Veterinary Practice

PetWheelz Inc.

21853 42nd Ave.
Lexington Hills, Kentucky 40500

Paul Greenland

PetWheelz Inc. is a mobile veterinary practice. Instead of pet owners bringing their animals to a brick-and-mortar location for check-ups and treatment, we bring the clinic to them, saving them both time and money.

EXECUTIVE SUMMARY

Business Overview

There are many benefits associated with owning a pet. However, obtaining veterinary care can be inconvenient, challenging, and sometimes, nearly impossible. This is especially true for busy families with small children, disabled individuals, and senior citizens. In addition, some pets get car sick or are difficult to transport.

PetWheelz Inc. is a mobile veterinary practice. Instead of pet owners bringing their animals to a brick-and-mortar location for check-ups and treatment, we bring the clinic to them, saving them both time and money. PetWheelz provides a wide range of basic services, including physical pet examinations, vaccinations, micro-chipping (technology for identifying lost pets), preventative/routine care, treatment of minor wounds and injuries, diagnostic laboratory testing, and euthanasia.

In addition to added convenience for pet owners, a mobile business model allows veterinarians to see pets in their natural environment. This sometimes provides key insight regarding behavioral problems, as well as allergies.

Company History

PetWheelz Inc. is a new business established by Sherry Thompson, DVM, a veterinarian with more than 10 years of experience. Prior to establishing her own mobile practice, Thompson worked for a traditional veterinary clinic in Mobile, Alabama. When her father passed away, Thompson decided to relocate to the growing community of Lexington Hills, Kentucky, to be closer to her mother. Establishing a mobile practice will provide her with a more flexible schedule and allow her to develop her entrepreneurial skills. In addition, Thompson will be able to provide a much-needed service in a community with larger than average dual-income families and senior citizens.

MARKET ANALYSIS

According to data from the American Pet Products Manufacturers Association (APPMA), by the late 2000s there were 360 million pets in the United States, outnumbering the number of people (300 million). At that time, the nation was home to 44.8 million dogs owners and 38.4 million cat owners.

After growing to $38.5 billion in 2006, consumer spending on pets was expected to reach $40.8 million in 2007 and $52.0 billion by 2009. Spending on veterinary care was estimated at $9.8 billion in 2007, slightly behind supplies and over-the-counter medications ($9.9 billion) and food ($16.1 billion). According to the APPMA, 63 percent of U.S. households contained a pet.

U.S. Census data indicates that the community of Lexington Hills, Kentucky, consists of approximately 12,200 households. Using formulas from the 2007 U.S. Pet Ownership & Demographics Sourcebook, the community includes an estimated 4,538 dog-owning households (7,715 dogs), some 3,953 cat-owning households (8,697 cats), and 476 bird-owning households (1,190 birds).

Estimated veterinarian visits total 7,715 for dogs; 6,720 for cats; and 143 for birds. In terms of annual veterinarian-related expenditures, residents spend approximately $1.62 million for the care of their dogs; $751,070 for the care of their cats; and $4,284 for the care of their birds. Total annual veterinarian-related expenditures total $2.375 million.

INDUSTRY ANALYSIS

Mobile veterinary services have been in existence for many years. Although statistics regarding this specific type of practice are not available, there is ample data regarding veterinarians in general.

According to the American Veterinary Medical Association, there were 85,977 veterinarians practicing in the United States in 2008. Of these, 42,690 were females and 43,287 were males. Those veterinarians in private practice totaled 59,711. Median earnings (professional income before taxes) totaled $91,000 in 2007. Of this total, 67.3 percent of veterinarians focused exclusively on companion animals, while 9.9 percent focused predominantly on companion animals. Another 7.3 percent worked in mixed animal practices, and 6.1 percent had an equine focus.

According to the Bureau of Labor Statistics' Occupational Outlook Handbook, 2008-09 Edition, the veterinary profession is poised for explosive growth. Between 2006 and 2016, the employment of veterinarians is projected to rise 35 percent. One trend that is contributing to this growth is the rising popularity of cats as pets, the growth of pet insurance, and increased expenditures on advanced care by affluent pet owners.

The primary professional organization within our field is the American Veterinary Medical Association (AVMA), which represents more than 78,000 veterinarians. Members of the association, which was formed in 1863, work in a variety of settings, including private practice, corporate practice, industry, uniformed services, academia, and government.

PERSONNEL

Dr. Sherry Thompson, DVM

Dr. Sherry Thompson, DVM, graduated from veterinary school in Texas in 1998. She completed an internship in small animal medicine and surgery at the University of Pennsylvania, where she also completed a special species and emergency critical care fellowship. Dr. Thompson later relocated to

Mobile, Alabama, where she first worked as an emergency veterinarian before becoming an associate in a traditional veterinary practice. PetWheelz is Dr. Thompson's first business venture.

Professional & Advisory Support

PetWheelz has established a business banking account with Lexington Hills Community Bank, as well as a merchant account for accepting credit card payments. Legal services are provided by the firm of Johnson & Smith, and tax advisory services are provided by Bowen Tax Service.

GROWTH STRATEGY

Although some of the services we provide in our mobile unit (e.g., X-ray, laboratory, ultrasound, etc.) are relatively advanced, PetWheelz will provide mostly routine veterinary care during its initial years of operations. Dr. Thompson performs surgical procedures for a local animal hospital on an as-needed basis. However, she is not able to provide these services through her mobile practice.

After three years, her goal is to purchase a 26-foot RV that will accommodate the additional equipment needed to perform surgical procedures at customers' homes. At that time, it may be possible to retain her current vehicle and hire an additional veterinarian and/or or a veterinary technician. In fact, a staff veterinarian at a local horse racing track has expressed an interest in picking up occasional hours for Dr. Thompson, so that she can balance her schedule. It's possible that this arrangement may result in a new business partner after several years.

One key growth strategy for our practice will be to host mobile clinics in neighborhoods and in the parking lots of area retailers (especially pet supply stores and grooming centers). By doing this on a regular basis, we will be able to significantly increase our annual patient volumes.

SERVICES

PetWheelz provides a wide range of basic services, including:

- Physical pet examinations
- Vaccinations (Rabies, Distemper/Parvo, Kennel Cough, etc.)
- Heartworm tests
- Basic dental care
- Micro-chipping (technology for identifying lost pets)
- Preventative/routine care
- Minor wound and injury treatments
- Eye and ear care
- Diagnostic laboratory testing
- Euthanasia

We treat a wide range animal health conditions including:

- Arthritis
- Bloat
- Canine Distemper

- Cancer

- Canine Parvovirus

- Diabetes

- Epilepsy

- Eye and ear problems

- Feline Distemper

- Fleas

- Heartworm

- Hip Dysplasia

- Hookworm

- Mites

- Obesity

- Parasites

- Rabies

- Roundworms

- Salmonella

- Skin conditions

- Tapeworms

- Ticks

- Vertigo

MARKETING & SALES

We have developed a marketing plan that involves the following primary tactics:

- Printed collateral describing our business.

- A half-page Yellow Page advertisement featuring a photo of our mobile veterinarian unit, as well as a bulleted list of services offered and the advantages associated with using our business.

- The development of professional relationships with local veterinarians who operate traditional clinics, as well as a nearby animal hospital, in order to secure referrals when they encounter patients who are unable to travel to their clinics.

- A Web site with complete details about our business and the services we offer.

- A monthly pet care e-mail newsletter for area pet owners.

- Flyers distributed via area pet grooming businesses and pet supply stores, in order to promote mobile veterinary clinics and general awareness of our practice.

- Highly targeted direct mail campaigns to area pet owners. For this purpose, we will rent the names of subscribers to popular pet-related magazines, as well as the customer files from local pet grooming businesses and supply stores.

- A public relations campaign that involves the submission of periodic human interest stories to local newspapers, illustrating how we were able to help busy pet owners, or those unable to transport their pet to a traditional veterinary clinic for care.

- A customer loyalty program that provides a 15 percent discount to those referring a friend or family member to our business. The discount will apply to both the existing customer and the new customer.

- Mobile marketing (displaying our business name, Web site address, phone number, and tagline on the outside of our vehicle).

OPERATIONS

Facility & Location

Our business is unique in that we are a "location on wheels." Specifically, operations are based in a 2000 Ford 3-450 Dodgen Mobile Vet Tech Van. Acquired for $45,600, the vehicle has only 32,000 miles and is equipped with:

- V10 gas engine
- Auto transmission
- Heat/AC
- Bathroom
- Generator
- Electronic pet scale
- Small x-ray machine
- Large animal x-ray
- Centrufuse for urine and blood
- Flatbed scanner
- Computer station
- Oxygen breathing station
- Animal examination station with large sink
- Patient label writer
- Alarm system

In addition to providing mobile care for pets, we perform most of our office work from our mobile office as well. Telephone calls are received at a traditional landline in Sherry Thompson's home. During the day, her mother helps to field telephone calls from pet owners and various suppliers. When her mother is not available, Thompson utilizes an answering service that takes messages and forwards calls to her cell phone. Thompson's mobile veterinary unit also is equipped with a laptop computer with wireless Internet access, allowing her to access clinical research, e-mail messages, and other Web sites as needed.

Payment & Fees

Our practice charges $55 for a basic home visit. This includes a full exam for a maximum of up to five family pets. Beyond the examination, all additional services are provided for a specific fee. Examples of charges for common services include:

- X-ray ($75, first film/consultation)

- Rabies shots ($34)

- Distemper shots ($39)

- Heartworm tests ($45)

In addition to cash and checks, we accept all major credit cards, as well as many veterinary insurance plans.

LEGAL

Dr. Thompson is licensed to practice veterinary medicine in the state of Kentucky. In addition to holding a DVM degree and having passed a national board exam, she adheres to all of the requirements established by the Kentucky Board of Veterinary Examiners, which examines and licenses all eligible candidates for entry into the veterinary medicine profession. Dr. Thompson pays a biennial renewal fee of $200 and meets all applicable continuing education requirements.

FINANCIAL ANALYSIS

Start-up Budget
- Advertising & Marketing—$3,250

- Vehicle (first-year loan payments)—$11,712

- Drugs & Supplies—$70,000

- Fuel—$18,000

- Miscellaneous Items—$1,000

- Legal—$1,250

- Health Insurance—$5,800

- Accounting—$1,325

- Office Supplies—$500

- Laptop Computers/Peripherals—$3,400

- Liability Insurance—$7,500

- Automotive Insurance—$11,765

- Salary—$100,000

Based on an analysis of the local market and conversations with owners of mobile veterinary practices in similar communities, Dr. Thompson anticipates that PetWheelz will grow at a compound annual rate of 12.5 percent during its first three years of operation. Considering this, projected gross revenues and expenses for the first three years of operations are as follows:

Revenues
- 2010—$375,000

- 2011—$421,875

- 2012—$474,609

Expenses

- 2010—$235,502
- 2011—$247,277
- 2012—$259,641

Net Profits

Based on the above revenues and expenses, we anticipate strong profits during our first three years of operations:

- 2010—$139,498
- 2011—$174,598
- 2012—$241,918

Financing for PetWheelz will consist of a commercial loan from Lexington Hills Community Bank, which also has agreed to supply us with a line of credit. In addition, Dr. Thompson is contributing $45,000 from her personal savings.

SWOT ANALYSIS

- *Strengths:* As a mobile veterinary business, we are unique in the local marketplace; no other veterinarians are currently offering a mobile service. This model provides the owner with considerable flexibility and significantly reduced overhead.

- *Weaknesses:* Under the mobile business model, we are not able to see as many patients as a traditional brick-and-mortar clinic can.

- *Opportunities:* We are in a unique position to corner the market for busy families and those unable to travel to traditional clinics. In addition, by occasionally hosting mobile clinics near popular retail locations, we can help bridge the lower patient volume gap noted above.

- *Threats:* We are at the mercy of market volatility, in terms of fuel costs. In addition, the risk of an accident (especially during unfavorable weather conditions) is an ever present risk.

Mortgage Banking Firm

Stiles Mortgage Banking Firm, Inc.

4567 State St.
Albany, New York 12201

BizPlanDB.com

The purpose of this business plan is to raise $1,250,000 for the development of a mortgage banking firm while showcasing the expected financials and operations over the next three years. Stiles Mortgage Banking Firm, Inc. is a New York-based corporation that will provide residential and commercial mortgages to customers in its targeted market.

EXECUTIVE SUMMARY

The purpose of this business plan is to raise $1,250,000 for the development of a mortgage banking firm while showcasing the expected financials and operations over the next three years. Stiles Mortgage Banking Firm, Inc. is a New York-based corporation that will provide residential and commercial mortgages to customers in its targeted market. The Company was founded in 2009 by Joe Stiles.

The Services

The primary revenue stream for the Stiles Mortgage Banking Firm will come from the closing of loans for residences and commercial properties. The Company will use its warehouse line of credit in order to fund these loans, which will be immediately resold to secondary investors. The Company will earn fees from both the sale of the loan and fees charged to borrowers.

The Company's secondary income stream will come from the interest generated on held loans until they are sold to secondary and third party inventors.

The third section of the business plan will further describe the services offered by the Stiles Mortgage Banking Firm.

Financing

Mr. Stiles is seeking to raise $1,250,000 as a working capital line of credit, which will be primarily secured by the loans closed by the business. The interest rate and loan agreement are to be further discussed during negotiation. This business plan assumes that the business will receive a 10 year credit line with a 5% fixed interest rate. The financing will be used for the following:

- Development of the Company's office location.
- Financing for the first six months of operation.
- Capital to close loans for residential and commercial borrowers.

Mr. Stiles will contribute $250,000 to the venture.

Mission Statement

Stiles Mortgage Banking Firm's mission is to become the recognized leader in its targeted market for mortgage services.

Management Team

The Company was founded by Joe Stiles. Mr. Stiles has more than 25 years of experience in the mortgage industry. Through his expertise, he will be able to bring the operations of the business to profitability within its first year of operations.

Sales Forecasts

Mr. Stiles expects a strong rate of growth at the start of operations. Below are the expected financials over the next three years.

Proforma profit and loss (yearly)

Year	2009	2010	2011
Sales	$1,201,500	$1,345,680	$1,480,248
Operating costs	$ 364,443	$ 381,842	$ 399,242
EBITDA	$ 196,258	$ 246,142	$ 291,540
Taxes, interest, and depreciation	$ 188,294	$ 202,468	$ 219,673
Net profit	$ 7,963	$ 43,674	$ 71,867

Sales, operating costs, and profit forecast

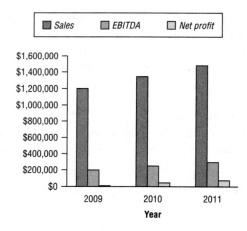

Expansion Plan

The Founder expects that the business will aggressively expand during the first three years of operation. As the real estate market returns to normal conditions, the Stiles Mortgage Banking Firm will be an excellent position to capture a significant portion of its targeted market.

COMPANY AND FINANCING SUMMARY

Registered Name and Corporate Structure

Stiles Mortgage Banking Firm, Inc. is registered as a corporation in the State of New York.

Required Funds

At this time, the Stiles Mortgage Banking Firm requires $1.25 million of debt funds in addition to the $250,000 put forth by Mr. Stiles. Below is a breakdown of how these funds will be used:

Projected startup costs

Business startup year	2009
Initial lease payments and deposits	$ 15,000
Working capital	$ 65,000
FF&E	$ 30,000
Leasehold improvements	$ 7,500
Security deposits	$ 5,000
Insurance	$ 5,000
Warehouse line of credit	$ 1,350,000
Marketing budget	$ 17,500
Miscellaneous and unforeseen costs	$ 5,000
Total startup costs	**$1,500,000**

Investor Equity

Mr. Stiles is not seeking an investment from a third party at this time.

Management Equity

Joe Stiles owns 100% of the Stiles Mortgage Banking Firm, Inc.

Exit Strategy

If the business is very successful, Mr. Stiles may seek to sell the business to a third party for a significant earnings multiple. Most likely, the Company will hire a qualified business broker to sell the business on behalf of the Stiles Mortgage Banking Firm. Based on historical numbers, the business could fetch a sales premium of up to 4 times earnings.

MORTGAGE BANKING OPERATIONS

The business of the Company is to assist homebuyers and investors in the acquisition and financing of real estate assets. These services will allow investors and homebuyers access to the capital markets. To some extent, this business will have a more erratic revenue stream as this business is dependent on deal flow and not guaranteed payments by debtors or tenants. The Company will operate an affinity mortgage banking facility (in association with its associated lenders) that will include a warehouse line of credit for financing transactions. This will be in addition to the $1.35 million of capital sought in this business plan.

Mr. Stiles expects that each financing deal made by the Company will yield approximately 5.2% of the face value of any transaction. The risks associated with this business are low as the Company does not plan on holding long term debt instruments unless the credit quality of the mortgagee is excellent.

Most loans that are made by the Company will be immediately sold to investors in the secondary market. Revenue from these operations are received from both the debtor and the investor that purchases the loan. In a typical transaction, the debtor will pay 2-3% of the loan amount to the Company. Additionally, a markup of 2-3% is applied to the loan when it is sold to an investor. The holding period of these loans is very short, with most loans packaged a sold to investors within a three to six week period.

STRATEGIC AND MARKET ANALYSIS

Economic Outlook

This section of the analysis will detail the economic climate, the mortgage industry, the customer profile, and the competition that the business will face as it progresses through its business operations.

Currently, the real estate market is undergoing a severe correction. Delinquencies and defaults on sub-prime and Alt-A mortgages issued over the last five years have increased dramatically. As such, the result has been a substantial decrease in the value of real estate across the United States. The market has seen serious corrections in price. This trend is expected to continue through out 2009 as the credit markets and the real estate markets adjust to the new risk pricing.

Industry Analysis

The market for real estate is one of the largest economic markets in the world. In the United States, the market for mortgages is the largest consumer and commercial finance market. For most people, a purchase of real estate (for both primary residence or investment purposes) is the largest financial transactions that they will ever conduct. Any standing structure has monetary value and can be used as an investment. Offices and homes are a necessity for all people and businesses. The overall market for real estate will continue to grow as the population continues to grow despite the current economic conditions. Additionally, there has been a shift in taste among Americans such that people now desire to have more than one home. While this concept has been a dream among many people, the ability for a middle income family to purchase a second home has become a reality with the change in how lending works. However, recent changes in the credit market, namely the sub prime mortgage melt-down, have resulted in difficulty for middle and upper middle income borrowers to refinance and acquire second mortgages. As such, the business may have issues with top line income generation at the onset of operations.

A study conducted by the Mortgage Bankers Association of America estimated that $2.5 trillion dollars of mortgages will be closed in 2009. This is a decrease from 2008. The decline in mortgage volume is attributed to exhaustion of consumers seeking to purchase new properties coupled with the severe issues with the credit markets.

The market for mortgages is an extremely large market, and no single competitor commands a distinct advantage over another competitor. The products offered by each business are relatively similar, and as stated before—there is no real distinction made by borrowers as to which mortgage facility to use to obtain financing. The primary distinction is made by price of closing costs, and the efficiency in which a loan can be closed by a broker or banker.

Customer Profile

Many people require the services of mortgage banks. As many people require mortgages, the demographics of this market are excessively large. These demographics include:

- Annual Household income of $45,000+ per year.

- Is seeking to purchase a home value exceeding $250,000+.

- Has a down payment equal to 10% to 20% of the value of the home they are seeking to purchase.

Within the Company's targeted market of the New York metropolitan area, there are approximately 300,000 people that fall into the Company's demographic profile. These are people that are actively seeking to purchase homes. As of 2008, the estimated population of the New York metropolitan area is 18 million people. Among these residents, the annual household income is $47,000 while median family income is $54,000.

Competition

There is a tremendous amount of competition among lending companies to acquire, finance, and sell mortgages. However, there are not many mortgage banking firms that specialize solely on small and medium sized real estate transactions. Mr. Stiles feels that the Stiles Mortgage Banking Firm can use its lending and advisory service for each client so that they receive more than just the financing they need. Management will seek to essentially partner with clients in their real estate endeavors, rather than just provide a one time financing. By allowing clients services beyond traditional lending, Mr. Stiles hopes to ensure that the will have repeat business from previous clients.

MARKETING PLAN

The Stiles Mortgage Banking Firm intends to maintain an extensive marketing campaign that will ensure maximum visibility for the business in its targeted New York metropolitan area market. Below is an overview of the marketing strategies and objectives of the Stiles Mortgage Banking Firm.

Marketing Objectives

- Develop an online presence by acquiring accounts for major online real estate portals.

- Establish relationships with real estate brokers and agents within the targeted market.

- Develop relationships with accountants, lawyers, and title companies within the Company's targeted New York metropolitan area market.

Marketing Strategies

As the competition among mortgage banking firms is very strong, it is imperative that the Company focus a significant portion of its marketing campaigns and messages on the fact that the business seeks to develop long term relationships with real estate companies, investors, and developers.

Among individual homebuyers, the Company will use traditional marketing strategies including newspaper/circular advertising throughout the New York metropolitan area. In equal importance to media marketing, Management intends to develop very close relationships with New York-based accountants, attorneys, realtors, and title companies that can refer clients to the Stiles Mortgage Banking Firm.

Finally, the business will maintain a highly interactive website that will feature information about the Stiles Mortgage Banking Firm, its offered credit facilities, and pertinent contact information. The website will also feature specialized calculators that can provide general estimates of how much a mortgage will cost based on credit quality, size of the down payment, amount of principal borrowed, and length of loan. This type of web technology has become common place and can be readily integrated into the Company's website.

Pricing

For each closed loan, the business will generate fees equal to 1% to 2% of the face value of the loan with an additional 1% to 3% of fees generated from the sale of the closed mortgage to an institutional investor.

ORGANIZATIONAL PLAN AND PERSONNEL SUMMARY

Corporate Organization

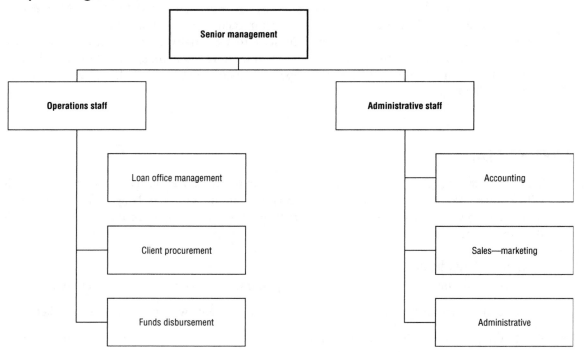

Organizational Budget

Personnel plan—yearly

Year	2009	2010	2011
Owner	$ 40,000	$ 41,200	$ 42,436
Loan processing manager	$ 35,000	$ 36,050	$ 37,132
Loan processing staff	$ 65,000	$ 66,950	$ 68,959
Bookkeeper	$ 12,500	$ 12,875	$ 13,261
Administrative	$ 50,000	$ 51,500	$ 53,045
Total	**$202,500**	**$208,575**	**$214,832**
Numbers of personnel			
Owner	1	1	1
Loan processing manager	1	1	1
Loan processing staff	2	2	2
Bookkeeper	1	1	1
Administrative	2	2	2
Totals	**7**	**7**	**7**

Personnel expense breakdown

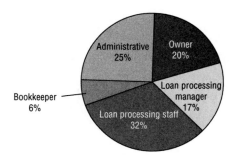

Management Biographies

Mr. Joe Stiles is a highly experienced financial professional with more than 25 years in the industry. Since beginning his career in the mortgage and finance industry, Mr. Stiles has become well versed in every aspect of real estate finance and economics. Mr. Stiles's skill set includes, but is not limited to:

- The ability to oversee agents and employees.

- A complete understanding of accounting of the complex legal and accounting issues that the Stiles Mortgage Banking Firm will face on a day to day basis.

- Licensure to operate as a mortgage banker within the State of New York.

FINANCIAL PLAN

Underlying Assumptions

The Company has based its proforma financial statements on the following:

- Stiles Mortgage Banking Firm, Inc. will have an annual revenue growth rate of 10% per year.

- The Owner will acquire $1.25 million of debt funds to develop the business. An additional affinity line of credit may be sought to further fuel loan closings.

- The credit line will have a 10 year term and a 5% fixed interest rate.

Sensitivity Analysis

The Company's revenues can change depending on the general economic climate of the real estate industry. In times of economic recession, the Stiles Mortgage Banking Firm may have issues with its top line income as fewer sales will be made.

Source of Funds

Financing

Equity contributions	
Management investment	$ 250,000.00
Total equity financing	**$ 250,000.00**
Banks and lenders	
Banks and lenders	$ 1,250,000.00
Total debt financing	**$1,250,000.00**
Total financing	**$1,500,000.00**

General Assumptions

General assumptions

Year	2009	2010	2011
Short term interest rate	9.5%	9.5%	9.5%
Long term interest rate	10.0%	10.0%	10.0%
Federal tax rate	33.0%	33.0%	33.0%
State tax rate	5.0%	5.0%	5.0%
Personnel taxes	15.0%	15.0%	15.0%

Profit and Loss Statements

Proforma profit and loss (yearly)

Year	2009	2010	2011
Sales	$1,201,500	$1,345,680	$1,480,248
Cost of goods sold	$ 640,800	$ 717,696	$ 789,466
Gross margin	46.67%	46.67%	46.67%
Operating income	$ 560,700	$ 627,984	$ 690,782
Expenses			
Payroll	$ 202,500	$ 208,575	$ 214,832
General and administrative	$ 20,000	$ 20,800	$ 21,632
Marketing expenses	$ 48,060	$ 53,827	$ 59,210
Professional fees and licensure	$ 7,500	$ 7,725	$ 7,957
Insurance costs	$ 12,000	$ 12,600	$ 13,230
Travel and vehicle costs	$ 8,000	$ 8,800	$ 9,680
Rent and utilities	$ 30,000	$ 31,500	$ 33,075
Miscellaneous costs	$ 6,008	$ 6,728	$ 7,401
Payroll taxes	$ 30,375	$ 31,286	$ 32,225
Total operating costs	**$ 364,443**	**$ 381,842**	**$ 399,242**
EBITDA	**$ 196,258**	**$ 246,142**	**$ 291,540**
Federal income tax	$ 64,765	$ 77,137	$ 92,143
State income tax	$ 9,813	$ 11,687	$ 13,961
Interest expense	$ 12,467	$ 12,393	$ 12,319
Depreciation expenses	$ 101,250	$ 101,250	$ 101,250
Net profit	**$ 7,963**	**$ 43,674**	**$ 71,867**
Profit margin	**0.66%**	**3.25%**	**4.86%**

Cash Flow Analysis

Proforma cash flow analysis—yearly

Year	2009	2010	2011
Cash from operations	$ 109,213	$144,924	$173,117
Cash from receivables	$ 0	$ 0	$ 0
Operating cash inflow	**$ 109,213**	**$144,924**	**$173,117**
Other cash inflows			
Equity investment	$ 250,000	$ 0	$ 0
Increased borrowings	$1,250,000	$ 0	$ 0
Sales of business assets	$ 0	$ 0	$ 0
A/P increases	$ 37,902	$ 43,587	$ 50,125
Total other cash inflows	**$1,537,902**	**$ 43,587**	**$ 50,125**
Total cash inflow	**$1,647,115**	**$188,512**	**$223,243**
Cash outflows			
Repayment of principal	$ 7,313	$ 7,386	$ 7,461
A/P decreases	$ 24,897	$ 29,876	$ 35,852
A/R increases	$ 0	$ 0	$ 0
Asset purchases	$1,417,500	$ 36,231	$ 43,279
Dividends	$ 76,449	$101,447	$121,182
Total cash outflows	**$1,526,159**	**$174,941**	**$207,774**
Net cash flow	**$ 120,956**	**$ 13,571**	**$ 15,469**
Cash balance	**$ 120,956**	**$134,527**	**$149,996**

Balance Sheet

Proforma balance sheet—yearly

Year	2009	2010	2011
Assets			
Cash	$ 120,956	$ 134,527	$ 149,996
Amortized development/expansion costs	$ 37,500	$ 41,123	$ 45,451
Mortgage portfolio	$1,350,000	$1,368,116	$1,389,755
FF&E	$ 30,000	$ 44,492	$ 61,804
Accumulated depreciation	($ 101,250)	($ 202,500)	($ 303,750)
Total assets	**$1,437,206**	**$1,385,758**	**$1,343,256**
Liabilities and equity			
Accounts payable	$ 13,005	$ 26,716	$ 40,990
Long term liabilities	$1,242,687	$1,235,301	$1,227,914
Other liabilities	$ 0	$ 0	$ 0
Total liabilities	**$1,255,692**	**$1,262,017**	**$1,268,904**
Net worth	**$ 181,514**	**$ 123,741**	**$ 74,352**
Total liabilities and equity	**$1,437,206**	**$1,385,758**	**$1,343,256**

Breakeven Analysis

Monthly break even analysis

Year	2009	2010	2011
Monthly revenue	$ 65,079	$ 68,186	$ 71,293
Yearly revenue	$780,948	$818,233	$855,519

MORTGAGE BANKING FIRM

Business Ratios

Business ratios—yearly

Year	2009	2010	2011
Sales			
Sales growth	0.0%	12.0%	10.0%
Gross margin	46.7%	46.7%	46.7%
Financials			
Profit margin	0.66%	3.25%	4.86%
Assets to liabilities	1.14%	1.10%	1.06%
Equity to liabilities	0.14%	0.10%	0.06%
Assets to equity	7.92%	11.20%	18.07%
Liquidity			
Acid test	0.10%	0.11%	0.12%
Cash to assets	0.08%	0.10%	0.11%

Three Year Profit and Loss Statement

Profit and loss statement (first year)

Months	1	2	3	4	5	6	7
Sales	$67,500	$72,000	$76,500	$81,000	$85,500	$90,000	$99,000
Cost of goods sold	$36,000	$38,400	$40,800	$43,200	$45,600	$48,000	$52,800
Gross margin	46.7%	46.7%	46.7%	46.7%	46.7%	46.7%	46.7%
Operating income	$31,500	$33,600	$35,700	$37,800	$39,900	$42,000	$46,200
Expenses							
Payroll	$16,875	$16,875	$16,875	$16,875	$16,875	$16,875	$16,875
General and administrative	$ 1,667	$ 1,667	$ 1,667	$ 1,667	$ 1,667	$ 1,667	$ 1,667
Marketing expenses	$ 4,005	$ 4,005	$ 4,005	$ 4,005	$ 4,005	$ 4,005	$ 4,005
Professional fees and licensure	$ 625	$ 625	$ 625	$ 625	$ 625	$ 625	$ 625
Insurance costs	$ 1,000	$ 1,000	$ 1,000	$ 1,000	$ 1,000	$ 1,000	$ 1,000
Travel and vehicle costs	$ 667	$ 667	$ 667	$ 667	$ 667	$ 667	$ 667
Rent and utilities	$ 2,500	$ 2,500	$ 2,500	$ 2,500	$ 2,500	$ 2,500	$ 2,500
Miscellaneous costs	$ 501	$ 501	$ 501	$ 501	$ 501	$ 501	$ 501
Payroll taxes	$ 2,531	$ 2,531	$ 2,531	$ 2,531	$ 2,531	$ 2,531	$ 2,531
Total operating costs	$30,370	$30,370	$30,370	$30,370	$30,370	$30,370	$30,370
EBITDA	$ 1,130	$ 3,230	$ 5,330	$ 7,430	$ 9,530	$11,630	$15,830
Federal income tax	$ 3,638	$ 3,881	$ 4,124	$ 4,366	$ 4,609	$ 4,851	$ 5,336
State income tax	$ 551	$ 588	$ 625	$ 662	$ 698	$ 735	$ 809
Interest expense	$ 1,042	$ 1,041	$ 1,041	$ 1,040	$ 1,040	$ 1,039	$ 1,039
Depreciation expense	$ 8,438	$ 8,438	$ 8,438	$ 8,438	$ 8,438	$ 8,438	$ 8,438
Net profit	−$12,539	−$10,718	−$ 8,897	−$ 7,076	−$ 5,254	−$ 3,433	$ 209

Months	8	9	10	11	12	2009
Sales	$108,000	$117,000	$126,000	$135,000	$144,000	$1,201,500
Cost of goods sold	$ 57,600	$ 62,400	$ 67,200	$ 72,000	$ 76,800	$ 640,800
Gross margin	46.7%	46.7%	46.7%	46.7%	46.7%	46.7%
Operating income	$ 50,400	$ 54,600	$ 58,800	$ 63,000	$ 67,200	$ 560,700
Expenses						
Payroll	$ 16,875	$ 16,875	$ 16,875	$ 16,875	$ 16,875	$ 202,500
General and administrative	$ 1,667	$ 1,667	$ 1,667	$ 1,667	$ 1,667	$ 20,000
Marketing expenses	$ 4,005	$ 4,005	$ 4,005	$ 4,005	$ 4,005	$ 48,060
Professional fees and licensure	$ 625	$ 625	$ 625	$ 625	$ 625	$ 7,500
Insurance costs	$ 1,000	$ 1,000	$ 1,000	$ 1,000	$ 1,000	$ 12,000
Travel and vehicle costs	$ 667	$ 667	$ 667	$ 667	$ 667	$ 8,000
Rent and utilities	$ 2,500	$ 2,500	$ 2,500	$ 2,500	$ 2,500	$ 30,000
Miscellaneous costs	$ 501	$ 501	$ 501	$ 501	$ 501	$ 6,008
Payroll taxes	$ 2,531	$ 2,531	$ 2,531	$ 2,531	$ 2,531	$ 30,375
Total operating costs	$ 30,370	$ 30,370	$ 30,370	$ 30,370	$ 30,370	$ 364,443
EBITDA	$ 20,030	$ 24,230	$ 28,430	$ 32,630	$ 36,830	$ 196,258
Federal income tax	$ 5,822	$ 6,307	$ 6,792	$ 7,277	$ 7,762	$ 64,765
State income tax	$ 882	$ 956	$ 1,029	$ 1,103	$ 1,176	$ 9,813
Interest expense	$ 1,038	$ 1,038	$ 1,037	$ 1,037	$ 1,036	$ 12,467
Depreciation expense	$ 8,438	$ 8,438	$ 8,438	$ 8,438	$ 8,438	$ 101,250
Net profit	$ 3,851	$ 7,492	$ 11,134	$ 14,776	$ 18,418	$ 7,963

Profit and loss statement (second year)

2010

Quarter	Q1	Q2	Q3	Q4	2010
Sales	$269,136	$336,420	$363,334	$376,790	$1,345,680
Cost of goods sold	$143,539	$179,424	$193,778	$200,955	$ 717,696
Gross margin	46.7%	46.7%	46.7%	46.7%	46.7%
Operating income	**$125,597**	**$156,996**	**$169,556**	**$175,836**	**$ 627,984**
Expenses					
Payroll	$ 41,715	$ 52,144	$ 56,315	$ 58,401	$ 208,575
General and administrative	$ 4,160	$ 5,200	$ 5,616	$ 5,824	$ 20,800
Marketing expenses	$ 10,765	$ 13,457	$ 14,533	$ 15,072	$ 53,827
Professional fees and licensure	$ 1,545	$ 1,931	$ 2,086	$ 2,163	$ 7,725
Insurance costs	$ 2,520	$ 3,150	$ 3,402	$ 3,528	$ 12,600
Travel and vehicle costs	$ 1,760	$ 2,200	$ 2,376	$ 2,464	$ 8,800
Rent and utilities	$ 6,300	$ 7,875	$ 8,505	$ 8,820	$ 31,500
Miscellaneous costs	$ 1,346	$ 1,682	$ 1,817	$ 1,884	$ 6,728
Payroll taxes	$ 6,257	$ 7,822	$ 8,447	$ 8,760	$ 31,286
Total operating costs	**$ 76,368**	**$ 95,460**	**$103,097**	**$106,916**	**$ 381,842**
EBITDA	**$ 49,228**	**$ 61,536**	**$ 66,458**	**$ 68,920**	**$ 246,142**
Federal income tax	$ 15,427	$ 19,284	$ 20,827	$ 21,598	$ 77,137
State income tax	$ 2,337	$ 2,922	$ 3,156	$ 3,272	$ 11,687
Interest expense	$ 3,105	$ 3,101	$ 3,096	$ 3,091	$ 12,393
Depreciation expense	$ 25,313	$ 25,313	$ 25,313	$ 25,313	$ 101,250
Net profit	**$ 3,046**	**$ 10,916**	**$ 14,067**	**$ 15,645**	**$ 43,674**

Profit and loss statement (third year)

2011

Quarter	Q1	Q2	Q3	Q4	2011
Sales	$296,050	$370,062	$399,667	$414,469	$1,480,248
Cost of goods sold	$157,893	$197,366	$213,156	$221,050	$ 789,466
Gross margin	46.7%	46.7%	46.7%	46.7%	46.7%
Operating income	**$138,156**	**$172,696**	**$186,511**	**$193,419**	**$ 690,782**
Expenses					
Payroll	$ 42,966	$ 53,708	$ 58,005	$ 60,153	$ 214,832
General and administrative	$ 4,326	$ 5,408	$ 5,841	$ 6,057	$ 21,632
Marketing expenses	$ 11,842	$ 14,802	$ 15,987	$ 16,579	$ 59,210
Professional fees and licensure	$ 1,591	$ 1,989	$ 2,148	$ 2,228	$ 7,957
Insurance costs	$ 2,646	$ 3,308	$ 3,572	$ 3,704	$ 13,230
Travel and vehicle costs	$ 1,936	$ 2,420	$ 2,614	$ 2,710	$ 9,680
Rent and utilities	$ 6,615	$ 8,269	$ 8,930	$ 9,261	$ 33,075
Miscellaneous costs	$ 1,480	$ 1,850	$ 1,998	$ 2,072	$ 7,401
Payroll taxes	$ 6,445	$ 8,056	$ 8,701	$ 9,023	$ 32,225
Total operating costs	**$ 79,848**	**$ 99,810**	**$107,795**	**$111,788**	**$ 399,242**
EBITDA	**$ 58,308**	**$ 72,885**	**$ 78,716**	**$ 81,631**	**$ 291,540**
Federal income tax	$ 18,429	$ 23,036	$ 24,879	$ 25,800	$ 92,143
State income tax	$ 2,792	$ 3,490	$ 3,769	$ 3,909	$ 13,961
Interest expense	$ 3,087	$ 3,082	$ 3,077	$ 3,073	$ 12,319
Depreciation expense	$ 25,313	$ 25,313	$ 25,313	$ 25,313	$ 101,250
Net profit	**$ 8,688**	**$ 17,965**	**$ 21,678**	**$ 23,537**	**$ 71,867**

Three Year Cash Flow Analysis

Cash flow analysis (first year)

Months	1	2	3	4	5	6	7
Cash from operations	−$ 4,102	−$ 2,280	−$ 459	$ 1,362	$ 3,183	$ 5,004	$ 8,646
Cash from receivables	$ 0	$ 0	$ 0	$ 0	$ 0	$ 0	$ 0
Operating cash inflow	**−$ 4,102**	**−$ 2,280**	**−$ 459**	**$ 1,362**	**$ 3,183**	**$ 5,004**	**$ 8,646**
Other cash inflows							
Equity investment	$ 250,000	$ 0	$ 0	$ 0	$ 0	$ 0	$ 0
Increased borrowings	$ 1,250,000	$ 0	$ 0	$ 0	$ 0	$ 0	$ 0
Sales of business assets	$ 0	$ 0	$ 0	$ 0	$ 0	$ 0	$ 0
A/P increases	$ 3,159	$ 3,159	$ 3,159	$ 3,159	$ 3,159	$ 3,159	$ 3,159
Total other cash inflows	**$1,503,159**	**$ 3,159**	**$ 3,159**	**$ 3,159**	**$ 3,159**	**$ 3,159**	**$ 3,159**
Total cash inflow	**$1,499,057**	**$ 878**	**$ 2,699**	**$ 4,520**	**$ 6,342**	**$ 8,163**	**$11,805**
Cash outflows							
Repayment of principal	$ 607	$ 607	$ 608	$ 608	$ 609	$ 609	$ 610
A/P decreases	$ 2,075	$ 2,075	$ 2,075	$ 2,075	$ 2,075	$ 2,075	$ 2,075
A/R increases	$ 0	$ 0	$ 0	$ 0	$ 0	$ 0	$ 0
Asset purchases	$ 1,000,000	$ 0	$ 0	$ 0	$417,500	$ 0	$ 0
Dividends	$ 0	$ 0	$ 0	$ 0	$ 0	$ 0	$ 0
Total cash outflows	**$1,002,681**	**$ 2,682**	**$ 2,682**	**$ 2,683**	**$420,183**	**$ 2,684**	**$ 2,684**
Net cash flow	**$ 496,375**	**−$ 1,804**	**$ 17**	**$ 1,838**	**−$413,842**	**$ 5,479**	**$ 9,120**
Cash balance	**$ 496,375**	**$494,572**	**$494,588**	**$496,426**	**$ 82,584**	**$88,063**	**$97,183**

Months	8	9	10	11	12	2009
Cash from operations	$ 12,288	$ 15,930	$ 19,572	$ 23,214	$ 26,856	$ 109,213
Cash from receivables	$ 0	$ 0	$ 0	$ 0	$ 0	$ 0
Operating cash inflow	**$ 12,288**	**$ 15,930**	**$ 19,572**	**$ 23,214**	**$ 26,856**	**$ 109,213**
Other cash inflows						
Equity investment	$ 0	$ 0	$ 0	$ 0	$ 0	$ 250,000
Increased borrowings	$ 0	$ 0	$ 0	$ 0	$ 0	$ 1,250,000
Sales of business assets	$ 0	$ 0	$ 0	$ 0	$ 0	$ 0
A/P increases	$ 3,159	$ 3,159	$ 3,159	$ 3,159	$ 3,159	$ 37,902
Total other cash inflows	**$ 3,159**	**$ 3,159**	**$ 3,159**	**$ 3,159**	**$ 3,159**	**$1,537,902**
Total cash inflow	**$ 15,447**	**$ 19,088**	**$ 22,730**	**$ 26,372**	**$ 30,014**	**$1,647,115**
Cash outflows						
Repayment of principal	$ 610	$ 611	$ 611	$ 612	$ 612	$ 7,313
A/P decreases	$ 2,075	$ 2,075	$ 2,075	$ 2,075	$ 2,075	$ 24,897
A/R increases	$ 0	$ 0	$ 0	$ 0	$ 0	$ 0
Asset purchases	$ 0	$ 0	$ 0	$ 0	$ 0	$1,417,500
Dividends	$ 0	$ 0	$ 0	$ 0	$ 76,449	$ 76,449
Total cash outflows	**$ 2,685**	**$ 2,685**	**$ 2,686**	**$ 2,686**	**$ 79,136**	**$1,526,159**
Net cash flow	**$ 12,762**	**$ 16,403**	**$ 20,044**	**$ 23,686**	**−$ 49,122**	**$ 120,956**
Cash balance	**$109,945**	**$126,348**	**$146,392**	**$170,078**	**$120,956**	**$ 120,956**

Cash flow analysis (second year)

2010

Quarter	Q1	Q2	Q3	Q4	2010
Cash from operations	$ 28,985	$ 36,231	$ 39,130	$ 40,579	$144,924
Cash from receivables	$ 0	$ 0	$ 0	$ 0	$ 0
Operating cash inflow	**$ 28,985**	**$ 36,231**	**$ 39,130**	**$ 40,579**	**$144,924**
Other cash inflows					
Equity investment	$ 0	$ 0	$ 0	$ 0	$ 0
Increased borrowings	$ 0	$ 0	$ 0	$ 0	$ 0
Sales of business assets	$ 0	$ 0	$ 0	$ 0	$ 0
A/P increases	$ 8,717	$ 10,897	$ 11,769	$ 12,204	$ 43,587
Total other cash inflows	**$ 8,717**	**$ 10,897**	**$ 11,769**	**$ 12,204**	**$ 43,587**
Total cash inflow	**$ 37,702**	**$ 47,128**	**$ 50,898**	**$ 52,783**	**$188,512**
Cash outflows					
Repayment of principal	$ 1,840	$ 1,844	$ 1,849	$ 1,854	$ 7,386
A/P decreases	$ 5,975	$ 7,469	$ 8,067	$ 8,365	$ 29,876
A/R increases	$ 0	$ 0	$ 0	$ 0	$ 0
Asset purchases	$ 7,246	$ 9,058	$ 9,782	$ 10,145	$ 36,231
Dividends	$ 20,289	$ 25,362	$ 27,391	$ 28,405	$101,447
Total cash outflows	**$ 35,351**	**$ 43,733**	**$ 47,089**	**$ 48,769**	**$174,941**
Net cash flow	**$ 2,352**	**$ 3,395**	**$ 3,810**	**$ 4,014**	**$ 13,571**
Cash balance	**$123,308**	**$126,703**	**$130,512**	**$134,527**	**$134,527**

Cash flow analysis (third year)

2011

Quarter	Q1	Q2	Q3	Q4	2011
Cash from operations	$ 34,623	$ 43,279	$ 46,742	$ 48,473	$173,117
Cash from receivables	$ 0	$ 0	$ 0	$ 0	$ 0
Operating cash inflow	**$ 34,623**	**$ 43,279**	**$ 46,742**	**$ 48,473**	**$173,117**
Other cash inflows					
Equity investment	$ 0	$ 0	$ 0	$ 0	$ 0
Increased borrowings	$ 0	$ 0	$ 0	$ 0	$ 0
Sales of business assets	$ 0	$ 0	$ 0	$ 0	$ 0
A/P increases	$ 10,025	$ 12,531	$ 13,534	$ 14,035	$ 50,125
Total other cash inflows	**$ 10,025**	**$ 12,531**	**$ 13,534**	**$ 14,035**	**$ 50,125**
Total cash inflow	**$ 44,649**	**$ 55,811**	**$ 60,276**	**$ 62,508**	**$223,243**
Cash outflows					
Repayment of principal	$ 1,858	$ 1,863	$ 1,867	$ 1,872	$ 7,461
A/P decreases	$ 7,170	$ 8,963	$ 9,680	$ 10,038	$ 35,852
A/R increases	$ 0	$ 0	$ 0	$ 0	$ 0
Asset purchases	$ 8,656	$ 10,820	$ 11,685	$ 12,118	$ 43,279
Dividends	$ 24,236	$ 30,296	$ 32,719	$ 33,931	$121,182
Total cash outflows	**$ 41,921**	**$ 51,941**	**$ 55,952**	**$ 57,960**	**$207,774**
Net cash flow	**$ 2,728**	**$ 3,870**	**$ 4,324**	**$ 4,548**	**$ 15,469**
Cash balance	**$137,254**	**$141,124**	**$145,447**	**$149,996**	**$149,996**

Oil and Gas Manufacturing and Services Co.

Russel Oil and Gas Valves Co. Inc.

456 First St.
Toronto, Ontario, Canada

Gerald Rekve

Russel Oil and Gas Valves Co. Inc. is a new company that was formed by two former oil and gas employees.

EXECUTIVE SUMMARY

Russel Oil and Gas Valves Co. Inc. is a new company that was formed by two former oil and gas employees. Both have extensive experience in the technical part of understanding all the aspects of the business.

Based on an investment by investors, both partners plan to raise $3 million dollars; this will go toward the setup of the company, build the required production facilities, and hire the staff.

The sector Russel Oil and Gas Valves Co. Inc. will be operating in is the valve business. The products and services are going to be very specific to the oil and gas business. The partners designed a special in valve company that allows for better flow of the liquid in the pipe lines. Right now the flow is slowed by 23% based on studies. This new patent-pending attachment will reduce the slowed liquid by 19%. Based on studies this will mean an average increase in revenue by $768.00 per minute of flow.

There have been letters of interest signed by major oil and gas companies for the product we will be producing. In 2008 there was a great hit to the stock market and oil went down to $55 per barrel from a high of $125 a barrel in 2007. Our plan is to have a plant up and running early 2010.

COMPANY SUMMARY

Russel Oil and Gas Valves Co. Inc. was established by recently laid–off employees of Shell Canada. Ben Wedge and partner George Russel both were laid off after 10 years with Shell Canada. While both regretted leaving the comfort of a steady income of employment of a large firm, they realized that this was a great opportunity to take their large severance pay and take the chance to start a company they both talked about while working together for Shell.

The main focus of this firm will be to take products from existing suppliers of valves to the oil and gas market, and then customize the fabrication of the end flow units that control the supply and pressure just as the gas leaves the valves.

Right now this is done by the installing company. The installation by the company of this is done by a welder onsite building one large pipe custom to the pipe line, where the valve is being installed. This slows done the valve installation quite a bit. We believe our process will allow for us to eliminate this altogether.

COMPANY OWNERSHIP

Russel Oil and Gas Valves Co. Inc. was established Ben Wedge and partner George Russel.

Both partners will be 24% shareholders, totaling 48%; the balance of ownership will be new investors in the firm. The partners are willing to give up ownership in order to secure the funding required to get the business off the ground.

The company will be registered in Ontario as a Limited Liability Company and incorporated thus thereafter.

START–UP SUMMARY

The company will be started by investments from each partner of $50,000. This will total $100,000 as start-up capital, along with another $100,000 from an outside investor who has already been brought on board. This investor has agreed to take a 10% equity stake in the company in exchange for this investment. Additional investors will be offered a lesser stake in exchange for investment with the two partners and the first large investor who owns 10%.

The partners have already chosen a location to operate their office out of, along with the required facilities that will be used to manufacture the products the firm will be selling. Russel Oil and Gas Valves Co. Inc. partners both have engineering backgrounds. This allowed them to draw the blueprints for the valve product. Therefore the next stage will be product of the unit for sale to the end users.

PRODUCTS

Russel Oil and Gas Valves Co. Inc. has designed a number of products it will be selling to the oil and gas market. Here is what has been designed and is waiting to be manufactured.

- Gas valve adapter for exit

- Gas valve adapter for entrance

- Oil valve for exit

- Oil value for entrance

- Minimize valve slower

- Flow valve constrictor

Each one of these units is new to the market today; that is the main reason the large oil and gas firms hire or have on staff welders who custom-make these as they are required.

MARKET ANALYSIS SUMMARY

This is a new market product, with no real products on the market at present. We understand that once we hit the market there will be competitors who will see the market and try to enter it. The size of the market annually based on number of pipeline projects being either constructed or serviced. We believe the market size for our products and services to be $1,000,000 in the first year, then $3,000,000 year two and as our services and products become more widely known our third year sales will rise to $5,000,000.

MARKET SEGMENTATION

With the oil and gas market being so high, we have defined the market we are going after as a very small niche market. Our segment will be in the valve market. This being only a small part of the industry, along with the fact that our products are only to be a small segment of this area.

We understand there are the water and steam as well industrial applications for our products; however we will only focus on the oil and gas business for the first 5 years. If, as we move along, we see that moving into these other markets will be advantageous for us and we have the required staffing and funding with out affecting our core market, we may then move into these other markets.

TARGET MARKET SEGMENT STRATEGY

Our primary method for the first six months in business will be to target trade shows, send out mailers to clients and finally hire sales consultants to call on potential clients and show them our products. In general here are a few ideas we have to target our market.

- Attend trade shows for Oil and Gas
- Hire sales staff
- Mail info sheets on our products
- Build and maintain a website showing all our products
- Make sure search engines have been paid for keyword searches
- Send editorial ideas to trade magazines, hoping they will run a story on our products

SALES STRATEGY

Russel Oil and Gas Valves Co. Inc. sales strategy is going to be one of consultation and education to our clients. While we understand a vast majority of our clients will be non-technical in nature, we feel that the best approach will be to first educate them so they can see the value of not having onsite welders build the adaptation units custom for each application as it is not required.

Installation of our product will cost the client about 40% of what the current cost is, also and most importantly installation of our product for a single application will reduce the amount of time it takes to work through this problem. The time savings is anywhere from a present 2 and a half day job off this application as long as the welder does not run into any hiccups when installing his custom made device, to ours which will only take 1 day.

We will attend trade shows promoting our products; these shows will be all across North America and the world. We will also mail out information pieces to clients along with follow up telephone calls.

Finally we will focus energies on building and maintaining a great website that will allow us to promote our products via the internet.

SALES FORECAST

Our sales forecast is as follows.

- Year one—$1,000,000

- Year two—$3,000,000

- Year three—$5,000,000

MANAGEMENT SUMMARY

Russel Oil and Gas Valves Co. Inc. will be set up as a LLC company with a structure similar to that of a public company.

Two partners will share in the management rolls of the company with one being the president and CEO and the other being the Vice President.

President and CEO, Ben Wedge

Ben Wedge has considerable experience in oil and gas. Having worked for Shell Canada ever since he graduated from the University of Saskatchewan Engineering Program. Ben focused all his time when working with Shell on refinement as well as distribution. When Shell offered early retirement to their staff, it was felt that this would be a good time for Ben to leave.

Vice President, George Russel

George Russel also has considerable experience in the oil and gas area. George worked for Sonoco for seven years in the distribution area, as well four years with Chevron and finally the last 12 years with Shell Canada in the distribution area and the refinement area. George went to the University of Calgary and got his engineering degree in chemical engineering. While this was not a direct match to his skills, George was able to quickly get the required understanding of his field.

Other positions include:

- CFO—TBD

- Business Startup Manager—TBD

- Director of Manufacturing—TBD

- Sales Director—TBD

FINANCIAL PLAN

The sector that Russel Oil and Gas Valves Co. Inc. will be operating in, is considered a new sector, in that the market has already using options, however we believe that our option to install this special equipment for the valve business will revolutionize the industry.

The investment in the production of this equipment will be approximately $2,000,000. This will cover the set up of the production plant, the equipment required to produce the products, and operating cash as the company ramps up. The money will be secured from primary investors in the financial markets.

There will be a secured loan from bank lending alliance headed by one of Canada's smaller banks. This investment will be secured by the equipment and buildings. The balance of the investment $2 million will be secured by equity in the business.

The two partners, who are starting the firm, will be supplying the patent technology and their experience to the start up company.

PRODUCTION ROLLOUT AND SETUP

The first step will be to locate a piece of land that will be used to build the production facility on. Once chosen, we will then use the blueprints that were drawn up by our engineering firm and architectural firm to build the facility. This process will take about nine months for the search and then another 13 months to build the buildings.

Customer research has already indicated that there is an extensive market for our products and services. Once we hire the marketing staff we will be focusing on contracts to move into the market.

Once the facilities are built up, then we will start the hiring process. We will hire all the required management and production staff, and all the marketing staff to promote the products.

Pro forma profit and loss	Year 2	Year 3	Year 4	Year 5	Year 6
Sales	$1,354,705	$1,461,550	$2,601,569	$2,729,944	$3,902,842
Direct cost of sales	$ 499,051	$ 529,974	$ 879,739	$ 842,839	$1,119,700
Production payroll	$ 444,000	$ 757,000	$ 959,000	$1,063,000	$1,566,000
Other costs of goods	$ 0	$ 0	$ 0	$ 0	$ 0
Total cost of sales	$ 243,051	$ 286,974	$ 338,739	$ 405,839	$ 485,700
Gross margin	$ 111,654	$ 174,576	$ 262,830	$ 324,105	$ 417,142
Gross margin %	31.48%	37.82%	43.69%	44.40%	46.20%
Operating expenses					
Sales and marketing expenses					
Sales and marketing payroll	$ 275,000	$ 400,000	$ 60,000	$ 80,000	$ 100,000
Advertising/promotion	$ 4,950	$ 6,000	$ 7,500	$ 8,500	$ 9,500
Other sales and marketing expenses	$ 0	$ 0	$ 0	$ 0	$ 0
Total sales and marketing expenses	$ 7,700	$ 10,000	$ 13,500	$ 16,500	$ 19,500
Sales and marketing %	2.17%	2.17%	2.24%	2.26%	2.16%
General and administrative expenses					
General and administrative payroll	$ 43,200	$ 43,500	$ 44,000	$ 45,000	$ 45,000
Sales and marketing and other expenses	$ 5,400	$ 7,200	$ 8,500	$ 9,500	$ 10,200
Depreciation	$ 7,750	$ 7,750	$ 7,750	$ 7,750	$ 7,750
Rent	$ 8,400	$ 8,400	$ 8,400	$ 8,400	$ 8,400
Equipment lease	$ 35,988	$ 35,988	$ 35,988	$ 35,988	$ 35,988
Utilities	$ 7,200	$ 7,200	$ 7,200	$ 7,200	$ 7,200
Insurance	$ 4,800	$ 5,400	$ 7,200	$ 9,000	$ 9,600
Payroll taxes	$ 0	$ 0	$ 0	$ 0	$ 0
Other general and administrative expenses	$ 0	$ 0	$ 0	$ 0	$ 0
Total general and administrative expenses	$ 112,738	$ 115,438	$ 119,038	$ 122,838	$ 124,138
General and administrative %	31.78%	25.01%	19.79%	16.83%	13.75%
Other expenses:					
Other payroll	$ 0	$ 0	$ 0	$ 0	$ 0
Consultants	$ 0	$ 6,000	$ 6,000	$ 6,000	$ 6,000
Other other expenses	$ 0	$ 0	$ 0	$ 0	$ 0
Total other expenses	$ 0	$ 6,000	$ 6,000	$ 6,000	$ 6,000
Other %	0.00%	1.30%	1.00%	0.82%	0.66%

PROJECTED BALANCE SHEET

Russel Oil and Gas Valves Co. Inc. products and services' projected balance sheet shows a strong cash development capability over the projected five year plan. The projected balance sheet, like the rest of the business plan, assumes the business remains at its startup location during the first five years of operations, keeping costs relatively fixed for the projections. Again management still feels it can develop a stronger situation than what is reflected.

As projected in the Balance Sheet, the products and services division builds its cash position while also developing a sound net worth. As the industrial Products and Services Division is a manufacturing setting, this business plan reflects the development of a large amount of hard, non–cash assets, excluding ending year five receivables.

During the life of the plan, inventory requirements may change as we offer our clients different purchasing options and build our inventory of used products; any differences in cash flow and inventory would show that the cash is tied up in inventory. With this in mind, we would try to keep the required inventory down to reasonable levels wherever possible.

This division is also a service-oriented segment of the business; many of the services offered are tied to particular product lines offered, allowing the business to create multiple income streams throughout the development of the plan. For segmentation purposes some products have both labor and materials to manufacture a product, some have labor only when providing a service. We have chosen not to show the breakdown of these finer details in the plan.

Pro forma balance sheet	Year 1	Year 2	Year 3	Year 4	Year 5
Assets					
Current assets					
Cash	$300,453	$1,001,547	$101,429	$130,763	$226,983
Accounts receivable	$ 58,857	$ 76,586	$ 99,820	$121,121	$149,811
Inventory	$ 37,048	$ 42,803	$ 52,066	$ 63,177	$ 78,141
Other current assets	$ 5,000	$ 5,000	$ 5,000	$ 5,000	$ 5,000
Total current assets	$213,358	$ 225,937	$301,184	$385,061	$503,335
Long-term assets					
Long-term assets	$ 45,000	$ 45,000	$ 45,000	$ 45,000	$ 45,000
Accumulated depreciation	$ 7,750	$ 15,500	$ 23,250	$ 31,000	$ 38,750
Total long-term assets	$ 37,250	$ 29,500	$ 21,750	$ 14,000	$ 6,250
Total assets	**$250,608**	**$ 255,437**	**$322,934**	**$399,061**	**$509,585**
Liabilities and capital					
Current liabilities					
Accounts payable	$ 45,789	$ 26,927	$ 33,663	$ 40,636	$ 49,625
Current borrowing	$ 0	$ 0	$ 0	$ 0	$ 0
Other current liabilities	$ 0	$ 0	$ 0	$ 0	$ 0
Subtotal current liabilities	$ 45,789	$ 26,927	$ 33,663	$ 40,636	$ 49,625
Long-term liabilities					
Long-term liabilities	$ 41,250	$ 37,500	$ 33,750	$ 30,000	$ 26,250
Total liabilities	**$ 87,039**	**$ 64,427**	**$ 67,413**	**$ 70,636**	**$ 75,875**
Paid-in capital	$230,000	$ 230,000	$230,000	$230,000	$230,000
Retained earnings	($ 53,350)	($ 66,431)	($ 58,990)	($ 24,480)	$ 18,426
Earnings	($ 13,081)	$ 27,440	$ 84,511	$122,906	$185,284

BUSINESS RATIOS

The following table shows standard business ratios for the years of our plan, and a comparison column for data from Manufacturing Industries.

The Products and Services Division's ratios reflect a strong growth with regards to its Gross Margins.

In the long term, our Long Term Assets decline below industry profiles as equipment is paid down, but our overall Debt to Asset ratios are better than the industry in overall results as leaner manufacturing and better coordinated use of our channel partners come into play allowing for more growth without incurring additional expense.

Our General and Administrative ratios are much higher than the industry, but personnel plays an essential role as the business grows towards its growth and outsourcing goals. Also the industry standard profile could reflect more automation than we have at this point, thus our requirement for more personnel.

Ratio analysis	Year 1	Year 2	Year 3	Year 4	Year 5	Industry profile
Sales growth	0.00%	30.12%	30.34%	21.34%	23.69%	−0.33%
Percent of total assets						
Accounts receivable	23.49%	29.98%	30.91%	30.35%	29.40%	23.08%
Inventory	14.78%	16.76%	16.12%	15.83%	15.33%	15.97%
Other current assets	2.00%	1.96%	1.55%	1.25%	0.98%	34.94%
Total current assets	85.14%	88.45%	93.26%	96.49%	98.77%	73.99%
Long-term assets	14.86%	11.55%	6.74%	3.51%	1.23%	26.01%
Total assets	100.00%	100.00%	100.00%	100.00%	100.00%	100.00%
Current liabilities	18.27%	10.54%	10.42%	10.18%	9.74%	23.82%
Long-term liabilities	16.46%	14.68%	10.45%	7.52%	5.15%	17.66%
Total liabilities	34.73%	25.22%	20.88%	17.70%	14.89%	41.48%
Net worth	65.27%	74.78%	79.12%	82.30%	85.11%	58.52%
Percent of sales						
Sales	100.00%	100.00%	100.00%	100.00%	100.00%	100.00%
Gross margin	31.48%	37.82%	43.69%	44.40%	46.20%	36.34%
Selling, general & administrative expenses	39.96%	31.88%	29.64%	27.56%	25.68%	17.49%
Advertising expenses	2.22%	2.31%	2.42%	2.44%	2.35%	1.27%
Profit before interest and taxes	−2.48%	9.35%	20.66%	24.49%	29.63%	3.23%
Main ratios						
Current	4.66	8.39	8.95	9.48	10.14	2.18
Quick	3.85	6.80	7.40	7.92	8.57	1.33
Total debt to total assets	34.73%	25.22%	20.88%	17.70%	14.89%	50.82%
Pre-tax return on net worth	−8.00%	20.52%	47.25%	53.46%	61.03%	7.44%
Pre-tax return on assets	−5.22%	15.35%	37.39%	44.00%	51.94%	15.13%
Additional ratios						
Net profit margin	−3.69%	5.95%	14.05%	16.84%	20.52%	n.a.
Return on equity	−8.00%	14.37%	33.07%	37.42%	42.72%	n.a.
Activity ratios						
Accounts receivable turnover	4.52	4.52	4.52	4.52	4.52	n.a.
Collection days	38	71	71	74	73	n.a.
Inventory turnover	12.00	5.36	5.90	5.95	5.44	n.a.
Accounts payable turnover	6.69	12.17	12.17	12.17	12.17	n.a.
Payment days	27	41	27	27	27	n.a.
Total asset turnover	1.22	1.85	1.26	1.83	1.77	n.a.
Debt ratios						
Debt to net worth	0.53	0.34	0.26	0.22	0.17	n.a.
Current liab. to liab.	0.52	0.41	0.50	0.58	0.65	n.a.
Liquidity ratios						
Net working capital	$165,529	$149,010	$227,520	$364,426	$413,710	n.a.
Interest coverage	−2.04	10.96	34.89	56.08	95.11	n.a.
Additional ratios						
Assets to sales	0.75	0.35	0.64	0.65	0.86	n.a.
Current debt/total assets	18%	11%	10%	10%	10%	n.a.
Acid test	2.57	3.96	4.44	4.94	5.55	n.a.
Sales/net worth	1.17	3.42	2.55	2.72	2.18	n.a.
Dividend payout	0.00	0.00	0.24	0.41	0.43	n.a.

Organic Lawn Care Services

Evergreen Organic Lawn Care Services

5400 Hillshire Road
Columbia, Missouri 65201

Kari Lucke

Evergreen Organic Lawn Care Services will provide a variety of lawn care and related services to consumers in the Columbia, Missouri, area using nontoxic and organic methods and products.

INTRODUCTION

Mission Statement

Evergreen Organic Lawn Care Services will provide a variety of lawn care and related services to consumers in the Columbia, Missouri, area using nontoxic and organic methods and products.

Executive Summary

An increasing number of homeowners are concerned about the environment and the "carbon footprint" they are leaving during their daily lives. They are also more aware of the type of chemicals and toxins that are being used on an everyday basis and their resulting effects on their family's health. Many of these same people own homes and have a vested interest in maintaining their outdoor surroundings. As a result, organic lawn care has become a high demand market. Through their new lawn care service business, John and Karen Purdue will provide the services people need to keep their lawn looking good without harming the environment or using substances that may have a detrimental effect on human health or the health of the environment.

Business Philosophy

Evergreen Organic Lawn Care will operate based on two basic philosophies. The first is: "Timely Service, Every Time." Owners John and Karen Purdue recognize that people are busy and that providing almost immediate responses to inquiries, problems, and requests will give them an edge in the lawn care market. Calls are returned and e–mails will be answered on the same day they are received. Karen will be in charge of this part of the business, and she is prepared to make responding to customers her number–one priority.

The other core business philosophy at Evergreen is represented by the slogan "You and Your Lawn Can be Green." In other words, people can have a nice lawn and still be environmentally responsible by using Evergreen's services.

Goals and Objectives

First Year:

- Gain at least 20 regular clients

Second Year:

- Service at least 30 regular clients

- Have enough business to justify hiring one part–time employee

Third Year:

- Service at least 40 regular clients

- Have enough business to justify hiring a second part–time employee

Organization Structure

At its inception, Evergreen will consist of only two employees: owners John and Karen Purdue. John will provide the actual lawn care services and Karen will do all the record–keeping and bookwork.

INDUSTRY AND MARKET

Industry Analysis

"Organic" has become the buzz word in many American industries, including lawn care. Information from such popular figures as Dr. Mehmet Oz, a regular guest on "The Oprah Winfrey Show," are making people think about their health and the outside world's effects on it. In a recent broadcast, Dr. Oz recommended people take off their shoes when entering the house, in order to avoid exposing themselves and their family members to the toxins from lawn treatments. This type of information has caused homeowners to rethink the way they are handling their lawn care and to question whether they really want toxins and chemicals on their lawns and homes. These are the kinds of questions that are helping the organic lawn care industry grow in the United States.

Market Analysis

The market for Evergreen consists of upper–middle and upper–class families in Columbia, Missouri. Columbia's population grew from 69,000 in 1990 approximately 94,000 in 2007. The median household income of Columbia residents is $42,163, with a race distribution of 83 percent White, 9 percent Black, and 8 percent other. Fifteen percent of the Boone County population has an annual income of $100,000 or more.

Columbia has experienced a boom in construction since the early 2000s. Dozens of new homes and businesses are being built as the city grows and develops. The increase in population has caused an increase in the demand for lawn care services.

Competition

Lawn care services that advertise "organic" services in the Columbia area include a few franchise operations, such as TruGreen Lawn Care and Professional Landscaping Inc., and several private small businesses, such as Southside Lawn Care and Tiger Turf of Mid–Missouri. However, all of the current lawn care service companies offer their organic services as an alternative to their regular service: Evergreen will be the first lawn care service in Columbia that uses organic methods exclusively.

PERSONNEL

Management

Karen Purdue will act as business manager for Evergreen. Karen has a Bachelor of Arts degree in accounting from the University of Missouri and has worked at several businesses as office manager and accountant. John Purdue will perform the physical work of the lawn care business. John has a Bachelor's degree in agriculture from the University of Missouri and worked as a landscaper for the University for six years; thus he has the knowledge and skills necessary to complete all the services offered by Evergreen. In addition, John has completed training through the University of Missouri Extension Service on organic agriculture, farming, and lawn care.

Staffing

John and Karen Purdue will be the only employees initially. As the business grows, the Purdues will hire additional staff. They expect to hire one part–time employee to assist John with services after the first year of operation and a second part–time employee by the third year. Employees will be recruited via online ads and through the local newspaper, the *Columbia Daily Tribune*. Applicants will not be required to have experience in lawn care, and John will provide on–the–job training specific to Evergreen's services. However, those who do have lawn care experience will be eligible for a slightly higher hourly wage, which will be between $10 to $12 an hour based on experience. As per industry standard, no benefits, such as vacation time or health insurance, will be provided to the part–time employees. As home to two four–year private colleges and one large state university, Columbia has no shortage of young people looking for part–time jobs, especially in the spring and summer months during which Evergreen will be operating, so the Purdues anticipate a relatively large pool of applicants from which to hire.

Professional and Advisory Support

John and Karen Purdue are members of the Professional Landcare Network (PLANET), a trade organization dedicated to helping members manage and succeed in their lawn care business. PLANET offers a variety of resources, including an annual conference, publications, training programs, and an online community for those involved in the industry, as well as a certification program for lawn care specialists.

BUSINESS STRATEGY

According to LandscapeAmerica.com, the key to organic lawn care is treating the soil, whereas traditional lawn care companies treat the grass. For example, a regular lawn care company will spray quick—release chemical fertilizer to help grass grow; chemical weed killers to destroy undesirables such as weeds and crabgrass; and chemical pesticides to kill insects that may destroy grass, shrubs, trees, and so on. Evergreen, on the other hand, will focus on maintaining a healthy soil, which in turn will produce healthy grass.

The goal of organic lawn care is to use ecological options, including such concepts as Integrated Pest Management and using the "least toxic pest management" process available. The underlying basis of organic lawn care practices is soil management where the biotic character of the soil is at least preserved and more importantly improved. Organic matter provides nutrients, moisture retention, texture, and an environment to sustain high populations of microorganisms. In organic lawn care, when corrective methods become necessary, they tend to be "natural" as opposed to the synthetic ones used in conventional lawn care programs.

When necessary Evergreen will use slow–release organic fertilizer, composting, aerating, and integrated pest management (IPM) to improve the soil and reduce weeds and pests. IPM involves "the coordinated use of pest and environmental information with available pest control methods to prevent unacceptable levels of pest damage by the most economical means and with the least possible hazard to people, property, and the environment," according to the EPA. It involves using such methods as mechanical trapping devices, insect growth regulators, mating disruption substances (pheromones), and biological pesticides.

PRODUCTS AND SERVICES

Description

Evergreen's basic service includes weekly mowing, trimming, and edging; application of organic fertilizer four times a year (late May, early July, early September, and late October); composting; and ongoing integrated pest management. Additional services offered will include tree and shrubbery maintenance; aeration; pH soil treatments; and other services as needed.

All products and methods used by Evergreen will be chemical–free and natural. Evergreen will also offer a guarantee of customer satisfaction.

Unique Features/Niche

Evergreen will be the only all–organic lawn care company in Columbia.

Product/Service Life Cycle

Because lawn care is a seasonal business, most activity will take place in the months of March through September.

Pricing

Pricing will be based on the size and features of clients' yards and the desired services. The basic service package will include weekly mowing/edging/trimming, fertilizer four times a year; composing; and integrated pest control, and prices will be determined based on the size of the yard and any special features that may increase the time or labor needed to service it. The fee will start at $49.95 for yards up to 5,000 square feet, with $10 for each additional 1,000 square feet. Ten percent will be added for extenuating features such as numerous trees, hills, and/or other special considerations.

MARKETING AND SALES

Advertising and Promotion

The main forms of advertising will be a web site, brochures, and newspaper ads. The web site will list services included, reasons to use a lawn care service—as well as reasons to use Evergreen—and other pertinent information. A photo of John, Karen, and, later, the other employees will be posted to give customers a personal link to the company. Photos will also be used to inspire and convince potential customers that they would benefit from the service. Brochures will contain the same basic information as the web site in a condensed and printed form.

At the outset, Evergreen will also run regular ads in the local paper, the *Columbia Daily Tribune*. In addition, word of mouth will be considered an important form of advertising. As people use Evergreen's services and are satisfied, they will recommend the company to friends and family.

Cost

Advertising costs are expected to include approximately $100 for web site fees, $250 a year for brochure printing, and $400 for newspaper ads.

OPERATIONS

Customers

People who use lawn care services tend to be homeowners with annual household incomes above $75,000. Although elderly people who are not physically able to or do not desire to perform their own mowing are common users of lawn care services, they are not typically as interested in the organic movement as the younger generation. In Columbia, which hosts a relatively young population, homeowners constitute 47 percent of the population (44,180 households), and 27 percent of households have incomes over $75,000 (25,380 households).

Supplies

Evergreen will use Milorganite Organic Nitrogen Fertilizer with 4% Iron, sold at home improvement stores such as Home Depot. One 36–pound bag of Milorganite costs about $10, covers about 2,500 square feet, and is applied to a lawn four times a year. The product will be applied according to spreader settings listed on the company's website.

Other supplies will be purchased on an as–needed basis.

Equipment

The following equipment will be required to begin the business:

- Truck and trailer

- Riding lawn mower

- Push lawn mower

- Weed–eater

- Edger

- Electric shrub trimmers

- Leaf blower

- Seeder/fertilizer spreader

- Other equipment: Shovels, rakes, etc.

Hours

Evergreen will operate an appointment basis on all days expect Sunday.

Facility and Location

The Purdues will operate the business out of their home at 5400 Hillshire Road, Columbia, Missouri. Because their property includes 5 acres and two metal outbuildings that have been erected in the past three years, they will have adequate and secure storage for all equipment.

Legal Environment

Evergreen will use a contract prepared by attorney George Smith for all clients. It will state basic information regarding liability, services contracted, fee, time frame/dates of service, and other relevant information and will be signed by the client and Evergreen representative before any services, not including a free estimate, are performed.

FINANCIAL ANALYSIS

Start—Up Expenses

Start-up expenses

Lawn care equipment	$ 7,000
Lawn care supplies	$ 800
Office equipment and supplies	$ 500
Uniforms	$ 100
Advertising	$ 700
Pick-up truck and trailer	$25,000
Legal fees	$ 500
Insurance	$ 500
Business license	$ 100
Closing costs on loan	$ 1,000
Total start-up expenses	**$36,200**

Half the funding for start—up costs ($18,100) will be provided by money from the Purdues' personal savings account and half from a low—interest business loan.

Monthly Expenses

First year monthly expenses

Lawn care supplies	$ 200
Office supplies	$ 100
Gas and oil for equipment	$ 500
Insurance	$ 100
Equipment maintenance/Repair	$ 100
Loan payment	$ 500
Total monthly expenses, first year	**$1,500**

Estimated incomes are based on low figures using the average cost of $50 per client per week for 20 weeks of lawn care. Service time is approximately May through September (5 months). Add—on services include those not covered under the basic service plan and are estimated conservatively at $200 per month the first year, $300 per month the second year, and $400 per month the third year. Expenses are increased 10 percent for each additional 10 clients.

Year	No. lawns serviced weekly	Add-on services	Total income	Minus expenses	Total profit
Year 1	20	$1,000	$21,000	$7,500	$13,500
Year 2	30	$1,500	$31,500	$12,250*	$19,250
Year 3	40	$2,000	$42,000	$18,675**	$23,325

*$8,250 expenses plus salary for one part-time employee for 20 hours a week at a rate of $10 an hour
**$9,075 expenses plus salary for two part-time employees for 20 hours a week each at a rate of $12 an hour

Pipeline Fracture Testing Service

ADSL Pipeline Services Inc.

6712 Hidalgo
Houston, Texas 77056

Gerald Rekve

The sole purpose of this business plan is to raise $4,000,000 of which $2,000,000 has already been secured by client investments with service purchases.

EXECUTIVE SUMMARY

ADSL Pipeline Services Inc. is an existing company that was started in 2007 by Ben Francis. The company is a LLC that is held privately by Ben Francis. As part of the growth strategy Mr. Francis is requiring an investment of $4 million dollars to take the company to the next stage. There are no current plans to take the company public. This being said at some point in the future this will be a possibility and at that time the ownership and investors will make that decision.

At present ADSL Pipeline Services Inc. has clients lined up to buy their products and services. All the patents are held by Ben Francis and are not going to be included in the company's assets. The use of the patent will be leased to ADSL Pipeline Services Inc. for a period of 10 years. Until such point this changes, Ben Francis will be paid annually for the use of the patent for the VidoMonitor9001.

The sole purpose of this business plan is to raise $4,000,000 of which $2,000,000 has already been secured by client investments with service purchases.

With the Middle East, as well as increased security pressure local and abroad, we are very confident that our technology is in the right place at the right time.

MISSION STATEMENT

Our mission statement is to provide our clients with state-of-the-art monitoring and tracking equipment that is matched by no other in the market. We have no down times that are due to any event.

We will provide the best in customer service and provide our clients with fast and up-to-date tracking and monitoring.

We will not let our information get in the hands of any third party that has no right to view our client information.

THE PRODUCTS AND SERVICES

This business plan was written after considerable increase in requests for testing pipelines across North America.

Presently there has been an increase in the numbers of pipelines that are getting damaged either by natural earth events or vandalism. ADSL Pipeline Services Inc. will send out teams of trained staff to test pipelines, but also install newly engineered monitoring equipment that can not only in nano seconds determine there has been a breach to the pipeline, but also direct a satellite to actually turn and focus in on the fractured pipeline. This will serve two purposes—first, the engineers can quickly identify the level of damage to the site, and, second, be able to take pictures as well video of the location within minutes of the fracture happening. This will allow for any vandals to be caught in the act and the police can use this in court to prosecute the vandals.

The VidoMonitor9001 has been produced by ADSL Pipeline Services Inc. team of engineers. This device has the ability to send signals for up to 3,000 miles using the existing Satellite telephone service and the cellular networks. Working agreements have been reached with all cellular providers in North America. This in itself took considerable amount of work by the customer service staff. The technology used to build the VidoMonitor9001 was considerable. First, the monitor had to have the ability to differentiate between cell calls and Satellite calls by existing clients of the networks. One of the biggest issues with was that fact the crowded cell market left little room for a separate radio signal. Given that fact that there are still people in North America using the CB Radio technology from the 70's also complicated the matter. There was about $1.2 million dollars invested in the VidoMonitor9001.

The quality of the video and pictures are incredible based on the current technology of digital cameras.

COMPANY START-UP

ADSL Pipeline Services Inc. is already in business and operating for the past two years, starting in 2007 by Ben Francis with him investing $1.5 million into the business. Today—late 2009—the company has the products and is in the position to roll out across North America and also in Iraq and other oil producing countries that required this type of monitoring services.

The head office of ADSL Pipeline Services Inc. is located in Houston, Texas with regional monitoring stations setup in Prud Homme, Saskatchewan and Paris, France.

The company is requiring additional investments of $4 million dollars in order to roll out the services in a timely matter. The entire infrastructure is in place; the money will be used to increase the number of clients, the installation of the monitors, and the monitoring of the systems. Client acquisition is the easy part; with only a limited number of pipeline companies, the customer demand for our products is high.

COMPANY START UP BUDGET

ADSL Pipeline Services Inc. start up budget is as follows. While the company already has an existing infrastructure in place, the requirement to increase the volume of monitor installation is at a critical stage. The clients are requesting urgent rollout of the monitors and are willing to pay extra for the installation of them. This being said, we will use the $4 million invested capital that hire both staff and contractors to facilitate the installation of the monitors.

- 3rd & 4th Quarter of 2009—Spend $1 million on production of the monitors.

- 1st quarter 2010—Spend $2 million on subcontractors to start the install.

- The balance of the $4 million will be $1 million—this will be used as an operating budget to keep the company liquid while we roll out the installation.

The clients that we have signed contracts with are willing to advance approximately $2 million of payments to us. This will mean our cash flow for the first 6 months of 2010 will be nil. This is where the $1 million extra we raise will be used to run the day-to-day operations for 6 months.

Future clients have indicated to us that they are also willing to sign similar agreements, however, we feel this will not be required because of the short timeline we will be bringing in the required revenues to sustain our business.

START-UP BUDGET

Start-up requirements

Start-up expenses

Legal	$ 5,000
Stationery etc.	$ 1,000
Brochures	$ 3,000
Insurance	$ 1,000
Rent	$ 10,000
Equipment and tools	$ 50,000
Vans (2)	$ 50,000
Total start-up expenses	**$120,000**

Start-up assets

Cash required	$100,000
Start-up inventory	$ 0
Other current assets	$ 0
Long-term assets	$ 50,000
Total assets	$150,000
Total requirements	**$270,000**

START-UP FUNDING

Start-up funding

Start-up expenses to fund	$100,000
Start-up assets to fund	$115,000
Total funding required	$215,000

Assets

Non-cash assets from start-up	$ 50,000
Cash requirements from start-up	$ 50,000
Additional cash raised	$ 0
Cash balance on starting date	$100,000

Liabilities and capital

Liabilities

Current borrowing	$ 0
Long-term liabilities	$100,000
Accounts payable (outstanding bills)	$ 0
Other current liabilities (interest-free)	$ 0
Total liabilities	$100,000

Capital

Planned investment	$ 0
Owner	$ 60,000
Total planned investment	$ 60,000
Loss at start-up (start-up expenses)	$100,000
Total capital	$ 60,000
Total funding	**$500,000**

STAFFING COSTS

Staffing costs

Subcontractors	$ 2,000,000
Product production	$ 1,000,000
Staffing existing	$ 2,450,000 (1 year)
Increase in office cost	$ 340,000
Travel	$ 120,000
New staff hire cost	$ 2,500,000

EQUIPMENT INSTALLATION

ADSL Pipeline Services Inc. is a new company and was formed by Ben Francis, former CEO of a large gas company based in Texas. Mr. Francis invested $1.5 million of his own money to launch this business. After about two years of R & D Mr. Francis launched his company in 2009. Right now ADSL Pipeline Services Inc. has about 45 employees. The employees are in all departments from engineering to production and customer service. What is required at the moment is the installation of 1,000 miles of pipe monitors. Each monitor must be installed every 800 feet in areas where there is a straight line or level ground. In areas where there are curves, tree coverage or any obstruction between monitor, the monitor must be installed in eyes sight each other. This task is considerable considering it takes about 40 minutes to install one monitor. Add the drive time and it adds another 15 minutes. So on an average 10 hour work day, a two man crew can install 10 monitors.

Because the set up and installation is considerably more labor intensive, installation staff will be required before we can sign on more clients. This is one of the reasons for this business plan—to attract investors in order to pay our staff or contractors to install the monitors.

THE MONITORING OF THIS NETWORK

Once all the monitors for a client pipeline have been installed, this client pipeline will be 100% secure.

The monitoring will be done at our North American geographically-central location. The reason we do it here instead of at our head office in Houston, Texas is simple. We need to make sure the monitoring office is central to all the satellites that fly over North America both day and night. The location chosen is a small town called Prud Homme, Saskatchewan. This location will employ over 100 staff, all of which will work shifts around the clock.

Each staff person hired to work in the monitoring station will be required to pass background checks and physiological tests to determine if they have the required strength to work in an environment where the combination of burden and sudden call to attention is required.

On a six-hour shift each one of the staff will monitor anywhere from 500—700 miles of pipeline. When an event happens, that staff member will call it up on the closest satellite to determine what type of event happened, and then start the required process to deal with the event.

STAFFING

The company ADSL Pipeline Services Inc. has approximately 45 staff at the time of this business plan. Here is a breakdown of where the staff is located.

Houston, Texas (Head Office)

- Ben Francis—CEO & Chairmen of the board

- Hadley Brown—CFO

- Betty White—CIO

- Darren Quarters—VP IT

- Mandern Gui—Chief Tech Officer & VP Production

- Harry Brewster—Regional Manager Rollout North America

- Funi Ugiuti—Regional Manager Rollout Middle East

- Franco Dolomote—Regional Manager Rollout UK & Europe & Russia

Prud Homme Monitor Station, Saskatchewan, Canada

- Lily Wasman—Monitor Station Manager

- Gina Grasser—Assistant Station Manager

- Plus 8 monitoring staff

- Will grow to 81 staff when in full operation

UK & Europe—Paris, France Monitor Station

- Manscion Deomo—Monitor Station Manager

- Asitin Grows—Assistant Station Manager

- Plus 4 monitoring staff

- Will grow to 56 staff when in full operation

Kuit Monitoring Station

- Jicy Waitiui—Monitor Station Manager

- Kiuaty Gancty—Assistant Station Manager

- Plus 5 monitoring staff

- Will grow to 39 staff when in full operation

There is the potential to add new monitoring stations throughout the world. These will be determined on an as needed basis.

Right now we have 12 crews of 20 contract staff installing the devices where required. Once we get the funding we are requesting, we will see this number grow to about 1,200 installers working from January to July, 2010.

The biggest expense will be the installation of the monitors.

SALES & MARKETING

We will be renting out this monitor service to our clients. The rental fee will be based on a number of factors.

DETERMINANTS TO FEES

- Number of monitors required
- Location of monitors
- Accessibility of monitors to install crew

The fees for monitoring these devises are as follows.

Installed monitors

- 1—500 = $36 each, monthly
- 501—1000 = $33 each, monthly
- 1001—2000 = $31 each, monthly
- 2001—5000 = $29 each, monthly
- 5000—10,000 = $24 each, monthly
- 10,001 + = $18 each, monthly

Location of monitors

- If location is easy access—meaning less than 1 kilometer from road—no extra fee
- If location is medium hard access—1–3 kilometer from road—one time $6.00 extra fee per monitor
- If terrain is heavy treed/mountain/desert or any other hard access determined by client and us, extra one time fee of $12.00 per monitor
- If in war zone or area staff is at risk of injury, between $45 and $120 per monitor extra one time fee

SALES FORECAST

Our sales forecast for the first year will be in $2 million dollars; year two we will have sales of $3.5 million dollars. Year three we will target to have $4.5 million dollars in sales.

There is some assumptions about our sales—that there is no break down in any of our contracts. This means the contracts not broken by war, weather, earth events, or so on.

MARKETING OF OUR PRODUCTS

Already we have clients signed up for our service; we also have a waiting list of clients who want our service. There is no other competitor out there that offers a direct product to ours. This we are sure will change as new companies develop their own technology as to ours. Right now we have a monopoly for our products and services.

Having said this, we are certain once our clients sign on to our products we will keep them for a long time. In order to insure this as well to make certain that all our clients are happy, we will have on-staff marketing experts who will focus all their energy on winning clients and then retaining them as we move our company forward. Getting the message out about our products and services will be done as follows.

1. **Trade Show exposure.** We will attend all the trade shows of the products and services for anything to do with oil, gas, etc.

2. Sales executives who will target clients across North America and UK, Europe, and the world.

3. **Website and Inter-Network**. The website will be public place where potential clients, media and investors can get information on our company. The Inter-Network will be the place existing clients can get live information on their pipelines; this will also be used to show potential clients how our services work. The Inter-Network will be that of a high security. In fact the security for this network will be similar to that of a bank, because of the potential of the wrong people getting our pipeline information. Only high-level people in the clients' business will be given short-term access to this network and each time a client wants access, one of the senior security staff will actually visit the client site and provide them with short-term access. Short-term means 4 hour limits. Because of the required high security even the senior security staff will have a limit of 2–4 hours per client per visit.

4. **Trade publications advertising**. We will target a variety of trade publications in the oil and gas field and run info-type advertising.

5. We will send mailers to potential clients teaching them about our products

COMPETITION

Investment Capital Required

We are targeting to raise $2 million via investor money and $2 million from prepaid client services. We are very confidant that we will achieve our goals. The $2 million from investors will be paid back over a term of 4 years at 12% interest and monthly installments payments of $10,000 starting month 7 after we have installed all the required monitors for this rollout. The balance of the 12% added to $21,000 per month will start at the end of month 12 after we have installed all the monitors.

The $2 million from clients will be paid back in terms of free service for 6 months. This will mean for 6 months after all monitors are installed, we will operating with no cash flow other that of new clients who sign up to our service. We know this may be considered risky however we know going into month 7 we will have certain cash flow and also we have a $1 million dollar reserve in place.

The contractors who have signed on to install the monitors have also put some skin in the game, using an acronym. The contractors will be taking 1st stage payment for all work on a monthly basis, based on 70% of contract. Then once the contract is done and all monitors are installed, the contractors will be paid the balance of the 30% in monthly installments over an 8 month period at 3% interest.

We first did not account for this, however the contractors came to us and offered this, knowing that as we roll out more contracts over the years, this will play favor in our books and we will most likely continue to use these contractors in the future-a win-win situation for both us and our contractors.

Our production facilities are already in place and we have subcontracted out certain components of our product, therefore reducing the required investment of capital and equipment as well as staff. We have signed long-term contracts with manufacturers of these extra components.

CLIENTS

Our clients list includes both large and small types of clients.

- Western Pipelines
- Houston Gas Co.
- Wynargard Oil & Gas

- Shell

- Imperial Oil

- Esso

- TransCanada Pipe Lines

- North One Pipe Line

- Kuit Pipe Line Inc.

- Euro Pipes LLC

- UK Petro

- BMO Gas

- AGM Oil Services

STAFF TRAINING & RECRUITMENT

All of our staff will undergo an extensive background check and training prior to gaining employment with our firm. The background check will be done by CSIS in Canada, FBI In USA, and Interpol in UK & Europe. While some think this is over doing it, we maintain that we manage the pipeline infra-structure that could cripple an economy if it is broken down. We have been told by all these agencies that this is a minimum requirement in order for us to operate in this sector. We understand that this is a concern for potential employees; however we know once our staff sees our full services they will understand and adopt the background checks.

The training will be extensive for software training, security training, and distribution training. On average the training will take place over a period of 8 weeks off site. Each employee is required to achieve a minimum of 75% level of success on any tests conducted during the 8 week training. This will be paid training similar to other oil and gas paid training. If the potential staffer does not achieve the 75%, then they will be retested in the areas they failed. The retesting will be paid by the company. Our goal is that if one of our hiring managers see the potential in you, and they hire you, we will do all we can to make sure you pass the 8 week course. Once employed we will maintain a success follow up every 6 months; this will be to insure our staff is happy and we are happy with their work.

NETWORK MANAGEMENT

Because we are operating a one-of-a-kind network, that not only involves clients, it involves countries, security agencies, satellite tracking, and so on, we will install a number of failsafe stop gaps to insure our network never goes down. If there is ever a breach in one of our clients lines, we will be there to offer quick as well correct action to correct the event. To track the event, this means we are policing a large and vast global network. We are certain that our follow through services ensure 100% customer satisfaction. The stop gap measures we will implement are not included in this document for security reasons. However we are certain that they will meet all the regularities requirements.

RATIO ANALYSIS

Ratio analysis	Year 1	Year 2	Year 3	Industry profile
Sales growth	0.00%	10.29%	10.20%	4.70%
Percent of total assets				
Accounts receivable	18.84%	17.96%	18.26%	11.20%
Inventory	4.64%	4.38%	4.30%	1.40%
Other current assets	0.00%	0.00%	0.00%	36.30%
Total current assets	66.72%	73.93%	78.43%	48.90%
Long-term assets	33.28%	26.07%	21.57%	51.10%
Total assets	100.00%	100.00%	100.00%	100.00%
Current liabilities	8.57%	9.01%	8.87%	26.90%
Long-term liabilities	65.52%	50.34%	40.65%	22.20%
Total liabilities	74.09%	59.36%	49.52%	49.10%
Net worth	25.91%	40.64%	50.48%	50.90%
Percent of sales				
Sales	100.00%	100.00%	100.00%	100.00%
Gross margin	72.03%	72.30%	73.28%	64.10%
Selling, general & administrative			67.37%	45.40%
expenses	63.05%	63.85%	4.76%	0.20%
Advertising expenses	3.86%	4.37%	10.43%	5.20%
Profit before interest and taxes	15.86%	14.55%		
Main ratios				
Current	7.79	8.20	8.84	1.79
Quick	7.24	7.71	8.36	1.44
Total debt to total assets	74.09%	59.36%	49.52%	49.10%
Pre-tax return on net worth	111.96%	64.12%	36.71%	4.70%
Pre-tax return on assets	29.01%	26.06%	18.53%	9.30%
Additional ratios				
Net profit margin	8.97%	8.45%	5.91%	n.a.
Return on equity	78.37%	44.88%	25.70%	n.a.
Activity ratios				
Accounts receivable turnover	9.01	9.01	9.01	n.a.
Collection days	58	39	39	n.a.
Inventory turnover	6.00	14.24	14.05	n.a.
Accounts payable turnover	10.64	12.17	12.17	n.a.
Payment days	27	27	29	n.a.
Total asset turnover	2.26	2.16	2.19	n.a.
Debt ratios				
Debt to net worth	2.86	1.46	0.98	n.a.
Current liab. to liab.	0.12	0.15	0.18	n.a.
Liquidity ratios				
Net working capital	$79,888	$103,167	$119,795	n.a.
Interest coverage	5.21	5.87	5.25	n.a.
Additional ratios				
Assets to sales	0.44	0.46	0.46	n.a.
Current debt/Total assets	9%	9%	9%	n.a.
Acid test	5.05	5.72	6.30	n.a.
Sales/Net worth	8.74	5.31	4.35	n.a.
Dividend payout	0.00	0.00	0.00	n.a.

PROJECTED PROFIT AND LOSS

The following table and chart highlights the projected profit and loss for three years.

Pro forma profit and loss	Year 1	Year 2	Year 3
Sales			
Direct cost of sales	$400,000	$600,000	$900,000
Other production expenses	$ 0	$ 0	$ 0
Total cost of sales	$400,000	$600,000	$900,000
Gross margin	$290,000	$340,000	$440,000
Gross margin %	72.03%	72.30%	73.28%
Expenses			
Payroll	$120,000	$136,000	$166,000
Sales and marketing and other expenses	$ 18,000	$ 23,000	$ 28,000
Utilities	$ 12,000	$ 42,000	$ 62,000
Payroll taxes	$ 18,000	$ 20,400	$ 24,900

PROJECTED CASH FLOW

The following is the projected cash flow for three years.

Pro forma cash flow	Year 1	Year 2	Year 3
Cash from operations			
Cash sales	$ 77,750	$ 85,750	$ 94,500
Cash from receivables	$207,375	$254,588	$280,588
Subtotal cash from operations	$285,125	$340,338	$375,088
Additional cash received			
New investment received	$ 5,000	$ 0	$ 0
Subtotal cash received	$290,125	$340,338	$375,088
Expenditures from operations			
Cash spending	$120,000	$136,000	$166,000
Bill payments	$110,000	$180,000	$190,000

Safety Consulting Firm

Peters, Marsh & McLellan LLC

3333 Chestnut Ave.
Rogers Hill, Pennsylvania 19105

Paul Greenland

Peters, Marsh & McLellan LLC is an independent safety consulting firm focusing primarily on OSHA compliance, ergonomics, and transportation safety.

EXECUTIVE SUMMARY

Business Overview

By 2010, companies of all sizes, and in every industry, were required to comply with state and federal laws pertaining to occupational health and safety. By taking proactive measures to ensure the safety of their employees, the environment, and the larger public, companies benefit in numerous ways. For example, businesses are able to minimize or eliminate operational-related risks, reduce accident rates, prevent job-related diseases and injuries, reduce workers compensation payments, lower insurance premiums, and avoid government fines. In addition, companies that make occupational health and safety a priority can often increase employee morale and productivity, and realize a higher return on investment.

Established in 2004, Peters, Marsh & McLellan LLC is an independent safety consulting firm focusing primarily on OSHA compliance, ergonomics, and transportation safety. Although we work with organizations of all sizes, we concentrate mainly on small- and medium-sized companies that do not have full-time safety directors or departments.

Organizational Structure

Peters, Marsh & McLellan LLC is a limited liability corporation based in the Commonwealth of Pennsylvania. This type of business structure provides us with the liability protection of a corporation, along with the advantage of being treated as a partnership. Our firm is owned by John Peters, CSP, CPE; Rick Marsh, CSP, CDS; and Mary McLellan, CSHM, CSP. Together, the owners have more than 60 years of combined experience in the occupational health and safety industry.

MARKET ANALYSIS

In 2008 the U.S. Department of Labor's Bureau of Labor Statistics (BLS) reported that there were 3.7 million nonfatal occupational injuries and illnesses in 2008. This compared to 4.0 million cases in 2007. Injuries accounted for nearly 95 percent of the total (3.5 million).

BLS data reveals that, in 2008, four industry sectors were responsible for approximately 75 percent of all injuries and illnesses resulting in days away from work. Among these are trade, transportation, and utilities (30%) and manufacturing (15%). In terms of occupations, eight accounted for 30 percent of all injuries and illnesses with days away from work. These include laborers and freight, stock, and material movers, as well as heavy and tractor-trailer truck drivers.

The $4 trillion U.S. manufacturing sector has accounted for the lion's share (83%) of our revenues to date. Within manufacturing, our firm specializes in two primary areas, including:

1. *Beverage Manufacturing & Bottling*—With annual sales of approximately $70 million, this segment includes several thousand companies that bottle everything from beer, wine, and spirits, to soft drinks, juice, and water. Most of our clients are smaller operations that perform both production and bottling operations at one facility. We are very familiar with the equipment and technology used for bottling and packaging. In most cases, operations are characterized by a high degree of automation.

2. *Candy Manufacturing*—This $17 billion industry segment is dominated by several large players, including the Hershey Company and Nestlé. However, there were approximately 1,600 companies operating within the candy manufacturing segment during the late 2000s. A wide variety of specialized machines are used on candy production lines, which we are knowledgeable about. Historically, we have provided services to a number of smaller and mid-sized candy companies.

Other important segments for our consulting firm are transportation & logistics and general office workers:

1. *Transportation & Logistics*—Within this $200 billion industry segment, we focus heavily on both long–distance and local trucking (truckload and less–than–truckload) operations. Many of our clients operate trucks equipped with advanced technology, including on–board computer systems and GPS scheduling systems. In addition to trucking, we also focus on warehouse operations. As with trucking, many of our clients' warehousing operations are highly automated and computer-ized, utilizing conveyor systems and radio frequency identification (RFID) technology.

2. *General Office*—Although not technically an industry segment in its own right, we provide consultation to many companies in order to improve optimal environments for employees who spend the majority of their workday behind a desk. Executive secretaries and administrative assistants comprise one major category within this area. According to the U.S. Department of Labor's Occupational Outlook Handbook, 2008–09 Edition, employment of secretaries and admin-istrative assistants totaled 4.24 million in 2006, and was expected to reach 4.60 million by 2016.

INDUSTRY ANALYSIS

Many of the consultants in our field formerly worked as occupational health and safety specialists or safety managers with organizations. In addition to undergraduate degrees in occupational health or safety, consultants may have degrees in specific fields, including chemistry, engineering, or biology.

According to the U.S. Department of Labor, 56,000 occupational health and safety specialists and technicians were employed in 2006. By 2016 this figure is expected to rise about 9 percent, reaching 61,000. In addition, 678,000 management analysts were employed in 2006. By 2016, this figure is expected to increase 22 percent, reaching 827,000. Although this total includes management analysts of all kinds, it illustrates rapid growth within the consulting field.

The primary professional organization within our field is the American Society of Safety Engineers (ASSE). Established in 1911, ASSE is the oldest and largest professional safety organization. With approximately 32,000 members, it offers 14 practice specialties, 151 chapters, 28 sections, and 58 student sections.

PERSONNEL

Peters, Marsh & McLellan LLC is owned by John Peters, CSP, CPE; Rick Marsh, CSP, CDS; and Mary McLellan, CSHM, CSP. Together, the owners have more than 60 years of combined experience in the occupational health and safety industry.

John Peters, CSP, CPE

A safety industry veteran with more than 20 years of experience, John Peters, CSP, CPE, is a Certified Safety Professional, as well as a Certified Professional Ergonomist. Peters received his undergraduate training at Central University, where he graduated with a Masters in Science in 1979. After working as the safety director for a large packaged goods company, he completed additional graduate coursework in the field of ergonomics. Peters specializes in several areas, including occupational safety ergonomics, human factors industrial engineering, and safety management. He is a member of the Human Factors and Ergonomics Society, as well as the American Society of Safety Engineers. Peters has authored numerous white papers and journal articles within the safety field.

Rick Marsh, CSP, CDS

Rick Marsh, CSP, CDS, brings transportation-related expertise to our firm. Marsh is a 1982 graduate of Smithfield College, where he earned an undergraduate degree in business. During the early years of his career, he went to work for a mid-sized trucking company. Ultimately becoming an operations manager, he later specialized in transportation safety, becoming a Certified Safety Professional, as well as a Certified Motor Vehicle Fleet Safety Director. Marsh has specialized expertise in motor vehicle/fleet operations, negligent maintenance, negligent method of operation, accident investigation, truck loading/unloading, material handling, DOT compliance, fleet safety, forklifts, and warehouse safety. He is a frequent national presenter on matters related to transportation safety.

Mary McLellan, CSHM, CSP

Mary McLellan, CSHM, CSP, is a Certified Safety and Health Manager, as well as a Certified Safety Professional. A 1988 graduate of Southwest Texas State University, McClellan has special expertise in the areas of regulatory compliance; rules, policies, and procedures; OSHA recordkeeping; safety training; accident investigation; emergency preparedness and response; and contractor safety programs. Over the course of her career, she has worked as a safety manager at several large organizations, including candy and beverage companies. She is the author of a forthcoming book titled *Workplace Safety: What You Need to Know* (Johnson Publishers, 2011).

Professional & Advisory Support

Peters, Marsh & McLellan operates in a complicated legal environment. As such, we rely upon the law office of McCarthy, Scrivano & Holm for advising on legal matters pertaining to safety issues. Specifically, this firm specializes in employment, as well as occupational safety and health. The firm's attorneys are admitted to practice in the states where we do the majority of our business. In addition, McCarthy, Scrivano & Holm handles OSHA/MSHA administrative law cases nationwide.

In addition, our firm has established a business banking account with Rogers Hill Community Bank, including a merchant account for credit card payments. Tax advisement is provided by Bottom Line Accounting Services.

GROWTH STRATEGY

Peters, Marsh & McLellan's billable hours and revenues have been relatively flat since our third year of operations. We realize that additional consultants are needed to further our long–term growth. With this in mind, we have established plans to add one additional consultant in 2010, followed by another in 2011. In addition to having a positive impact on our net income, as revealed in the Financial Analysis section of this plan, our objective is to expand the scope of consulting services offered, and the types of industry clients served. In our view, this strategy will allow us to become a more comprehensive safety consulting firm.

SERVICES

The consulting services provided by our firm pertain to a seemingly endless list of job-related accidents, injuries, and illnesses. Examples include, but are not limited to:

- Asphyxiation
- Burns
- Cave-ins
- Crushing (by falling walls, falling machinery, steel beams, dump truck bodies, etc.)
- Drowning
- Electrical shock
- Electrocution
- Falls (from elevations, towers, scaffolds, roofs, etc.)
- Fires
- Striking (by nails, collapsing crane booms, falling objects, etc.)
- Trench cave-ins

The services we offer include:

- Contractor reviews
- DOT compliance
- Emergency action plans
- Ergonomic programs
- Expert testimony
- Hand injury prevention
- Incident analysis
- Incident and case management strategy
- Job site safety inspections
- OSHA pre-audit inspections
- OSHA recordkeeping
- Policy & procedure development
- Regulatory interpretation
- Safe work permits
- Safety awareness programs
- Safety plan development
- Task hazard analysis

MARKETING & SALES

We have developed a marketing plan that involves the following primary tactics:

- Printed collateral describing our business.

- Advertisements in several print and online industry and professional directories, including the ASSE Environmental Health and Safety Consultants Directory.

- A Web site with complete details about our firm and the services we offer.

- A monthly e-mail newsletter for safety managers, which provides case studies, tips, and insight from our field experiences.

- The use of appropriate social media channels such as LinkedIn to stay connected with other professionals and key prospects.

- Highly targeted direct mail campaigns to key decision-makers within the industry sub-segments we serve (e.g., beverage bottling and manufacturing, candy manufacturing, transportation, etc.).

- Expert columns (in trade magazines read by professionals within the industries we serve), white papers, and other publications to showcase our consultants' expertise.

- A public relations campaign that involves the submission of successful case studies (in the form of press releases) to appropriate business and trade magazines. Specifically, case studies illustrate how we helped a client to lower accident or injury rates, increase productivity, etc.

- Tradeshow/exhibition marketing (making presentations and engaging in relationship building activities with key prospects).

OPERATIONS

Facility & Location

Peters, Marsh & McLellan is located in Rogers Hill, Pennsylvania, a smaller town located approximately 20 miles northwest of Philadelphia. Our office at 3333 Chestnut Ave. is based in an old house that has been zoned for commercial use. The location is ideal because rent is very affordable, and we have easy access to the Philadelphia International Airport and major highways.

LEGAL

As a limited liability company (LLC) based in the Commonwealth of Pennsylvania, we have filed a certificate of organization with the Pennsylvania State Department's Corporation Bureau. In addition, each year we file a Certificate of Annual Registration, along with a corresponding annual registration fee, on or before April 15.

As stated in the Professional & Advisory Support section of this plan, we rely upon the law office of McCarthy, Scrivano & Holm for advice on legal matters pertaining to safety issues.

Finally, Peters, Marsh & McLellan has secured appropriate business liability insurance coverage.

FINANCIAL ANALYSIS

Following is Peters, Marsh & McLellan's balance sheet for 2009, followed by several two–year projections that take into account the addition of one new consultant per year in 2010 and 2011.

Revenue

- Consulting—$596,700
- Public Speaking—$18,456
- Royalty Income—$4,569
- Total Revenue—$619,725

Expenses

- Salaries—$300,000
- Utilities—$2,675
- Rent—$11,500
- Insurance—$21,540
- Office Supplies—$1,560
- Equipment—$6,200
- Marketing & Advertising—$15,567
- Telecommunications & Internet—$5,256
- Professional Development—$15,600
- Travel & Entertainment—$41,237
- Subscriptions & Dues—$2,765
- Taxes & Fees—$3,678
- Total Expenses—$427,578
- Net Income—$192,147

Revenue Projections

- 2010—$837,256
- 2011—$1,057,479

Net Income Projections

- 2010—$289,978
- 2011—$390,501

Self-Service Laundry Business

Wash 'N Go

7 Clent Street
Burlington, Vermont 05401

Laura Becker

In addition to the basic wash and dry machines, Wash 'N Go will offer add–on services including a wash and fold service, a send out dry cleaning service, vending machines, television viewing, and free internet access.

BUSINESS OBJECTIVE

The business objective is to establish a self service laundry business. This will entail providing coin or card operated washing machines and dryers to local residents (renters) in surrounding apartment complexes including college students from the local university.

In addition to the basic wash and dry machines, Wash 'N Go will offer add–on services including a wash and fold service, a send-out dry cleaning service, vending machines, television viewing, and free internet access.

EXECUTIVE SUMMARY

The self service laundry or coin/card operated laundry business can be a profitable business for the independent owner operator. The ideal location for retail space is in a high–traffic area populated by a rental community.

The current trends in the industry include larger storefronts offering value-added services. Therefore, in addition to the standard washer and dryer self service equipment, businesses today are catering to busy consumers and offering premium services such as pick up and delivery; wash and fold and dry cleaning. In addition, conveniences such as Internet access, television viewing and food service are now provided in some stores. Full–time attendants may also be utilized in stores to provide extra levels of customer service.

Generally speaking, for an independent operator looking to establish a business it makes more sense to purchase an existing laundry business. Establishing a laundry business initially involves high start up costs with relatively expensive construction and equipment fees. Thus it usually makes sense to evaluate existing businesses.

The keys to success will be a good location; a high number of turns per day (uses per machine per day); revenue from value added services (that can provide a higher profit margin); and energy efficiency.

INDUSTRY ANALYSIS

According to the Coin Laundry Association, a coin laundry business is defined as one which provides commercial–grade, self–service laundry equipment to customers in a retail space. There are currently over 35,000 coin laundry businesses in the United States. It is estimated that the industry generates approximately $5 billion in gross annual revenue.

The amount of money generated by a laundry business can vary tremendously. According to the Coin Laundry Association's President and CEO, Brian Wallace, the annual gross income from one store can range from $30,000 to $1 million. Expenses generally range from between 65 to 115 percent of the gross income. For example, if a store makes $30,000 in revenue in one year, at best it would have a net profit of $10,500 and at worst it would lose $4,500.

Generally speaking, coin laundry businesses do best in geographic areas that are surrounded by people who live in rental buildings and who do not have their own laundry equipment. According to the Coin Laundry Association, "the self–service laundry market consists of an estimated primary customer base of 86 million people living in rental housing, as of the 2000 U.S. Census."

The outlook for the coin laundry industry is strong as population growth and an increase in rental housing (along with the current recession preventing many people from buying their own homes equipped with equipment) will provide an increase in potential customer demand for coin laundries.

In the article, "How to Start a Coin–Operated Laundry," the industry outlook is discussed as follows: "Industry growth is based on the demographics of population density, population mix and population income. The more concentrated the population, the greater the need for quality coin laundry facilities. National and regional demographics indicate renters, the primary users of coin laundries, are the fastest–growing segment in the nation. As of the 2000 U.S. Census, 31 percent of the nation's 116 million households were renter occupied. The number of coin laundry stores built over the past 60 years has grown steadily as the population has increased and shifted to more concentrated areas. The end result has been a mature, stabilized industry with predictable rates of turnover and values of existing coin laundries, development of new turn–key facilities, and equipment expansion and replacement."

The current self service laundry market is composed primarily of independent owners, not franchises. Entrepeneur.com reports that 75% of coin laundry owners own only one store. There are a few local chains throughout the United States, but none are national and only some have a sizable number of stores.

About 50% of business owners operate the store as a full–time job. This is becoming more common, however, as stores get bigger in size and offer value–added services (such as wash/dry/fold and dry cleaning) which can generate additional revenue streams.

TRENDS

Larger Stores and Value–Added Services

The future for the industry looks bright. New and existing owners are looking to establish larger storefronts and also to provide value–added services to create additional revenue streams (with greater profit margins). The larger spaces allow for more equipment and for greater comfort for the consumer. Value–added services such as pick up and delivery services; wash and fold; dry cleaning and others provide premium services as conveniences for customers with tight schedules (perhaps families where both adults work, etc.). Stores also now may offer Internet access, television viewing, video games, food service such as coffee and snacks and play areas for children. Some owners are providing more attendants in the store to provide a greater level of service as well.

According to Brian Wallace, President and CEO of the Coin Laundry Association, "The industry is now getting a facelift. There's a trend toward coin laundries being more comfortable for the customer." A recent survey from the Coin Laundry Association showed that more than half of existing coin laundry businesses now offer wash–and–fold service.

According to Entrepeneur.com, "Many owners around the country are serving food, renting mailboxes and offering free Internet access. Because the new laundries are bigger than in the past —often 3,000 or 4,000 square feet—overhead is higher, and owners are looking for ways to cover the cost. These additional services demand little increase in overhead because the rent is already paid for."

Paul Partyka, Editor of American Coin–Op, a magazine devoted to self–service laundries, says that "Trying to generate additional revenue per square foot has always been an issue. But it's even more so now with tighter competition and utility bills growing. Everybody wants to squeeze as much money as possible out of their space. Looking for an extra service that will work is always on their mind."

Equipment Trends

Coin and Card Systems

In addition, many laundry businesses are moving to card systems rather than coin systems. Customers use swipe cards that subtract the cost of the wash or dry, much like a phone card or debit card.

For the owner, the card systems allow for easy price adjustments which can translate into additional income. For instance, a slight 2 cent increase per washing machine and dryer turn per machine can add up to be significant and relatively unnoticed by the customer. For customers, the benefit of the cards are that they can purchase cards and not be concerned with having to have so much change.

Top Load and Front Load Washers

The industry is moving toward more front load washers. Generally, although front load washers are initially more expensive they have several benefits including: greater capacity, and greater water and energy efficiency.

Trends Summary

In summary, Brian Brunckhorst, creator of "Own a Laundromat Teleseminar on CD," believes that the emergence of larger stores will provide for larger capacity equipment; and for the use card systems because it will be difficult to pay for the larger fees in coins. Brunckhorst states, "The average store is about 2,300 square feet, and we're starting to see more and more stores that are bigger than 4,000 square feet opening, so I would expect to see more of that in the future. I think that we'll see a lot less top–loading washers and more stores that don't have any of those, moving towards the front–loading type of washers, and stores that have larger equipment capacities, where in the past, you might have a store that it maybe has one or two large capacity, say, fifty pound washers. Now stores are opening up with sixty, eighty pound washers, even up to one hundred and twenty–five pound washers. And so just larger capacity, bigger stores, I see more of that, and I also see the store owners starting to move more and more towards some sort of a card system, rather than using coins, because with the larger capacity machines, they vend for a higher price, then could you imagine having a washer that costs ten dollars and having to put forty quarters in?"

MARKET ANALYSIS

Buy Existing Business or Create New Business

Most industry experts will advise a new owner to purchase an existing business, rather than start from scratch. The high costs of space renovation and equipment purchases can be prohibitive.

New coin laundries are valued based on actual construction and equipment costs, and existing coin laundries are valued based primarily on profit and loss statements including detailed water usage analyses.

When considering the purchase of an existing business, many prospective owners/operators choose to work with a broker. The broker will charge a sales commission which is usually between 8 and 10 percent of the purchase price. According to the Coin Laundry Association, the marketing time for store sales averages between 60 to 90 days.

How to Value an Existing Business

According to the Coin Laundry Association, coin laundries normally sell for a multiple of their net earnings. The multiple may vary between three to five times the net cash flow depending on several valuation factors.

The following primary components establish market value as stated by the Coin Laundry Association:

- Net earnings

- The existing lease, particularly length; frequency and amount of increases; expense provisions; and overall ratio of rent to gross income

- The condition of the equipment and facility

- Vend price structure

- Demographics

Replacement cost and land usage issues With regard to the equipment, the standard of useful life for commercial coin laundry equipment is as follows:

- Topload Washers (12 lbs. to 14 lbs.): 5—8 years

- Frontload Washers (18 lbs. to 50 lbs.): 10—15 years

- Dryers (30 lbs. to 60 lbs.): 15—20 years

- Heating Systems: 10—15 years

- Coin Changers: 10—15 years

This schedule will vary upon usage, sales volume and maintenance. Useful life may differ for accounting or tax purposes.

Many distributors also act as brokers. For instance, Huebsch Financial Services (finance arm of Huebsch the distributor) will finance up to 65% of the valuation of the business. Huebsch assesses the value of the laundromat based on a detailed analysis of the utility bills, trailing twelve months EBITDA from Profit & Loss Statement, and tax returns of the business. Laundromats typically are valued at three to five times trailing twelve months EBITDA.

Analyzing Turns Per Day and Dryer Income

Turns per day (TPD) refers to the number of times on average each machine is used each day. National surveys, conducted by the Coin Laundry Association, indicate a wide range of performance for individual stores and types of equipment. The range for washing machines is usually three to eight turns per day.

Dryer income varies widely and is usually calculated as a percentage of income from the washing machines. Dryer income can vary from between 40 to 60 percent of total washer income.

According to Brian Brunckhost, a prospective owner can evaluate dryer income by making some assumptions. "In most stores, the average dryer income is somewhere between 40% and 60% of the wash income, so if you were to take 50% of the wash income as the average, if the wash income is $10,000 a month, then you can figure ballpark–wise, the dryer income would be another $5,000 for $15,000."

In purchasing an existing business, the equipment is in place. The new owner may choose to add or replace some machines but the infrastructure is in place.

Reviewing a Profit and Loss Statement

According to Brian Brunckhorst who owns several laundromats and is the creator of the "Own a Laundromat Teleseminar on CD" and the "Laundromat Success Newsletter," when evaluating a business owner's profit and loss statement it is important to make some key assumptions about the equipment. For example, the industry standard for number of turns (how many times a machine is used each day) is three to five times a day. When evaluating a business then it may make sense to assume four turns per day. Other important information will be the fee per machine (how many quarters does each machine take per turn). Then one can determine what the gross revenue should be. For instance, if one were to assume that each machine costs $3 per turn and there are twenty machines that would equate to $60 per turn or $240 (when multiplied by four turns per day). Then the $240 can be multiplied by thirty to obtain an estimate of monthly gross revenue or $7,200.

Performing a Water Analysis

An important way to estimate business revenue is based on an analysis of water usage. The prospective owner will need to review a year's worth of water bills to determine the actual business income. The analysis involves looking at how much water was used in total; then how much water is used for each machine; and then determining how many times each machine is used per month. Once that is estimated, then one can multiply the water price per machine by the vend price (fee charged per machine) to get a solid estimate of washer income generated.

Building a New Laundromat

If the prospective owner opts to build out a new laundromat, construction costs and new equipment costs must be assessed. One can expect to pay between $150,000 and $300,000 to fill an average–size laundromat with washers and dryers.

According to Entrepeneur.com, average costs for the establishment of a new business are as follows:

- Top–load washers: $500—$700 each

- Front–load washers: $3,500—$20,000 each depending on size

- Stacked dryer (two dryers stacked): $5,000—$6,000

- Card systems: $40,000—$80,000 including readers on machines, card dispenser and cards and software to monitor equipment usage and change prices

- Change machine: $1,000—$3,000

- Water heating system: $15,000—$40,000

- Soap vending machine: $500—$1,500

- Laundry carts: $50—$75 each

- Miscellaneous supplies (trash cans, soap, etc.) $750—$1,000

- License fees (which can include the following depending on location): Business license, Health department license (if you are serving food), Fire department permit, Air and water pollution control permit, Sign permit, Public improvement fees, Impact fees, Other construction costs

OPERATIONS

Coin laundry operations consist of three basic areas: janitorial, maintenance and the handling of money (which consists of collections and loading coin changers). Bookkeeping, administration and banking are typically handled outside of the actual store.

Retail Space and Location

According to Wascomat, an equipment manufacturer, a coin laundry business should be located in a "high–traffic, densely populated, predominately renter–occupied, middle– to low–income area with parking next to or within a neighborhood shopping area. Coin laundries have also performed well in middle– to high–income areas when located near condominiums, co–ops, and apartment buildings. Many two income families find it faster, safer, and more convenient to use the local laundromats which provide bigger, more efficient, and better washers and dryers than found in the home or in a building laundry room."

According to the Coin Laundry Association, coin laundries generally occupy the retail space on long–term leases (10–25 years) and generate steady cash flow over the life of the lease. It is important to secure a long term lease for the business because setting up a new location can be very expensive. New space needs to be outfit with the following: machine pad construction; providing gas lines for dryer operations; lawful waste–water egress; plumbing (including sufficient water supply); three phase and single–phase electrical layouts; dryer venting system; flooring, ceiling, and counter space.

Stores generally occupy 1,000 to 5,000 square feet of retail space, with the 2002 average being 2,260 square feet according to the Coin Laundry Association. The current trend is to larger retail space.

Lease

When operating a self service laundry business, a vital component to its success will be a long term lease. This is because it is costly to establish the business infrastructure so the owner will not want to have to endure moving to a new location after a short period of time.

Laundromats should always have a long and easily assignable leases explains Gary Ruff, a lawyer who provides advice on establishing self service laundry businesses.

According to Brian Brunckhorst, creator of the "Own a Laundromat Teleseminar on CD," the length of the lease should be at least 15 years. The main reason, again, is that the owner will want to recoup the initial investment costs. The useful life on most equipment is 15 to 20 years. The goal is to stay in one location for the "life" of the machines so that they don't need to be moved.

The best lease is a fixed lease for a period of time such as five years (with no annual ties to the consumer price index). In this scenario, every five years, the lease payments would increase by an agreed upon percentage. If possible, the owner will also want to avoid leases with triple net. Triple net is a lease in which the lessee pays rent and taxes, insurance and maintenance expenses (for common areas such as landscaping, etc.) that arise from the use of the property.

Cash Flow

Coin laundries can range in market value from $50,000 to more than $1 million, and can generate cash flow between $15,000 and $200,000 per year.

Hours of Operation

Business hours typically run from 6 a.m. to 10 p.m. If located near a college campus, the evening hours may be extended.

Coin Systems Versus Card Systems

According to industry manufacter Wascomat, "A tremendous industry innovation is the card system. It lets you change your vend prices in penny increments (vend price changes in a regular coin meter system are in quarter increments). The card system allows you to change your prices for different times and days of the week, so, for example, you can run specials on slow days. You can also easily determine which machines are getting the most use and when they are most busy. The card system saves owners hours of collecting coins from each machine—it's all computerized with a paper trail for easy accounting."

Many operators are migrating from coin systems (customers use coins to pay for machines) to card systems (customers use cards to pay for machines). There are many advantages to the card systems, particularly for larger stores. The two main advantages are the ability of the owner to manipulate prices more efficiently; and for the owner to get the "float" from the balance on the cards.

The company, Card Concepts, Inc., provides a product called LaundryCard. The company discusses the advantages of investing in a card system on its web site. Although the initial investment is significant, there are long term benefits. "Investing in a LaundryCard system pays for it's many ways but the two simplest factors are 'penny incremental pricing' and 'float.' Penny incremental pricing basically allows store owners to vend machines in non quarter increments, so rather than vend a 30 pound washer at $3.25 vend it at $3.32. In this example, the small seven cent increase in vend price could equate to an extraordinary profit gain over the course of a month. Imagine raising all of your vend prices by $.07, the impact is very minimal to your customer but could have a tremendous positive impact on your bottom line...The second strong ROI factor is 'float'. Float refers to the amount of money that customers put onto their cards but have not yet spent. For example, a customer may add $20 to their card but only spend $18 on any given day. Customers realize that this remaining $2 will stay on their card and most will return to the store in a following week to use it. The key factor is that the store owner holds this value for the customer, multiply this across thousands of customers and the float can get substantial. There is always a percentage of cards that are lost, moved away, or forgotten about that goes directly to the store owner, but the most important factor is that the cards with unused balances on them represent a 'Loyalty' of returning customers. The float percentage varies from store to store but it is not uncommon for float to reach two to four percent of the stores gross machine sales."

Equipment

Evaluating Washers: Front load versus Top Load Washers

A big trend in the industry is the front load machine, rather than the traditional washer that opens from the top. Front load washers have two advantages over top load washers. First, they use less water. Second, they get clothes cleaner (the clothes in the laundry are actually shifted from the top of the basket to the bottom which provides for better cleaning action). However, front loaders are more expensive than top loaders.

A comparison of the two types of washers is below.

Front Load:

- Can be stacked with a dryer on top to conserve space.

- Spins clothes faster than a top–load, extracting more water. This saves energy (and money), because it allows you to dry a load of clothes in a shorter amount of time.

- Uses a wash process that is more gentle on clothing.

- Requires a special type of detergent made for front–load machines. These detergents are becoming more common on grocery store shelves, but they might not be available everywhere. They also might cost a little more.

- Costs more. Prices vary, but expect to pay 30 percent to 40 percent more for a front–load machine than you would for a comparable top–load machine.

- Uses less water, which lowers utility bills. This savings can offset the additional cost of the machine, but it usually takes several years for the numbers to balance.

Top Load:

- Includes a wider variety of available models, colors and features.

- Costs less initially, but is less energy–efficient.

- Offers easier access to the wash tub.

- Uses regular detergent.

- Cannot easily be stacked to save space.

In addition, according to Michaelbluejay.com, front load machines are much more energy efficient, "front–loading washers use 40–75% less water and 30–85% less energy than typical top–loaders (10 to 24 gallons vs. up to 40 gallons, and 120–560 kWh/yr. vs. 800 kWh/yr.)"

Front–load washers are also known to get more of the water out of clothes, so drying expenses will be lower. Last, front load machines can more easily wash large items such as rugs because they do not have the central agitator.

Equipment Vendors

Owners should purchase machines that have a fast spin speed to get as much water out of the clothes as possible. This will result in shorter drying times (saving time and energy/utility costs).

Major equipment vendors include Maytag, Speed Queen, Dexter and Wascomat.

Business Web Sites

The Coin Laundry Association is now hosting web sites for its members.

Publications

The Coin Laundry Association's, *The Journal. Coin Laundry News*, and American Coin–Op's *Laundry* are the major publication for the industry.

Insurance

The Coin Laundry Association's CLA Insurance (http://coinlaundryinsurance.com/) provides members with insurance including:

- Property / Liability Insurance

- Worker's Compensation

- Umbrella Insurance

- Auto Insurance for Company Vehicles

- CLA Insurance Benefits

- Loss Control

There are also other insurance providers. Another company that specializes in this industry is NIE Insurance. NIE began as a dry cleaning insurer and has moving into the self service laundry business.

Unique Insurance Risks When Operating a Laundry

Some of the unique risks found at a coin laundry are the ones you might expect with the public operating washers and dryers all day every day. They include:

- Wet floors from leaking washers

- Uneven floor surface due to drains located in path of customers

- Dryer fires due to greasy fabrics, excessive lint, plastic or other combustible items being left in clothing
- Children playing with equipment and/or running through the laundry
- Tables and chairs that are all connected with little support (customers like to sit on the table section)
- Tanning beds
- Pool tables
- Rides
- Climbing toys

Professional Support

As with any small business, the hiring of an outside accountant and an outside lawyer for professional advice is highly recommended.

Solar Energy Farm

Ward Solar Energy Farm, Inc.

2354 Rotary Rd.
Chemung, New York 14825

BizPlanDB.com

The purpose of this business plan is to raise $5,000,000 for the development of an alternative energy business that produces electricity from photovoltaic cells while showcasing the expected financials and operations over the next three years. Ward Solar Energy Farm, Inc. is a New York-based corporation that will sell electricity into the power grid from the power produced from its photovoltaic cell structures. The Company was founded in 2009 by Mike Ward.

EXECUTIVE SUMMARY

The purpose of this business plan is to raise $5,000,000 for the development of an alternative energy business that produces electricity from photovoltaic cells while showcasing the expected financials and operations over the next three years. Ward Solar Energy Farm, Inc. is a New York-based corporation that will sell electricity into the power grid from the power produced from its photovoltaic cell structures. The Company was founded in 2009 by Mike Ward.

The Services

As the prices of traditional fuels has skyrocketed (oil, natural gas, and coal), the demand among consumers for ecologically friendly and economically viable alternatives has increased. As of late 2009, the prices of crude oil and its related energy products have remained a multiyear highs (although much lower than its highest point of $150 per barrel). As such, companies like Ward Solar Energy Farm, Inc. have recognized a tremendous opportunity to develop facilities that produce electricity from renewable and infinite sources of energy like solar power.

The Company intends to develop approximately 1,500 individual solar energy producing structures that will sit on approximately 4 acres of land. The Company anticipates that this field will produce approximately 2MW of electricity to be sold into the power grid.

The third section of the business plan will further describe the production of the Ward Solar Energy Farm.

Financing

Mr. Ward is seeking to raise $5,000,000 from an investor. The preliminary terms of this agreement call for an investor to receive a 45% ownership interest in the business coupled with a recurring stream of dividends starting in the first year of operations. The investor will also receive a seat on the board of directors. The financing will be used for the following:

- Development of Ward Solar Energy Farm location.

- Financing for the first six months of operation.

- Capital to purchase photovoltaic cell structures.

Mission Statement

Management's mission is to develop the Ward Solar Energy Farm into a profitable and ecologically friendly venture that will provide the Company and its owners with a steady stream of income from the sale of environmentally friendly energy productions services.

Management Team

The Company was founded by Mike Ward. Mr. Ward has more than 10 years of experience in the alternative energy industry. Through his expertise, he will be able to bring the operations of the business to profitability within its first year of operations.

Sales Forecasts

Mr. Ward expects a strong rate of growth at the start of operations. Below are the expected financials over the next three years.

Proforma profit and loss (yearly)

Year	2009	2010	2011
Sales	$2,106,600	$2,211,930	$2,322,527
Operating costs	$1,113,433	$1,152,762	$1,193,562
EBITDA	$ 782,507	$ 837,975	$ 896,712
Taxes, interest, and depreciation	$ 390,803	$ 411,880	$ 434,201
Net profit	$ 391,704	$ 426,094	$ 462,511

Expansion Plan

The Founder expects that the business will aggressively expand during the first three years of operation. Mr. Ward intends to aggressively solicit additional rounds of capital will concurrently reinvesting a significant portion of the Company's after tax income into the acquisition of new photovoltaic cell structures.

COMPANY AND FINANCING SUMMARY

Registered Name and Corporate Structure

Ward Solar Energy Farm, Inc. is registered as a corporation in the State of New York.

Required Funds

At this time, Ward Solar Energy Farm requires $5,000,000 of investor funds. Below is a breakdown of how these funds will be used:

Projected startup costs

Business startup year	2009
Initial lease payments and deposits	$ 60,000
Working capital	$ 300,000
FF&E	$ 500,000
Leasehold improvements	$ 75,000
Security deposits	$ 25,000
Insurance	$ 20,000
Photovoltaic cells	$4,000,000
Marketing budget	$ 17,500
Miscellaneous and unforeseen costs	$ 2,500
Total startup costs	**$5,000,000**

Investor Equity

At this time, Mr. Ward is seeking to sell a 45% interest in the business in exchange for the capital sought in this business plan. The investor will also receive a seat on the board of directors as well as a recurring stream of dividends starting in the first year of operations.

Management Equity

Mike Ward owns 100% of the Ward Solar Energy Farm, Inc. Once the requisite capital is raised, he will retain a 55% ownership interest in the business.

Exit Strategy

If the business is very successful, Mr. Ward may seek to sell the business to a third party for a significant earnings multiple. Most likely, the Company will hire a qualified business broker to sell the business on behalf of Ward Solar Energy Farm. Based on historical numbers, the business could fetch a sales premium of up to 4 to 6 times the previous year's net earnings.

SOLAR ENERGY PRODUCTION

As stated in the executive summary, the Company intends to acquire/lease 4 acres of property which will house 700 photovoltaic cell structures for the production of electricity harnessed through the sun. These photovoltaic cells capture solar energy (photons) and then convert them to electricity. This process is known as the photovoltaic effect and it was first discovered by Albert Einstein in the early 20th century.

The retail energy price of electricity is $.09–$0.16 KWh, which is what residential customers pay on average within the United States. Wholesale pricing is lower than that based on the utilities expenses and profits. Management believes $.07 – $.09 per KWh is possible price that the Company can sell its energy to the local utilities and municipalities.

The expected cost of the 700 photovoltaic cell structures is $4,000,000. Despite this high cost, the Company will recognize tremendous revenues from the continued operation of its photovoltaic structures on a 12 to 16 hour per day basis. Management will have a team of 8 to 12 employees that continually oversee the ongoing operation of the solar energy capturing structures on a daily basis.

In the future, Management intends to expand its facility to accommodate up to 2,000 photovoltaic cell structures The business may solicit additional rounds of capital or it may lease the cells to generate a higher return on investment.

STRATEGIC AND MARKET ANALYSIS

Economic Outlook

This section of the analysis will detail the economic climate, the alternative energy industry, the customer profile, and the competition that the business will face as it progresses through its business operations.

The current geopolitical environment has led Management to believe that energy prices will continue to increase in the near future. The war in Iraq, faltering nuclear production talks with Iran, and general Middle Eastern instability has led many economists to believe that there is a fifteen to twenty percent risk premium now associated with the price of crude oil and related energy products. While these issues bring worry to the general economy, Management sees a significant opportunity to enter the market with a source of alternative energy. Many politicians and special interest groups have promoted the development of alterative energy solutions to combat the continually increasing energy prices in the United States. Additionally, the fast growth of Asian nations (namely India and China) has prompted further increases in the global demand for energy. This trend is expected to continue in perpetuity.

Inflation is also concern for the Company. As the inflation rate decreases, the purchasing power parity of the American dollar decreases in relation to other currencies. This may pose a significant risk to the Company should rampant inflation, much like the inflation experienced in the late 1970s, occur again. In this event, the Company will enlist the services of a qualified derivatives focused investment bank to manage large scale currency transactions that would offset the risks normally associated with the distribution of energy products to foreign buyers. The primary risk of rapid inflation in the economy would contribute to a slow down in spending among consumers, but it would also affect the Company's ability to borrow funds for the expansion of the number of photovoltaic structures operated by the business.

Industry Analysis

There are approximately 400 companies that provide non–nuclear and non–fossil fuel power generation to the general public. Each year, these businesses aggregately provide more than $18 billion dollars of energy to the open market. The trend among these alternative energy sources is expected to grow significantly as the need for alternative fuels and power grows. Currently, the price of oil and other fossil fuels has skyrocketed to the point where many consumers are looking for alternative methods of power.

Collectively, the industry employs more than 18,000 people. Aggregate payrolls exceed $4 billion dollars per year.

Customer Profile

For the Company's solar electricity production capabilities, Management expects two core groups of purchasers: government agencies and electricity wholesalers. Among the first group, Management expects that agencies such as counties, state governments, and the US federal government will acquire large scale electricity delivery contracts from the Company with the intent to use the energy within their large scale applications. At the onset of operations, the Company will immediately begin developing relationships with local county governments as well as the state government for ongoing divestiture and purchase agreements.

Competition

Energy production is one of the freest markets in the economy. These markets operate on a global scale, and as such, it is difficult to determine the exact competitors that the Company will face as it progresses through its business operations. Any business that produces electricity is a potential competitor for the business. However, solar energy is becoming an increasingly popular method of producing electricity, and the Company's primary competitive advantage will be its low cost operating infrastructure, its completely renewable input (solar), and the demand among consumers for cleaner alternatives to traditional oil, natural gas, coal, and nuclear energy power plants.

MARKETING PLAN

As Ward Solar Energy Farm intends to sell its produced energy directly into the electrical grid, the marketing required by the business will be minimal. However, Management is committed to increasing the awareness of solar energy usage. Below is a brief overview of the ways that Ward Solar Energy Farm will market its operations and alternative energy production.

Marketing Objectives

- Develop an online presence by developing a website and placing the Company's name and contact information with online directories to further increase awareness of solar energy.

- Establish relationships with energy wholesalers and government agencies within the Company's targeted market.

Marketing Strategies

Currently, there are a number of organizations, including the Solar Energy Industries Association that are pushing initiatives, lobbying legislatures, and informing the general public about the benefits about alternative energy products. Management feels that it is important to invest in these public relations campaigns (even though they will not affect direct sales). Additionally, the increased awareness of solar produced electricity, its zero emissions, and ability to wean the United States off of foreign energy sources may prompt consumers and lawmakers to further expand the rebates, tax credits, and other incentive programs available for making solar produced electricity an economy viable energy product now and in the future. Approximately $10,000 to $20,000 per year will be spent to support these causes.

Additionally, industry conventions, energy product trade shows, and other public relations campaigns will be enacted in order to promote the business.

Pricing

The Company anticipates that it will receive approximately $150 per MwH delivered into the national power grid.

ORGANIZATIONAL PLAN AND PERSONNEL SUMMARY

Corporate Organization

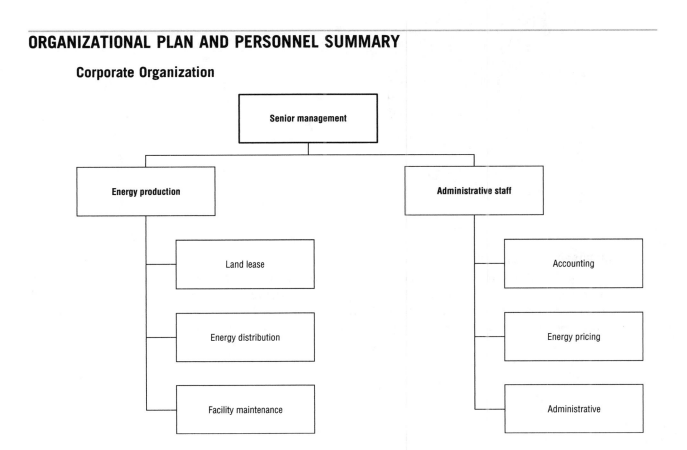

Organizational Budget

Personnel plan—yearly

Year	2009	2010	2011
Senior management	$100,000	$103,000	$106,090
Facility manager	$130,000	$133,900	$137,917
Facility maintenance staff	$232,000	$238,960	$246,129
Scientific staff	$130,000	$133,900	$137,917
Administrative and accounting	$ 70,000	$ 72,100	$ 74,263
Total	**$662,000**	**$681,860**	**$702,316**
Numbers of personnel			
Senior management	1	1	1
Facility manager	2	2	2
Facility maintenance staff	8	8	8
Scientific staff	2	2	2
Administrative and accounting	2	2	2
Totals	**15**	**15**	**15**

Personnel expense breakdown

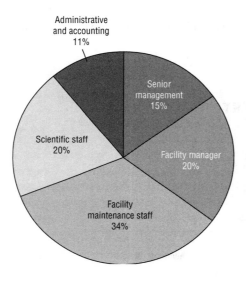

Management Biographies

Mr. Ward has been involved with the production and development of renewable and alternative energy sources over the past ten years. Through his duel experience/education in energy engineering and business, he will be able to quickly bring the operations of the business to profitability with a focus on expanding bottom line income through several additional capital raisings.

FINANCIAL PLAN

Underlying Assumptions

The Company has based its proforma financial statements on the following:

- Ward Solar Energy Farm, Inc. will have an annual revenue growth rate of 5% per year.

- The Owner will solicit $5,000,000 of equity funds to develop the business.

- The Company will invest 25% of its after–tax profits back into the Company's operating infrastructure.

Sensitivity Analysis

The Company's revenues are moderately sensitive to changes in the general economy. Solar produced electricity is comparatively priced with their petroleum/coal based counterparts, and in the event that prices decline, the Company may see a reduction in its revenues. Only in the event of a steep drop in the price of petrol based energy products does Management anticipate that the Company will have issues regarding top line income.

Source of Funds

Financing

Equity contributions	
Investor(s)	$ 5,000,000.00
Total equity financing	**$5,000,000.00**
Banks and lenders	
Total debt financing	**$ 0.00**
Total financing	**$5,000,000.00**

General Assumptions

General assumptions

Year	2009	2010	2011
Short term interest rate	9.5%	9.5%	9.5%
Long term interest rate	10.0%	10.0%	10.0%
Federal tax rate	33.0%	33.0%	33.0%
State tax rate	5.0%	5.0%	5.0%
Personnel taxes	15.0%	15.0%	15.0%

Profit and Loss Statements

Proforma profit and loss (yearly)

Year	2009	2010	2011
Sales	**$2,106,600**	**$2,211,930**	**$2,322,527**
Cost of goods sold	$ 210,660	$ 221,193	$ 232,253
Gross margin	90.00%	90.00%	90.00%
Operating income	**$1,895,940**	**$1,990,737**	**$2,090,274**
Expenses			
Payroll	$ 662,000	$ 681,860	$ 702,316
General and administrative	$ 61,200	$ 63,648	$ 66,194
Marketing expenses	$ 21,066	$ 22,119	$ 23,225
Professional fees and licensure	$ 25,219	$ 25,976	$ 26,755
Insurance costs	$ 51,987	$ 54,586	$ 57,316
Energy distribution expenses	$ 42,132	$ 44,239	$ 46,451
Leases and utilities	$ 125,250	$ 131,513	$ 138,088
Miscellaneous costs	$ 25,279	$ 26,543	$ 27,870
Payroll taxes	$ 99,300	$ 102,279	$ 105,347
Total operating costs	**$1,113,433**	**$1,152,762**	**$1,193,562**
EBITDA	**$ 782,507**	**$ 837,975**	**$ 896,712**
Federal income tax	$ 258,227	$ 276,532	$ 295,915
State income tax	$ 39,125	$ 41,899	$ 44,836
Interest expense	$ 0	$ 0	$ 0
Depreciation expenses	$ 93,450	$ 93,450	$ 93,450
Net profit	**$ 391,704**	**$ 426,094**	**$ 462,511**
Profit margin	**18.59%**	**19.26%**	**19.91%**

Cash Flow Analysis

Proforma cash flow analysis—yearly

Year	2009	2010	2011
Cash from operations	$ 485,154	$519,544	$555,961
Cash from receivables	$ 0	$ 0	$ 0
Operating cash inflow	**$ 485,154**	**$519,544**	**$555,961**
Other cash inflows			
Equity investment	$5,000,000	$ 0	$ 0
Increased borrowings	$ 0	$ 0	$ 0
Sales of business assets	$ 0	$ 0	$ 0
A/P increases	$ 37,902	$ 43,587	$ 50,125
Total other cash inflows	**$5,037,902**	**$ 43,587**	**$ 50,125**
Total cash inflow	**$5,523,056**	**$563,132**	**$606,087**
Cash outflows			
Repayment of principal	$ 0	$ 0	$ 0
A/P decreases	$ 24,897	$ 29,876	$ 35,852
A/R increases	$ 0	$ 0	$ 0
Asset purchases	$4,672,500	$129,886	$138,990
Dividends	$ 291,093	$311,727	$333,577
Total cash outflows	**$4,988,490**	**$471,489**	**$508,419**
Net cash flow	**$ 534,567**	**$ 91,643**	**$ 97,668**
Cash balance	**$ 534,567**	**$626,209**	**$723,877**

Balance Sheet

Proforma balance sheet—yearly

Year	2009	2010	2011
Assets			
Cash	$ 534,567	$ 626,209	$ 723,877
Amortized expansion costs	$ 172,500	$ 185,489	$ 199,388
Photovoltaic cell structures	$4,000,000	$4,097,415	$4,201,657
FF&E	$ 500,000	$ 519,483	$ 540,331
Accumulated depreciation	($ 93,450)	($ 186,900)	($ 280,350)
Total assets	**$5,113,617**	**$5,241,695**	**$5,384,904**
Liabilities and equity			
Accounts payable	$ 13,005	$ 26,716	$ 40,990
Long term liabilities	$ 0	$ 0	$ 0
Other liabilities	$ 0	$ 0	$ 0
Total liabilities	**$ 13,005**	**$ 26,716**	**$ 40,990**
Net worth	**$5,100,612**	**$5,214,979**	**$5,343,914**
Total liabilities and equity	**$5,113,617**	**$5,241,695**	**$5,384,904**

Breakeven Analysis

Monthly break even analysis

Year	2009	2010	2011
Monthly revenue	$ 103,096	$ 106,737	$ 110,515
Yearly revenue	$1,237,148	$1,280,847	$1,326,180

Business Ratios

Business ratios—yearly

Year	2009	2010	2011
Sales			
Sales growth	0.0%	5.0%	5.0%
Gross margin	90.0%	90.0%	90.0%
Financials			
Profit margin	18.59%	19.26%	19.91%
Assets to liabilities	393.20%	196.20%	131.37%
Equity to liabilities	392.20%	195.20%	130.37%
Assets to equity	1.00%	1.01%	1.01%
Liquidity			
Acid test	41.10%	23.44%	17.66%
Cash to assets	0.10%	0.12%	0.13%

Utilities Reclamation Services

Hydro Power Lines Reclamation Services Inc.

789 Main St.
Seattle, Washington 98101

Gerald Rekve

Hydro Power Lines Reclamation Services Inc. is a Limited Liability Company set up to operate in Seattle, Washington.

THE COMPANY

Hydro Power Lines Reclamation Services Inc. is a Limited Liability Company set up to operate in Seattle, Washington. The company is a new one formed by Greg Mann. Greg Mann is a former employee of Seattle Power & Utilities.

Greg worked with Seattle Power for 12 years in a variety of jobs. Then in 2008 a letter was sent out to all employees that the government–owned utility was going to need to upgrade all the transmission lines in an escalated fashion over the next 20 years. The primary reason for this was that 50% lines were installed over 70 years ago, meaning the increase in power failure was increasing at a higher rate than originally thought.

So with the backing of a few family members, Greg quickly formed Hydro Power Lines Reclamation Services Inc. and asked his employer for a three month leave of absence while he put together the tender for the contracts that was posted. Seattle Power decided to allow this leave of absence simply because if they were going to trust anyone with the rebuilding of the network, they would feel more comfortable if they were someone they knew.

After two months of research, a business plan was prepared, and the tender was submitted. Greg went back to work at Seattle Power while he waited the fate of his tender. Then six weeks later, the news came down. Greg had won the contract to rebuild 8% of the network. Based on the success as well quality of work, this would open the door for other tenders down the road.

This meant that now Greg Mann would need to resign from his job at Seattle Power, simply because the contract he had won would take 5—7 years to complete.

THE NETWORK

The power grid for Seattle and surrounding area is covered with trees, mountains, lakes, and bridges. You name it, the area has all the makings of a lot of work.

Originally the construction of the electrical grid started in the early 1900's, however most of the early lines were replaced in the 1940's with larger capacity lines. At this point Seattle was still a small city. Then in the 1940's—1960's there was a population boom and the city grew at a high rate. The transmission lines put into place to handle this extra capacity. Along came the 1970's, 1980's and the 1990's which all started to push the capacity of the old equipment to its maximum. In the early 2000's a couple of events happened that forced Seattle Power to look closely at all their network and plan for major changes. Some of these changes had to do with security due to the attacks of 2001 in New York by terrorists.

The end result was a requirement by current electrical standards to rebuild and replace over 50% of the transmission lines and equipment. There have been a lot of power outages in all regions, mostly due to failure of old equipment or lines. So far there have been no injuries associated with these outages, however at the pace they are happening the government decided to make the investment to get the network rebuilt to meet the high energy demands of one of the America's fastest-growing cities with population that demands a lot of energy to run a high-tech environment.

THE MARKET

Winning the contract put Hydro Power Lines Reclamation Services Inc. in an odd position for a new company. For a new company to yet to have one employee other than the owner and to have the first 7 years in business to have annual revenue to be guaranteed at $5 million per year. This is not normal; however this is where Greg Mann is today.

Seattle Power has awarded 8% of the rebuilding of the network to Hydro Power Lines Reclamation Services Inc. This represents about $35 Million dollars in gross sales. There may be opportunity to increase this number based on Hydro Power Lines Reclamation Services Inc.'s ability to hire more crews, buy more equipment, and win the further trust of Seattle Power and other communities in the region where they will do business.

COMPETITION

The uniqueness of this business and the fact that Greg Mann has already secured a 7-year contract means that competition is not a factor; the only competition would be the quality of work his crews do over the next few years. Good quality work is a guarantee of more work.

START UP

The start up of Hydro Power Lines Reclamation Services Inc. will be a textbook case of a company starting from scratch. Here is what it will require for Hydro Power Lines Reclamation Services Inc. to be successful.

In order to do the required work, there will be a number of pieces of equipment required. These pieces of equipment will be specialized in order to do the required work. Also what will be required will be highly trained staff. These staff will be sought out over the region and into other states.

Start-up budget

Heavy equipment	$6,000,000
Light equipment	$1,500,000
Staff training	$ 200,000
Tools	$ 700,000
Warehouse & office & storage facility	$ 200,000
Legal	$ 10,000
Admin	$ 5,000
Travel & accommodations	$ 40,000
Advertising for staff	$ 10,000
Recruiters retainers	$ 20,000
Hiring costs	$ 50,000
Insurance for vehicles	$ 25,000
Insurance for buildings	$ 2,700
Insurance & workers comp	$ 1,800

Moving costs for new employees where they came from out of state is budgeted for $200,000. Note this is spread among new hires and there is a cap of $2,500 per employee to real estate and up to $4,500 for movers, etc.

WORKFLOW

The volume of work carried out by the crews of Hydro Power Lines Reclamation Services Inc. will be done in stages. Because of the danger of working with high voltage, the need to stay focused, have teams of crews who work well together and who consistently look out for each other is of utmost importance.

Here are the names of the crews and the work that they perform on a daily, weekly, and monthly basis.

- The Planner

- The Inspector

- The Take Down Techs

- The Installer Techs

- The Cleaners

While these titles seem simple, they each play a vital role in the installation of new lines for the hydro business in Seattle region.

THE PLANNER

The planners are just that—they review the grid/network of the various locations. After reviewing the grid, the planner sends out an inspector. There will be four planners, each responsible for a different region in Seattle.

THE INSPECTOR

The inspector will go to the locations as requested by the planner, review the lines as well equipment, and then go back to the field office and notify the planner with the possible requirements of the job. The planner then sends in a team of take down techs. There will be a total of eight inspectors.

THE TAKE DOWN TECHS

The take down techs will then go to the site and set up all the equipment required to do the job. While on site, they will begin the job of removing the old equipment; at the same time the installer techs are arriving onsite to install the new lines and other equipment. There will be eight take down crews, each having a total of ten take down techs.

THE INSTALLER TECHS

The installer techs will start working behind the take down techs, following where they have removed the old equipment and then installing new equipment. The flow of work in this type of environment is very dangerous. While all this work is taking place with high voltage of electricity and safety is concerned, all measures are taken to insure the crews are provided a very safe work environment. There will be eight installer crews, each having twenty crew members.

THE CLEANERS

As the crews move through the job, the cleaners come in and make sure there is no debris left on the job site. This will help reduce the possibly of any injuries on the job site. There will be eight cleaning crews, each having six members per crew.

PAYROLL

Job	Yearly salary	Total no. of staff	Total cost
Planners	$125,000	4	$ 500,000
Inspectors	$ 95,000	8	$ 760,000
Take-down techs	$ 82,000	80	$ 6,560,000
Installer techs	$ 91,000	160	$14,560,000
Cleaners	$ 56,000	48	$ 2,688,000
President & CEO	$150,000 + bonuses	1	$ 150,000 + bonuses
VP of operations	$120,000	1	$ 120,000
HR manager	$ 90,000	1	$ 90,000
Office support staff	$ 34,000	8	$ 272,000
Warehouse staff	$ 31,000	4	$ 124,000
Equipment techs	$ 76,000	4	$ 304,000

Business Plan Template

USING THIS TEMPLATE

A business plan carefully spells out a company's projected course of action over a period of time, usually the first two to three years after the start-up. In addition, banks, lenders, and other investors examine the information and financial documentation before deciding whether or not to finance a new business venture. Therefore, a business plan is an essential tool in obtaining financing and should describe the business itself in detail as well as all important factors influencing the company, including the market, industry, competition, operations and management policies, problem solving strategies, financial resources and needs, and other vital information. The plan enables the business owner to anticipate costs, plan for difficulties, and take advantage of opportunities, as well as design and implement strategies that keep the company running as smoothly as possible.

This template has been provided as a model to help you construct your own business plan. Please keep in mind that there is no single acceptable format for a business plan, and that this template is in no way comprehensive, but serves as an example.

The business plans provided in this section are fictional and have been used by small business agencies as models for clients to use in compiling their own business plans.

GENERIC BUSINESS PLAN

Main headings included below are topics that should be covered in a comprehensive business plan. They include:

Business Summary

Purpose
Provides a brief overview of your business, succinctly highlighting the main ideas of your plan.

Includes

- Name and Type of Business
- Description of Product/Service
- Business History and Development
- Location
- Market

- Competition
- Management
- Financial Information
- Business Strengths and Weaknesses
- Business Growth

Table of Contents

Purpose
Organized in an Outline Format, the Table of Contents illustrates the selection and arrangement of information contained in your plan.

Includes

- Topic Headings and Subheadings
- Page Number References

Business History and Industry Outlook

Purpose

Examines the conception and subsequent development of your business within an industry specific context.

Includes

- Start-up Information
- Owner/Key Personnel Experience
- Location
- Development Problems and Solutions
- Investment/Funding Information
- Future Plans and Goals
- Market Trends and Statistics
- Major Competitors
- Product/Service Advantages
- National, Regional, and Local Economic Impact

Product/Service

Purpose

Introduces, defines, and details the product and/or service that inspired the information of your business.

Includes

- Unique Features
- Niche Served
- Market Comparison
- Stage of Product/Service Development
- Production
- Facilities, Equipment, and Labor
- Financial Requirements
- Product/Service Life Cycle
- Future Growth

Market Examination

Purpose

Assessment of product/service applications in relation to consumer buying cycles.

Includes

- Target Market
- Consumer Buying Habits
- Product/Service Applications
- Consumer Reactions
- Market Factors and Trends
- Penetration of the Market
- Market Share
- Research and Studies
- Cost
- Sales Volume and Goals

Competition

Purpose

Analysis of Competitors in the Marketplace.

Includes

- Competitor Information
- Product/Service Comparison
- Market Niche
- Product/Service Strengths and Weaknesses
- Future Product/Service Development

Marketing

Purpose

Identifies promotion and sales strategies for your product/service.

Includes

- Product/Service Sales Appeal
- Special and Unique Features
- Identification of Customers
- Sales and Marketing Staff
- Sales Cycles
- Type of Advertising/ Promotion
- Pricing
- Competition
- Customer Services

Operations

Purpose

Traces product/service development from production/inception to the market environment.

Includes

- Cost Effective Production Methods
- Facility
- Location
- Equipment
- Labor
- Future Expansion

Administration and Management

Purpose

Offers a statement of your management philosophy with an in-depth focus on processes and procedures.

Includes

- Management Philosophy
- Structure of Organization
- Reporting System
- Methods of Communication
- Employee Skills and Training
- Employee Needs and Compensation
- Work Environment
- Management Policies and Procedures
- Roles and Responsibilities

Key Personnel

Purpose

Describes the unique backgrounds of principle employees involved in business.

Includes

- Owner(s)/Employee Education and Experience
- Positions and Roles
- Benefits and Salary
- Duties and Responsibilities
- Objectives and Goals

Potential Problems and Solutions

Purpose

Discussion of problem solving strategies that change issues into opportunities.

Includes

- Risks
- Litigation
- Future Competition
- Economic Impact
- Problem Solving Skills

Financial Information

Purpose

Secures needed funding and assistance through worksheets and projections detailing financial plans, methods of repayment, and future growth opportunities.

Includes

- Financial Statements
- Bank Loans
- Methods of Repayment
- Tax Returns

- Start-up Costs
- Projected Income (3 years)
- Projected Cash Flow (3 Years)
- Projected Balance Statements (3 years)

Appendices

Purpose

Supporting documents used to enhance your business proposal.

Includes

- Photographs of product, equipment, facilities, etc.
- Copyright/Trademark Documents
- Legal Agreements
- Marketing Materials
- Research and or Studies

- Operation Schedules
- Organizational Charts
- Job Descriptions
- Resumes
- Additional Financial Documentation

Fictional Food Distributor

Commercial Foods, Inc.

3003 Avondale Ave.
Knoxville, TN 37920

This plan demonstrates how a partnership can have a positive impact on a new business. It demonstrates how two individuals can carve a niche in the specialty foods market by offering gourmet foods to upscale restaurants and fine hotels. This plan is fictional and has not been used to gain funding from a bank or other lending institution.

STATEMENT OF PURPOSE

Commercial Foods, Inc. seeks a loan of $75,000 to establish a new business. This sum, together with $5,000 equity investment by the principals, will be used as follows:

- Merchandise inventory $25,000

- Office fixture/equipment $12,000

- Warehouse equipment $14,000

- One delivery truck $10,000

- Working capital $39,000

- Total $100,000

DESCRIPTION OF THE BUSINESS

Commercial Foods, Inc. will be a distributor of specialty food service products to hotels and upscale restaurants in the geographical area of a 50 mile radius of Knoxville. Richard Roberts will direct the sales effort and John Williams will manage the warehouse operation and the office. One delivery truck will be used initially with a second truck added in the third year. We expect to begin operation of the business within 30 days after securing the requested financing.

MANAGEMENT

A. Richard Roberts is a native of Memphis, Tennessee. He is a graduate of Memphis State University with a Bachelor's degree from the School of Business. After graduation, he worked for a major manufacturer of specialty food service products as a detail sales person for five years, and, for the past three years, he has served as a product sales manager for this firm.

B. John Williams is a native of Nashville, Tennessee. He holds a B.S. Degree in Food Technology from the University of Tennessee. His career includes five years as a product development chemist in gourmet food products and five years as operations manager for a food service distributor.

Both men are healthy and energetic. Their backgrounds complement each other, which will ensure the success of Commercial Foods, Inc. They will set policies together and personnel decisions will be made jointly. Initial salaries for the owners will be $1,000 per month for the first few years. The spouses of both principals are successful in the business world and earn enough to support the families.

They have engaged the services of Foster Jones, CPA, and William Hale, Attorney, to assist them in an advisory capacity.

PERSONNEL

The firm will employ one delivery truck driver at a wage of $8.00 per hour. One office worker will be employed at $7.50 per hour. One part-time employee will be used in the office at $5.00 per hour. The driver will load and unload his own trucks. Mr. Williams will assist in the warehouse operation as needed to assist one stock person at $7.00 per hour. An additional delivery truck and driver will be added the third year.

LOCATION

The firm will lease a 20,000 square foot building at 3003 Avondale Ave., in Knoxville, which contains warehouse and office areas equipped with two-door truck docks. The annual rental is $9,000. The building was previously used as a food service warehouse and very little modification to the building will be required.

PRODUCTS AND SERVICES

The firm will offer specialty food service products such as soup bases, dessert mixes, sauce bases, pastry mixes, spices, and flavors, normally used by upscale restaurants and nice hotels. We are going after a niche in the market with high quality gourmet products. There is much less competition in this market than in standard run of the mill food service products. Through their work experiences, the principals have contacts with supply sources and with local chefs.

THE MARKET

We know from our market survey that there are over 200 hotels and upscale restaurants in the area we plan to serve. Customers will be attracted by a direct sales approach. We will offer samples of our products and product application data on use of our products in the finished prepared foods. We will cultivate the chefs in these establishments. The technical background of John Williams will be especially useful here.

COMPETITION

We find that we will be only distributor in the area offering a full line of gourmet food service products. Other foodservice distributors offer only a few such items in conjunction with their standard product line. Our survey shows that many of the chefs are ordering products from Atlanta and Memphis because of a lack of adequate local supply.

SUMMARY

Commercial Foods, Inc. will be established as a foodservice distributor of specialty food in Knoxville. The principals, with excellent experience in the industry, are seeking a $75,000 loan to establish the business. The principals are investing $25,000 as equity capital.

The business will be set up as an S Corporation with each principal owning 50% of the common stock in the corporation.

Fictional Hardware Store

Oshkosh Hardware, Inc.

123 Main St.
Oshkosh, WI 54901

The following plan outlines how a small hardware store can survive competition from large discount chains by offering products and providing expert advice in the use of any product it sells. This plan is fictional and has not been used to gain funding from a bank or other lending institution.

EXECUTIVE SUMMARY

Oshkosh Hardware, Inc. is a new corporation that is going to establish a retail hardware store in a strip mall in Oshkosh, Wisconsin. The store will sell hardware of all kinds, quality tools, paint, and housewares. The business will make revenue and a profit by servicing its customers not only with needed hardware but also with expert advice in the use of any product it sells.

Oshkosh Hardware, Inc. will be operated by its sole shareholder, James Smith. The company will have a total of four employees. It will sell its products in the local market. Customers will buy our products because we will provide free advice on the use of all of our products and will also furnish a full refund warranty.

Oshkosh Hardware, Inc. will sell its products in the Oshkosh store staffed by three sales representatives. No additional employees will be needed to achieve its short and long range goals. The primary short range goal is to open the store by October 1, 1994. In order to achieve this goal a lease must be signed by July 1, 1994 and the complete inventory ordered by August 1, 1994.

Mr. James Smith will invest $30,000 in the business. In addition, the company will have to borrow $150,000 during the first year to cover the investment in inventory, accounts receivable, and furniture and equipment. The company will be profitable after six months of operation and should be able to start repayment of the loan in the second year.

THE BUSINESS

The business will sell hardware of all kinds, quality tools, paint, and housewares. We will purchase our products from three large wholesale buying groups.

In general our customers are homeowners who do their own repair and maintenance, hobbyists, and housewives. Our business is unique in that we will have a complete line of all hardware items and will be able to get special orders by overnight delivery. The business makes revenue and profits by servicing our customers not only with needed hardware but also with expert advice in the use of any product we sell. Our major costs for bringing our products to market are cost of merchandise of 36%, salaries of $45,000, and occupancy costs of $60,000.

Oshkosh Hardware, Inc.'s retail outlet will be located at 1524 Frontage Road, which is in a newly developed retail center of Oshkosh. Our location helps facilitate accessibility from all parts of town and reduces our delivery costs. The store will occupy 7500 square feet of space. The major equipment involved in our business is counters and shelving, a computer, a paint mixing machine, and a truck.

THE MARKET

Oshkosh Hardware, Inc. will operate in the local market. There are 15,000 potential customers in this market area. We have three competitors who control approximately 98% of the market at present. We feel we can capture 25% of the market within the next four years. Our major reason for believing this is that our staff is technically competent to advise our customers in the correct use of all products we sell.

After a careful market analysis, we have determined that approximately 60% of our customers are men and 40% are women. The percentage of customers that fall into the following age categories are:

Under 16: 0%
17-21: 5%
22-30: 30%
31-40: 30%
41-50: 20%
51-60: 10%
61-70: 5%
Over 70: 0%

The reasons our customers prefer our products is our complete knowledge of their use and our full refund warranty.

We get our information about what products our customers want by talking to existing customers. There seems to be an increasing demand for our product. The demand for our product is increasing in size based on the change in population characteristics.

SALES

At Oshkosh Hardware, Inc. we will employ three sales people and will not need any additional personnel to achieve our sales goals. These salespeople will need several years experience in home repair and power tool usage. We expect to attract 30% of our customers from newspaper ads, 5% of our customers from local directories, 5% of our customers from the yellow pages, 10% of our customers from family and friends, and 50% of our customers from current customers. The most cost effect source will be current customers. In general our industry is growing.

MANAGEMENT

We would evaluate the quality of our management staff as being excellent. Our manager is experienced and very motivated to achieve the various sales and quality assurance objectives we have set. We will use a management information system that produces key inventory, quality assurance, and sales data on a weekly basis. All data is compared to previously established goals for that week, and deviations are the primary focus of the management staff.

GOALS IMPLEMENTATION

The short term goals of our business are:

1. Open the store by October 1, 1994
2. Reach our breakeven point in two months
3. Have sales of $100,000 in the first six months

In order to achieve our first short term goal we must:

1. Sign the lease by July 1, 1994
2. Order a complete inventory by August 1, 1994

In order to achieve our second short term goal we must:

1. Advertise extensively in Sept. and Oct.
2. Keep expenses to a minimum

In order to achieve our third short term goal we must:

1. Promote power tool sales for the Christmas season
2. Keep good customer traffic in Jan. and Feb.

The long term goals for our business are:

1. Obtain sales volume of $600,000 in three years
2. Become the largest hardware dealer in the city
3. Open a second store in Fond du Lac

The most important thing we must do in order to achieve the long term goals for our business is to develop a highly profitable business with excellent cash flow.

FINANCE

Oshkosh Hardware, Inc. Faces some potential threats or risks to our business. They are discount house competition. We believe we can avoid or compensate for this by providing quality products complimented by quality advice on the use of every product we sell. The financial projections we have prepared are located at the end of this document.

JOB DESCRIPTION-GENERAL MANAGER

The General Manager of the business of the corporation will be the president of the corporation. He will be responsible for the complete operation of the retail hardware store which is owned by the corporation. A detailed description of his duties and responsibilities is as follows.

Sales

Train and supervise the three sales people. Develop programs to motivate and compensate these employees. Coordinate advertising and sales promotion effects to achieve sales totals as outlined in budget. Oversee purchasing function and inventory control procedures to insure adequate merchandise at all times at a reasonable cost.

Finance

Prepare monthly and annual budgets. Secure adequate line of credit from local banks. Supervise office personnel to insure timely preparation of records, statements, all government reports, control of receivables and payables, and monthly financial statements.

Administration

Perform duties as required in the areas of personnel, building leasing and maintenance, licenses and permits, and public relations.

Organizations, Agencies, & Consultants

A listing of Associations and Consultants of interest to entrepreneurs, followed by the ten Small Business Administration Regional Offices, Small Business Development Centers, Service Corps of Retired Executives offices, and Venture Capital and Finance Companies.

Associations

This section contains a listing of associations and other agencies of interest to the small business owner. Entries are listed alphabetically by organization name.

American Business Women's Association
9100 Ward Pkwy.
PO Box 8728
Kansas City, MO 64114-0728
(800)228-0007
E-mail: abwa@abwa.org
Website: http://www.abwa.org
Jeanne Banks, National President

American Franchisee Association
53 W Jackson Blvd., Ste. 1157
Chicago, IL 60604
(312)431-0545
E-mail: info@franchisee.org
Website: http://www.franchisee.org
Susan P. Kezios, President

American Independent Business Alliance
222 S Black Ave.
Bozeman, MT 59715
(406)582-1255
E-mail: info@amiba.net
Website: http://www.amiba.net
Jennifer Rockne, Director

American Small Businesses Association
206 E College St., Ste. 201
Grapevine, TX 76051
800-942-2722
E-mail: info@asbaonline.org
Website: http://www.asbaonline.org/

American Women's Economic Development Corporation
216 East 45th St., 10th Floor
New York, NY 10017
(917)368-6100

Fax: (212)986-7114
E-mail: info@awed.org
Website: http://www.awed.org
Roseanne Antonucci, Exec. Dir.

Association for Enterprise Opportunity
1601 N Kent St., Ste. 1101
Arlington, VA 22209
(703)841-7760
Fax: (703)841-7748
E-mail: aeo@assoceo.org
Website: http://www.micro enterpriseworks.org
Bill Edwards, Exec.Dir.

Association of Small Business Development Centers
c/o Don Wilson
8990 Burke Lake Rd.
Burke, VA 22015
(703)764-9850
Fax: (703)764-1234
E-mail: info@asbdc-us.org
Website: http://www.asbdc-us.org
Don Wilson, Pres./CEO

BEST Employers Association
2505 McCabe Way
Irvine, CA 92614
(949)253-4080
800-433-0088
Fax: (714)553-0883
E-mail: info@bestlife.com
Website: http://www.bestlife.com
Donald R. Lawrenz, CEO

Center for Family Business
PO Box 24219
Cleveland, OH 44124
(440)460-5409
E-mail: grummi@aol.com
Dr. Leon A. Danco, Chm.

Coalition for Government Procurement
1990 M St. NW, Ste. 400
Washington, DC 20036
(202)331-0975
E-mail: info@thecgp.org
Website: http://www.coalgovpro.org
Paul Caggiano, Pres.

Employers of America
PO Box 1874
Mason City, IA 50402-1874
(641)424-3187
800-728-3187
Fax: (641)424-1673
E-mail: employer@employerhelp.org
Website: http://www.employerhelp.org
Jim Collison, Pres.

Family Firm Institute
200 Lincoln St., Ste. 201
Boston, MA 02111
(617)482-3045
Fax: (617)482-3049
E-mail: ffi@ffi.org
Website: http://www.ffi.org
Judy L. Green, Ph.D., Exec.Dir.

Independent Visually Impaired Enterprisers
500 S 3rd St., Apt. H
Burbank, CA 91502
(818)238-9321
E-mail: abazyn@bazyn communications.com
http://www.acb.org/affiliates
Adris Bazyn, Pres.

International Association for Business Organizations
3 Woodthorn Ct., Ste. 12
Owings Mills, MD 21117
(410)581-1373
E-mail: nahbb@msn.com
Rudolph Lewis, Exec. Officer

International Council for Small Business
The George Washington University
School of Business and Public
Management
2115 G St. NW, Ste. 403
Washington, DC 20052
(202)994-0704
Fax: (202)994-4930
E-mail: icsb@gwu.edu
Website: http://www.icsb.org
Susan G. Duffy. Admin.

International Small Business Consortium
3309 Windjammer St.
Norman, OK 73072
E-mail: sb@isbc.com
Website: http://www.isbc.com

Kauffman Center for Entrepreneurial Leadership
4801 Rockhill Rd.
Kansas City, MO 64110-2046
(816)932-1000
E-mail: info@kauffman.org
Website: http://www.entreworld.org

National Alliance for Fair Competition
3 Bethesda Metro Center, Ste. 1100
Bethesda, MD 20814
(410)235-7116
Fax: (410)235-7116
E-mail: ampesq@aol.com
Tony Ponticelli, Exec.Dir.

National Association for the Self-Employed
PO Box 612067
DFW Airport
Dallas, TX 75261-2067
(800)232-6273
E-mail: mpetron@nase.org
Website: http://www.nase.org
Robert Hughes, Pres.

National Association of Business Leaders
4132 Shoreline Dr., Ste. J & H
Earth City, MO 63045
Fax: (314)298-9110
E-mail: nabl@nabl.com
Website: http://www.nabl.com/
Gene Blumenthal, Contact

National Association of Private Enterprise
PO Box 15550
Long Beach, CA 90815
888-224-0953

Fax: (714)844-4942
Website: http://www.napeonline.net
Laura Squiers, Exec.Dir.

National Association of Small Business Investment Companies
666 11th St. NW, Ste. 750
Washington, DC 20001
(202)628-5055
Fax: (202)628-5080
E-mail: nasbic@nasbic.org
Website: http://www.nasbic.org
Lee W. Mercer, Pres.

National Business Association
PO Box 700728
5151 Beltline Rd., Ste. 1150
Dallas, TX 75370
(972)458-0900
800-456-0440
Fax: (972)960-9149
E-mail: info@nationalbusiness.org
Website: http://www.national
business.org
Raj Nisankarao, Pres.

National Business Owners Association
PO Box 111
Stuart, VA 24171
(276)251-7500
(866)251-7505
Fax: (276)251-2217
E-mail: membershipservices@nboa.org
Website: http://www.rvmdb.com.nboa
Paul LaBarr, Pres.

National Center for Fair Competition
PO Box 220
Annandale, VA 22003
(703)280-4622
Fax: (703)280-0942
E-mail: kentonp1@aol.com
Kenton Pattie, Pres.

National Family Business Council
1640 W. Kennedy Rd.
Lake Forest, IL 60045
(847)295-1040
Fax: (847)295-1898
E-mail: lmsnfbc@email.msn.com
Jogn E. Messervey, Pres.

National Federation of Independent Business
53 Century Blvd., Ste. 250
Nashville, TN 37214
(615)872-5800
800-NFIBNOW
Fax: (615)872-5353
Website: http://www.nfib.org
Jack Faris, Pres. and CEO

National Small Business Association
1156 15th St. NW, Ste. 1100
Washington, DC 20005
(202)293-8830
800-345-6728
Fax: (202)872-8543
E-mail: press@nsba.biz
Website: http://www.nsba.biz
Rob Yunich, Dir. of Communications

PUSH Commercial Division
930 E 50th St.
Chicago, IL 60615-2702
(773)373-3366
Fax: (773)373-3571
E-mail: info@rainbowpush.org
Website: http://www.rainbowpush.org
Rev. Willie T. Barrow, Co-Chm.

Research Institute for Small and Emerging Business
722 12th St. NW
Washington, DC 20005
(202)628-8382
Fax: (202)628-8392
E-mail: info@riseb.org
Website: http://www.riseb.org
Allan Neece, Jr., Chm.

Sales Professionals USA
PO Box 149
Arvada, CO 80001
(303)534-4937
888-736-7767
E-mail: salespro@salesprofessionals-usa.com
Website: http://www.salesprofessionals-usa.com
Sharon Herbert, Natl. Pres.

Score Association - Service Corps of Retired Executives
409 3rd St. SW, 6th Fl.
Washington, DC 20024
(202)205-6762
800-634-0245
Fax: (202)205-7636
E-mail: media@score.org
Website: http://www.score.org
W. Kenneth Yancey, Jr., CEO

Small Business and Entrepreneurship Council
1920 L St. NW, Ste. 200
Washington, DC 20036
(202)785-0238
Fax: (202)822-8118
E-mail: membership@sbec.org
Website: http://www.sbecouncil.org
Karen Kerrigan, Pres./CEO

Small Business in Telecommunications
1331 H St. NW, Ste. 500
Washington, DC 20005
(202)347-4511
Fax: (202)347-8607
E-mail: sbt@sbthome.org
Website: http://www.sbthome.org
Lonnie Danchik, Chm.

Small Business Legislative Council
1010 Massachusetts Ave. NW, Ste. 540
Washington, DC 20005
(202)639-8500
Fax: (202)296-5333
E-mail: email@sblc.org
Website: http://www.sblc.org
John Satagaj, Pres.

Small Business Service Bureau
554 Main St.
PO Box 15014
Worcester, MA 01615-0014
(508)756-3513
800-343-0939
Fax: (508)770-0528
E-mail: membership@sbsb.com
Website: http://www.sbsb.com
Francis R. Carroll, Pres.

Small Publishers Association of North America
1618 W COlorado Ave.
Colorado Springs, CO 80904
(719)475-1726
Fax: (719)471-2182
E-mail: span@spannet.org
Website: http://www.spannet.org
Scott Flora, Exec. Dir.

SOHO America
PO Box 941
Hurst, TX 76053-0941
800-495-SOHO
E-mail: soho@1sas.com
Website: http://www.soho.org

Structured Employment Economic Development Corporation
915 Broadway, 17th Fl.
New York, NY 10010
(212)473-0255
Fax: (212)473-0357
E-mail: info@seedco.org
Website: http://www.seedco.org
William Grinker, CEO

Support Services Alliance
107 Prospect St.
Schoharie, NY 12157
800-836-4772

E-mail: info@ssamembers.com
Website: http://www.ssainfo.com
Steve COle, Pres.

United States Association for Small Business and Entrepreneurship
975 University Ave., No. 3260
Madison, WI 53706
(608)262-9982
Fax: (608)263-0818
E-mail: jgillman@wisc.edu
Website: http://www.ususbe.org
Joan Gillman, Exec. Dir.

Consultants

This section contains a listing of consultants specializing in small business development. It is arranged alphabetically by country, then by state or province, then by city, then by firm name.

Canada

Alberta

Common Sense Solutions
3405 16A Ave.
Edmonton, AB, Canada
(403)465-7330
Fax: (403)465-7380
E-mail: gcoulson@comsense solutions.com
Website: http://www.comsense solutions.com

Varsity Consulting Group
School of Business
University of Alberta
Edmonton, AB, Canada T6G 2R6
(780)492-2994
Fax: (780)492-5400
Website: http://www.bus.ualberta.ca/vcg

Viro Hospital Consulting
42 Commonwealth Bldg., 9912 - 106 St. NW
Edmonton, AB, Canada T5K 1C5
(403)425-3871
Fax: (403)425-3871
E-mail: rpb@freenet.edmonton.ab.ca

British Columbia

SRI Strategic Resources Inc.
4330 Kingsway, Ste. 1600
Burnaby, BC, Canada V5H 4G7
(604)435-0627
Fax: (604)435-2782

E-mail: inquiry@sri.bc.ca
Website: http://www.sri.com

Andrew R. De Boda Consulting
1523 Milford Ave.
Coquitlam, BC, Canada V3J 2V9
(604)936-4527
Fax: (604)936-4527
E-mail: deboda@intergate.bc.ca
Website: http://www.ourworld. compuserve.com/homepages/deboda

The Sage Group Ltd.
980 - 355 Burrard St.
744 W Haistings, Ste. 410
Vancouver, BC, Canada V6C 1A5
(604)669-9269
Fax: (604)669-6622

Tikkanen-Bradley
1345 Nelson St., Ste. 202
Vancouver, BC, Canada V6E 1J8
(604)669-0583
E-mail: webmaster@tikkanen bradley.com
Website: http://www.tikkanenbradley.com

Ontario

The Cynton Co.
17 Massey St.
Brampton, ON, Canada L6S 2V6
(905)792-7769
Fax: (905)792-8116
E-mail: cynton@home.com
Website: http://www.cynton.com

Begley & Associates
RR 6
Cambridge, ON, Canada N1R 5S7
(519)740-3629
Fax: (519)740-3629
E-mail: begley@in.on.ca
Website: http://www.in.on.ca/~begley/ index.htm

CRO Engineering Ltd.
1895 William Hodgins Ln.
Carp, ON, Canada K0A 1L0
(613)839-1108
Fax: (613)839-1406
E-mail: J.Grefford@ieee.ca
Website: http://www.geocities.com/ WallStreet/District/7401/

Task Enterprises
Box 69, RR 2 Hamilton
Flamborough, ON, Canada L8N 2Z7
(905)659-0153
Fax: (905)659-0861

HST Group Ltd.
430 Gilmour St.
Ottawa, ON, Canada K2P 0R8
(613)236-7303
Fax: (613)236-9893

Harrison Associates
BCE Pl.
181 Bay St., Ste. 3740
PO Box 798
Toronto, ON, Canada M5J 2T3
(416)364-5441
Fax: (416)364-2875

TCI Convergence Ltd. Management Consultants
99 Crown's Ln.
Toronto, ON, Canada M5R 3P4
(416)515-4146
Fax: (416)515-2097
E-mail: tci@inforamp.net
Website: http://tciconverge.com/index.1.html

Ken Wyman & Associates Inc.
64B Shuter St., Ste. 200
Toronto, ON, Canada M5B 1B1
(416)362-2926
Fax: (416)362-3039
E-mail: kenwyman@compuserve.com

JPL Business Consultants
82705 Metter Rd.
Wellandport, ON, Canada L0R 2J0
(905)386-7450
Fax: (905)386-7450
E-mail: plamarch@freenet.npiec.on.ca

Quebec

The Zimmar Consulting Partnership Inc.
Westmount
PO Box 98
Montreal, QC, Canada H3Z 2T1
(514)484-1459
Fax: (514)484-3063

Saskatchewan

Trimension Group
No. 104-110 Research Dr.
Innovation Place, SK, Canada S7N 3R3
(306)668-2560
Fax: (306)975-1156
E-mail: trimension@trimension.ca
Website: http://www.trimension.ca

Corporate Management Consultants
40 Government Road - PO Box 185
Prud Homme, SK, Canada, S0K 3K0
(306)654-4569

E-mail: cmccorporatemanagement@shaw.ca
Website: http://www.Corporate managementconsultants.com
Gerald Rekve

United States

Alabama

Business Planning Inc.
300 Office Park Dr.
Birmingham, AL 35223-2474
(205)870-7090
Fax: (205)870-7103

Tradebank of Eastern Alabama
546 Broad St., Ste. 3
Gadsden, AL 35901
(205)547-8700
Fax: (205)547-8718
E-mail: mansion@webex.com
Website: http://www.webex.com/~tea

Alaska

AK Business Development Center
3335 Arctic Blvd., Ste. 203
Anchorage, AK 99503
(907)562-0335
Free: 800-478-3474
Fax: (907)562-6988
E-mail: abdc@gci.net
Website: http://www.abdc.org

Business Matters
PO Box 287
Fairbanks, AK 99707
(907)452-5650

Arizona

Carefree Direct Marketing Corp.
8001 E Serene St.
PO Box 3737
Carefree, AZ 85377-3737
(480)488-4227
Fax: (480)488-2841

Trans Energy Corp.
1739 W 7th Ave.
Mesa, AZ 85202
(480)827-7915
Fax: (480)967-6601
E-mail: aha@clean-air.org
Website: http://www.clean-air.org

CMAS
5125 N 16th St.
Phoenix, AZ 85016

(602)395-1001
Fax: (602)604-8180

Comgate Telemanagement Ltd.
706 E Bell Rd., Ste. 105
Phoenix, AZ 85022
(602)485-5708
Fax: (602)485-5709
E-mail: comgate@netzone.com
Website: http://www.comgate.com

Moneysoft Inc.
1 E Camelback Rd. #550
Phoenix, AZ 85012
Free: 800-966-7797
E-mail: mbray@moneysoft.com

Harvey C. Skoog
PO Box 26439
Prescott Valley, AZ 86312
(520)772-1714
Fax: (520)772-2814

LMC Services
8711 E Pinnacle Peak Rd., No. 340
Scottsdale, AZ 85255-3555
(602)585-7177
Fax: (602)585-5880
E-mail: louws@earthlink.com

Sauerbrun Technology Group Ltd.
7979 E Princess Dr., Ste. 5
Scottsdale, AZ 85255-5878
(602)502-4950
Fax: (602)502-4292
E-mail: info@sauerbrun.com
Website: http://www.sauerbrun.com

Gary L. McLeod
PO Box 230
Sonoita, AZ 85637
Fax: (602)455-5661

Van Cleve Associates
6932 E 2nd St.
Tucson, AZ 85710
(520)296-2587
Fax: (520)296-3358

California

Acumen Group Inc.
(650)949-9349
Fax: (650)949-4845
E-mail: acumen-g@ix.netcom.com
Website: http://pw2.netcom.com/~janed/acumen.html

On-line Career and Management Consulting
420 Central Ave., No. 314
Alameda, CA 94501

(510)864-0336
Fax: (510)864-0336
E-mail: career@dnai.com
Website: http://www.dnai.com/~career

Career Paths-Thomas E. Church & Associates Inc.
PO Box 2439
Aptos, CA 95001
(408)662-7950
Fax: (408)662-7955
E-mail: church@ix.netcom.com
Website: http://www.careerpaths-tom.com

Keck & Co. Business Consultants
410 Walsh Rd.
Atherton, CA 94027
(650)854-9588
Fax: (650)854-7240
E-mail: info@keckco.com
Website: http://www.keckco.com

Ben W. Laverty III, PhD, REA, CEI
4909 Stockdale Hwy., Ste. 132
Bakersfield, CA 93309
(661)283-8300
Free: 800-833-0373
Fax: (661)283-8313
E-mail: cstc@cstcsafety.com
Website: http://www.cstcsafety.com/cstc

Lindquist Consultants-Venture Planning
225 Arlington Ave.
Berkeley, CA 94707
(510)524-6685
Fax: (510)527-6604

Larson Associates
PO Box 9005
Brea, CA 92822
(714)529-4121
Fax: (714)572-3606
E-mail: ray@consultlarson.com
Website: http://www.consultlarson.com

Kremer Management Consulting
PO Box 500
Carmel, CA 93921
(408)626-8311
Fax: (408)624-2663
E-mail: ddkremer@aol.com

W and J PARTNERSHIP
PO Box 2499
18876 Edwin Markham Dr.
Castro Valley, CA 94546
(510)583-7751
Fax: (510)583-7645
E-mail: wamorgan@wjpartnership.com
Website: http://www.wjpartnership.com

JB Associates
21118 Gardena Dr.
Cupertino, CA 95014
(408)257-0214
Fax: (408)257-0216
E-mail: semarang@sirius.com

House Agricultural Consultants
PO Box 1615
Davis, CA 95617-1615
(916)753-3361
Fax: (916)753-0464
E-mail: infoag@houseag.com
Website: http://www.houseag.com/

3C Systems Co.
16161 Ventura Blvd., Ste. 815
Encino, CA 91436
(818)907-1302
Fax: (818)907-1357
E-mail: mark@3CSysCo.com
Website: http://www.3CSysCo.com

Technical Management Consultants
3624 Westfall Dr.
Encino, CA 91436-4154
(818)784-0626
Fax: (818)501-5575
E-mail: tmcrs@aol.com

RAINWATER-GISH & Associates, Business Finance & Development
317 3rd St., Ste. 3
Eureka, CA 95501
(707)443-0030
Fax: (707)443-5683

Global Tradelinks
451 Pebble Beach Pl.
Fullerton, CA 92835
(714)441-2280
Fax: (714)441-2281
E-mail: info@globaltradelinks.com
Website: http://www.globaltradelinks.com

Strategic Business Group
800 Cienaga Dr.
Fullerton, CA 92835-1248
(714)449-1040
Fax: (714)525-1631

Burnes Consulting
20537 Wolf Creek Rd.
Grass Valley, CA 95949
(530)346-8188
Free: 800-949-9021
Fax: (530)346-7704
E-mail: kent@burnesconsulting.com
Website: http://www.burnesconsulting.com

Pioneer Business Consultants
9042 Garfield Ave., Ste. 312
Huntington Beach, CA 92646
(714)964-7600

Beblie, Brandt & Jacobs Inc.
16 Technology, Ste. 164
Irvine, CA 92618
(714)450-8790
Fax: (714)450-8799
E-mail: darcy@bbjinc.com
Website: http://198.147.90.26

Fluor Daniel Inc.
3353 Michelson Dr.
Irvine, CA 92612-0650
(949)975-2000
Fax: (949)975-5271
E-mail: sales.consulting@fluordaniel.com
Website: http://www.fluordaniel consulting.com

MCS Associates
18300 Von Karman, Ste. 710
Irvine, CA 92612
(949)263-8700
Fax: (949)263-0770
E-mail: info@mcsassociates.com
Website: http://www.mcsassociates.com

Inspired Arts Inc.
4225 Executive Sq., Ste. 1160
La Jolla, CA 92037
(619)623-3525
Free: 800-851-4394
Fax: (619)623-3534
E-mail: info@inspiredarts.com
Website: http://www.inspiredarts.com

The Laresis Companies
PO Box 3284
La Jolla, CA 92038
(619)452-2720
Fax: (619)452-8744

RCL & Co.
PO Box 1143
737 Pearl St., Ste. 201
La Jolla, CA 92038
(619)454-8883
Fax: (619)454-8880

Comprehensive Business Services
3201 Lucas Cir.
Lafayette, CA 94549
(925)283-8272
Fax: (925)283-8272

The Ribble Group
27601 Forbes Rd., Ste. 52
Laguna Niguel, CA 92677

(714)582-1085
Fax: (714)582-6420
E-mail: ribble@deltanet.com

Norris Bernstein, CMC
9309 Marina Pacifica Dr. N
Long Beach, CA 90803
(562)493-5458
Fax: (562)493-5459
E-mail: norris@ctecomputer.com
Website: http://foodconsultants.com/
bernstein/

Horizon Consulting Services
1315 Garthwick Dr.
Los Altos, CA 94024
(415)967-0906
Fax: (415)967-0906

Brincko Associates Inc.
1801 Avenue of the Stars, Ste. 1054
Los Angeles, CA 90067
(310)553-4523
Fax: (310)553-6782

Rubenstein/Justman Management Consultants
2049 Century Park E, 24th Fl.
Los Angeles, CA 90067
(310)282-0800
Fax: (310)282-0400
E-mail: info@rjmc.net
Website: http://www.rjmc.net

F.J. Schroeder & Associates
1926 Westholme Ave.
Los Angeles, CA 90025
(310)470-2655
Fax: (310)470-6378
E-mail: fjsacons@aol.com
Website: http://www.mcninet.com/
GlobalLook/Fjschroe.html

Western Management Associates
5959 W Century Blvd., Ste. 565
Los Angeles, CA 90045-6506
(310)645-1091
Free: (888)788-6534
Fax: (310)645-1092
E-mail: gene@cfoforrent.com
Website: http://www.cfoforrent.com

Darrell Sell and Associates
Los Gatos, CA 95030
(408)354-7794
E-mail: darrell@netcom.com

Leslie J. Zambo
3355 Michael Dr.
Marina, CA 93933
(408)384-7086

Fax: (408)647-4199
E-mail: 104776.1552@compuserve.com

Marketing Services Management
PO Box 1377
Martinez, CA 94553
(510)370-8527
Fax: (510)370-8527
E-mail: markserve@biotechnet.com

William M. Shine Consulting Service
PO Box 127
Moraga, CA 94556-0127
(510)376-6516

Palo Alto Management Group Inc.
2672 Bayshore Pky., Ste. 701
Mountain View, CA 94043
(415)968-4374
Fax: (415)968-4245
E-mail: mburwen@pamg.com

BizplanSource
1048 Irvine Ave., Ste. 621
Newport Beach, CA 92660
Free: 888-253-0974
Fax: 800-859-8254
E-mail: info@bizplansource.com
Website: http://www.bizplansource.com
Adam Greengrass, President

The Market Connection
4020 Birch St., Ste. 203
Newport Beach, CA 92660
(714)731-6273
Fax: (714)833-0253

Muller Associates
PO Box 7264
Newport Beach, CA 92658
(714)646-1169
Fax: (714)646-1169

International Health Resources
PO Box 329
North San Juan, CA 95960-0329
(530)292-1266
Fax: (530)292-1243
Website: http://www.futureof
healthcare.com

NEXUS - Consultants to Management
PO Box 1531
Novato, CA 94948
(415)897-4400
Fax: (415)898-2252
E-mail: jimnexus@aol.com

Aerospcace.Org
PO Box 28831
Oakland, CA 94604-8831

(510)530-9169
Fax: (510)530-3411
Website: http://www.aerospace.org

Intelequest Corp.
722 Gailen Ave.
Palo Alto, CA 94303
(415)968-3443
Fax: (415)493-6954
E-mail: frits@iqix.com

McLaughlin & Associates
66 San Marino Cir.
Rancho Mirage, CA 92270
(760)321-2932
Fax: (760)328-2474
E-mail: jackmcla@msn.com

Carrera Consulting Group, a division of Maximus
2110 21st St., Ste. 400
Sacramento, CA 95818
(916)456-3300
Fax: (916)456-3306
E-mail: central@carreraconsulting.com
Website: http://www.carreraconsulting.com

Bay Area Tax Consultants and Bayhill Financial Consultants
1150 Bayhill Dr., Ste. 1150
San Bruno, CA 94066-3004
(415)952-8786
Fax: (415)588-4524
E-mail: baytax@compuserve.com
Website: http://www.baytax.com/

AdCon Services, LLC
8871 Hillery Dr.
Dan Diego, CA 92126
(858)433-1411
E-mail: adam@adconservices.com
Website: http://www.adconservices.com
Adam Greengrass

California Business Incubation Network
101 W Broadway, No. 480
San Diego, CA 92101
(619)237-0559
Fax: (619)237-0521

G.R. Gordetsky Consultants Inc.
11414 Windy Summit Pl.
San Diego, CA 92127
(619)487-4939
Fax: (619)487-5587
E-mail: gordet@pacbell.net

Freeman, Sullivan & Co.
131 Steuart St., Ste. 500
San Francisco, CA 94105
(415)777-0707

Free: 800-777-0737
Fax: (415)777-2420
Website: http://www.fsc-research.com

Ideas Unlimited
2151 California St., Ste. 7
San Francisco, CA 94115
(415)931-0641
Fax: (415)931-0880

Russell Miller Inc.
300 Montgomery St., Ste. 900
San Francisco, CA 94104
(415)956-7474
Fax: (415)398-0620
E-mail: rmi@pacbell.net
Website: http://www.rmisf.com

PKF Consulting
425 California St., Ste. 1650
San Francisco, CA 94104
(415)421-5378
Fax: (415)956-7708
E-mail: callahan@pkfc.com
Website: http://www.pkfonline.com

Welling & Woodard Inc.
1067 Broadway
San Francisco, CA 94133
(415)776-4500
Fax: (415)776-5067

Highland Associates
16174 Highland Dr.
San Jose, CA 95127
(408)272-7008
Fax: (408)272-4040

ORDIS Inc.
6815 Trinidad Dr.
San Jose, CA 95120-2056
(408)268-3321
Free: 800-446-7347
Fax: (408)268-3582
E-mail: ordis@ordis.com
Website: http://www.ordis.com

Stanford Resources Inc.
20 Great Oaks Blvd., Ste. 200
San Jose, CA 95119
(408)360-8400
Fax: (408)360-8410
E-mail: sales@stanfordsources.com
Website: http://www.stanfordresources.com

Technology Properties Ltd. Inc.
PO Box 20250
San Jose, CA 95160
(408)243-9898
Fax: (408)296-6637
E-mail: sanjose@tplnet.com

Helfert Associates
1777 Borel Pl., Ste. 508
San Mateo, CA 94402-3514
(650)377-0540
Fax: (650)377-0472

Mykytyn Consulting Group Inc.
185 N Redwood Dr., Ste. 200
San Rafael, CA 94903
(415)491-1770
Fax: (415)491-1251
E-mail: info@mcgi.com
Website: http://www.mcgi.com

Omega Management Systems Inc.
3 Mount Darwin Ct.
San Rafael, CA 94903-1109
(415)499-1300
Fax: (415)492-9490
E-mail: omegamgt@ix.netcom.com

The Information Group Inc.
4675 Stevens Creek Blvd., Ste. 100
Santa Clara, CA 95051
(408)985-7877
Fax: (408)985-2945
E-mail: dvincent@tig-usa.com
Website: http://www.tig-usa.com

Cast Management Consultants
1620 26th St., Ste. 2040N
Santa Monica, CA 90404
(310)828-7511
Fax: (310)453-6831

Cuma Consulting Management
Box 724
Santa Rosa, CA 95402
(707)785-2477
Fax: (707)785-2478

The E-Myth Academy
131B Stony Cir., Ste. 2000
Santa Rosa, CA 95401
(707)569-5600
Free: 800-221-0266
Fax: (707)569-5700
E-mail: info@e-myth.com
Website: http://www.e-myth.com

Reilly, Connors & Ray
1743 Canyon Rd.
Spring Valley, CA 91977
(619)698-4808
Fax: (619)460-3892
E-mail: davidray@adnc.com

Management Consultants
Sunnyvale, CA 94087-4700
(408)773-0321

RJR Associates
1639 Lewiston Dr.
Sunnyvale, CA 94087
(408)737-7720
E-mail: bobroy@rjrassoc.com
Website: http://www.rjrassoc.com

Schwafel Associates
333 Cobalt Way, Ste. 21
Sunnyvale, CA 94085
(408)720-0649
Fax: (408)720-1796
E-mail: schwafel@ricochet.net
Website: http://www.patca.org

Staubs Business Services
23320 S Vermont Ave.
Torrance, CA 90502-2940
(310)830-9128
Fax: (310)830-9128
E-mail: Harry_L_Staubs@Lamg.com

Out of Your Mind...and Into the Marketplace
13381 White Sands Dr.
Tustin, CA 92780-4565
(714)544-0248
Free: 800-419-1513
Fax: (714)730-1414
E-mail: lpinson@aol.com
Website: http://www.business-plan.com

Independent Research Services
PO Box 2426
Van Nuys, CA 91404-2426
(818)993-3622

Ingman Company Inc.
7949 Woodley Ave., Ste. 120
Van Nuys, CA 91406-1232
(818)375-5027
Fax: (818)894-5001

Innovative Technology Associates
3639 E Harbor Blvd., Ste. 203E
Ventura, CA 93001
(805)650-9353

Grid Technology Associates
20404 Tufts Cir.
Walnut, CA 91789
(909)444-0922
Fax: (909)444-0922
E-mail: grid_technology@msn.com

Ridge Consultants Inc.
100 Pringle Ave., Ste. 580
Walnut Creek, CA 94596
(925)274-1990
Fax: (510)274-1956
E-mail: info@ridgecon.com
Website: http://www.ridgecon.com

Bell Springs Publishing
PO Box 1240
Willits, CA 95490
(707)459-6372
E-mail: bellsprings@sabernet
Website: http://www.bellsprings.com

Hutchinson Consulting and Appraisal
23245 Sylvan St., Ste. 103
Woodland Hills, CA 91367
(818)888-8175
Free: 800-977-7548
Fax: (818)888-8220
E-mail: r.f.hutchinson-cpa@worldnet.
att.net

Colorado

Sam Boyer & Associates
4255 S Buckley Rd., No. 136
Aurora, CO 80013
Free: 800-785-0485
Fax: (303)766-8740
E-mail: samboyer@samboyer.com
Website: http://www.samboyer.com/

Ameriwest Business Consultants Inc.
PO Box 26266
Colorado Springs, CO 80936
(719)380-7096
Fax: (719)380-7096
E-mail: email@abchelp.com
Website: http://www.abchelp.com

GVNW Consulting Inc.
2270 La Montana Way
Colorado Springs, CO 80936
(719)594-5800
Fax: (719)594-5803
Website: http://www.gvnw.com

M-Squared Inc.
755 San Gabriel Pl.
Colorado Springs, CO 80906
(719)576-2554
Fax: (719)576-2554

Thornton Financial FNIC
1024 Centre Ave., Bldg. E
Fort Collins, CO 80526-1849
(970)221-2089
Fax: (970)484-5206

TenEyck Associates
1760 Cherryville Rd.
Greenwood Village, CO 80121-1503
(303)758-6129
Fax: (303)761-8286

Associated Enterprises Ltd.
13050 W Ceder Dr., Unit 11
Lakewood, CO 80228

(303)988-6695
Fax: (303)988-6739
E-mail: ael1@classic.msn.com

The Vincent Company Inc.
200 Union Blvd., Ste. 210
Lakewood, CO 80228
(303)989-7271
Free: 800-274-0733
Fax: (303)989-7570
E-mail: vincent@vincentco.com
Website: http://www.vincentco.com

Johnson & West Management Consultants Inc.
7612 S Logan Dr.
Littleton, CO 80122
(303)730-2810
Fax: (303)730-3219

Western Capital Holdings Inc.
10050 E Applwood Dr.
Parker, CO 80138
(303)841-1022
Fax: (303)770-1945

Connecticut

Stratman Group Inc.
40 Tower Ln.
Avon, CT 06001-4222
(860)677-2898
Free: 800-551-0499
Fax: (860)677-8210

Cowherd Consulting Group Inc.
106 Stephen Mather Rd.
Darien, CT 06820
(203)655-2150
Fax: (203)655-6427

Greenwich Associates
8 Greenwich Office Park
Greenwich, CT 06831-5149
(203)629-1200
Fax: (203)629-1229
E-mail: lisa@greenwich.com
Website: http://www.greenwich.com

Follow-up News
185 Pine St., Ste. 818
Manchester, CT 06040
(860)647-7542
Free: 800-708-0696
Fax: (860)646-6544
E-mail: Followupnews@aol.com

Lovins & Associates Consulting
309 Edwards St.
New Haven, CT 06511
(203)787-3367

Fax: (203)624-7599
E-mail: Alovinsphd@aol.com
Website: http://www.lovinsgroup.com

JC Ventures Inc.
4 Arnold St.
Old Greenwich, CT 06870-1203
(203)698-1990
Free: 800-698-1997
Fax: (203)698-2638

Charles L. Hornung Associates
52 Ned's Mountain Rd.
Ridgefield, CT 06877
(203)431-0297

Manus
100 Prospect St., S Tower
Stamford, CT 06901
(203)326-3880
Free: 800-445-0942
Fax: (203)326-3890
E-mail: manus1@aol.com
Website: http://www.RightManus.com

RealBusinessPlans.com
156 Westport Rd.
Wilton, CT 06897
(914)837-2886
E-mail: ct@realbusinessplans.com
Website: http://www.RealBusinessPlans.com
Tony Tecce

Delaware

Focus Marketing
61-7 Habor Dr.
Claymont, DE 19703
(302)793-3064

Daedalus Ventures Ltd.
PO Box 1474
Hockessin, DE 19707
(302)239-6758
Fax: (302)239-9991
E-mail: daedalus@mail.del.net

The Formula Group
PO Box 866
Hockessin, DE 19707
(302)456-0952
Fax: (302)456-1354
E-mail: formula@netaxs.com

Selden Enterprises Inc.
2502 Silverside Rd., Ste. 1
Wilmington, DE 19810-3740
(302)529-7113
Fax: (302)529-7442
E-mail: selden2@bellatlantic.net
Website: http://www.seldenenterprises.com

District of Columbia

Bruce W. McGee and Associates
7826 Eastern Ave. NW, Ste. 30
Washington, DC 20012
(202)726-7272
Fax: (202)726-2946

McManis Associates Inc.
1900 K St. NW, Ste. 700
Washington, DC 20006
(202)466-7680
Fax: (202)872-1898
Website: http://www.mcmanis-mmi.com

Smith, Dawson & Andrews Inc.
1000 Connecticut Ave., Ste. 302
Washington, DC 20036
(202)835-0740
Fax: (202)775-8526
E-mail: webmaster@sda-inc.com
Website: http://www.sda-inc.com

Florida

BackBone, Inc.
20404 Hacienda Court
Boca Raton, FL 33498
(561)470-0965
Fax: 516-908-4038
E-mail: BPlans@backboneinc.com
Website: http://www.backboneinc.com
Charles Epstein, President

Whalen & Associates Inc.
4255 Northwest 26 Ct.
Boca Raton, FL 33434
(561)241-5950
Fax: (561)241-7414
E-mail: drwhalen@ix.netcom.com

E.N. Rysso & Associates
180 Bermuda Petrel Ct.
Daytona Beach, FL 32119
(386)760-3028
E-mail: erysso@aol.com

Virtual Technocrats LLC
560 Lavers Circle, #146
Delray Beach, FL 33444
(561)265-3509
E-mail: josh@virtualtechnocrats.com;
info@virtualtechnocrats.com
Website: http://www.virtualtechno
crats.com
Josh Eikov, Managing Director

Eric Sands Consulting Services
6193 Rock Island Rd., Ste. 412
Fort Lauderdale, FL 33319
(954)721-4767

Fax: (954)720-2815
E-mail: easands@aol.com
Website: http://www.ericsandsconsultig.com

Professional Planning Associates, Inc.
1975 E. Sunrise Blvd. Suite 607
Fort Lauderdale, FL 33304
(954)764-5204
Fax: 954-463-4172
E-mail: Mgoldstein@proplana.com
Website: http://proplana.com
Michael Goldstein, President

Host Media Corp.
3948 S 3rd St., Ste. 191
Jacksonville Beach, FL 32250
(904)285-3239
Fax: (904)285-5618
E-mail: msconsulting@compuserve.com
Website: http://www.media
servicesgroup.com

William V. Hall
1925 Brickell, Ste. D-701
Miami, FL 33129
(305)856-9622
Fax: (305)856-4113
E-mail: williamvhall@compuserve.com

F.A. McGee Inc.
800 Claughton Island Dr., Ste. 401
Miami, FL 33131
(305)377-9123

Taxplan Inc.
Mirasol International Ctr.
2699 Collins Ave.
Miami Beach, FL 33140
(305)538-3303

T.C. Brown & Associates
8415 Excalibur Cir., Apt. B1
Naples, FL 34108
(941)594-1949
Fax: (941)594-0611
E-mail: tcater@naples.net.com

RLA International Consulting
713 Lagoon Dr.
North Palm Beach, FL 33408
(407)626-4258
Fax: (407)626-5772

Comprehensive Franchising Inc.
2465 Ridgecrest Ave.
Orange Park, FL 32065
(904)272-6567
Free: 800-321-6567
Fax: (904)272-6750
E-mail: theimp@cris.com
Website: http://www.franchise411.com

Hunter G. Jackson Jr. - Consulting Environmental Physicist
PO Box 618272
Orlando, FL 32861-8272
(407)295-4188
E-mail: hunterjackson@juno.com

F. Newton Parks
210 El Brillo Way
Palm Beach, FL 33480
(561)833-1727
Fax: (561)833-4541

Avery Business Development Services
2506 St. Michel Ct.
Ponte Vedra Beach, FL 32082
(904)285-6033
Fax: (904)285-6033

Strategic Business Planning Co.
PO Box 821006
South Florida, FL 33082-1006
(954)704-9100
Fax: (954)438-7333
E-mail: info@bizplan.com
Website: http://www.bizplan.com

Dufresne Consulting Group Inc.
10014 N Dale Mabry, Ste. 101
Tampa, FL 33618-4426
(813)264-4775
Fax: (813)264-9300
Website: http://www.dcgconsult.com

Agrippa Enterprises Inc.
PO Box 175
Venice, FL 34284-0175
(941)355-7876
E-mail: webservices@agrippa.com
Website: http://www.agrippa.com

Center for Simplified Strategic Planning Inc.
PO Box 3324
Vero Beach, FL 32964-3324
(561)231-3636
Fax: (561)231-1099
Website: http://www.cssp.com

Georgia

Marketing Spectrum Inc.
115 Perimeter Pl., Ste. 440
Atlanta, GA 30346
(770)395-7244
Fax: (770)393-4071

Business Ventures Corp.
1650 Oakbrook Dr., Ste. 405
Norcross, GA 30093
(770)729-8000
Fax: (770)729-8028

Informed Decisions Inc.
100 Falling Cheek
Sautee Nacoochee, GA 30571
(706)878-1905
Fax: (706)878-1802
E-mail: skylake@compuserve.com

Tom C. Davis & Associates, P.C.
3189 Perimeter Rd.
Valdosta, GA 31602
(912)247-9801
Fax: (912)244-7704
E-mail: mail@tcdcpa.com
Website: http://www.tcdcpa.com/

Illinois

TWD and Associates
431 S Patton
Arlington Heights, IL 60005
(847)398-6410
Fax: (847)255-5095
E-mail: tdoo@aol.com

Management Planning Associates Inc.
2275 Half Day Rd., Ste. 350
Bannockburn, IL 60015-1277
(847)945-2421
Fax: (847)945-2425

Phil Faris Associates
86 Old Mill Ct.
Barrington, IL 60010
(847)382-4888
Fax: (847)382-4890
E-mail: pfaris@meginsnet.net

Seven Continents Technology
787 Stonebridge
Buffalo Grove, IL 60089
(708)577-9653
Fax: (708)870-1220

Grubb & Blue Inc.
2404 Windsor Pl.
Champaign, IL 61820
(217)366-0052
Fax: (217)356-0117

ACE Accounting Service Inc.
3128 N Bernard St.
Chicago, IL 60618
(773)463-7854
Fax: (773)463-7854

AON Consulting Worldwide
200 E Randolph St., 10th Fl.
Chicago, IL 60601
(312)381-4800
Free: 800-438-6487
Fax: (312)381-0240
Website: http://www.aon.com

FMS Consultants
5801 N Sheridan Rd., Ste. 3D
Chicago, IL 60660
(773)561-7362
Fax: (773)561-6274

Grant Thornton
800 1 Prudential Plz.
130 E Randolph St.
Chicago, IL 60601
(312)856-0001
Fax: (312)861-1340
E-mail: gtinfo@gt.com
Website: http://www.grantthornton.com

Kingsbury International Ltd.
5341 N Glenwood Ave.
Chicago, IL 60640
(773)271-3030
Fax: (773)728-7080
E-mail: jetlag@mcs.com
Website: http://www.kingbiz.com

MacDougall & Blake Inc.
1414 N Wells St., Ste. 311
Chicago, IL 60610-1306
(312)587-3330
Fax: (312)587-3699
E-mail: jblake@compuserve.com

James C. Osburn Ltd.
6445 N. Western Ave., Ste. 304
Chicago, IL 60645
(773)262-4428
Fax: (773)262-6755
E-mail: osburnltd@aol.com

Tarifero & Tazewell Inc.
211 S Clark
Chicago, IL 60690
(312)665-9714
Fax: (312)665-9716

Human Energy Design Systems
620 Roosevelt Dr.
Edwardsville, IL 62025
(618)692-0258
Fax: (618)692-0819

China Business Consultants Group
931 Dakota Cir.
Naperville, IL 60563
(630)778-7992
Fax: (630)778-7915
E-mail: cbcq@aol.com

Center for Workforce Effectiveness
500 Skokie Blvd., Ste. 222
Northbrook, IL 60062
(847)559-8777
Fax: (847)559-8778

E-mail: office@cwelink.com
Website: http://www.cwelink.com

Smith Associates
1320 White Mountain Dr.
Northbrook, IL 60062
(847)480-7200
Fax: (847)480-9828

Francorp Inc.
20200 Governors Dr.
Olympia Fields, IL 60461
(708)481-2900
Free: 800-372-6244
Fax: (708)481-5885
E-mail: francorp@aol.com
Website: http://www.francorpinc.com

Camber Business Strategy Consultants
1010 S Plum Tree Ct
Palatine, IL 60078-0986
(847)202-0101
Fax: (847)705-7510
E-mail: camber@ameritech.net

Partec Enterprise Group
5202 Keith Dr.
Richton Park, IL 60471
(708)503-4047
Fax: (708)503-9468

Rockford Consulting Group Ltd.
Century Plz., Ste. 206
7210 E State St.
Rockford, IL 61108
(815)229-2900
Free: 800-667-7495
Fax: (815)229-2612
E-mail: rligus@RockfordConsulting.com
Website: http://www.Rockford
Consulting.com

RSM McGladrey Inc.
1699 E Woodfield Rd., Ste. 300
Schaumburg, IL 60173-4969
(847)413-6900
Fax: (847)517-7067
Website: http://www.rsmmcgladrey.com

A.D. Star Consulting
320 Euclid
Winnetka, IL 60093
(847)446-7827
Fax: (847)446-7827
E-mail: startwo@worldnet.att.net

Indiana

Modular Consultants Inc.
3109 Crabtree Ln.
Elkhart, IN 46514

(219)264-5761
Fax: (219)264-5761
E-mail: sasabo5313@aol.com

Midwest Marketing Research
PO Box 1077
Goshen, IN 46527
(219)533-0548
Fax: (219)533-0540
E-mail: 103365.654@compuserve

Ketchum Consulting Group
8021 Knue Rd., Ste. 112
Indianapolis, IN 46250
(317)845-5411
Fax: (317)842-9941

**MDI Management
Consulting**
1519 Park Dr.
Munster, IN 46321
(219)838-7909
Fax: (219)838-7909

Iowa

McCord Consulting Group Inc.
4533 Pine View Dr. NE
PO Box 11024
Cedar Rapids, IA 52410
(319)378-0077
Fax: (319)378-1577
E-mail: smmccord@hom.com
Website: http://www.mccordgroup.com

Management Solutions L.C.
3815 Lincoln Pl. Dr.
Des Moines, IA 50312
(515)277-6408
Fax: (515)277-3506
E-mail: wasunimers@uswest.net

Grandview Marketing
15 Red Bridge Dr.
Sioux City, IA 51104
(712)239-3122
Fax: (712)258-7578
E-mail: eandrews@pionet.net

Kansas

Assessments in Action
513A N Mur-Len
Olathe, KS 66062
(913)764-6270
Free: (888)548-1504
Fax: (913)764-6495
E-mail: lowdene@qni.com
Website: http://www.assessments-
in-action.com

Maine

Edgemont Enterprises
PO Box 8354
Portland, ME 04104
(207)871-8964
Fax: (207)871-8964

Pan Atlantic Consultants
5 Milk St.
Portland, ME 04101
(207)871-8622
Fax: (207)772-4842
E-mail: pmurphy@maine.rr.com
Website: http://www.panatlantic.net

Maryland

Clemons & Associates Inc.
5024-R Campbell Blvd.
Baltimore, MD 21236
(410)931-8100
Fax: (410)931-8111
E-mail: info@clemonsmgmt.com
Website: http://www.clemonsmgmt.com

Imperial Group Ltd.
305 Washington Ave., Ste. 204
Baltimore, MD 21204-6009
(410)337-8500
Fax: (410)337-7641

Leadership Institute
3831 Yolando Rd.
Baltimore, MD 21218
(410)366-9111
Fax: (410)243-8478
E-mail: behconsult@aol.com

Burdeshaw Associates Ltd.
4701 Sangamore Rd.
Bethesda, MD 20816-2508
(301)229-5800
Fax: (301)229-5045
E-mail: jstacy@burdeshaw.com
Website: http://www.burdeshaw.com

Michael E. Cohen
5225 Pooks Hill Rd., Ste. 1119 S
Bethesda, MD 20814
(301)530-5738
Fax: (301)530-2988
E-mail: mecohen@crosslink.net

World Development Group Inc.
5272 River Rd., Ste. 650
Bethesda, MD 20816-1405
(301)652-1818
Fax: (301)652-1250
E-mail: wdg@has.com
Website: http://www.worlddg.com

Swartz Consulting
PO Box 4301
Crofton, MD 21114-4301
(301)262-6728

Software Solutions International Inc.
9633 Duffer Way
Gaithersburg, MD 20886
(301)330-4136
Fax: (301)330-4136

Strategies Inc.
8 Park Center Ct., Ste. 200
Owings Mills, MD 21117
(410)363-6669
Fax: (410)363-1231
E-mail: strategies@strat1.com
Website: http://www.strat1.com

Hammer Marketing Resources
179 Inverness Rd.
Severna Park, MD 21146
(410)544-9191
Fax: (305)675-3277
E-mail: info@gohammer.com
Website: http://www.gohammer.com

Andrew Sussman & Associates
13731 Kretsinger
Smithsburg, MD 21783
(301)824-2943
Fax: (301)824-2943

Massachusetts

Geibel Marketing and Public Relations
PO Box 611
Belmont, MA 02478-0005
(617)484-8285
Fax: (617)489-3567
E-mail: jgeibel@geibelpr.com
Website: http://www.geibelpr.com

Bain & Co.
2 Copley Pl.
Boston, MA 02116
(617)572-2000
Fax: (617)572-2427
E-mail: corporate.inquiries@bain.com
Website: http://www.bain.com

Mehr & Co.
62 Kinnaird St.
Cambridge, MA 02139
(617)876-3311
Fax: (617)876-3023
E-mail: mehrco@aol.com

Monitor Company Inc.
2 Canal Park
Cambridge, MA 02141

(617)252-2000
Fax: (617)252-2100
Website: http://www.monitor.com

Information & Research Associates
PO Box 3121
Framingham, MA 01701
(508)788-0784

Walden Consultants Ltd.
252 Pond St.
Hopkinton, MA 01748
(508)435-4882
Fax: (508)435-3971
Website: http://www.waldencon
sultants.com

Jeffrey D. Marshall
102 Mitchell Rd.
Ipswich, MA 01938-1219
(508)356-1113
Fax: (508)356-2989

Consulting Resources Corp.
6 Northbrook Park
Lexington, MA 02420
(781)863-1222
Fax: (781)863-1441
E-mail: res@consultingresources.net
Website: http://www.consulting
resources.net

Planning Technologies Group L.L.C.
92 Hayden Ave.
Lexington, MA 02421
(781)778-4678
Fax: (781)861-1099
E-mail: ptg@plantech.com
Website: http://www.plantech.com

Kalba International Inc.
23 Sandy Pond Rd.
Lincoln, MA 01773
(781)259-9589
Fax: (781)259-1460
E-mail: info@kalbainternational.com
Website: http://www.kalbainter
national.com

VMB Associates Inc.
115 Ashland St.
Melrose, MA 02176
(781)665-0623
Fax: (425)732-7142
E-mail: vmbinc@aol.com

The Company Doctor
14 Pudding Stone Ln.
Mendon, MA 01756
(508)478-1747
Fax: (508)478-0520

Data and Strategies Group Inc.
190 N Main St.
Natick, MA 01760
(508)653-9990
Fax: (508)653-7799
E-mail: dsginc@dsggroup.com
Website: http://www.dsggroup.com

The Enterprise Group
73 Parker Rd.
Needham, MA 02494
(617)444-6631
Fax: (617)433-9991
E-mail: lsacco@world.std.com
Website: http://www.enterprise-group.com

PSMJ Resources Inc.
10 Midland Ave.
Newton, MA 02458
(617)965-0055
Free: 800-537-7765
Fax: (617)965-5152
E-mail: psmj@tiac.net
Website: http://www.psmj.com

Scheur Management Group Inc.
255 Washington St., Ste. 100
Newton, MA 02458-1611
(617)969-7500
Fax: (617)969-7508
E-mail: smgnow@scheur.com
Website: http://www.scheur.com

I.E.E.E., Boston Section
240 Bear Hill Rd., 202B
Waltham, MA 02451-1017
(781)890-5294
Fax: (781)890-5290

Business Planning and Consulting Services
20 Beechwood Ter.
Wellesley, MA 02482
(617)237-9151
Fax: (617)237-9151

Michigan

Walter Frederick Consulting
1719 South Blvd.
Ann Arbor, MI 48104
(313)662-4336
Fax: (313)769-7505

Fox Enterprises
6220 W Freeland Rd.
Freeland, MI 48623
(517)695-9170
Fax: (517)695-9174
E-mail: foxjw@concentric.net
Website: http://www.cris.com/~foxjw

G.G.W. and Associates
1213 Hampton
Jackson, MI 49203
(517)782-2255
Fax: (517)782-2255

Altamar Group Ltd.
6810 S Cedar, Ste. 2-B
Lansing, MI 48911
(517)694-0910
Free: 800-443-2627
Fax: (517)694-1377

Sheffieck Consultants Inc.
23610 Greening Dr.
Novi, MI 48375-3130
(248)347-3545
Fax: (248)347-3530
E-mail: cfsheff@concentric.net

Rehmann, Robson PC
5800 Gratiot
Saginaw, MI 48605
(517)799-9580
Fax: (517)799-0227
Website: http://www.rrpc.com

Francis & Co.
17200 W 10 Mile Rd., Ste. 207
Southfield, MI 48075
(248)559-7600
Fax: (248)559-5249

Private Ventures Inc.
16000 W 9 Mile Rd., Ste. 504
Southfield, MI 48075
(248)569-1977
Free: 800-448-7614
Fax: (248)569-1838
E-mail: pventuresi@aol.com

JGK Associates
14464 Kerner Dr.
Sterling Heights, MI 48313
(810)247-9055
Fax: (248)822-4977
E-mail: kozlowski@home.com

Minnesota

Health Fitness Corp.
3500 W 80th St., Ste. 130
Bloomington, MN 55431
(612)831-6830
Fax: (612)831-7264

Consatech Inc.
PO Box 1047
Burnsville, MN 55337
(612)953-1088
Fax: (612)435-2966

Robert F. Knotek
14960 Ironwood Ct.
Eden Prairie, MN 55346
(612)949-2875

DRI Consulting
7715 Stonewood Ct.
Edina, MN 55439
(612)941-9656
Fax: (612)941-2693
E-mail: dric@dric.com
Website: http://www.dric.com

Markin Consulting
12072 87th Pl. N
Maple Grove, MN 55369
(612)493-3568
Fax: (612)493-5744
E-mail: markin@markinconsulting.com
Website: http://www.markin
consulting.com

**Minnesota Cooperation Office for
Small Business & Job Creation Inc.**
5001 W 80th St., Ste. 825
Minneapolis, MN 55437
(612)830-1230
Fax: (612)830-1232
E-mail: mncoop@msn.com
Website: http://www.mnco.org

Enterprise Consulting Inc.
PO Box 1111
Minnetonka, MN 55345
(612)949-5909
Fax: (612)906-3965

Amdahl International
724 1st Ave. SW
Rochester, MN 55902
(507)252-0402
Fax: (507)252-0402
E-mail: amdahl@best-service.com
Website: http://www.wp.com/amdahl_int

Power Systems Research
1365 Corporate Center Curve, 2nd Fl.
St. Paul, MN 55121
(612)905-8400
Free: (888)625-8612
Fax: (612)454-0760
E-mail: Barb@Powersys.com
Website: http://www.powersys.com

Missouri

**Business Planning and Development
Corp.**
4030 Charlotte St.
Kansas City, MO 64110
(816)753-0495

E-mail: humph@bpdev.demon.co.uk
Website: http://www.bpdev.demon.co.uk

CFO Service
10336 Donoho
St. Louis, MO 63131
(314)750-2940
E-mail: jskae@cfoservice.com
Website: http://www.cfoservice.com

Nebraska

**International Management Consulting
Group Inc.**
1309 Harlan Dr., Ste. 205
Bellevue, NE 68005
(402)291-4545
Free: 800-665-IMCG
Fax: (402)291-4343
E-mail: imcg@neonramp.com
Website: http://www.mgtcon
sulting.com

**Heartland Management Consulting
Group**
1904 Barrington Pky.
Papillion, NE 68046
(402)339-2387
Fax: (402)339-1319

Nevada

The DuBois Group
865 Tahoe Blvd., Ste. 108
Incline Village, NV 89451
(775)832-0550
Free: 800-375-2935
Fax: (775)832-0556
E-mail: DuBoisGrp@aol.com

New Hampshire

Wolff Consultants
10 Buck Rd.
Hanover, NH 03755
(603)643-6015

BPT Consulting Associates Ltd.
12 Parmenter Rd., Ste. B-6
Londonderry, NH 03053
(603)437-8484
Free: (888)278-0030
Fax: (603)434-5388
E-mail: bptcons@tiac.net
Website: http://www.bptconsulting.com

New Jersey

Bedminster Group Inc.
1170 Rte. 22 E
Bridgewater, NJ 08807

(908)500-4155
Fax: (908)766-0780
E-mail: info@bedminstergroup.com
Website: http://www.bedminster
group.com
Fax: (202)806-1777
Terry Strong, Acting Regional Dir.

Delta Planning Inc.
PO Box 425
Denville, NJ 07834
(913)625-1742
Free: 800-672-0762
Fax: (973)625-3531
E-mail: DeltaP@worldnet.att.net
Website: http://deltaplanning.com

Kumar Associates Inc.
1004 Cumbermeade Rd.
Fort Lee, NJ 07024
(201)224-9480
Fax: (201)585-2343
E-mail: mail@kumarassociates.com
Website: http://kumarassociates.com

John Hall & Company Inc.
PO Box 187
Glen Ridge, NJ 07028
(973)680-4449
Fax: (973)680-4581
E-mail: jhcompany@aol.com

Market Focus
PO Box 402
Maplewood, NJ 07040
(973)378-2470
Fax: (973)378-2470
E-mail: mcss66@marketfocus.com

Vanguard Communications Corp.
100 American Rd.
Morris Plains, NJ 07950
(973)605-8000
Fax: (973)605-8329
Website: http://www.vanguard.net/

ConMar International Ltd.
1901 US Hwy. 130
North Brunswick, NJ 08902
(732)940-8347
Fax: (732)274-1199

KLW New Products
156 Cedar Dr.
Old Tappan, NJ 07675
(201)358-1300
Fax: (201)664-2594
E-mail: lrlarsen@usa.net
Website: http://www.klwnew
products.com

PA Consulting Group
315A Enterprise Dr.
Plainsboro, NJ 08536
(609)936-8300
Fax: (609)936-8811
E-mail: info@paconsulting.com
Website: http://www.pa-consulting.com

Aurora Marketing Management Inc.
66 Witherspoon St., Ste. 600
Princeton, NJ 08542
(908)904-1125
Fax: (908)359-1108
E-mail: aurora2@voicenet.com
Website: http://www.auroramarketing.net

Smart Business Supersite
88 Orchard Rd., CN-5219
Princeton, NJ 08543
(908)321-1924
Fax: (908)321-5156
E-mail: irv@smartbiz.com
Website: http://www.smartbiz.com

Tracelin Associates
1171 Main St., Ste. 6K
Rahway, NJ 07065
(732)381-3288

Schkeeper Inc.
130-6 Bodman Pl.
Red Bank, NJ 07701
(732)219-1965
Fax: (732)530-3703

Henry Branch Associates
2502 Harmon Cove Twr.
Secaucus, NJ 07094
(201)866-2008
Fax: (201)601-0101
E-mail: hbranch161@home.com

Robert Gibbons & Company Inc.
46 Knoll Rd.
Tenafly, NJ 07670-1050
(201)871-3933
Fax: (201)871-2173
E-mail: crisisbob@aol.com

PMC Management Consultants Inc.
6 Thistle Ln.
Three Bridges, NJ 08887-0332
(908)788-1014
Free: 800-PMC-0250
Fax: (908)806-7287
E-mail: int@pmc-management.com
Website: http://www.pmc-management.com

R.W. Bankart & Associates
20 Valley Ave., Ste. D-2

Westwood, NJ 07675-3607
(201)664-7672

New Mexico

Vondle & Associates Inc.
4926 Calle de Tierra, NE
Albuquerque, NM 87111
(505)292-8961
Fax: (505)296-2790
E-mail: vondle@aol.com

InfoNewMexico
2207 Black Hills Rd., NE
Rio Rancho, NM 87124
(505)891-2462
Fax: (505)896-8971

New York

Powers Research and Training Institute
PO Box 78
Bayville, NY 11709
(516)628-2250
Fax: (516)628-2252
E-mail: powercocch@compuserve.com
Website: http://www.nancypowers.com

Consortium House
296 Wittenberg Rd.
Bearsville, NY 12409
(845)679-8867
Fax: (845)679-9248
E-mail: eugenegs@aol.com
Website: http://www.chpub.com

Progressive Finance Corp.
3549 Tiemann Ave.
Bronx, NY 10469
(718)405-9029
Free: 800-225-8381
Fax: (718)405-1170

Wave Hill Associates Inc.
2621 Palisade Ave., Ste. 15-C
Bronx, NY 10463
(718)549-7368
Fax: (718)601-9670
E-mail: pepper@compuserve.com

Management Insight
96 Arlington Rd.
Buffalo, NY 14221
(716)631-3319
Fax: (716)631-0203
E-mail: michalski@foodservice insight.com
Website: http://www.foodservice insight.com

Samani International Enterprises, Marions Panyaught Consultancy
2028 Parsons
Flushing, NY 11357-3436
(917)287-8087
Fax: 800-873-8939
E-mail: vjp2@biostrategist.com
Website: http://www.biostrategist.com

Marketing Resources Group
71-58 Austin St.
Forest Hills, NY 11375
(718)261-8882

Mangabay Business Plans & Development Subsidiary of Innis Asset Allocation
125-10 Queens Blvd., Ste. 2202
Kew Gardens, NY 11415
(905)527-1947
Fax: 509-472-1935
E-mail: mangabay@mangabay.com
Website: http://www.mangabay.com
Lee Toh, Managing Partner

ComputerEase Co.
1301 Monmouth Ave.
Lakewood, NY 08701
(212)406-9464
Fax: (914)277-5317
E-mail: crawfordc@juno.com

Boice Dunham Group
30 W 13th St.
New York, NY 10011
(212)924-2200
Fax: (212)924-1108

Elizabeth Capen
27 E 95th St.
New York, NY 10128
(212)427-7654
Fax: (212)876-3190

Haver Analytics
60 E 42nd St., Ste. 2424
New York, NY 10017
(212)986-9300
Fax: (212)986-5857
E-mail: data@haver.com
Website: http://www.haver.com

The Jordan, Edmiston Group Inc.
150 E 52nd Ave., 18th Fl.
New York, NY 10022
(212)754-0710
Fax: (212)754-0337

KPMG International
345 Park Ave.
New York, NY 10154-0102
(212)758-9700

Fax: (212)758-9819
Website: http://www.kpmg.com

Mahoney Cohen Consulting Corp.
111 W 40th St., 12th Fl.
New York, NY 10018
(212)490-8000
Fax: (212)790-5913

Management Practice Inc.
342 Madison Ave.
New York, NY 10173-1230
(212)867-7948
Fax: (212)972-5188
Website: http://www.mpiweb.com

Moseley Associates Inc.
342 Madison Ave., Ste. 1414
New York, NY 10016
(212)213-6673
Fax: (212)687-1520

Practice Development Counsel
60 Sutton Pl. S
New York, NY 10022
(212)593-1549
Fax: (212)980-7940
E-mail: pwhaserot@pdcounsel.com
Website: http://www.pdcounsel.com

Unique Value International Inc.
575 Madison Ave., 10th Fl.
New York, NY 10022-1304
(212)605-0590
Fax: (212)605-0589

The Van Tulleken Co.
126 E 56th St.
New York, NY 10022
(212)355-1390
Fax: (212)755-3061
E-mail: newyork@vantulleken.com

Vencon Management Inc.
301 W 53rd St.
New York, NY 10019
(212)581-8787
Fax: (212)397-4126
Website: http://www.venconinc.com

Werner International Inc.
55 E 52nd, 29th Fl.
New York, NY 10055
(212)909-1260
Fax: (212)909-1273
E-mail: richard.downing@rgh.com
Website: http://www.wernertex.com

Zimmerman Business Consulting Inc.
44 E 92nd St., Ste. 5-B
New York, NY 10128

(212)860-3107
Fax: (212)860-7730
E-mail: ljzzbci@aol.com
Website: http://www.zbcinc.com

Overton Financial
7 Allen Rd.
Peekskill, NY 10566
(914)737-4649
Fax: (914)737-4696

Stromberg Consulting
2500 Westchester Ave.
Purchase, NY 10577
(914)251-1515
Fax: (914)251-1562
E-mail: strategy@stromberg_consul
ting.com
Website: http://www.stromberg_
consulting.com

Innovation Management Consulting Inc.
209 Dewitt Rd.
Syracuse, NY 13214-2006
(315)425-5144
Fax: (315)445-8989
E-mail: missonneb@axess.net

M. Clifford Agress
891 Fulton St.
Valley Stream, NY 11580
(516)825-8955
Fax: (516)825-8955

Destiny Kinal Marketing Consultancy
105 Chemung St.
Waverly, NY 14892
(607)565-8317
Fax: (607)565-4083

Valutis Consulting Inc.
5350 Main St., Ste. 7
Williamsville, NY 14221-5338
(716)634-2553
Fax: (716)634-2554
E-mail: valutis@localnet.com
Website: http://www.valutisconsulting.com

North Carolina

Best Practices L.L.C.
6320 Quadrangle Dr., Ste. 200
Chapel Hill, NC 27514
(919)403-0251
Fax: (919)403-0144
E-mail: best@best:in/class
Website: http://www.best-in-class.com

Norelli & Co.
Bank of America Corporate Ctr.
100 N Tyron St., Ste. 5160

Charlotte, NC 28202-4000
(704)376-5484
Fax: (704)376-5485
E-mail: consult@norelli.com
Website: http://www.norelli.com

North Dakota

Center for Innovation
4300 Dartmouth Dr.
PO Box 8372
Grand Forks, ND 58202
(701)777-3132
Fax: (701)777-2339
E-mail: bruce@innovators.net
Website: http://www.innovators.net

Ohio

Transportation Technology Services
208 Harmon Rd.
Aurora, OH 44202
(330)562-3596

Empro Systems Inc.
4777 Red Bank Expy., Ste. 1
Cincinnati, OH 45227-1542
(513)271-2042
Fax: (513)271-2042

Alliance Management International Ltd.
1440 Windrow Ln.
Cleveland, OH 44147-3200
(440)838-1922
Fax: (440)838-0979
E-mail: bgruss@amiltd.com
Website: http://www.amiltd.com

Bozell Kamstra Public Relations
1301 E 9th St., Ste. 3400
Cleveland, OH 44114
(216)623-1511
Fax: (216)623-1501
E-mail: jfeniger@cleveland.bozellk
amstra.com
Website: http://www.bozellk
amstra.com

Cory Dillon Associates
111 Schreyer Pl. E
Columbus, OH 43214
(614)262-8211
Fax: (614)262-3806

Holcomb Gallagher Adams
300 Marconi, Ste. 303
Columbus, OH 43215
(614)221-3343
Fax: (614)221-3367
E-mail: riadams@acme.freenet.oh.us

Young & Associates
PO Box 711
Kent, OH 44240
(330)678-0524
Free: 800-525-9775
Fax: (330)678-6219
E-mail: online@younginc.com
Website: http://www.younginc.com

Robert A. Westman & Associates
8981 Inversary Dr. SE
Warren, OH 44484-2551
(330)856-4149
Fax: (330)856-2564

Oklahoma

Innovative Partners L.L.C.
4900 Richmond Sq., Ste. 100
Oklahoma City, OK 73118
(405)840-0033
Fax: (405)843-8359
E-mail: ipartners@juno.com

Oregon

**INTERCON - The International
Converting Institute**
5200 Badger Rd.
Crooked River Ranch, OR 97760
(541)548-1447
Fax: (541)548-1618
E-mail: johnbowler@
crookedriverranch.com

Talbott ARM
HC 60, Box 5620
Lakeview, OR 97630
(541)635-8587
Fax: (503)947-3482

Management Technology Associates Ltd.
2768 SW Sherwood Dr, Ste. 105
Portland, OR 97201-2251
(503)224-5220
Fax: (503)224-5334
E-mail: lcuster@mta-ltd.com
Website: http://www.mgmt-tech.com

Pennsylvania

Healthscope Inc.
400 Lancaster Ave.
Devon, PA 19333
(610)687-6199
Fax: (610)687-6376
E-mail: health@voicenet.com
Website: http://www.healthscope.net/

Elayne Howard & Associates Inc.
3501 Masons Mill Rd., Ste. 501

Huntingdon Valley, PA 19006-3509
(215)657-9550

GRA Inc.
115 West Ave., Ste. 201
Jenkintown, PA 19046
(215)884-7500
Fax: (215)884-1385
E-mail: gramail@gra-inc.com
Website: http://www.gra-inc.com

**Mifflin County Industrial Development
Corp.**
Mifflin County Industrial Plz.
6395 SR 103 N
Bldg. 50
Lewistown, PA 17044
(717)242-0393
Fax: (717)242-1842
E-mail: mcide@acsworld.net

Autech Products
1289 Revere Rd.
Morrisville, PA 19067
(215)493-3759
Fax: (215)493-9791
E-mail: autech4@yahoo.com

Advantage Associates
434 Avon Dr.
Pittsburgh, PA 15228
(412)343-1558
Fax: (412)362-1684
E-mail: ecocba1@aol.com

Regis J. Sheehan & Associates
Pittsburgh, PA 15220
(412)279-1207

James W. Davidson Company Inc.
23 Forest View Rd.
Wallingford, PA 19086
(610)566-1462

Puerto Rico

Diego Chevere & Co.
Metro Parque 7, Ste. 204
Metro Office
Caparra Heights, PR 00920
(787)774-9595
Fax: (787)774-9566
E-mail: dcco@coqui.net

Manuel L. Porrata and Associates
898 Munoz Rivera Ave., Ste. 201
San Juan, PR 00927
(787)765-2140
Fax: (787)754-3285
E-mail: m_porrata@manuelporrata.com
Website: http://manualporrata.com

South Carolina

Aquafood Business Associates
PO Box 13267
Charleston, SC 29422
(843)795-9506
Fax: (843)795-9477
E-mail: rraba@aol.com

Profit Associates Inc.
PO Box 38026
Charleston, SC 29414
(803)763-5718
Fax: (803)763-5719
E-mail: bobrog@awod.com
Website: http://www.awod.com/gallery/
business/proasc

Strategic Innovations International
12 Executive Ct.
Lake Wylie, SC 29710
(803)831-1225
Fax: (803)831-1177
E-mail: stratinnov@aol.com
Website: http://www.
strategicinnovations.com

Minus Stage
Box 4436
Rock Hill, SC 29731
(803)328-0705
Fax: (803)329-9948

Tennessee

Daniel Petchers & Associates
8820 Fernwood CV
Germantown, TN 38138
(901)755-9896

Business Choices
1114 Forest Harbor, Ste. 300
Hendersonville, TN 37075-9646
(615)822-8692
Free: 800-737-8382
Fax: (615)822-8692
E-mail: bz-ch@juno.com

**RCFA Healthcare Management
Services L.L.C.**
9648 Kingston Pke., Ste. 8
Knoxville, TN 37922
(865)531-0176
Free: 800-635-4040
Fax: (865)531-0722
E-mail: info@rcfa.com
Website: http://www.rcfa.com

Growth Consultants of America
3917 Trimble Rd.
Nashville, TN 37215

(615)383-0550
Fax: (615)269-8940
E-mail: 70244.451@compuserve.com

Texas

**Integrated Cost Management
Systems Inc.**
2261 Brookhollow Plz. Dr., Ste. 104
Arlington, TX 76006
(817)633-2873
Fax: (817)633-3781
E-mail: abm@icms.net
Website: http://www.icms.net

Lori Williams
1000 Leslie Ct.
Arlington, TX 76012
(817)459-3934
Fax: (817)459-3934

Business Resource Software Inc.
2013 Wells Branch Pky., Ste. 305
Austin, TX 78728
Free: 800-423-1228
Fax: (512)251-4401
E-mail: info@brs-inc.com
Website: http://www.brs-inc.com

Erisa Adminstrative Services Inc.
12325 Hymeadow Dr., Bldg. 4
Austin, TX 78750-1847
(512)250-9020
Fax: (512)250-9487
Website: http://www.cserisa.com

R. Miller Hicks & Co.
1011 W 11th St.
Austin, TX 78703
(512)477-7000
Fax: (512)477-9697
E-mail: millerhicks@rmhicks.com
Website: http://www.rmhicks.com

Pragmatic Tactics Inc.
3303 Westchester Ave.
College Station, TX 77845
(409)696-5294
Free: 800-570-5294
Fax: (409)696-4994
E-mail: ptactics@aol.com
Website: http://www.ptatics.com

Perot Systems
12404 Park Central Dr.
Dallas, TX 75251
(972)340-5000
Free: 800-688-4333
Fax: (972)455-4100
E-mail: corp.comm@ps.net
Website: http://www.perotsystems.com

ReGENERATION Partners
3838 Oak Lawn Ave.
Dallas, TX 75219
(214)559-3999
Free: 800-406-1112
E-mail: info@regeneration-partner.com
Website: http://www.regeneration-partners.com

**High Technology Associates - Division
of Global Technologies Inc.**
1775 St. James Pl., Ste. 105
Houston, TX 77056
(713)963-9300
Fax: (713)963-8341
E-mail: hta@infohwy.com

MasterCOM
103 Thunder Rd.
Kerrville, TX 78028
(830)895-7990
Fax: (830)443-3428
E-mail: jmstubblefield@master
training.com
Website: http://www.mastertraining.com

PROTEC
4607 Linden Pl.
Pearland, TX 77584
(281)997-9872
Fax: (281)997-9895
E-mail: p.oman@ix.netcom.com

Alpha Quadrant Inc.
10618 Auldine
San Antonio, TX 78230
(210)344-3330
Fax: (210)344-8151
E-mail: mbussone@sbcglobal.net
Website:http://www.a-quadrant.com
Michele Bussone

Bastian Public Relations
614 San Dizier
San Antonio, TX 78232
(210)404-1839
E-mail: lisa@bastianpr.com
Website: http://www.bastianpr.com
Lisa Bastian CBC

**Business Strategy Development
Consultants**
PO Box 690365
San Antonio, TX 78269
(210)696-8000
Free: 800-927-BSDC
Fax: (210)696-8000

Tom Welch, CPC
6900 San Pedro Ave., Ste. 147
San Antonio, TX 78216-6207

(210)737-7022
Fax: (210)737-7022
E-mail: bplan@iamerica.net
Website: http://www.moneywords.com

Utah

Business Management Resource
PO Box 521125
Salt Lake City, UT 84152-1125
(801)272-4668
Fax: (801)277-3290
E-mail: pingfong@worldnet.att.net

Virginia

Tindell Associates
209 Oxford Ave.
Alexandria, VA 22301
(703)683-0109
Fax: 703-783-0219
E-mail: scott@tindell.net
Website: http://www.tindell.net
Scott Lockett, President

Elliott B. Jaffa
2530-B S Walter Reed Dr.
Arlington, VA 22206
(703)931-0040
E-mail: thetrainingdoctor@excite.com
Website: http://www.tregistry.com/jaffa.htm

Koach Enterprises - USA
5529 N 18th St.
Arlington, VA 22205
(703)241-8361
Fax: (703)241-8623

Federal Market Development
5650 Chapel Run Ct.
Centreville, VA 20120-3601
(703)502-8930
Free: 800-821-5003
Fax: (703)502-8929

Huff, Stuart & Carlton
2107 Graves Mills Rd., Ste. C
Forest, VA 24551
(804)316-9356
Free: (888)316-9356
Fax: (804)316-9357
Website: http://www.wealthmgt.net

AMX International Inc.
1420 Spring Hill Rd. , Ste. 600
McLean, VA 22102-3006
(703)690-4100
Fax: (703)643-1279
E-mail: amxmail@amxi.com
Website: http://www.amxi.com

Charles Scott Pugh (Investor)
4101 Pittaway Dr.
Richmond, VA 23235-1022
(804)560-0979
Fax: (804)560-4670

John C. Randall and Associates Inc.
PO Box 15127
Richmond, VA 23227
(804)746-4450
Fax: (804)730-8933
E-mail: randalljcx@aol.com
Website: http://www.johncrandall.com

McLeod & Co.
410 1st St.
Roanoke, VA 24011
(540)342-6911
Fax: (540)344-6367
Website: http://www.mcleodco.com/

Salzinger & Company Inc.
8000 Towers Crescent Dr., Ste. 1350
Vienna, VA 22182
(703)442-5200
Fax: (703)442-5205
E-mail: info@salzinger.com
Website: http://www.salzinger.com

The Small Business Counselor
12423 Hedges Run Dr., Ste. 153
Woodbridge, VA 22192
(703)490-6755
Fax: (703)490-1356

Washington

Burlington Consultants
10900 NE 8th St., Ste. 900
Bellevue, WA 98004
(425)688-3060
Fax: (425)454-4383
E-mail: partners@burlington
consultants.com
Website: http://www.burlington
consultants.com

Perry L. Smith Consulting
800 Bellevue Way NE, Ste. 400
Bellevue, WA 98004-4208
(425)462-2072
Fax: (425)462-5638

St. Charles Consulting Group
1420 NW Gilman Blvd.
Issaquah, WA 98027
(425)557-8708
Fax: (425)557-8731
E-mail: info@stcharlesconsulting.com
Website: http://www.stcharlescon
sulting.com

Independent Automotive Training Services
PO Box 334
Kirkland, WA 98083
(425)822-5715
E-mail: ltunney@autosvccon.com
Website: http://www.autosvccon.com

Kahle Associate Inc.
6203 204th Dr. NE
Redmond, WA 98053
(425)836-8763
Fax: (425)868-3770
E-mail: randykahle@kahleassociates.com
Website: http://www.kahleassociates.com

Dan Collin
3419 Wallingord Ave N, No. 2
Seattle, WA 98103
(206)634-9469
E-mail: dc@dancollin.com
Website: http://members.home.net/
dcollin/

ECG Management Consultants Inc.
1111 3rd Ave., Ste. 2700
Seattle, WA 98101-3201
(206)689-2200
Fax: (206)689-2209
E-mail: ecg@ecgmc.com
Website: http://www.ecgmc.com

Northwest Trade Adjustment Assistance Center
900 4th Ave., Ste. 2430
Seattle, WA 98164-1001
(206)622-2730
Free: 800-667-8087
Fax: (206)622-1105
E-mail: matchingfunds@nwtaac.org
Website: http://www.taacenters.org

Business Planning Consultants
S 3510 Ridgeview Dr.
Spokane, WA 99206
(509)928-0332
Fax: (509)921-0842
E-mail: bpci@nextdim.com

West Virginia

**Stanley & Associates Inc./
BusinessandMarketingPlans.com**
1687 Robert C. Byrd Dr.
Beckley, WV 25801
(304)252-0324
Free: 888-752-6720
Fax: (304)252-0470
E-mail: cclay@charterinternet.com

Website: http://www.Businessand
MarketingPlans.com
Christopher Clay

Wisconsin

White & Associates Inc.
5349 Somerset Ln. S
Greenfield, WI 53221
(414)281-7373
Fax: (414)281-7006
E-mail: wnaconsult@aol.com

Small business administration regional offices

This section contains a listing of Small Business Administration offices arranged numerically by region. Service areas are provided. Contact the appropriate office for a referral to the nearest field office, or visit the Small Business Administration online at www.sba.gov.

Region 1

U.S. Small Business Administration
Region I Office
10 Causeway St., Ste. 812
Boston, MA 02222-1093
Phone: (617)565-8415
Fax: (617)565-8420
Serves Connecticut, Maine, Massachusetts, New Hampshire, Rhode Island, and Vermont.

Region 2

U.S. Small Business Administration
Region II Office
26 Federal Plaza, Ste. 3108
New York, NY 10278
Phone: (212)264-1450
Fax: (212)264-0038
Serves New Jersey, New York, Puerto Rico, and the Virgin Islands.

Region 3

U.S. Small Business Administration
Region III Office
Robert N C Nix Sr. Federal Building
900 Market St., 5th Fl.
Philadelphia, PA 19107
(215)580-2807
Serves Delaware, the District of Columbia, Maryland, Pennsylvania, Virginia, and West Virginia.

Region 4

U.S. Small Business Administration
Region IV Office
233 Peachtree St. NE
Harris Tower 1800
Atlanta, GA 30303
Phone: (404)331-4999
Fax: (404)331-2354
Serves Alabama, Florida, Georgia, Kentucky, Mississippi, North Carolina, South Carolina, and Tennessee.

Region 5

U.S. Small Business Administration
Region V Office
500 W. Madison St.
Citicorp Center, Ste. 1240
Chicago, IL 60661-2511
Phone: (312)353-0357
Fax: (312)353-3426
Serves Illinois, Indiana, Michigan, Minnesota, Ohio, and Wisconsin.

Region 6

U.S. Small Business Administration
Region VI Office
4300 Amon Carter Blvd., Ste. 108
Fort Worth, TX 76155
Phone: (817)684-5581
Fax: (817)684-5588
Serves Arkansas, Louisiana, New Mexico, Oklahoma, and Texas.

Region 7

U.S. Small Business Administration
Region VII Office
323 W. 8th St., Ste. 307
Kansas City, MO 64105-1500
Phone: (816)374-6380
Fax: (816)374-6339
Serves Iowa, Kansas, Missouri, and Nebraska.

Region 8

U.S. Small Business Administration
Region VIII Office
721 19th St., Ste. 400
Denver, CO 80202
Phone: (303)844-0500
Fax: (303)844-0506
Serves Colorado, Montana, North Dakota, South Dakota, Utah, and Wyoming.

Region 9

U.S. Small Business Administration
Region IX Office
330 N Brand Blvd., Ste. 1270
Glendale, CA 91203-2304
Phone: (818)552-3434
Fax: (818)552-3440
Serves American Samoa, Arizona, California, Guam, Hawaii, Nevada, and the Trust Territory of the Pacific Islands.

Region 10

U.S. Small Business Administration
Region X Office
2401 Fourth Ave., Ste. 400
Seattle, WA 98121
Phone: (206)553-5676
Fax: (206)553-4155
Serves Alaska, Idaho, Oregon, and Washington.

Small business development centers

This section contains a listing of all Small Business Development Centers, organized alphabetically by state/U.S. territory, then by city, then by agency name.

Alabama

Alabama SBDC
UNIVERSITY OF ALABAMA
2800 Milan Court Suite 124
Birmingham, AL 35211-6908
Phone: 205-943-6750
Fax: 205-943-6752
E-Mail: wcampbell@provost.uab.edu
Website: http://www.asbdc.org
Mr. William Campbell Jr, State Director

Alaska

Alaska SBDC
UNIVERSITY OF ALASKA - ANCHORAGE
430 West Seventh Avenue, Suite 110
Anchorage, AK 99501
Phone: 907-274 -7232
Fax: 907-274-9524
E-Mail: anerw@uaa.alaska.edu
Website: http://www.aksbdc.org
Ms. Jean R. Wall, State Director

American Samoa

American Samoa SBDC
AMERICAN SAMOA COMMUNITY COLLEGE
P.O. Box 2609
Pago Pago, American Samoa 96799
Phone: 011-684-699-4830
Fax: 011-684-699-6132
E-Mail: htalex@att.net
Mr. Herbert Thweatt, Director

Arizona

Arizona SBDC
MARICOPA COUNTY COMMUNITY COLLEGE
2411 West 14th Street, Suite 132
Tempe, AZ 85281
Phone: 480-731-8720
Fax: 480-731-8729
E-Mail: mike.york@domail.maricopa.edu
Website: http://www.dist.maricopa.edu.sbdc
Mr. Michael York, State Director

Arkansas

Arkansas SBDC
UNIVERSITY OF ARKANSAS
2801 South University Avenue
Little Rock, AR 72204
Phone: 501-324-9043
Fax: 501-324-9049
E-Mail: jmroderick@ualr.edu
Website: http://asbdc.ualr.edu
Ms. Janet M. Roderick, State Director

California

California - San Francisco SBDC
Northern California SBDC Lead Center
HUMBOLDT STATE UNIVERSITY
Office of Economic Development
1 Harpst Street 2006A, Siemens Hall
Arcata, CA, 95521
Phone: 707-826-3922
Fax: 707-826-3206
E-Mail: gainer@humboldt.edu
Ms. Margaret A. Gainer, Regional Director

California - Sacramento SBDC
CALIFORNIA STATE UNIVERSITY - CHICO
Chico, CA 95929-0765
Phone: 530-898-4598
Fax: 530-898-4734

E-Mail: dripke@csuchico.edu
Website: http://gsbdc.csuchico.edu
Mr. Dan Ripke, Interim Regional Director

California - San Diego SBDC
SOUTHWESTERN COMMUNITY COLLEGE DISTRICT
900 Otey Lakes Road
Chula Vista, CA 91910
Phone: 619-482-6388
Fax: 619-482-6402
E-Mail: dtrujillo@swc.cc.ca.us
Website: http://www.sbditc.org
Ms. Debbie P. Trujillo, Regional Director

California - Fresno SBDC
UC Merced Lead Center
UNIVERSITY OF CALIFORNIA - MERCED
550 East Shaw, Suite 105A
Fresno, CA 93710
Phone: 559-241-6590
Fax: 559-241-7422
E-Mail: crosander@ucmerced.edu
Website: http://sbdc.ucmerced.edu
Mr. Chris Rosander, State Director

California - Santa Ana SBDC
Tri-County Lead SBDC
CALIFORNIA STATE UNIVERSITY - FULLERTON
800 North State College Boulevard, LH640
Fullerton, CA 92834
Phone: 714-278-2719
Fax: 714-278-7858
E-Mail: vpham@fullerton.edu
Website: http://www.leadsbdc.org
Ms. Vi Pham, Lead Center Director

California - Los Angeles Region SBDC
LONG BEACH COMMUNITY COLLEGE DISTRICT
3950 Paramount Boulevard, Ste 101
Lakewood, CA 90712
Phone: 562-938-5004
Fax: 562-938-5030
E-Mail: ssloan@lbcc.edu
Ms. Sheneui Sloan, Interim Lead Center Director

Colorado

Colorado SBDC
OFFICE OF ECONOMIC DEVELOPMENT
1625 Broadway, Suite 170
Denver, CO 80202
Phone: 303-892-3864
Fax: 303-892-3848
E-Mail: Kelly.Manning@state.co.us

Website: http://www.state.co.us/oed/sbdc
Ms. Kelly Manning, State Director

Connecticut

Connecticut SBDC
UNIVERSITY OF CONNECTICUT
1376 Storrs Road, Unit 4094
Storrs, CT 06269-1094
Phone: 860-870-6370
Fax: 860-870-6374
E-Mail: richard.cheney@uconn.edu
Website: http://www.sbdc.uconn.edu
Mr. Richard Cheney, Interim State Director

Delaware

Delaware SBDC
DELAWARE TECHNOLOGY PARK
1 Innovation Way, Suite 301
Newark, DE 19711
Phone: 302-831-2747
Fax: 302-831-1423
E-Mail: Clinton.tymes@mvs.udel.edu
Website: http://www.delawaresbdc.org
Mr. Clinton Tymes, State Director

District of Columbia

District of Columbia SBDC
HOWARD UNIVERSITY
2600 6th Street, NW Room 128
Washington, DC 20059
Phone: 202-806-1550
Fax: 202-806-1777
E-Mail: hturner@howard.edu
Website: http://www.dcsbdc.com/
Mr. Henry Turner, Executive Director

Florida

Florida SBDC
UNIVERSITY OF WEST FLORIDA
401 East Chase Street, Suite 100
Pensacola, FL 32502
Phone: 850-473-7800
Fax: 850-473-7813
E-Mail: jcartwri@uwf.edu
Website: http://www.floridasbdc.com
Mr. Jerry Cartwright, State Director

Georgia

Georgia SBDC
UNIVERSITY OF GEORGIA
1180 East Broad Street
Athens, GA 30602
Phone: 706-542-6762
Fax: 706-542-6776
E-mail: aadams@sbdc.uga.edu

Website: http://www.sbdc.uga.edu
Mr. Allan Adams, Interim State Director

Guam

Guam Small Business Development Center
UNIVERSITY OF GUAM
Pacific Islands SBDC
P.O. Box 5014 - U.O.G. Station
Mangilao, GU 96923
Phone: 671-735-2590
Fax: 671-734-2002
E-mail: casey@pacificsbdc.com
Website: http://www.uog.edu/sbdc
Mr. Casey Jeszenka, Director

Hawaii

Hawaii SBDC
UNIVERSITY OF HAWAII - HILO
308 Kamehameha Avenue, Suite 201
Hilo, HI 96720
Phone: 808-974-7515
Fax: 808-974-7683
E-Mail: darrylm@interpac.net
Website: http://www.hawaii-sbdc.org
Mr. Darryl Mleynek, State Director

Idaho

Idaho SBDC
BOISE STATE UNIVERSITY
1910 University Drive
Boise, ID 83725
Phone: 208-426-3799
Fax: 208-426-3877
E-mail: jhogge@boisestate.edu
Website: http://www.idahosbdc.org
Mr. Jim Hogge, State Director

Illinois

Illinois SBDC
DEPARTMENT OF COMMERCE AND ECONOMIC OPPORTUNITY
620 E. Adams, S-4
Springfield, IL 62701
Phone: 217-524-5700
Fax: 217-524-0171
E-mail: mpatrilli@ildceo.net
Website: http://www.ilsbdc.biz
Mr. Mark Petrilli, State Director

Indiana

Indiana SBDC
INDIANA ECONOMIC DEVELOPMENT CORPORATION
One North Capitol, Suite 900
Indianapolis, IN 46204

Phone: 317-234-8872
Fax: 317-232-8874
E-mail: dtrocha@isbdc.org
Website: http://www.isbdc.org
Ms. Debbie Bishop Trocha, State Director

Iowa

Iowa SBDC
IOWA STATE UNIVERSITY
340 Gerdin Business Bldg.
Ames, IA 50011-1350
Phone: 515-294-2037
Fax: 515-294-6522
E-mail: jonryan@iastate.edu
Website: http://www.iabusnet.org
Mr. Jon Ryan, State Director

Kansas

Kansas SBDC
FORT HAYS STATE UNIVERSITY
214 SW Sixth Street, Suite 301
Topeka, KS 66603
Phone: 785-296-6514
Fax: 785-291-3261
E-mail: ksbdc.wkearns@fhsu.edu
Website: http://www.fhsu.edu/ksbdc
Mr. Wally Kearns, State Director

Kentucky

Kentucky SBDC
UNIVERSITY OF KENTUCKY
225 Gatton College of Business
Economics Building
Lexington, KY 40506-0034
Phone: 859-257-7668
Fax: 859-323-1907
E-mail: lrnaug0@pop.uky.edu
Website: http://www.ksbdc.org
Ms. Becky Naugle, State Director

Louisiana

Louisiana SBDC
UNIVERSITY OF LOUISIANA - MONROE
College of Business Administration
700 University Avenue
Monroe, LA 71209
Phone: 318-342-5506
Fax: 318-342-5510
E-mail: wilkerson@ulm.edu
Website: http://www.lsbdc.org
Ms. Mary Lynn Wilkerson, State Director

Maine

Maine SBDC
UNIVERSITY OF SOUTHERN MAINE
96 Falmouth Street P.O. Box 9300
Portland, ME 04103
Phone: 207-780-4420
Fax: 207-780-4810
E-mail: jrmassaua@maine.edu
Website: http://www.mainesbdc.org
Mr. John Massaua, State Director

Maryland

Maryland SBDC
UNIVERSITY OF MARYLAND
7100 Baltimore Avenue, Suite 401
College Park, MD 20742
Phone: 301-403-8300
Fax: 301-403-8303
E-mail: rsprow@mdsbdc.umd.edu
Website: http://www.mdsbdc.umd.edu
Ms. Renee Sprow, State Director

Massachusetts

Massachusetts SBDC
UNIVERSITY OF MASSACHUSETTS
School of Management, Room 205
Amherst, MA 01003-4935
Phone: 413-545-6301
Fax: 413-545-1273
E-mail: gep@msbdc.umass.edu
Website: http://msbdc.som.umass.edu
Ms. Georgianna Parkin, State Director

Michigan

Michigan SBTDC
GRAND VALLEY STATE UNIVERSITY
510 West Fulton Avenue
Grand Rapids, MI 49504
Phone: 616-331-7485
Fax: 616-331-7389
E-mail: lopuckic@gvsu.edu
Website: http://www.misbtdc.org
Ms. Carol Lopucki, State Director

Minnesota

Minnesota SBDC
MINNESOTA SMALL BUSINESS DEVELOPMENT CENTER
1st National Bank Building
332 Minnesota Street, Suite E200
St. Paul, MN 55101-1351
Phone: 651-297-5773
Fax: 651-296-5287

E-mail: michael.myhre@state.mn.us
Website: http://www.mnsbdc.com
Mr. Michael Myhre, State Director

Mississippi

Mississippi SBDC
UNIVERSITY OF MISSISSIPPI
B-19 Jeanette Phillips Drive
P.O. Box 1848
University, MS 38677
Phone: 662-915-5001
Fax: 662-915-5650
E-mail: wgurley@olemiss.edu
Website: http://www.olemiss.edu/depts/mssbdc
Mr. Doug Gurley, Jr., State Director

Missouri

Missouri SBDC
UNIVERSITY OF MISSOURI
1205 University Avenue, Suite 300
Columbia, MO 65211
Phone: 573-882-1348
Fax: 573-884-4297
E-mail: summersm@missouri.edu
Website: http://www.mo-sbdc.org/index.shtml
Mr. Max Summers, State Director

Montana

Montana SBDC
DEPARTMENT OF COMMERCE
301 South Park Avenue, Room 114 /
P.O. Box 200505
Helena, MT 59620
Phone: 406-841-2746
Fax: 406-444-1872
E-mail: adesch@state.mt.us
Website: http://commerce.state.mt.us/brd/BRD_SBDC.html
Ms. Ann Desch, State Director

Nebraska

Nebraska SBDC
UNIVERSITY OF NEBRASKA - OMAHA
60th & Dodge Street, CBA Room 407
Omaha, NE 68182
Phone: 402-554-2521
Fax: 402-554-3473
E-mail: rbernier@unomaha.edu
Website: http://nbdc.unomaha.edu
Mr. Robert Bernier, State Director

Nevada

Nevada SBDC
UNIVERSITY OF NEVADA - RENO
Reno College of Business
Administration, Room 411
Reno, NV 89557-0100
Phone: 775-784-1717
Fax: 775-784-4337
E-mail: males@unr.edu
Website: http://www.nsbdc.org
Mr. Sam Males, State Director

New Hampshire

New Hampshire SBDC
UNIVERSITY OF NEW HAMPSHIRE
108 McConnell Hall
Durham, NH 03824-3593
Phone: 603-862-4879
Fax: 603-862-4876
E-mail: Mary.Collins@unh.edu
Website: http://www.nhsbdc.org
Ms. Mary Collins, State Director

New Jersey

New Jersey SBDC
RUTGERS UNIVERSITY
49 Bleeker Street
Newark, NJ 07102-1993
Phone: 973-353-5950
Fax: 973-353-1110
E-mail: bhopper@njsbdc.com
Website: http://www.njsbdc.com/home
Ms. Brenda Hopper, State Director

New Mexico

New Mexico SBDC
SANTA FE COMMUNITY COLLEGE
6401 Richards Avenue
Santa Fe, NM 87505
Phone: 505-428-1362
Fax: 505-471-9469
E-mail: rmiller@santa-fe.cc.nm.us
Website: http://www.nmsbdc.org
Mr. Roy Miller, State Director

New York

New York SBDC
STATE UNIVERSITY OF NEW YORK
SUNY Plaza, S-523
Albany, NY 12246
Phone: 518-443-5398
Fax: 518-443-5275
E-mail: j.king@nyssbdc.org
Website: http://www.nyssbdc.org
Mr. Jim King, State Director

North Carolina

North Carolina SBDTC
UNIVERSITY OF NORTH CAROLINA
5 West Hargett Street, Suite 600
Raleigh, NC 27601
Phone: 919-715-7272
Fax: 919-715-7777
E-mail: sdaugherty@sbtdc.org
Website: http://www.sbtdc.org
Mr. Scott Daugherty, State Director

North Dakota

North Dakota SBDC
UNIVERSITY OF NORTH DAKOTA
1600 E. Century Avenue, Suite 2
Bismarck, ND 58503
Phone: 701-328-5375
Fax: 701-328-5320
E-mail: christine.martin@und.nodak.edu
Website: http://www.ndsbdc.org
Ms. Christine Martin-Goldman, State
Director

Ohio

Ohio SBDC
**OHIO DEPARTMENT
OF DEVELOPMENT**
77 South High Street
Columbus, OH 43216
Phone: 614-466-5102
Fax: 614-466-0829
E-mail: mabraham@odod.state.oh.us
Website: http://www.ohiosbdc.org
Ms. Michele Abraham, State Director

Oklahoma

Oklahoma SBDC
**SOUTHEAST OKLAHOMA STATE
UNIVERSITY**
517 University, Box 2584, Station A
Durant, OK 74701
Phone: 580-745-7577
Fax: 580-745-7471
E-mail: gpennington@sosu.edu
Website: http://www.osbdc.org
Mr. Grady Pennington, State Director

Oregon

Oregon SBDC
LANE COMMUNITY COLLEGE
99 West Tenth Avenue, Suite 390
Eugene, OR 97401-3021
Phone: 541-463-5250
Fax: 541-345-6006
E-mail: carterb@lanecc.edu

Website: http://www.bizcenter.org
Mr. William Carter, State Director

Pennsylvania

Pennsylvania SBDC
UNIVERSITY OF PENNSYLVANIA
The Wharton School
3733 Spruce Street
Philadelphia, PA 19104-6374
Phone: 215-898-1219
Fax: 215-573-2135
E-mail: ghiggins@wharton.upenn.edu
Website: http://pasbdc.org
Mr. Gregory Higgins, State Director

Puerto Rico

Puerto Rico SBDC
**INTER-AMERICAN UNIVERSITY
OF PUERTO RICO**
416 Ponce de Leon Avenue, Union Plaza,
Seventh Floor
Hato Rey, PR 00918
Phone: 787-763-6811
Fax: 787-763-4629
E-mail: cmarti@prsbdc.org
Website: http://www.prsbdc.org
Ms. Carmen Marti, Executive Director

Rhode Island

Rhode Island SBDC
BRYANT UNIVERSITY
1150 Douglas Pike
Smithfield, RI 02917
Phone: 401-232-6923
Fax: 401-232-6933
E-mail: adawson@bryant.edu
Website: http://www.risbdc.org
Ms. Diane Fournaris, Interim State Director

South Carolina

South Carolina SBDC
UNIVERSITY OF SOUTH CAROLINA
College of Business Administration
1710 College Street
Columbia, SC 29208
Phone: 803-777-4907
Fax: 803-777-4403
E-mail: lenti@moore.sc.edu
Website: http://scsbdc.moore.sc.edu
Mr. John Lenti, State Director

South Dakota

South Dakota SBDC
UNIVERSITY OF SOUTH DAKOTA
414 East Clark Street, Patterson Hall
Vermillion, SD 57069

Phone: 605-677-6256
Fax: 605-677-5427
E-mail: jshemmin@usd.edu
Website: http://www.sdsbdc.org
Mr. John S. Hemmingstad, State
Director

Tennessee

Tennessee SBDC
TENNESSEE BOARD OF REGENTS
1415 Murfressboro Road, Suite 540
Nashville, TN 37217-2833
Phone: 615-898-2745
Fax: 615-893-7089
E-mail: pgeho@mail.tsbdc.org
Website: http://www.tsbdc.org
Mr. Patrick Geho, State Director

Texas

Texas-North SBDC
**DALLAS COUNTY COMMUNITY
COLLEGE**
1402 Corinth Street
Dallas, TX 75215
Phone: 214-860-5835
Fax: 214-860-5813
E-mail: emk9402@dcccd.edu
Website: http://www.ntsbdc.org
Ms. Liz Klimback, Region Director

Texas-Houston SBDC
UNIVERSITY OF HOUSTON
2302 Fannin, Suite 200
Houston, TX 77002
Phone: 713-752-8425
Fax: 713-756-1500
E-mail: fyoung@uh.edu
Website: http://sbdcnetwork.uh.edu
Mr. Mike Young, Executive Director

Texas-NW SBDC
TEXAS TECH UNIVERSITY
2579 South Loop 289, Suite 114
Lubbock, TX 79423
Phone: 806-745-3973
Fax: 806-745-6207
E-mail: c.bean@nwtsbdc.org
Website: http://www.nwtsbdc.org
Mr. Craig Bean, Executive Director

**Texas-South-West Texas Border
Region SBDC**
**UNIVERSITY OF TEXAS -
SAN ANTONIO**
501 West Durango Boulevard
San Antonio, TX 78207-4415
Phone: 210-458-2742
Fax: 210-458-2464

E-mail: albert.salgado@utsa.edu
Website: http://www.iedtexas.org
Mr. Alberto Salgado, Region Director

Utah

Utah SBDC
SALT LAKE COMMUNITY COLLEGE
9750 South 300 West
Sandy, UT 84070
Phone: 801-957-3493
Fax: 801-957-3488
E-mail: Greg.Panichello@slcc.edu
Website:http://www.slcc.edu/sbdc
Mr. Greg Panichello, State Director

Vermont

Vermont SBDC
VERMONT TECHNICAL COLLEGE
PO Box 188, 1 Main Street
Randolph Center, VT 05061-0188
Phone: 802-728-9101
Fax: 802-728-3026
E-mail: lquillen@vtc.edu
Website: http://www.vtsbdc.org
Ms. Lenae Quillen-Blume, State Director

Virgin Islands

Virgin Islands SBDC
**UNIVERSITY OF THE VIRGIN
ISLANDS**
8000 Nisky Center, Suite 720
St. Thomas, VI 00802-5804
Phone: 340-776-3206
Fax: 340-775-3756
E-mail: wbush@webmail.uvi.edu
Website: http://rps.uvi.edu/SBDC
Mr. Warren Bush, State Director

Virginia

Virginia SBDC
GEORGE MASON UNIVERSITY
4031 University Drive, Suite 200
Fairfax, VA 22030-3409
Phone: 703-277-7727
Fax: 703-352-8515
E-mail: jkeenan@gmu.edu
Website: http://www.virginiasbdc.org
Ms. Jody Keenan, Director

Washington

Washington SBDC
WASHINGTON STATE UNIVERSITY
534 E. Trent Avenue
P.O. Box 1495
Spokane, WA 99210-1495

Phone: 509-358-7765
Fax: 509-358-7764
E-mail: barogers@wsu.edu
Website: http://www.wsbdc.org
Mr. Brett Rogers, State Director

West Virginia

West Virginia SBDC
**WEST VIRGINIA DEVELOPMENT
OFFICE**
Capital Complex, Building 6, Room 652
Charleston, WV 25301
Phone: 304-558-2960
Fax: 304-558-0127
E-mail: csalyer@wvsbdc.org
Website: http://www.wvsbdc.org
Mr. Conley Salyor, State Director

Wisconsin

Wisconsin SBDC
UNIVERSITY OF WISCONSIN
432 North Lake Street, Room 423
Madison, WI 53706
Phone: 608-263-7794
Fax: 608-263-7830
E-mail: erica.kauten@uwex.edu
Website: http://www.wisconsinsbdc.org
Ms. Erica Kauten, State Director

Wyoming

Wyoming SBDC
UNIVERSITY OF WYOMING
P.O. Box 3922
Laramie, WY 82071-3922
Phone: 307-766-3505
Fax: 307-766-3406
E-mail: DDW@uwyo.edu
Website: http://www.uwyo.edu/sbdc
Ms. Debbie Popp, Acting State Director

Service corps of retired executives (score) offices

*This section contains a listing of all
SCORE offices organized alphabetically by
state/U.S. territory, then by city, then by
agency name.*

Alabama

SCORE Office (Northeast Alabama)
1330 Quintard Ave.
Anniston, AL 36202
(256)237-3536

SCORE Office (North Alabama)
901 South 15th St, Rm. 201
Birmingham, AL 35294-2060
(205)934-6868
Fax: (205)934-0538

SCORE Office (Baldwin County)
29750 Larry Dee Cawyer Dr.
Daphne, AL 36526
(334)928-5838

SCORE Office (Shoals)
612 S. COurt
Florence, AL 35630
(256)764-4661
Fax: (256)766-9017
E-mail: shoals@shoalschamber.com

SCORE Office (Mobile)
600 S Court St.
Mobile, AL 36104
(334)240-6868
Fax: (334)240-6869

SCORE Office (Alabama Capitol City)
600 S. Court St.
Montgomery, AL 36104
(334)240-6868
Fax: (334)240-6869

SCORE Office (East Alabama)
601 Ave. A
Opelika, AL 36801
(334)745-4861
E-mail: score636@hotmail.com
Website: http://www.angelfire.com/sc/
score636/

SCORE Office (Tuscaloosa)
2200 University Blvd.
Tuscaloosa, AL 35402
(205)758-7588

Alaska

SCORE Office (Anchorage)
510 L St., Ste. 310
Anchorage, AK 99501
(907)271-4022
Fax: (907)271-4545

Arizona

SCORE Office (Lake Havasu)
10 S. Acoma Blvd.
Lake Havasu City, AZ 86403
(520)453-5951
E-mail: SCORE@ctaz.com
Website: http://www.scorearizona.org/
lake_havasu/

SCORE Office (East Valley)
Federal Bldg., Rm. 104
26 N. MacDonald St.
Mesa, AZ 85201
(602)379-3100
Fax: (602)379-3143
E-mail: 402@aol.com
Website: http://www.scorearizona.
org/mesa/

SCORE Office (Phoenix)
2828 N. Central Ave., Ste. 800
Central & One Thomas
Phoenix, AZ 85004
(602)640-2329
Fax: (602)640-2360
E-mail: e-mail@SCORE-phoenix.org
Website: http://www.score-phoenix.org/

SCORE Office (Prescott Arizona)
1228 Willow Creek Rd., Ste. 2
Prescott, AZ 86301
(520)778-7438
Fax: (520)778-0812
E-mail: score@northlink.com
Website: http://www.scorearizona.org/
prescott/

SCORE Office (Tucson)
110 E. Pennington St.
Tucson, AZ 85702
(520)670-5008
Fax: (520)670-5011
E-mail: score@azstarnet.com
Website: http://www.scorearizona.org/
tucson/

SCORE Office (Yuma)
281 W. 24th St., Ste. 116
Yuma, AZ 85364
(520)314-0480
E-mail: score@C2i2.com
Website: http://www.scorearizona.org/
yuma

Arkansas

SCORE Office (South Central)
201 N. Jackson Ave.
El Dorado, AR 71730-5803
(870)863-6113
Fax: (870)863-6115

SCORE Office (Ozark)
Fayetteville, AR 72701
(501)442-7619

SCORE Office (Northwest Arkansas)
Glenn Haven Dr., No. 4
Ft. Smith, AR 72901
(501)783-3556

SCORE Office (Garland County)
Grand & Ouachita
PO Box 6012
Hot Springs Village, AR 71902
(501)321-1700

SCORE Office (Little Rock)
2120 Riverfront Dr., Rm. 100
Little Rock, AR 72202-1747
(501)324-5893
Fax: (501)324-5199

SCORE Office (Southeast Arkansas)
121 W. 6th
Pine Bluff, AR 71601
(870)535-7189
Fax: (870)535-1643

California

SCORE Office (Golden Empire)
1706 Chester Ave., No. 200
Bakersfield, CA 93301
(805)322-5881
Fax: (805)322-5663

SCORE Office (Greater Chico Area)
1324 Mangrove St., Ste. 114
Chico, CA 95926
(916)342-8932
Fax: (916)342-8932

SCORE Office (Concord)
2151-A Salvio St., Ste. B
Concord, CA 94520
(510)685-1181
Fax: (510)685-5623

SCORE Office (Covina)
935 W. Badillo St.
Covina, CA 91723
(818)967-4191
Fax: (818)966-9660

SCORE Office (Rancho Cucamonga)
8280 Utica, Ste. 160
Cucamonga, CA 91730
(909)987-1012
Fax: (909)987-5917

SCORE Office (Culver City)
PO Box 707
Culver City, CA 90232-0707
(310)287-3850
Fax: (310)287-1350

SCORE Office (Danville)
380 Diablo Rd., Ste. 103
Danville, CA 94526
(510)837-4400

SCORE Office (Downey)
11131 Brookshire Ave.
Downey, CA 90241
(310)923-2191
Fax: (310)864-0461

SCORE Office (El Cajon)
109 Rea Ave.
El Cajon, CA 92020
(619)444-1327
Fax: (619)440-6164

SCORE Office (El Centro)
1100 Main St.
El Centro, CA 92243
(619)352-3681
Fax: (619)352-3246

SCORE Office (Escondido)
720 N. Broadway
Escondido, CA 92025
(619)745-2125
Fax: (619)745-1183

SCORE Office (Fairfield)
1111 Webster St.
Fairfield, CA 94533
(707)425-4625
Fax: (707)425-0826

SCORE Office (Fontana)
17009 Valley Blvd., Ste. B
Fontana, CA 92335
(909)822-4433
Fax: (909)822-6238

SCORE Office (Foster City)
1125 E. Hillsdale Blvd.
Foster City, CA 94404
(415)573-7600
Fax: (415)573-5201

SCORE Office (Fremont)
2201 Walnut Ave., Ste. 110
Fremont, CA 94538
(510)795-2244
Fax: (510)795-2240

SCORE Office (Central California)
2719 N. Air Fresno Dr., Ste. 200
Fresno, CA 93727-1547
(559)487-5605
Fax: (559)487-5636

SCORE Office (Gardena)
1204 W. Gardena Blvd.
Gardena, CA 90247
(310)532-9905
Fax: (310)515-4893

SCORE Office (Lompoc)
330 N. Brand Blvd., Ste. 190
Glendale, CA 91203-2304

(818)552-3206
Fax: (818)552-3323

SCORE Office (Los Angeles)
330 N. Brand Blvd., Ste. 190
Glendale, CA 91203-2304
(818)552-3206
Fax: (818)552-3323

SCORE Office (Glendora)
131 E. Foothill Blvd.
Glendora, CA 91740
(818)963-4128
Fax: (818)914-4822

SCORE Office (Grover Beach)
177 S. 8th St.
Grover Beach, CA 93433
(805)489-9091
Fax: (805)489-9091

SCORE Office (Hawthorne)
12477 Hawthorne Blvd.
Hawthorne, CA 90250
(310)676-1163
Fax: (310)676-7661

SCORE Office (Hayward)
22300 Foothill Blvd., Ste. 303
Hayward, CA 94541
(510)537-2424

SCORE Office (Hemet)
1700 E. Florida Ave.
Hemet, CA 92544-4679
(909)652-4390
Fax: (909)929-8543

SCORE Office (Hesperia)
16367 Main St.
PO Box 403656
Hesperia, CA 92340
(619)244-2135

SCORE Office (Holloster)
321 San Felipe Rd., No. 11
Hollister, CA 95023

SCORE Office (Hollywood)
7018 Hollywood Blvd.
Hollywood, CA 90028
(213)469-8311
Fax: (213)469-2805

SCORE Office (Indio)
82503 Hwy. 111
PO Drawer TTT
Indio, CA 92202
(619)347-0676

SCORE Office (Inglewood)
330 Queen St.

Inglewood, CA 90301
(818)552-3206

SCORE Office (La Puente)
218 N. Grendanda St. D.
La Puente, CA 91744
(818)330-3216
Fax: (818)330-9524

SCORE Office (La Verne)
2078 Bonita Ave.
La Verne, CA 91750
(909)593-5265
Fax: (714)929-8475

SCORE Office (Lake Elsinore)
132 W. Graham Ave.
Lake Elsinore, CA 92530
(909)674-2577

SCORE Office (Lakeport)
PO Box 295
Lakeport, CA 95453
(707)263-5092

SCORE Office (Lakewood)
5445 E. Del Amo Blvd., Ste. 2
Lakewood, CA 90714
(213)920-7737

SCORE Office (Long Beach)
1 World Trade Center
Long Beach, CA 90831

SCORE Office (Los Alamitos)
901 W. Civic Center Dr., Ste. 160
Los Alamitos, CA 90720

SCORE Office (Los Altos)
321 University Ave.
Los Altos, CA 94022
(415)948-1455

SCORE Office (Manhattan Beach)
PO Box 3007
Manhattan Beach, CA 90266
(310)545-5313
Fax: (310)545-7203

SCORE Office (Merced)
1632 N. St.
Merced, CA 95340
(209)725-3800
Fax: (209)383-4959

SCORE Office (Milpitas)
75 S. Milpitas Blvd., Ste. 205
Milpitas, CA 95035
(408)262-2613
Fax: (408)262-2823

SCORE Office (Yosemite)
1012 11th St., Ste. 300
Modesto, CA 95354
(209)521-9333

SCORE Office (Montclair)
5220 Benito Ave.
Montclair, CA 91763

SCORE Office (Monterey Bay)
380 Alvarado St.
PO Box 1770
Monterey, CA 93940-1770
(408)649-1770

SCORE Office (Moreno Valley)
25480 Alessandro
Moreno Valley, CA 92553

SCORE Office (Morgan Hill)
25 W. 1st St.
PO Box 786
Morgan Hill, CA 95038
(408)779-9444
Fax: (408)778-1786

SCORE Office (Morro Bay)
880 Main St.
Morro Bay, CA 93442
(805)772-4467

SCORE Office (Mountain View)
580 Castro St.
Mountain View, CA 94041
(415)968-8378
Fax: (415)968-5668

SCORE Office (Napa)
1556 1st St.
Napa, CA 94559
(707)226-7455
Fax: (707)226-1171

SCORE Office (North Hollywood)
5019 Lankershim Blvd.
North Hollywood, CA 91601
(818)552-3206

SCORE Office (Northridge)
8801 Reseda Blvd.
Northridge, CA 91324
(818)349-5676

SCORE Office (Novato)
807 De Long Ave.
Novato, CA 94945
(415)897-1164
Fax: (415)898-9097

SCORE Office (East Bay)
519 17th St.
Oakland, CA 94612

(510)273-6611
Fax: (510)273-6015
E-mail: webmaster@eastbayscore.org
Website: http://www.eastbayscore.org

SCORE Office (Oceanside)
928 N. Coast Hwy.
Oceanside, CA 92054
(619)722-1534

SCORE Office (Ontario)
121 West B. St.
Ontario, CA 91762
Fax: (714)984-6439

SCORE Office (Oxnard)
PO Box 867
Oxnard, CA 93032
(805)385-8860
Fax: (805)487-1763

SCORE Office (Pacifica)
450 Dundee Way, Ste. 2
Pacifica, CA 94044
(415)355-4122

SCORE Office (Palm Desert)
72990 Hwy. 111
Palm Desert, CA 92260
(619)346-6111
Fax: (619)346-3463

SCORE Office (Palm Springs)
650 E. Tahquitz Canyon Way Ste. D
Palm Springs, CA 92262-6706
(760)320-6682
Fax: (760)323-9426

SCORE Office (Lakeside)
2150 Low Tree
Palmdale, CA 93551
(805)948-4518
Fax: (805)949-1212

SCORE Office (Palo Alto)
325 Forest Ave.
Palo Alto, CA 94301
(415)324-3121
Fax: (415)324-1215

SCORE Office (Pasadena)
117 E. Colorado Blvd., Ste. 100
Pasadena, CA 91105
(818)795-3355
Fax: (818)795-5663

SCORE Office (Paso Robles)
1225 Park St.
Paso Robles, CA 93446-2234
(805)238-0506
Fax: (805)238-0527

SCORE Office (Petaluma)
799 Baywood Dr., Ste. 3
Petaluma, CA 94954
(707)762-2785
Fax: (707)762-4721

SCORE Office (Pico Rivera)
9122 E. Washington Blvd.
Pico Rivera, CA 90660

SCORE Office (Pittsburg)
2700 E. Leland Rd.
Pittsburg, CA 94565
(510)439-2181
Fax: (510)427-1599

SCORE Office (Pleasanton)
777 Peters Ave.
Pleasanton, CA 94566
(510)846-9697

SCORE Office (Monterey Park)
485 N. Garey
Pomona, CA 91769

SCORE Office (Pomona)
485 N. Garey Ave.
Pomona, CA 91766
(909)622-1256

SCORE Office (Antelope Valley)
4511 West Ave. M-4
Quartz Hill, CA 93536
(805)272-0087
E-mail: avscore@ptw.com
Website: http://www.score.av.org/

SCORE Office (Shasta)
737 Auditorium Dr.
Redding, CA 96099
(916)225-2770

SCORE Office (Redwood City)
1675 Broadway
Redwood City, CA 94063
(415)364-1722
Fax: (415)364-1729

SCORE Office (Richmond)
3925 MacDonald Ave.
Richmond, CA 94805

SCORE Office (Ridgecrest)
PO Box 771
Ridgecrest, CA 93555
(619)375-8331
Fax: (619)375-0365

SCORE Office (Riverside)
3685 Main St., Ste. 350
Riverside, CA 92501
(909)683-7100

SCORE Office (Sacramento)
9845 Horn Rd., 260-B
Sacramento, CA 95827
(916)361-2322
Fax: (916)361-2164
E-mail: sacchapter@directcon.net

SCORE Office (Salinas)
PO Box 1170
Salinas, CA 93902
(408)424-7611
Fax: (408)424-8639

SCORE Office (Inland Empire)
777 E. Rialto Ave.
Purchasing
San Bernardino, CA 92415-0760
(909)386-8278

SCORE Office (San Carlos)
San Carlos Chamber of Commerce
PO Box 1086
San Carlos, CA 94070
(415)593-1068
Fax: (415)593-9108

SCORE Office (Encinitas)
550 W. C St., Ste. 550
San Diego, CA 92101-3540
(619)557-7272
Fax: (619)557-5894

SCORE Office (San Diego)
550 West C. St., Ste. 550
San Diego, CA 92101-3540
(619)557-7272
Fax: (619)557-5894
Website: http://www.score-sandiego.org

SCORE Office (Menlo Park)
1100 Merrill St.
San Francisco, CA 94105
(415)325-2818
Fax: (415)325-0920

SCORE Office (San Francisco)
455 Market St., 6th Fl.
San Francisco, CA 94105
(415)744-6827
Fax: (415)744-6750
E-mail: sfscore@sfscore.
Website: http://www.sfscore.com

SCORE Office (San Gabriel)
401 W. Las Tunas Dr.
San Gabriel, CA 91776
(818)576-2525
Fax: (818)289-2901

SCORE Office (San Jose)
Deanza College
208 S. 1st. St., Ste. 137
San Jose, CA 95113
(408)288-8479
Fax: (408)535-5541

SCORE Office (Silicon Valley)
84 W. Santa Clara St., Ste. 100
San Jose, CA 95113
(408)288-8479
Fax: (408)535-5541
E-mail: info@svscore.org
Website: http://www.svscore.org

SCORE Office (San Luis Obispo)
3566 S. Hiquera, No. 104
San Luis Obispo, CA 93401
(805)547-0779

SCORE Office (San Mateo)
1021 S. El Camino, 2nd Fl.
San Mateo, CA 94402
(415)341-5679

SCORE Office (San Pedro)
390 W. 7th St.
San Pedro, CA 90731
(310)832-7272

SCORE Office (Orange County)
200 W. Santa Anna Blvd., Ste. 700
Santa Ana, CA 92701
(714)550-7369
Fax: (714)550-0191
Website: http://www.score114.org

SCORE Office (Santa Barbara)
3227 State St.
Santa Barbara, CA 93130
(805)563-0084

SCORE Office (Central Coast)
509 W. Morrison Ave.
Santa Maria, CA 93454
(805)347-7755

SCORE Office (Santa Maria)
614 S. Broadway
Santa Maria, CA 93454-5111
(805)925-2403
Fax: (805)928-7559

SCORE Office (Santa Monica)
501 Colorado, Ste. 150
Santa Monica, CA 90401
(310)393-9825
Fax: (310)394-1868

SCORE Office (Santa Rosa)
777 Sonoma Ave., Rm. 115E
Santa Rosa, CA 95404

(707)571-8342
Fax: (707)541-0331
Website: http://www.pressdemo.com/community/score/score.html

SCORE Office (Scotts Valley)
4 Camp Evers Ln.
Scotts Valley, CA 95066
(408)438-1010
Fax: (408)438-6544

SCORE Office (Simi Valley)
40 W. Cochran St., Ste. 100
Simi Valley, CA 93065
(805)526-3900
Fax: (805)526-6234

SCORE Office (Sonoma)
453 1st St. E
Sonoma, CA 95476
(707)996-1033

SCORE Office (Los Banos)
222 S. Shepard St.
Sonora, CA 95370
(209)532-4212

SCORE Office (Tuolumne County)
39 North Washington St.
Sonora, CA 95370
(209)588-0128
E-mail: score@mlode.com

SCORE Office (South San Francisco)
445 Market St., Ste. 6th Fl.
South San Francisco, CA 94105
(415)744-6827
Fax: (415)744-6812

SCORE Office (Stockton)
401 N. San Joaquin St., Rm. 215
Stockton, CA 95202
(209)946-6293

SCORE Office (Taft)
314 4th St.
Taft, CA 93268
(805)765-2165
Fax: (805)765-6639

SCORE Office (Conejo Valley)
625 W. Hillcrest Dr.
Thousand Oaks, CA 91360
(805)499-1993
Fax: (805)498-7264

SCORE Office (Torrance)
3400 Torrance Blvd., Ste. 100
Torrance, CA 90503
(310)540-5858
Fax: (310)540-7662

SCORE Office (Truckee)
PO Box 2757
Truckee, CA 96160
(916)587-2757
Fax: (916)587-2439

SCORE Office (Visalia)
113 S. M St,
Tulare, CA 93274
(209)627-0766
Fax: (209)627-8149

SCORE Office (Upland)
433 N. 2nd Ave.
Upland, CA 91786
(909)931-4108

SCORE Office (Vallejo)
2 Florida St.
Vallejo, CA 94590
(707)644-5551
Fax: (707)644-5590

SCORE Office (Van Nuys)
14540 Victory Blvd.
Van Nuys, CA 91411
(818)989-0300
Fax: (818)989-3836

SCORE Office (Ventura)
5700 Ralston St., Ste. 310
Ventura, CA 93001
(805)658-2688
Fax: (805)658-2252
E-mail: scoreven@jps.net
Website: http://www.jps.net/scoreven

SCORE Office (Vista)
201 E. Washington St.
Vista, CA 92084
(619)726-1122
Fax: (619)226-8654

SCORE Office (Watsonville)
PO Box 1748
Watsonville, CA 95077
(408)724-3849
Fax: (408)728-5300

SCORE Office (West Covina)
811 S. Sunset Ave.
West Covina, CA 91790
(818)338-8496
Fax: (818)960-0511

SCORE Office (Westlake)
30893 Thousand Oaks Blvd.
Westlake Village, CA 91362
(805)496-5630
Fax: (818)991-1754

Colorado

SCORE Office (Colorado Springs)
2 N. Cascade Ave., Ste. 110
Colorado Springs, CO 80903
(719)636-3074
Website: http://www.cscc.org/score02/index.html

SCORE Office (Denver)
US Custom's House, 4th Fl.
721 19th St.
Denver, CO 80201-0660
(303)844-3985
Fax: (303)844-6490
E-mail: score62@csn.net
Website: http://www.sni.net/score62

SCORE Office (Tri-River)
1102 Grand Ave.
Glenwood Springs, CO 81601
(970)945-6589

SCORE Office (Grand Junction)
2591 B & 3/4 Rd.
Grand Junction, CO 81503
(970)243-5242

SCORE Office (Gunnison)
608 N. 11th
Gunnison, CO 81230
(303)641-4422

SCORE Office (Montrose)
1214 Peppertree Dr.
Montrose, CO 81401
(970)249-6080

SCORE Office (Pagosa Springs)
PO Box 4381
Pagosa Springs, CO 81157
(970)731-4890

SCORE Office (Rifle)
0854 W. Battlement Pky., Apt. C106
Parachute, CO 81635
(970)285-9390

SCORE Office (Pueblo)
302 N. Santa Fe
Pueblo, CO 81003
(719)542-1704
Fax: (719)542-1624
E-mail: mackey@iex.net
Website: http://www.pueblo.org/score

SCORE Office (Ridgway)
143 Poplar Pl.
Ridgway, CO 81432

SCORE Office (Silverton)
PO Box 480

Silverton, CO 81433
(303)387-5430

SCORE Office (Minturn)
PO Box 2066
Vail, CO 81658
(970)476-1224

Connecticut

SCORE Office (Greater Bridgeport)
230 Park Ave.
Bridgeport, CT 06601-0999
(203)576-4369
Fax: (203)576-4388

SCORE Office (Bristol)
10 Main St. 1st. Fl.
Bristol, CT 06010
(203)584-4718
Fax: (203)584-4722

SCORE office (Greater Danbury)
246 Federal Rd.
Unit LL2, Ste. 7
Brookfield, CT 06804
(203)775-1151

SCORE Office (Greater Danbury)
246 Federal Rd., Unit LL2, Ste. 7
Brookfield, CT 06804
(203)775-1151

SCORE Office (Eastern Connecticut)
Administration Bldg., Rm. 313
PO 625
61 Main St. (Chapter 579)
Groton, CT 06475
(203)388-9508

SCORE Office (Greater Hartford County)
330 Main St.
Hartford, CT 06106
(860)548-1749
Fax: (860)240-4659
Website: http://www.score56.org

SCORE Office (Manchester)
20 Hartford Rd.
Manchester, CT 06040
(203)646-2223
Fax: (203)646-5871

SCORE Office (New Britain)
185 Main St., Ste. 431
New Britain, CT 06051
(203)827-4492
Fax: (203)827-4480

SCORE Office (New Haven)
25 Science Pk., Bldg. 25, Rm. 366

New Haven, CT 06511
(203)865-7645

SCORE Office (Fairfield County)
24 Beldon Ave., 5th Fl.
Norwalk, CT 06850
(203)847-7348
Fax: (203)849-9308

SCORE Office (Old Saybrook)
146 Main St.
Old Saybrook, CT 06475
(860)388-9508

SCORE Office (Simsbury)
Box 244
Simsbury, CT 06070
(203)651-7307
Fax: (203)651-1933

SCORE Office (Torrington)
23 North Rd.
Torrington, CT 06791
(203)482-6586

Delaware

SCORE Office (Dover)
Treadway Towers
PO Box 576
Dover, DE 19903
(302)678-0892
Fax: (302)678-0189

SCORE Office (Lewes)
PO Box 1
Lewes, DE 19958
(302)645-8073
Fax: (302)645-8412

SCORE Office (Milford)
204 NE Front St.
Milford, DE 19963
(302)422-3301

SCORE Office (Wilmington)
824 Market St., Ste. 610
Wilmington, DE 19801
(302)573-6652
Fax: (302)573-6092
Website: http://www.scoredelaware.com

District of Columbia

SCORE Office (George Mason University)
409 3rd St. SW, 4th Fl.
Washington, DC 20024
800-634-0245

SCORE Office (Washington DC)
1110 Vermont Ave. NW, 9th Fl.

Washington, DC 20043
(202)606-4000
Fax: (202)606-4225
E-mail: dcscore@hotmail.com
Website: http://www.scoredc.org/

Florida

SCORE Office (Desota County Chamber of Commerce)
16 South Velucia Ave.
Arcadia, FL 34266
(941)494-4033

SCORE Office (Suncoast/Pinellas)
Airport Business Ctr.
4707 - 140th Ave. N, No. 311
Clearwater, FL 33755
(813)532-6800
Fax: (813)532-6800

SCORE Office (DeLand)
336 N. Woodland Blvd.
DeLand, FL 32720
(904)734-4331
Fax: (904)734-4333

SCORE Office (South Palm Beach)
1050 S. Federal Hwy., Ste. 132
Delray Beach, FL 33483
(561)278-7752
Fax: (561)278-0288

SCORE Office (Ft. Lauderdale)
Federal Bldg., Ste. 123
299 E. Broward Blvd.
Ft. Lauderdale, FL 33301
(954)356-7263
Fax: (954)356-7145

SCORE Office (Southwest Florida)
The Renaissance
8695 College Pky., Ste. 345 & 346
Ft. Myers, FL 33919
(941)489-2935
Fax: (941)489-1170

SCORE Office (Treasure Coast)
Professional Center, Ste. 2
3220 S. US, No. 1
Ft. Pierce, FL 34982
(561)489-0548

SCORE Office (Gainesville)
101 SE 2nd Pl., Ste. 104
Gainesville, FL 32601
(904)375-8278

SCORE Office (Hialeah Dade Chamber)
59 W. 5th St.
Hialeah, FL 33010

(305)887-1515
Fax: (305)887-2453

SCORE Office (Daytona Beach)
921 Nova Rd., Ste. A
Holly Hills, FL 32117
(904)255-6889
Fax: (904)255-0229
E-mail: score87@dbeach.com

SCORE Office (South Broward)
3475 Sheridian St., Ste. 203
Hollywood, FL 33021
(305)966-8415

SCORE Office (Citrus County)
5 Poplar Ct.
Homosassa, FL 34446
(352)382-1037

SCORE Office (Jacksonville)
7825 Baymeadows Way, Ste. 100-B
Jacksonville, FL 32256
(904)443-1911
Fax: (904)443-1980
E-mail: scorejax@juno.com
Website: http://www.scorejax.org/

SCORE Office (Jacksonville Satellite)
3 Independent Dr.
Jacksonville, FL 32256
(904)366-6600
Fax: (904)632-0617

SCORE Office (Central Florida)
5410 S. Florida Ave., No. 3
Lakeland, FL 33801
(941)687-5783
Fax: (941)687-6225

SCORE Office (Lakeland)
100 Lake Morton Dr.
Lakeland, FL 33801
(941)686-2168

SCORE Office (St. Petersburg)
800 W. Bay Dr., Ste. 505
Largo, FL 33712
(813)585-4571

SCORE Office (Leesburg)
9501 US Hwy. 441
Leesburg, FL 34788-8751
(352)365-3556
Fax: (352)365-3501

SCORE Office (Cocoa)
1600 Farno Rd., Unit 205
Melbourne, FL 32935
(407)254-2288

SCORE Office (Melbourne)
Melbourne Professional Complex
1600 Sarno, Ste. 205
Melbourne, FL 32935
(407)254-2288
Fax: (407)245-2288

SCORE Office (Merritt Island)
1600 Sarno Rd., Ste. 205
Melbourne, FL 32935
(407)254-2288
Fax: (407)254-2288

SCORE Office (Space Coast)
Melbourn Professional Complex
1600 Sarno, Ste. 205
Melbourne, FL 32935
(407)254-2288
Fax: (407)254-2288

SCORE Office (Dade)
49 NW 5th St.
Miami, FL 33128
(305)371-6889
Fax: (305)374-1882
E-mail: score@netrox.net
Website: http://www.netrox.net/~score/

SCORE Office (Naples of Collier)
International College
2654 Tamiami Trl. E
Naples, FL 34112
(941)417-1280
Fax: (941)417-1281
E-mail: score@naples.net
Website: http://www.naples.net/clubs/
score/index.htm

SCORE Office (Pasco County)
6014 US Hwy. 19, Ste. 302
New Port Richey, FL 34652
(813)842-4638

SCORE Office (Southeast Volusia)
115 Canal St.
New Smyrna Beach, FL 32168
(904)428-2449
Fax: (904)423-3512

SCORE Office (Ocala)
110 E. Silver Springs Blvd.
Ocala, FL 34470
(352)629-5959

Clay County SCORE Office
Clay County Chamber of Commerce
1734 Kingsdey Ave.
PO Box 1441
Orange Park, FL 32073
(904)264-2651
Fax: (904)269-0363

SCORE Office (Orlando)
80 N. Hughey Ave.
Rm. 445 Federal Bldg.
Orlando, FL 32801
(407)648-6476
Fax: (407)648-6425

SCORE Office (Emerald Coast)
19 W. Garden St., No. 325
Pensacola, FL 32501
(904)444-2060
Fax: (904)444-2070

SCORE Office (Charlotte County)
201 W. Marion Ave., Ste. 211
Punta Gorda, FL 33950
(941)575-1818
E-mail: score@gls3c.com
Website: http://www.charlotte-
florida.com/business/scorepg01.htm

SCORE Office (St. Augustine)
1 Riberia St.
St. Augustine, FL 32084
(904)829-5681
Fax: (904)829-6477

SCORE Office (Bradenton)
2801 Fruitville, Ste. 280
Sarasota, FL 34237
(813)955-1029

SCORE Office (Manasota)
2801 Fruitville Rd., Ste. 280
Sarasota, FL 34237
(941)955-1029
Fax: (941)955-5581
E-mail: score116@gte.net
Website: http://www.score-suncoast.org/

SCORE Office (Tallahassee)
200 W. Park Ave.
Tallahassee, FL 32302
(850)487-2665

SCORE Office (Hillsborough)
4732 Dale Mabry Hwy. N, Ste. 400
Tampa, FL 33614-6509
(813)870-0125

SCORE Office (Lake Sumter)
122 E. Main St.
Tavares, FL 32778-3810
(352)365-3556

SCORE Office (Titusville)
2000 S. Washington Ave.
Titusville, FL 32780
(407)267-3036
Fax: (407)264-0127

SCORE Office (Venice)
257 N. Tamiami Trl.
Venice, FL 34285
(941)488-2236
Fax: (941)484-5903

SCORE Office (Palm Beach)
500 Australian Ave. S, Ste. 100
West Palm Beach, FL 33401
(561)833-1672
Fax: (561)833-1712

SCORE Office (Wildwood)
103 N. Webster St.
Wildwood, FL 34785

Georgia

SCORE Office (Atlanta)
Harris Tower, Suite 1900
233 Peachtree Rd., NE
Atlanta, GA 30309
(404)347-2442
Fax: (404)347-1227

SCORE Office (Augusta)
3126 Oxford Rd.
Augusta, GA 30909
(706)869-9100

SCORE Office (Columbus)
School Bldg.
PO Box 40
Columbus, GA 31901
(706)327-3654

SCORE Office (Dalton-Whitfield)
305 S. Thorton Ave.
Dalton, GA 30720
(706)279-3383

SCORE Office (Gainesville)
PO Box 374
Gainesville, GA 30503
(770)532-6206
Fax: (770)535-8419

SCORE Office (Macon)
711 Grand Bldg.
Macon, GA 31201
(912)751-6160

SCORE Office (Brunswick)
4 Glen Ave.
St. Simons Island, GA 31520
(912)265-0620
Fax: (912)265-0629

SCORE Office (Savannah)
111 E. Liberty St., Ste. 103
Savannah, GA 31401
(912)652-4335

Fax: (912)652-4184
E-mail: info@scoresav.org
Website: http://www.coastalempire.com/
score/index.htm

Guam

SCORE Office (Guam)
Pacific News Bldg., Rm. 103
238 Archbishop Flores St.
Agana, GU 96910-5100
(671)472-7308

Hawaii

SCORE Office (Hawaii, Inc.)
1111 Bishop St., Ste. 204
PO Box 50207
Honolulu, HI 96813
(808)522-8132
Fax: (808)522-8135
E-mail: hnlscore@juno.com

SCORE Office (Kahului)
250 Alamaha, Unit N16A
Kahului, HI 96732
(808)871-7711

SCORE Office (Maui, Inc.)
590 E. Lipoa Pkwy., Ste. 227
Kihei, HI 96753
(808)875-2380

Idaho

SCORE Office (Treasure Valley)
1020 Main St., No. 290
Boise, ID 83702
(208)334-1696
Fax: (208)334-9353

SCORE Office (Eastern Idaho)
2300 N. Yellowstone, Ste. 119
Idaho Falls, ID 83401
(208)523-1022
Fax: (208)528-7127

Illinois

SCORE Office (Fox Valley)
40 W. Downer Pl.
PO Box 277
Aurora, IL 60506
(630)897-9214
Fax: (630)897-7002

SCORE Office (Greater Belvidere)
419 S. State St.
Belvidere, IL 61008
(815)544-4357
Fax: (815)547-7654

SCORE Office (Bensenville)
1050 Busse Hwy. Suite 100
Bensenville, IL 60106
(708)350-2944
Fax: (708)350-2979

SCORE Office (Central Illinois)
402 N. Hershey Rd.
Bloomington, IL 61704
(309)644-0549
Fax: (309)663-8270
E-mail: webmaster@central-illinois-
score.org
Website: http://www.central-illinois-
score.org/

SCORE Office (Southern Illinois)
150 E. Pleasant Hill Rd.
Box 1
Carbondale, IL 62901
(618)453-6654
Fax: (618)453-5040

SCORE Office (Chicago)
Northwest Atrium Ctr.
500 W. Madison St., No. 1250
Chicago, IL 60661
(312)353-7724
Fax: (312)886-5688
Website: http://www.mcs.net/~bic/

SCORE Office (Chicago–Oliver Harvey College)
Pullman Bldg.
1000 E. 11th St., 7th Fl.
Chicago, IL 60628
Fax: (312)468-8086

SCORE Office (Danville)
28 W. N. Street
Danville, IL 61832
(217)442-7232
Fax: (217)442-6228

SCORE Office (Decatur)
Milliken University
1184 W. Main St.
Decatur, IL 62522
(217)424-6297
Fax: (217)424-3993
E-mail: charding@mail.millikin.edu
Website: http://www.millikin.edu/
academics/Tabor/score.html

SCORE Office (Downers Grove)
925 Curtis
Downers Grove, IL 60515
(708)968-4050
Fax: (708)968-8368

SCORE Office (Elgin)
24 E. Chicago, 3rd Fl.
PO Box 648
Elgin, IL 60120
(847)741-5660
Fax: (847)741-5677

SCORE Office (Freeport Area)
26 S. Galena Ave.
Freeport, IL 61032
(815)233-1350
Fax: (815)235-4038

SCORE Office (Galesburg)
292 E. Simmons St.
PO Box 749
Galesburg, IL 61401
(309)343-1194
Fax: (309)343-1195

SCORE Office (Glen Ellyn)
500 Pennsylvania
Glen Ellyn, IL 60137
(708)469-0907
Fax: (708)469-0426

SCORE Office (Greater Alton)
Alden Hall
5800 Godfrey Rd.
Godfrey, IL 62035-2466
(618)467-2280
Fax: (618)466-8289
Website: http://www.altonweb.com/
score/

SCORE Office (Grayslake)
19351 W. Washington St.
Grayslake, IL 60030
(708)223-3633
Fax: (708)223-9371

SCORE Office (Harrisburg)
303 S. Commercial
Harrisburg, IL 62946-1528
(618)252-8528
Fax: (618)252-0210

SCORE Office (Joliet)
100 N. Chicago
Joliet, IL 60432
(815)727-5371
Fax: (815)727-5374

SCORE Office (Kankakee)
101 S. Schuyler Ave.
Kankakee, IL 60901
(815)933-0376
Fax: (815)933-0380

SCORE Office (Macomb)
216 Seal Hall, Rm. 214

Macomb, IL 61455
(309)298-1128
Fax: (309)298-2520

SCORE Office (Matteson)
210 Lincoln Mall
Matteson, IL 60443
(708)709-3750
Fax: (708)503-9322

SCORE Office (Mattoon)
1701 Wabash Ave.
Mattoon, IL 61938
(217)235-5661
Fax: (217)234-6544

SCORE Office (Quad Cities)
622 19th St.
Moline, IL 61265
(309)797-0082
Fax: (309)757-5435
E-mail: score@qconline.com
Website: http://www.qconline.com/
business/score/

SCORE Office (Naperville)
131 W. Jefferson Ave.
Naperville, IL 60540
(708)355-4141
Fax: (708)355-8355

SCORE Office (Northbrook)
2002 Walters Ave.
Northbrook, IL 60062
(847)498-5555
Fax: (847)498-5510

SCORE Office (Palos Hills)
10900 S. 88th Ave.
Palos Hills, IL 60465
(847)974-5468
Fax: (847)974-0078

SCORE Office (Peoria)
124 SW Adams, Ste. 300
Peoria, IL 61602
(309)676-0755
Fax: (309)676-7534

SCORE Office (Prospect Heights)
1375 Wolf Rd.
Prospect Heights, IL 60070
(847)537-8660
Fax: (847)537-7138

SCORE Office (Quincy Tri-State)
300 Civic Center Plz., Ste. 245
Quincy, IL 62301
(217)222-8093
Fax: (217)222-3033

SCORE Office (River Grove)
2000 5th Ave.
River Grove, IL 60171
(708)456-0300
Fax: (708)583-3121

SCORE Office (Northern Illinois)
515 N. Court St.
Rockford, IL 61103
(815)962-0122
Fax: (815)962-0122

SCORE Office (St. Charles)
103 N. 1st Ave.
St. Charles, IL 60174-1982
(847)584-8384
Fax: (847)584-6065

SCORE Office (Springfield)
511 W. Capitol Ave., Ste. 302
Springfield, IL 62704
(217)492-4416
Fax: (217)492-4867

SCORE Office (Sycamore)
112 Somunak St.
Sycamore, IL 60178
(815)895-3456
Fax: (815)895-0125

SCORE Office (University)
Hwy. 50 & Stuenkel Rd. Ste. C3305
University Park, IL 60466
(708)534-5000
Fax: (708)534-8457

Indiana

SCORE Office (Anderson)
205 W. 11th St.
Anderson, IN 46015
(317)642-0264

SCORE Office (Bloomington)
Star Center
216 W. Allen
Bloomington, IN 47403
(812)335-7334
E-mail: wtfische@indiana.edu
Website: http://www.brainfreezemedia.
com/score527/

SCORE Office (South East Indiana)
500 Franklin St.
Box 29
Columbus, IN 47201
(812)379-4457

SCORE Office (Corydon)
310 N. Elm St.
Corydon, IN 47112

(812)738-2137
Fax: (812)738-6438

SCORE Office (Crown Point)
Old Courthouse Sq. Ste. 206
PO Box 43
Crown Point, IN 46307
(219)663-1800

SCORE Office (Elkhart)
418 S. Main St.
Elkhart, IN 46515
(219)293-1531
Fax: (219)294-1859

SCORE Office (Evansville)
1100 W. Lloyd Expy., Ste. 105
Evansville, IN 47708
(812)426-6144

SCORE Office (Fort Wayne)
1300 S. Harrison St.
Ft. Wayne, IN 46802
(219)422-2601
Fax: (219)422-2601

SCORE Office (Gary)
973 W. 6th Ave., Rm. 326
Gary, IN 46402
(219)882-3918

SCORE Office (Hammond)
7034 Indianapolis Blvd.
Hammond, IN 46324
(219)931-1000
Fax: (219)845-9548

SCORE Office (Indianapolis)
429 N. Pennsylvania St., Ste. 100
Indianapolis, IN 46204-1873
(317)226-7264
Fax: (317)226-7259
E-mail: inscore@indy.net
Website: http://www.score-
indianapolis.org/

SCORE Office (Jasper)
PO Box 307
Jasper, IN 47547-0307
(812)482-6866

SCORE Office (Kokomo/Howard Counties)
106 N. Washington St.
Kokomo, IN 46901
(765)457-5301
Fax: (765)452-4564

SCORE Office (Logansport)
300 E. Broadway, Ste. 103
Logansport, IN 46947
(219)753-6388

SCORE Office (Madison)
301 E. Main St.
Madison, IN 47250
(812)265-3135
Fax: (812)265-2923

SCORE Office (Marengo)
Rt. 1 Box 224D
Marengo, IN 47140
Fax: (812)365-2793

SCORE Office (Marion/Grant Counties)
215 S. Adams
Marion, IN 46952
(765)664-5107

SCORE Office (Merrillville)
255 W. 80th Pl.
Merrillville, IN 46410
(219)769-8180
Fax: (219)736-6223

SCORE Office (Michigan City)
200 E. Michigan Blvd.
Michigan City, IN 46360
(219)874-6221
Fax: (219)873-1204

SCORE Office (South Central Indiana)
4100 Charleston Rd.
New Albany, IN 47150-9538
(812)945-0066

SCORE Office (Rensselaer)
104 W. Washington
Rensselaer, IN 47978

SCORE Office (Salem)
210 N. Main St.
Salem, IN 47167
(812)883-4303
Fax: (812)883-1467

SCORE Office (South Bend)
300 N. Michigan St.
South Bend, IN 46601
(219)282-4350
E-mail: chair@southbend-score.org
Website: http://www.southbend-score.org/

SCORE Office (Valparaiso)
150 Lincolnway
Valparaiso, IN 46383
(219)462-1105
Fax: (219)469-5710

SCORE Office (Vincennes)
27 N. 3rd
PO Box 553
Vincennes, IN 47591
(812)882-6440
Fax: (812)882-6441

SCORE Office (Wabash)
PO Box 371
Wabash, IN 46992
(219)563-1168
Fax: (219)563-6920

Iowa

SCORE Office (Burlington)
Federal Bldg.
300 N. Main St.
Burlington, IA 52601
(319)752-2967

SCORE Office (Cedar Rapids)
2750 1st Ave. NE, Ste 350
Cedar Rapids, IA 52401-1806
(319)362-6405
Fax: (319)362-7861
E:mail: score@scorecr.org
Website: http://www.scorecr.org

SCORE Office (Illowa)
333 4th Ave. S
Clinton, IA 52732
(319)242-5702

SCORE Office (Council Bluffs)
7 N. 6th St.
Council Bluffs, IA 51502
(712)325-1000

SCORE Office (Northeast Iowa)
3404 285th St.
Cresco, IA 52136
(319)547-3377

SCORE Office (Des Moines)
Federal Bldg., Rm. 749
210 Walnut St.
Des Moines, IA 50309-2186
(515)284-4760

SCORE Office (Ft. Dodge)
Federal Bldg., Rm. 436
205 S. 8th St.
Ft. Dodge, IA 50501
(515)955-2622

SCORE Office (Independence)
110 1st. St. east
Independence, IA 50644
(319)334-7178
Fax: (319)334-7179

SCORE Office (Iowa City)
210 Federal Bldg.
PO Box 1853
Iowa City, IA 52240-1853
(319)338-1662

SCORE Office (Keokuk)
401 Main St.
Pierce Bldg., No. 1
Keokuk, IA 52632
(319)524-5055

SCORE Office (Central Iowa)
Fisher Community College
709 S. Center
Marshalltown, IA 50158
(515)753-6645

SCORE Office (River City)
15 West State St.
Mason City, IA 50401
(515)423-5724

SCORE Office (South Central)
SBDC, Indian Hills Community College
525 Grandview Ave.
Ottumwa, IA 52501
(515)683-5127
Fax: (515)683-5263

SCORE Office (Dubuque)
10250 Sundown Rd.
Peosta, IA 52068
(319)556-5110

SCORE Office (Southwest Iowa)
614 W. Sheridan
Shenandoah, IA 51601
(712)246-3260

SCORE Office (Sioux City)
Federal Bldg.
320 6th St.
Sioux City, IA 51101
(712)277-2324
Fax: (712)277-2325

SCORE Office (Iowa Lakes)
122 W. 5th St.
Spencer, IA 51301
(712)262-3059

SCORE Office (Vista)
119 W. 6th St.
Storm Lake, IA 50588
(712)732-3780

SCORE Office (Waterloo)
215 E. 4th
Waterloo, IA 50703
(319)233-8431

Kansas

SCORE Office (Southwest Kansas)
501 W. Spruce
Dodge City, KS 67801
(316)227-3119

SCORE Office (Emporia)
811 Homewood
Emporia, KS 66801
(316)342-1600

SCORE Office (Golden Belt)
1307 Williams
Great Bend, KS 67530
(316)792-2401

SCORE Office (Hays)
PO Box 400
Hays, KS 67601
(913)625-6595

SCORE Office (Hutchinson)
1 E. 9th St.
Hutchinson, KS 67501
(316)665-8468
Fax: (316)665-7619

SCORE Office (Southeast Kansas)
404 Westminster Pl.
PO Box 886
Independence, KS 67301
(316)331-4741

SCORE Office (McPherson)
306 N. Main
PO Box 616
McPherson, KS 67460
(316)241-3303

SCORE Office (Salina)
120 Ash St.
Salina, KS 67401
(785)243-4290
Fax: (785)243-1833

SCORE Office (Topeka)
1700 College
Topeka, KS 66621
(785)231-1010

SCORE Office (Wichita)
100 E. English, Ste. 510
Wichita, KS 67202
(316)269-6273
Fax: (316)269-6499

SCORE Office (Ark Valley)
205 E. 9th St.
Winfield, KS 67156
(316)221-1617

Kentucky

SCORE Office (Ashland)
PO Box 830
Ashland, KY 41105
(606)329-8011
Fax: (606)325-4607

SCORE Office (Bowling Green)
812 State St.
PO Box 51
Bowling Green, KY 42101
(502)781-3200
Fax: (502)843-0458

SCORE Office (Tri-Lakes)
508 Barbee Way
Danville, KY 40422-1548
(606)231-9902

SCORE Office (Glasgow)
301 W. Main St.
Glasgow, KY 42141
(502)651-3161
Fax: (502)651-3122

SCORE Office (Hazard)
B & I Technical Center
100 Airport Gardens Rd.
Hazard, KY 41701
(606)439-5856
Fax: (606)439-1808

SCORE Office (Lexington)
410 W. Vine St., Ste. 290, Civic C
Lexington, KY 40507
(606)231-9902
Fax: (606)253-3190
E-mail: scorelex@uky.campus.mci.net

SCORE Office (Louisville)
188 Federal Office Bldg.
600 Dr. Martin L. King Jr. Pl.
Louisville, KY 40202
(502)582-5976

SCORE Office (Madisonville)
257 N. Main
Madisonville, KY 42431
(502)825-1399
Fax: (502)825-1396

SCORE Office (Paducah)
Federal Office Bldg.
501 Broadway, Rm. B-36
Paducah, KY 42001
(502)442-5685

Louisiana

SCORE Office (Central Louisiana)
802 3rd St.
Alexandria, LA 71309
(318)442-6671

SCORE Office (Baton Rouge)
564 Laurel St.
PO Box 3217
Baton Rouge, LA 70801

(504)381-7130
Fax: (504)336-4306

SCORE Office (North Shore)
2 W. Thomas
Hammond, LA 70401
(504)345-4457
Fax: (504)345-4749

SCORE Office (Lafayette)
804 St. Mary Blvd.
Lafayette, LA 70505-1307
(318)233-2705
Fax: (318)234-8671
E-mail: score302@aol.com

SCORE Office (Lake Charles)
120 W. Pujo St.
Lake Charles, LA 70601
(318)433-3632

SCORE Office (New Orleans)
365 Canal St., Ste. 3100
New Orleans, LA 70130
(504)589-2356
Fax: (504)589-2339

SCORE Office (Shreveport)
400 Edwards St.
Shreveport, LA 71101
(318)677-2536
Fax: (318)677-2541

Maine

SCORE Office (Augusta)
40 Western Ave.
Augusta, ME 04330
(207)622-8509

SCORE Office (Bangor)
Peabody Hall, Rm. 229
One College Cir.
Bangor, ME 04401
(207)941-9707

SCORE Office (Central & Northern Arroostock)
111 High St.
Caribou, ME 04736
(207)492-8010
Fax: (207)492-8010

SCORE Office (Penquis)
South St.
Dover Foxcroft, ME 04426
(207)564-7021

SCORE Office (Maine Coastal)
Mill Mall
Box 1105
Ellsworth, ME 04605-1105

(207)667-5800
E-mail: score@arcadia.net

SCORE Office (Lewiston-Auburn)
BIC of Maine-Bates Mill Complex
35 Canal St.
Lewiston, ME 04240-7764
(207)782-3708
Fax: (207)783-7745

SCORE Office (Portland)
66 Pearl St., Rm. 210
Portland, ME 04101
(207)772-1147
Fax: (207)772-5581
E-mail: Score53@score.maine.org
Website: http://www.score.maine.org/
chapter53/

SCORE Office (Western Mountains)
255 River St.
PO Box 252
Rumford, ME 04257-0252
(207)369-9976

SCORE Office (Oxford Hills)
166 Main St.
South Paris, ME 04281
(207)743-0499

Maryland

SCORE Office (Southern Maryland)
2525 Riva Rd., Ste. 110
Annapolis, MD 21401
(410)266-9553
Fax: (410)573-0981
E-mail: score390@aol.com
Website: http://members.aol.com/
score390/index.htm

SCORE Office (Baltimore)
The City Crescent Bldg., 6th Fl.
10 S. Howard St.
Baltimore, MD 21201
(410)962-2233
Fax: (410)962-1805

SCORE Office (Bel Air)
108 S. Bond St.
Bel Air, MD 21014
(410)838-2020
Fax: (410)893-4715

SCORE Office (Bethesda)
7910 Woodmont Ave., Ste. 1204
Bethesda, MD 20814
(301)652-4900
Fax: (301)657-1973

SCORE Office (Bowie)
6670 Race Track Rd.
Bowie, MD 20715
(301)262-0920
Fax: (301)262-0921

SCORE Office (Dorchester County)
203 Sunburst Hwy.
Cambridge, MD 21613
(410)228-3575

SCORE Office (Upper Shore)
210 Marlboro Ave.
Easton, MD 21601
(410)822-4606
Fax: (410)822-7922

SCORE Office (Frederick County)
43A S. Market St.
Frederick, MD 21701
(301)662-8723
Fax: (301)846-4427

SCORE Office (Gaithersburg)
9 Park Ave.
Gaithersburg, MD 20877
(301)840-1400
Fax: (301)963-3918

SCORE Office (Glen Burnie)
103 Crain Hwy. SE
Glen Burnie, MD 21061
(410)766-8282
Fax: (410)766-9722

SCORE Office (Hagerstown)
111 W. Washington St.
Hagerstown, MD 21740
(301)739-2015
Fax: (301)739-1278

SCORE Office (Laurel)
7901 Sandy Spring Rd. Ste. 501
Laurel, MD 20707
(301)725-4000
Fax: (301)725-0776

SCORE Office (Salisbury)
300 E. Main St.
Salisbury, MD 21801
(410)749-0185
Fax: (410)860-9925

Massachusetts

SCORE Office (NE Massachusetts)
100 Cummings Ctr., Ste. 101 K
Beverly, MA 01923
(978)922-9441
Website: http://www1.shore.net/~score/

SCORE Office (Boston)
10 Causeway St., Rm. 265
Boston, MA 02222-1093
(617)565-5591
Fax: (617)565-5598
E-mail: boston-score-20@worldnet.att.net
Website: http://www.scoreboston.org/

SCORE office (Bristol/Plymouth County)
53 N. 6th St., Federal Bldg.
Bristol, MA 02740
(508)994-5093

SCORE Office (SE Massachusetts)
60 School St.
Brockton, MA 02401
(508)587-2673
Fax: (508)587-1340
Website: http://www.metrosouth
chamber.com/score.html

SCORE Office (North Adams)
820 N. State Rd.
Cheshire, MA 01225
(413)743-5100

SCORE Office (Clinton Satellite)
1 Green St.
Clinton, MA 01510
Fax: (508)368-7689

SCORE Office (Greenfield)
PO Box 898
Greenfield, MA 01302
(413)773-5463
Fax: (413)773-7008

SCORE Office (Haverhill)
87 Winter St.
Haverhill, MA 01830
(508)373-5663
Fax: (508)373-8060

SCORE Office (Hudson Satellite)
PO Box 578
Hudson, MA 01749
(508)568-0360
Fax: (508)568-0360

SCORE Office (Cape Cod)
Independence Pk., Ste. 5B
270 Communications Way
Hyannis, MA 02601
(508)775-4884
Fax: (508)790-2540

SCORE Office (Lawrence)
264 Essex St.
Lawrence, MA 01840
(508)686-0900
Fax: (508)794-9953

SCORE Office (Leominster Satellite)
110 Erdman Way
Leominster, MA 01453
(508)840-4300
Fax: (508)840-4896

SCORE Office (Bristol/Plymouth Counties)
53 N. 6th St., Federal Bldg.
New Bedford, MA 02740
(508)994-5093

SCORE Office (Newburyport)
29 State St.
Newburyport, MA 01950
(617)462-6680

SCORE Office (Pittsfield)
66 West St.
Pittsfield, MA 01201
(413)499-2485

SCORE Office (Haverhill-Salem)
32 Derby Sq.
Salem, MA 01970
(508)745-0330
Fax: (508)745-3855

SCORE Office (Springfield)
1350 Main St.
Federal Bldg.
Springfield, MA 01103
(413)785-0314

SCORE Office (Carver)
12 Taunton Green, Ste. 201
Taunton, MA 02780
(508)824-4068
Fax: (508)824-4069

SCORE Office (Worcester)
33 Waldo St.
Worcester, MA 01608
(508)753-2929
Fax: (508)754-8560

Michigan

SCORE Office (Allegan)
PO Box 338
Allegan, MI 49010
(616)673-2479

SCORE Office (Ann Arbor)
425 S. Main St., Ste. 103
Ann Arbor, MI 48104
(313)665-4433

SCORE Office (Battle Creek)
34 W. Jackson Ste. 4A
Battle Creek, MI 49017-3505

(616)962-4076
Fax: (616)962-6309

SCORE Office (Cadillac)
222 Lake St.
Cadillac, MI 49601
(616)775-9776
Fax: (616)768-4255

SCORE Office (Detroit)
477 Michigan Ave., Rm. 515
Detroit, MI 48226
(313)226-7947
Fax: (313)226-3448

SCORE Office (Flint)
708 Root Rd., Rm. 308
Flint, MI 48503
(810)233-6846

SCORE Office (Grand Rapids)
111 Pearl St. NW
Grand Rapids, MI 49503-2831
(616)771-0305
Fax: (616)771-0328
E-mail: scoreone@iserv.net
Website: http://www.iserv.net/
~scoreone/

SCORE Office (Holland)
480 State St.
Holland, MI 49423
(616)396-9472

SCORE Office (Jackson)
209 East Washington
PO Box 80
Jackson, MI 49204
(517)782-8221
Fax: (517)782-0061

SCORE Office (Kalamazoo)
345 W. Michigan Ave.
Kalamazoo, MI 49007
(616)381-5382
Fax: (616)384-0096
E-mail: score@nucleus.net

SCORE Office (Lansing)
117 E. Allegan
PO Box 14030
Lansing, MI 48901
(517)487-6340
Fax: (517)484-6910

SCORE Office (Livonia)
15401 Farmington Rd.
Livonia, MI 48154
(313)427-2122
Fax: (313)427-6055

SCORE Office (Madison Heights)
26345 John R
Madison Heights, MI 48071
(810)542-5010
Fax: (810)542-6821

SCORE Office (Monroe)
111 E. 1st
Monroe, MI 48161
(313)242-3366
Fax: (313)242-7253

SCORE Office (Mt. Clemens)
58 S/B Gratiot
Mt. Clemens, MI 48043
(810)463-1528
Fax: (810)463-6541

SCORE Office (Muskegon)
PO Box 1087
230 Terrace Plz.
Muskegon, MI 49443
(616)722-3751
Fax: (616)728-7251

SCORE Office (Petoskey)
401 E. Mitchell St.
Petoskey, MI 49770
(616)347-4150

SCORE Office (Pontiac)
Executive Office Bldg.
1200 N. Telegraph Rd.
Pontiac, MI 48341
(810)975-9555

SCORE Office (Pontiac)
PO Box 430025
Pontiac, MI 48343
(810)335-9600

SCORE Office (Port Huron)
920 Pinegrove Ave.
Port Huron, MI 48060
(810)985-7101

SCORE Office (Rochester)
71 Walnut Ste. 110
Rochester, MI 48307
(810)651-6700
Fax: (810)651-5270

SCORE Office (Saginaw)
901 S. Washington Ave.
Saginaw, MI 48601
(517)752-7161
Fax: (517)752-9055

SCORE Office (Upper Peninsula)
2581 I-75 Business Spur
Sault Ste. Marie, MI 49783
(906)632-3301

SCORE Office (Southfield)
21000 W. 10 Mile Rd.
Southfield, MI 48075
(810)204-3050
Fax: (810)204-3099

SCORE Office (Traverse City)
202 E. Grandview Pkwy.
PO Box 387
Traverse City, MI 49685
(616)947-5075
Fax: (616)946-2565

SCORE Office (Warren)
30500 Van Dyke, Ste. 118
Warren, MI 48093
(810)751-3939

Minnesota

SCORE Office (Aitkin)
Aitkin, MN 56431
(218)741-3906

SCORE Office (Albert Lea)
202 N. Broadway Ave.
Albert Lea, MN 56007
(507)373-7487

SCORE Office (Austin)
PO Box 864
Austin, MN 55912
(507)437-4561
Fax: (507)437-4869

SCORE Office (South Metro)
Ames Business Ctr.
2500 W. County Rd., No. 42
Burnsville, MN 55337
(612)898-5645
Fax: (612)435-6972
E-mail: southmetro@scoreminn.org
Website: http://www.scoreminn.org/southmetro/

SCORE Office (Duluth)
1717 Minnesota Ave.
Duluth, MN 55802
(218)727-8286
Fax: (218)727-3113
E-mail: duluth@scoreminn.org
Website: http://www.scoreminn.org

SCORE Office (Fairmont)
PO Box 826
Fairmont, MN 56031
(507)235-5547
Fax: (507)235-8411

SCORE Office (Southwest Minnesota)
112 Riverfront St.

Box 999
Mankato, MN 56001
(507)345-4519
Fax: (507)345-4451
Website: http://www.scoreminn.org/

SCORE Office (Minneapolis)
North Plaza Bldg., Ste. 51
5217 Wayzata Blvd.
Minneapolis, MN 55416
(612)591-0539
Fax: (612)544-0436
Website: http://www.scoreminn.org/

SCORE Office (Owatonna)
PO Box 331
Owatonna, MN 55060
(507)451-7970
Fax: (507)451-7972

SCORE Office (Red Wing)
2000 W. Main St., Ste. 324
Red Wing, MN 55066
(612)388-4079

SCORE Office (Southeastern Minnesota)
220 S. Broadway, Ste. 100
Rochester, MN 55901
(507)288-1122
Fax: (507)282-8960
Website: http://www.scoreminn.org/

SCORE Office (Brainerd)
St. Cloud, MN 56301

SCORE Office (Central Area)
1527 Northway Dr.
St. Cloud, MN 56301
(320)240-1332
Fax: (320)255-9050
Website: http://www.scoreminn.org/

SCORE Office (St. Paul)
350 St. Peter St., No. 295
Lowry Professional Bldg.
St. Paul, MN 55102
(651)223-5010
Fax: (651)223-5048
Website: http://www.scoreminn.org/

SCORE Office (Winona)
Box 870
Winona, MN 55987
(507)452-2272
Fax: (507)454-8814

SCORE Office (Worthington)
1121 3rd Ave.
Worthington, MN 56187
(507)372-2919
Fax: (507)372-2827

Mississippi

SCORE Office (Delta)
915 Washington Ave.
PO Box 933
Greenville, MS 38701
(601)378-3141

SCORE Office (Gulfcoast)
1 Government Plaza
2909 13th St., Ste. 203
Gulfport, MS 39501
(228)863-0054

SCORE Office (Jackson)
1st Jackson Center, Ste. 400
101 W. Capitol St.
Jackson, MS 39201
(601)965-5533

SCORE Office (Meridian)
5220 16th Ave.
Meridian, MS 39305
(601)482-4412

Missouri

SCORE Office (Lake of the Ozark)
University Extension
113 Kansas St.
PO Box 1405
Camdenton, MO 65020
(573)346-2644
Fax: (573)346-2694
E-mail: score@cdoc.net
Website: http://sites.cdoc.net/score/

Chamber of Commerce (Cape Girardeau)
PO Box 98
Cape Girardeau, MO 63702-0098
(314)335-3312

SCORE Office (Mid-Missouri)
1705 Halstead Ct.
Columbia, MO 65203
(573)874-1132

SCORE Office (Ozark-Gateway)
1486 Glassy Rd.
Cuba, MO 65453-1640
(573)885-4954

SCORE Office (Kansas City)
323 W. 8th St., Ste. 104
Kansas City, MO 64105
(816)374-6675
Fax: (816)374-6692
E-mail: SCOREBIC@AOL.COM
Website: http://www.crn.org/score/

SCORE Office (Sedalia)
Lucas Place
323 W. 8th St., Ste.104
Kansas City, MO 64105
(816)374-6675

SCORE office (Tri-Lakes)
PO Box 1148
Kimberling, MO 65686
(417)739-3041

SCORE Office (Tri-Lakes)
HCRI Box 85
Lampe, MO 65681
(417)858-6798

SCORE Office (Mexico)
111 N. Washington St.
Mexico, MO 65265
(314)581-2765

SCORE Office (Southeast Missouri)
Rte. 1, Box 280
Neelyville, MO 63954
(573)989-3577

SCORE office (Poplar Bluff Area)
806 Emma St.
Poplar Bluff, MO 63901
(573)686-8892

SCORE Office (St. Joseph)
3003 Frederick Ave.
St. Joseph, MO 64506
(816)232-4461

SCORE Office (St. Louis)
815 Olive St., Rm. 242
St. Louis, MO 63101-1569
(314)539-6970
Fax: (314)539-3785
E-mail: info@stlscore.org
Website: http://www.stlscore.org/

SCORE Office (Lewis & Clark)
425 Spencer Rd.
St. Peters, MO 63376
(314)928-2900
Fax: (314)928-2900
E-mail: score01@mail.win.org

SCORE Office (Springfield)
620 S. Glenstone, Ste. 110
Springfield, MO 65802-3200
(417)864-7670
Fax: (417)864-4108

SCORE office (Southeast Kansas)
1206 W. First St.
Webb City, MO 64870
(417)673-3984

Montana

SCORE Office (Billings)
815 S. 27th St.
Billings, MT 59101
(406)245-4111

SCORE Office (Bozeman)
1205 E. Main St.
Bozeman, MT 59715
(406)586-5421

SCORE Office (Butte)
1000 George St.
Butte, MT 59701
(406)723-3177

SCORE Office (Great Falls)
710 First Ave. N
Great Falls, MT 59401
(406)761-4434
E-mail: scoregtf@in.tch.com

SCORE Office (Havre, Montana)
518 First St.
Havre, MT 59501
(406)265-4383

SCORE Office (Helena)
Federal Bldg.
301 S. Park
Helena, MT 59626-0054
(406)441-1081

SCORE Office (Kalispell)
2 Main St.
Kalispell, MT 59901
(406)756-5271
Fax: (406)752-6665

SCORE Office (Missoula)
723 Ronan
Missoula, MT 59806
(406)327-8806
E-mail: score@safeshop.com
Website: http://missoula.bigsky.net/
score/

Nebraska

SCORE Office (Columbus)
Columbus, NE 68601
(402)564-2769

SCORE Office (Fremont)
92 W. 5th St.
Fremont, NE 68025
(402)721-2641

SCORE Office (Hastings)
Hastings, NE 68901
(402)463-3447

SCORE Office (Lincoln)
8800 O St.
Lincoln, NE 68520
(402)437-2409

SCORE Office (Panhandle)
150549 CR 30
Minatare, NE 69356
(308)632-2133
Website: http://www.tandt.com/
SCORE

SCORE Office (Norfolk)
3209 S. 48th Ave.
Norfolk, NE 68106
(402)564-2769

SCORE Office (North Platte)
3301 W. 2nd St.
North Platte, NE 69101
(308)532-4466

SCORE Office (Omaha)
11145 Mill Valley Rd.
Omaha, NE 68154
(402)221-3606
Fax: (402)221-3680
E-mail: infoctr@ne.uswest.net
Website: http://www.tandt.com/score/

Nevada

SCORE Office (Incline Village)
969 Tahoe Blvd.
Incline Village, NV 89451
(702)831-7327
Fax: (702)832-1605

SCORE Office (Carson City)
301 E. Stewart
PO Box 7527
Las Vegas, NV 89125
(702)388-6104

SCORE Office (Las Vegas)
300 Las Vegas Blvd. S, Ste. 1100
Las Vegas, NV 89101
(702)388-6104

SCORE Office (Northern Nevada)
SBDC, College of Business
Administration
Univ. of Nevada
Reno, NV 89557-0100
(702)784-4436
Fax: (702)784-4337

New Hampshire

SCORE Office (North Country)
PO Box 34

Berlin, NH 03570
(603)752-1090

SCORE Office (Concord)
143 N. Main St., Rm. 202A
PO Box 1258
Concord, NH 03301
(603)225-1400
Fax: (603)225-1409

SCORE Office (Dover)
299 Central Ave.
Dover, NH 03820
(603)742-2218
Fax: (603)749-6317

SCORE Office (Monadnock)
34 Mechanic St.
Keene, NH 03431-3421
(603)352-0320

SCORE Office (Lakes Region)
67 Water St., Ste. 105
Laconia, NH 03246
(603)524-9168

SCORE Office (Upper Valley)
Citizens Bank Bldg., Rm. 310
20 W. Park St.
Lebanon, NH 03766
(603)448-3491
Fax: (603)448-1908
E-mail: billt@valley.net
Website: http://www.valley.net/~score/

SCORE Office (Merrimack Valley)
275 Chestnut St., Rm. 618
Manchester, NH 03103
(603)666-7561
Fax: (603)666-7925

SCORE Office (Mt. Washington Valley)
PO Box 1066
North Conway, NH 03818
(603)383-0800

SCORE Office (Seacoast)
195 Commerce Way, Unit-A
Portsmouth, NH 03801-3251
(603)433-0575

New Jersey

SCORE Office (Somerset)
Paritan Valley Community College,
Rte. 28
Branchburg, NJ 08807
(908)218-8874
E-mail: nj-score@grizbiz.com.
Website: http://www.nj-score.org/

SCORE Office (Chester)
5 Old Mill Rd.
Chester, NJ 07930
(908)879-7080

SCORE Office (Greater Princeton)
4 A George Washington Dr.
Cranbury, NJ 08512
(609)520-1776

SCORE Office (Freehold)
36 W. Main St.
Freehold, NJ 07728
(908)462-3030
Fax: (908)462-2123

SCORE Office (North West)
Picantinny Innovation Ctr.
3159 Schrader Rd.
Hamburg, NJ 07419
(973)209-8525
Fax: (973)209-7252
E-mail: nj-score@grizbiz.com
Website: http://www.nj-score.org/

SCORE Office (Monmouth)
765 Newman Springs Rd.
Lincroft, NJ 07738
(908)224-2573
E-mail: nj-score@grizbiz.com
Website: http://www.nj-score.org/

SCORE Office (Manalapan)
125 Symmes Dr.
Manalapan, NJ 07726
(908)431-7220

SCORE Office (Jersey City)
2 Gateway Ctr., 4th Fl.
Newark, NJ 07102
(973)645-3982
Fax: (973)645-2375

SCORE Office (Newark)
2 Gateway Center, 15th Fl.
Newark, NJ 07102-5553
(973)645-3982
Fax: (973)645-2375
E-mail: nj-score@grizbiz.com
Website: http://www.nj-score.org

SCORE Office (Bergen County)
327 E. Ridgewood Ave.
Paramus, NJ 07652
(201)599-6090
E-mail: nj-score@grizbiz.com
Website: http://www.nj-score.org/

SCORE Office (Pennsauken)
4900 Rte. 70

Pennsauken, NJ 08109
(609)486-3421

SCORE Office (Southern New Jersey)
4900 Rte. 70
Pennsauken, NJ 08109
(609)486-3421
E-mail: nj-score@grizbiz.com
Website: http://www.nj-score.org/

SCORE Office (Greater Princeton)
216 Rockingham Row
Princeton Forrestal Village
Princeton, NJ 08540
(609)520-1776
Fax: (609)520-9107
E-mail: nj-score@grizbiz.com
Website: http://www.nj-score.org/

SCORE Office (Shrewsbury)
Hwy. 35
Shrewsbury, NJ 07702
(908)842-5995
Fax: (908)219-6140

SCORE Office (Ocean County)
33 Washington St.
Toms River, NJ 08754
(732)505-6033
E-mail: nj-score@grizbiz.com
Website: http://www.nj-score.org/

SCORE Office (Wall)
2700 Allaire Rd.
Wall, NJ 07719
(908)449-8877

SCORE Office (Wayne)
2055 Hamburg Tpke.
Wayne, NJ 07470
(201)831-7788
Fax: (201)831-9112

New Mexico

SCORE Office (Albuquerque)
525 Buena Vista, SE
Albuquerque, NM 87106
(505)272-7999
Fax: (505)272-7963

SCORE Office (Las Cruces)
Loretto Towne Center
505 S. Main St., Ste. 125
Las Cruces, NM 88001
(505)523-5627
Fax: (505)524-2101
E-mail: score.397@zianet.com

SCORE Office (Roswell)
Federal Bldg., Rm. 237

Roswell, NM 88201
(505)625-2112
Fax: (505)623-2545

SCORE Office (Santa Fe)
Montoya Federal Bldg.
120 Federal Place, Rm. 307
Santa Fe, NM 87501
(505)988-6302
Fax: (505)988-6300

New York

SCORE Office (Northeast)
1 Computer Dr. S
Albany, NY 12205
(518)446-1118
Fax: (518)446-1228

SCORE Office (Auburn)
30 South St.
PO Box 675
Auburn, NY 13021
(315)252-7291

SCORE Office (South Tier Binghamton)
Metro Center, 2nd Fl.
49 Court St.
PO Box 995
Binghamton, NY 13902
(607)772-8860

SCORE Office (Queens County City)
12055 Queens Blvd., Rm. 333
Borough Hall, NY 11424
(718)263-8961

SCORE Office (Buffalo)
Federal Bldg., Rm. 1311
111 W. Huron St.
Buffalo, NY 14202
(716)551-4301
Website: http://www2.pcom.net/score/
buf45.html

SCORE Office (Canandaigua)
Chamber of Commerce Bldg.
113 S. Main St.
Canandaigua, NY 14424
(716)394-4400
Fax: (716)394-4546

SCORE Office (Chemung)
333 E. Water St., 4th Fl.
Elmira, NY 14901
(607)734-3358

SCORE Office (Geneva)
Chamber of Commerce Bldg.
PO Box 587

Geneva, NY 14456
(315)789-1776
Fax: (315)789-3993

SCORE Office (Glens Falls)
84 Broad St.
Glens Falls, NY 12801
(518)798-8463
Fax: (518)745-1433

SCORE Office (Orange County)
40 Matthews St.
Goshen, NY 10924
(914)294-8080
Fax: (914)294-6121

SCORE Office (Huntington Area)
151 W. Carver St.
Huntington, NY 11743
(516)423-6100

SCORE Office (Tompkins County)
904 E. Shore Dr.
Ithaca, NY 14850
(607)273-7080

SCORE Office (Long Island City)
120-55 Queens Blvd.
Jamaica, NY 11424
(718)263-8961
Fax: (718)263-9032

SCORE Office (Chatauqua)
101 W. 5th St.
Jamestown, NY 14701
(716)484-1103

SCORE Office (Westchester)
2 Caradon Ln.
Katonah, NY 10536
(914)948-3907
Fax: (914)948-4645
E-mail: score@w-w-w.com
Website: http://w-w-w.com/score/

SCORE Office (Queens County)
Queens Borough Hall
120-55 Queens Blvd. Rm. 333
Kew Gardens, NY 11424
(718)263-8961
Fax: (718)263-9032

SCORE Office (Brookhaven)
3233 Rte. 112
Medford, NY 11763
(516)451-6563
Fax: (516)451-6925

SCORE Office (Melville)
35 Pinelawn Rd., Rm. 207-W
Melville, NY 11747
(516)454-0771

SCORE Office (Nassau County)
400 County Seat Dr., No. 140
Mineola, NY 11501
(516)571-3303
E-mail: Counse1998@aol.com
Website: http://members.aol.com/
Counse1998/Default.htm

SCORE Office (Mt. Vernon)
4 N. 7th Ave.
Mt. Vernon, NY 10550
(914)667-7500

SCORE Office (New York)
26 Federal Plz., Rm. 3100
New York, NY 10278
(212)264-4507
Fax: (212)264-4963
E-mail: score1000@erols.com
Website: http://users.erols.com/
score-nyc/

SCORE Office (Newburgh)
47 Grand St.
Newburgh, NY 12550
(914)562-5100

SCORE Office (Owego)
188 Front St.
Owego, NY 13827
(607)687-2020

SCORE Office (Peekskill)
1 S. Division St.
Peekskill, NY 10566
(914)737-3600
Fax: (914)737-0541

SCORE Office (Penn Yan)
2375 Rte. 14A
Penn Yan, NY 14527
(315)536-3111

SCORE Office (Dutchess)
110 Main St.
Poughkeepsie, NY 12601
(914)454-1700

SCORE Office (Rochester)
601 Keating Federal Bldg., Rm. 410
100 State St.
Rochester, NY 14614
(716)263-6473
Fax: (716)263-3146
Website: http://www.ggw.org/score/

SCORE Office (Saranac Lake)
30 Main St.
Saranac Lake, NY 12983
(315)448-0415

SCORE Office (Suffolk)
286 Main St.
Setauket, NY 11733
(516)751-3886

SCORE Office (Staten Island)
130 Bay St.
Staten Island, NY 10301
(718)727-1221

SCORE Office (Ulster)
Clinton Bldg., Rm. 107
Stone Ridge, NY 12484
(914)687-5035
Fax: (914)687-5015
Website: http://www.scoreulster.org/

SCORE Office (Syracuse)
401 S. Salina, 5th Fl.
Syracuse, NY 13202
(315)471-9393

SCORE Office (Utica)
SUNY Institute of Technology, Route 12
Utica, NY 13504-3050
(315)792-7553

SCORE Office (Watertown)
518 Davidson St.
Watertown, NY 13601
(315)788-1200
Fax: (315)788-8251

North Carolina

SCORE office (Asheboro)
317 E. Dixie Dr.
Asheboro, NC 27203
(336)626-2626
Fax: (336)626-7077

SCORE Office (Asheville)
Federal Bldg., Rm. 259
151 Patton
Asheville, NC 28801-5770
(828)271-4786
Fax: (828)271-4009

SCORE Office (Chapel Hill)
104 S. Estes Dr.
PO Box 2897
Chapel Hill, NC 27514
(919)967-7075

SCORE Office (Coastal Plains)
PO Box 2897
Chapel Hill, NC 27515
(919)967-7075
Fax: (919)968-6874

SCORE Office (Charlotte)
200 N. College St., Ste. A-2015

Charlotte, NC 28202
(704)344-6576
Fax: (704)344-6769
E-mail: CharlotteSCORE47@AOL.com
Website: http://www.charweb.org/
business/score/

SCORE Office (Durham)
411 W. Chapel Hill St.
Durham, NC 27707
(919)541-2171

SCORE Office (Gastonia)
PO Box 2168
Gastonia, NC 28053
(704)864-2621
Fax: (704)854-8723

SCORE Office (Greensboro)
400 W. Market St., Ste. 103
Greensboro, NC 27401-2241
(910)333-5399

SCORE Office (Henderson)
PO Box 917
Henderson, NC 27536
(919)492-2061
Fax: (919)430-0460

SCORE Office (Hendersonville)
Federal Bldg., Rm. 108
W. 4th Ave. & Church St.
Hendersonville, NC 28792
(828)693-8702
E-mail: score@circle.net
Website: http://www.wncguide.com/
score/Welcome.html

SCORE Office (Unifour)
PO Box 1828
Hickory, NC 28603
(704)328-6111

SCORE Office (High Point)
1101 N. Main St.
High Point, NC 27262
(336)882-8625
Fax: (336)889-9499

SCORE Office (Outer Banks)
Collington Rd. and Mustain
Kill Devil Hills, NC 27948
(252)441-8144

SCORE Office (Down East)
312 S. Front St., Ste. 6
New Bern, NC 28560
(252)633-6688
Fax: (252)633-9608

SCORE Office (Kinston)
PO Box 95

New Bern, NC 28561
(919)633-6688

SCORE Office (Raleigh)
Century Post Office Bldg., Ste. 306
300 Federal St. Mall
Raleigh, NC 27601
(919)856-4739
E-mail: jendres@ibm.net
Website: http://www.intrex.net/score96/
score96.htm

SCORE Office (Sanford)
1801 Nash St.
Sanford, NC 27330
(919)774-6442
Fax: (919)776-8739

SCORE Office (Sandhills Area)
1480 Hwy. 15-501
PO Box 458
Southern Pines, NC 28387
(910)692-3926

SCORE Office (Wilmington)
Corps of Engineers Bldg.
96 Darlington Ave., Ste. 207
Wilmington, NC 28403
(910)815-4576
Fax: (910)815-4658

North Dakota

**SCORE Office
(Bismarck-Mandan)**
700 E. Main Ave., 2nd Fl.
PO Box 5509
Bismarck, ND 58506-5509
(701)250-4303

SCORE Office (Fargo)
657 2nd Ave., Rm. 225
Fargo, ND 58108-3083
(701)239-5677

SCORE Office (Upper Red River)
4275 Technology Dr., Rm. 156
Grand Forks, ND 58202-8372
(701)777-3051

SCORE Office (Minot)
100 1st St. SW
Minot, ND 58701-3846
(701)852-6883
Fax: (701)852-6905

Ohio

SCORE Office (Akron)
1 Cascade Plz., 7th Fl.
Akron, OH 44308

(330)379-3163
Fax: (330)379-3164

SCORE Office (Ashland)
Gill Center
47 W. Main St.
Ashland, OH 44805
(419)281-4584

SCORE Office (Canton)
116 Cleveland Ave. NW, Ste. 601
Canton, OH 44702-1720
(330)453-6047

SCORE Office (Chillicothe)
165 S. Paint St.
Chillicothe, OH 45601
(614)772-4530

SCORE Office (Cincinnati)
Ameritrust Bldg., Rm. 850
525 Vine St.
Cincinnati, OH 45202
(513)684-2812
Fax: (513)684-3251
Website: http://www.score.
chapter34.org/

SCORE Office (Cleveland)
Eaton Center, Ste. 620
1100 Superior Ave.
Cleveland, OH 44114-2507
(216)522-4194
Fax: (216)522-4844

SCORE Office (Columbus)
2 Nationwide Plz., Ste. 1400
Columbus, OH 43215-2542
(614)469-2357
Fax: (614)469-2391
E-mail: info@scorecolumbus.org
Website: http://www.scorecolumbus.org/

SCORE Office (Dayton)
Dayton Federal Bldg., Rm. 505
200 W. Second St.
Dayton, OH 45402-1430
(513)225-2887
Fax: (513)225-7667

SCORE Office (Defiance)
615 W. 3rd St.
PO Box 130
Defiance, OH 43512
(419)782-7946

SCORE Office (Findlay)
123 E. Main Cross St.
PO Box 923
Findlay, OH 45840
(419)422-3314

SCORE Office (Lima)
147 N. Main St.
Lima, OH 45801
(419)222-6045
Fax: (419)229-0266

SCORE Office (Mansfield)
55 N. Mulberry St.
Mansfield, OH 44902
(419)522-3211

SCORE Office (Marietta)
Thomas Hall
Marietta, OH 45750
(614)373-0268

SCORE Office (Medina)
County Administrative Bldg.
144 N. Broadway
Medina, OH 44256
(216)764-8650

SCORE Office (Licking County)
50 W. Locust St.
Newark, OH 43055
(614)345-7458

SCORE Office (Salem)
2491 State Rte. 45 S
Salem, OH 44460
(216)332-0361

SCORE Office (Tiffin)
62 S. Washington St.
Tiffin, OH 44883
(419)447-4141
Fax: (419)447-5141

SCORE Office (Toledo)
608 Madison Ave, Ste. 910
Toledo, OH 43624
(419)259-7598
Fax: (419)259-6460

SCORE Office (Heart of Ohio)
377 W. Liberty St.
Wooster, OH 44691
(330)262-5735
Fax: (330)262-5745

SCORE Office (Youngstown)
306 Williamson Hall
Youngstown, OH 44555
(330)746-2687

Oklahoma

SCORE Office (Anadarko)
PO Box 366
Anadarko, OK 73005
(405)247-6651

SCORE Office (Ardmore)
410 W. Main
Ardmore, OK 73401
(580)226-2620

SCORE Office (Northeast Oklahoma)
210 S. Main
Grove, OK 74344
(918)787-2796
Fax: (918)787-2796
E-mail: Score595@greencis.net

SCORE Office (Lawton)
4500 W. Lee Blvd., Bldg. 100, Ste. 107
Lawton, OK 73505
(580)353-8727
Fax: (580)250-5677

SCORE Office (Oklahoma City)
210 Park Ave., No. 1300
Oklahoma City, OK 73102
(405)231-5163
Fax: (405)231-4876
E-mail: score212@usa.net

SCORE Office (Stillwater)
439 S. Main
Stillwater, OK 74074
(405)372-5573
Fax: (405)372-4316

SCORE Office (Tulsa)
616 S. Boston, Ste. 406
Tulsa, OK 74119
(918)581-7462
Fax: (918)581-6908
Website: http://www.ionet.net/~tulscore/

Oregon

SCORE Office (Bend)
63085 N. Hwy. 97
Bend, OR 97701
(541)923-2849
Fax: (541)330-6900

SCORE Office (Willamette)
1401 Willamette St.
PO Box 1107
Eugene, OR 97401-4003
(541)465-6600
Fax: (541)484-4942

SCORE Office (Florence)
3149 Oak St.
Florence, OR 97439
(503)997-8444
Fax: (503)997-8448

SCORE Office (Southern Oregon)
33 N. Central Ave., Ste. 216

Medford, OR 97501
(541)776-4220
E-mail: pgr134f@prodigy.com

SCORE Office (Portland)
1515 SW 5th Ave., Ste. 1050
Portland, OR 97201
(503)326-3441
Fax: (503)326-2808
E-mail: gr134@prodigy.com

SCORE Office (Salem)
416 State St. (corner of Liberty)
Salem, OR 97301
(503)370-2896

Pennsylvania

SCORE Office (Altoona-Blair)
1212 12th Ave.
Altoona, PA 16601-3493
(814)943-8151

SCORE Office (Lehigh Valley)
Rauch Bldg. 37
Lehigh University
621 Taylor St.
Bethlehem, PA 18015
(610)758-4496
Fax: (610)758-5205

SCORE Office (Butler County)
100 N. Main St.
PO Box 1082
Butler, PA 16003
(412)283-2222
Fax: (412)283-0224

SCORE Office (Harrisburg)
4211 Trindle Rd.
Camp Hill, PA 17011
(717)761-4304
Fax: (717)761-4315

SCORE Office (Cumberland Valley)
75 S. 2nd St.
Chambersburg, PA 17201
(717)264-2935

SCORE Office (Monroe County-Stroudsburg)
556 Main St.
East Stroudsburg, PA 18301
(717)421-4433

SCORE Office (Erie)
120 W. 9th St.
Erie, PA 16501
(814)871-5650
Fax: (814)871-7530

SCORE Office (Bucks County)
409 Hood Blvd.
Fairless Hills, PA 19030
(215)943-8850
Fax: (215)943-7404

SCORE Office (Hanover)
146 Broadway
Hanover, PA 17331
(717)637-6130
Fax: (717)637-9127

SCORE Office (Harrisburg)
100 Chestnut, Ste. 309
Harrisburg, PA 17101
(717)782-3874

SCORE Office (East Montgomery County)
Baederwood Shopping Center
1653 The Fairways, Ste. 204
Jenkintown, PA 19046
(215)885-3027

SCORE Office (Kittanning)
2 Butler Rd.
Kittanning, PA 16201
(412)543-1305
Fax: (412)543-6206

SCORE Office (Lancaster)
118 W. Chestnut St.
Lancaster, PA 17603
(717)397-3092

SCORE Office (Westmoreland County)
300 Fraser Purchase Rd.
Latrobe, PA 15650-2690
(412)539-7505
Fax: (412)539-1850

SCORE Office (Lebanon)
252 N. 8th St.
PO Box 899
Lebanon, PA 17042-0899
(717)273-3727
Fax: (717)273-7940

SCORE Office (Lewistown)
3 W. Monument Sq., Ste. 204
Lewistown, PA 17044
(717)248-6713
Fax: (717)248-6714

SCORE Office (Delaware County)
602 E. Baltimore Pike
Media, PA 19063
(610)565-3677
Fax: (610)565-1606

SCORE Office (Milton Area)
112 S. Front St.
Milton, PA 17847

(717)742-7341
Fax: (717)792-2008

SCORE Office (Mon-Valley)
435 Donner Ave.
Monessen, PA 15062
(412)684-4277
Fax: (412)684-7688

SCORE Office (Monroeville)
William Penn Plaza
2790 Mosside Blvd., Ste. 295
Monroeville, PA 15146
(412)856-0622
Fax: (412)856-1030

SCORE Office (Airport Area)
986 Brodhead Rd.
Moon Township, PA 15108-2398
(412)264-6270
Fax: (412)264-1575

SCORE Office (Northeast)
8601 E. Roosevelt Blvd.
Philadelphia, PA 19152
(215)332-3400
Fax: (215)332-6050

SCORE Office (Philadelphia)
1315 Walnut St., Ste. 500
Philadelphia, PA 19107
(215)790-5050
Fax: (215)790-5057
E-mail: score46@bellatlantic.net
Website: http://www.pgweb.net/score46/

SCORE Office (Pittsburgh)
1000 Liberty Ave., Rm. 1122
Pittsburgh, PA 15222
(412)395-6560
Fax: (412)395-6562

SCORE Office (Tri-County)
801 N. Charlotte St.
Pottstown, PA 19464
(610)327-2673

SCORE Office (Reading)
601 Penn St.
Reading, PA 19601
(610)376-3497

SCORE Office (Scranton)
Oppenheim Bldg.
116 N. Washington Ave., Ste. 650
Scranton, PA 18503
(717)347-4611
Fax: (717)347-4611

SCORE Office (Central Pennsylvania)
200 Innovation Blvd., Ste. 242-B
State College, PA 16803

(814)234-9415
Fax: (814)238-9686
Website: http://countrystore.org/business/score.htm

SCORE Office (Monroe-Stroudsburg)
556 Main St.
Stroudsburg, PA 18360
(717)421-4433

SCORE Office (Uniontown)
Federal Bldg.
Pittsburg St.
PO Box 2065 DTS
Uniontown, PA 15401
(412)437-4222
E-mail: uniontownscore@lcsys.net

SCORE Office (Warren County)
315 2nd Ave.
Warren, PA 16365
(814)723-9017

SCORE Office (Waynesboro)
323 E. Main St.
Waynesboro, PA 17268
(717)762-7123
Fax: (717)962-7124

SCORE Office (Chester County)
Government Service Center, Ste. 281
601 Westtown Rd.
West Chester, PA 19382-4538
(610)344-6910
Fax: (610)344-6919
E-mail: score@locke.ccil.org

SCORE Office (Wilkes-Barre)
7 N. Wilkes-Barre Blvd.
Wilkes Barre, PA 18702-5241
(717)826-6502
Fax: (717)826-6287

SCORE Office (North Central Pennsylvania)
240 W. 3rd St., Rm. 227
PO Box 725
Williamsport, PA 17703
(717)322-3720
Fax: (717)322-1607
E-mail: score234@mail.csrlink.net
Website: http://www.lycoming.org/score/

SCORE Office (York)
Cyber Center
2101 Pennsylvania Ave.
York, PA 17404
(717)845-8830
Fax: (717)854-9333

Puerto Rico

SCORE Office (Puerto Rico & Virgin Islands)
PO Box 12383-96
San Juan, PR 00914-0383
(787)726-8040
Fax: (787)726-8135

Rhode Island

SCORE Office (Barrington)
281 County Rd.
Barrington, RI 02806
(401)247-1920
Fax: (401)247-3763

SCORE Office (Woonsocket)
640 Washington Hwy.
Lincoln, RI 02865
(401)334-1000
Fax: (401)334-1009

SCORE Office (Wickford)
8045 Post Rd.
North Kingstown, RI 02852
(401)295-5566
Fax: (401)295-8987

SCORE Office (J.G.E. Knight)
380 Westminster St.
Providence, RI 02903
(401)528-4571
Fax: (401)528-4539
Website: http://www.riscore.org

SCORE Office (Warwick)
3288 Post Rd.
Warwick, RI 02886
(401)732-1100
Fax: (401)732-1101

SCORE Office (Westerly)
74 Post Rd.
Westerly, RI 02891
(401)596-7761
800-732-7636
Fax: (401)596-2190

South Carolina

SCORE Office (Aiken)
PO Box 892
Aiken, SC 29802
(803)641-1111
800-542-4536
Fax: (803)641-4174

SCORE Office (Anderson)
Anderson Mall
3130 N. Main St.

Anderson, SC 29621
(864)224-0453

SCORE Office (Coastal)
284 King St.
Charleston, SC 29401
(803)727-4778
Fax: (803)853-2529

SCORE Office (Midlands)
Strom Thurmond Bldg., Rm. 358
1835 Assembly St., Rm 358
Columbia, SC 29201
(803)765-5131
Fax: (803)765-5962
Website: http://www.scoremidlands.org/

SCORE Office (Piedmont)
Federal Bldg., Rm. B-02
300 E. Washington St.
Greenville, SC 29601
(864)271-3638

SCORE Office (Greenwood)
PO Drawer 1467
Greenwood, SC 29648
(864)223-8357

SCORE Office (Hilton Head Island)
52 Savannah Trail
Hilton Head, SC 29926
(803)785-7107
Fax: (803)785-7110

SCORE Office (Grand Strand)
937 Broadway
Myrtle Beach, SC 29577
(803)918-1079
Fax: (803)918-1083
E-mail: score381@aol.com

SCORE Office (Spartanburg)
PO Box 1636
Spartanburg, SC 29304
(864)594-5000
Fax: (864)594-5055

South Dakota

SCORE Office (West River)
Rushmore Plz. Civic Ctr.
444 Mount Rushmore Rd., No. 209
Rapid City, SD 57701
(605)394-5311
E-mail: score@gwtc.net

SCORE Office (Sioux Falls)
First Financial Center
110 S. Phillips Ave., Ste. 200
Sioux Falls, SD 57104-6727

(605)330-4231
Fax: (605)330-4231

Tennessee

SCORE Office (Chattanooga)
Federal Bldg., Rm. 26
900 Georgia Ave.
Chattanooga, TN 37402
(423)752-5190
Fax: (423)752-5335

SCORE Office (Cleveland)
PO Box 2275
Cleveland, TN 37320
(423)472-6587
Fax: (423)472-2019

SCORE Office (Upper Cumberland Center)
1225 S. Willow Ave.
Cookeville, TN 38501
(615)432-4111
Fax: (615)432-6010

SCORE Office (Unicoi County)
PO Box 713
Erwin, TN 37650
(423)743-3000
Fax: (423)743-0942

SCORE Office (Greeneville)
115 Academy St.
Greeneville, TN 37743
(423)638-4111
Fax: (423)638-5345

SCORE Office (Jackson)
194 Auditorium St.
Jackson, TN 38301
(901)423-2200

SCORE Office (Northeast Tennessee)
1st Tennessee Bank Bldg.
2710 S. Roan St., Ste. 584
Johnson City, TN 37601
(423)929-7686
Fax: (423)461-8052

SCORE Office (Kingsport)
151 E. Main St.
Kingsport, TN 37662
(423)392-8805

SCORE Office (Greater Knoxville)
Farragot Bldg., Ste. 224
530 S. Gay St.
Knoxville, TN 37902
(423)545-4203
E-mail: scoreknox@ntown.com
Website: http://www.scoreknox.org/

SCORE Office (Maryville)
201 S. Washington St.
Maryville, TN 37804-5728
(423)983-2241
800-525-6834
Fax: (423)984-1386

SCORE Office (Memphis)
Federal Bldg., Ste. 390
167 N. Main St.
Memphis, TN 38103
(901)544-3588

SCORE Office (Nashville)
50 Vantage Way, Ste. 201
Nashville, TN 37228-1500
(615)736-7621

Texas

SCORE Office (Abilene)
2106 Federal Post Office and Court Bldg.
Abilene, TX 79601
(915)677-1857

SCORE Office (Austin)
2501 S. Congress
Austin, TX 78701
(512)442-7235
Fax: (512)442-7528

SCORE Office (Golden Triangle)
450 Boyd St.
Beaumont, TX 77704
(409)838-6581
Fax: (409)833-6718

SCORE Office (Brownsville)
3505 Boca Chica Blvd., Ste. 305
Brownsville, TX 78521
(210)541-4508

SCORE Office (Brazos Valley)
3000 Briarcrest, Ste. 302
Bryan, TX 77802
(409)776-8876
E-mail: 102633.2612@compuserve.com

SCORE Office (Cleburne)
Watergarden Pl., 9th Fl., Ste. 400
Cleburne, TX 76031
(817)871-6002

SCORE Office (Corpus Christi)
651 Upper North Broadway, Ste. 654
Corpus Christi, TX 78477
(512)888-4322
Fax: (512)888-3418

SCORE Office (Dallas)
6260 E. Mockingbird
Dallas, TX 75214-2619

(214)828-2471
Fax: (214)821-8033

SCORE Office (El Paso)
10 Civic Center Plaza
El Paso, TX 79901
(915)534-0541
Fax: (915)534-0513

SCORE Office (Bedford)
100 E. 15th St., Ste. 400
Ft. Worth, TX 76102
(817)871-6002

SCORE Office (Ft. Worth)
100 E. 15th St., No. 24
Ft. Worth, TX 76102
(817)871-6002
Fax: (817)871-6031
E-mail: fwbac@onramp.net

SCORE Office (Garland)
2734 W. Kingsley Rd.
Garland, TX 75041
(214)271-9224

SCORE Office (Granbury Chamber of Commerce)
416 S. Morgan
Granbury, TX 76048
(817)573-1622
Fax: (817)573-0805

SCORE Office (Lower Rio Grande Valley)
222 E. Van Buren, Ste. 500
Harlingen, TX 78550
(956)427-8533
Fax: (956)427-8537

SCORE Office (Houston)
9301 Southwest Fwy., Ste. 550
Houston, TX 77074
(713)773-6565
Fax: (713)773-6550

SCORE Office (Irving)
3333 N. MacArthur Blvd., Ste. 100
Irving, TX 75062
(214)252-8484
Fax: (214)252-6710

SCORE Office (Lubbock)
1205 Texas Ave., Rm. 411D
Lubbock, TX 79401
(806)472-7462
Fax: (806)472-7487

SCORE Office (Midland)
Post Office Annex
200 E. Wall St., Rm. P121
Midland, TX 79701
(915)687-2649

SCORE Office (Orange)
1012 Green Ave.
Orange, TX 77630-5620
(409)883-3536
800-528-4906
Fax: (409)886-3247

SCORE Office (Plano)
1200 E. 15th St.
PO Drawer 940287
Plano, TX 75094-0287
(214)424-7547
Fax: (214)422-5182

SCORE Office (Port Arthur)
4749 Twin City Hwy., Ste. 300
Port Arthur, TX 77642
(409)963-1107
Fax: (409)963-3322

SCORE Office (Richardson)
411 Belle Grove
Richardson, TX 75080
(214)234-4141
800-777-8001
Fax: (214)680-9103

SCORE Office (San Antonio)
Federal Bldg., Rm. A527
727 E. Durango
San Antonio, TX 78206
(210)472-5931
Fax: (210)472-5935

SCORE Office (Texarkana State College)
819 State Line Ave.
Texarkana, TX 75501
(903)792-7191
Fax: (903)793-4304

SCORE Office (East Texas)
RTDC
1530 SSW Loop 323, Ste. 100
Tyler, TX 75701
(903)510-2975
Fax: (903)510-2978

SCORE Office (Waco)
401 Franklin Ave.
Waco, TX 76701
(817)754-8898
Fax: (817)756-0776
Website: http://www.brc-waco.com/

SCORE Office (Wichita Falls)
Hamilton Bldg.
900 8th St.
Wichita Falls, TX 76307
(940)723-2741
Fax: (940)723-8773

Utah

SCORE Office (Northern Utah)
160 N. Main
Logan, UT 84321
(435)746-2269

SCORE Office (Ogden)
1701 E. Windsor Dr.
Ogden, UT 84604
(801)629-8613
E-mail: score158@netscape.net

SCORE Office (Central Utah)
1071 E. Windsor Dr.
Provo, UT 84604
(801)373-8660

SCORE Office (Southern Utah)
225 South 700 East
St. George, UT 84770
(435)652-7751

SCORE Office (Salt Lake)
310 S Main St.
Salt Lake City, UT 84101
(801)746-2269
Fax: (801)746-2273

Vermont

SCORE Office (Champlain Valley)
Winston Prouty Federal Bldg.
11 Lincoln St., Rm. 106
Essex Junction, VT 05452
(802)951-6762

SCORE Office (Montpelier)
87 State St., Rm. 205
PO Box 605
Montpelier, VT 05601
(802)828-4422
Fax: (802)828-4485

SCORE Office (Marble Valley)
256 N. Main St.
Rutland, VT 05701-2413
(802)773-9147

SCORE Office (Northeast Kingdom)
20 Main St.
PO Box 904
St. Johnsbury, VT 05819
(802)748-5101

Virgin Islands

SCORE Office (St. Croix)
United Plaza Shopping Center
PO Box 4010, Christiansted
St. Croix, VI 00822
(809)778-5380

SCORE Office (St. Thomas-St. John)
Federal Bldg., Rm. 21
Veterans Dr.
St. Thomas, VI 00801
(809)774-8530

Virginia

SCORE Office (Arlington)
2009 N. 14th St., Ste. 111
Arlington, VA 22201
(703)525-2400

SCORE Office (Blacksburg)
141 Jackson St.
Blacksburg, VA 24060
(540)552-4061

SCORE Office (Bristol)
20 Volunteer Pkwy.
Bristol, VA 24203
(540)989-4850

SCORE Office (Central Virginia)
1001 E. Market St., Ste. 101
Charlottesville, VA 22902
(804)295-6712
Fax: (804)295-7066

SCORE Office (Alleghany Satellite)
241 W. Main St.
Covington, VA 24426
(540)962-2178
Fax: (540)962-2179

SCORE Office (Central Fairfax)
3975 University Dr., Ste. 350
Fairfax, VA 22030
(703)591-2450

SCORE Office (Falls Church)
PO Box 491
Falls Church, VA 22040
(703)532-1050
Fax: (703)237-7904

SCORE Office (Glenns)
Glenns Campus
Box 287
Glenns, VA 23149
(804)693-9650

SCORE Office (Peninsula)
6 Manhattan Sq.
PO Box 7269
Hampton, VA 23666
(757)766-2000
Fax: (757)865-0339
E-mail: score100@seva.net

SCORE Office (Tri-Cities)
108 N. Main St.

Hopewell, VA 23860
(804)458-5536

SCORE Office (Lynchburg)
Federal Bldg.
1100 Main St.
Lynchburg, VA 24504-1714
(804)846-3235

SCORE Office (Greater Prince William)
8963 Center St
Manassas, VA 20110
(703)368-4813
Fax: (703)368-4733

SCORE Office (Martinsvile)
115 Broad St.
Martinsville, VA 24112-0709
(540)632-6401
Fax: (540)632-5059

SCORE Office (Hampton Roads)
Federal Bldg., Rm. 737
200 Grandby St.
Norfolk, VA 23510
(757)441-3733
Fax: (757)441-3733
E-mail: scorehr60@juno.com

SCORE Office (Norfolk)
Federal Bldg., Rm. 737
200 Granby St.
Norfolk, VA 23510
(757)441-3733
Fax: (757)441-3733

SCORE Office (Virginia Beach)
Chamber of Commerce
200 Grandby St., Rm 737
Norfolk, VA 23510
(804)441-3733

SCORE Office (Radford)
1126 Norwood St.
Radford, VA 24141
(540)639-2202

SCORE Office (Richmond)
Federal Bldg.
400 N. 8th St., Ste. 1150
PO Box 10126
Richmond, VA 23240-0126
(804)771-2400
Fax: (804)771-8018
E-mail: scorechapter12@yahoo.com
Website: http://www.cvco.org/score/

SCORE Office (Roanoke)
Federal Bldg., Rm. 716
250 Franklin Rd.
Roanoke, VA 24011

(540)857-2834
Fax: (540)857-2043
E-mail: scorerva@juno.com
Website: http://hometown.aol.com/
scorerv/Index.html

SCORE Office (Fairfax)
8391 Old Courthouse Rd., Ste. 300
Vienna, VA 22182
(703)749-0400

SCORE Office (Greater Vienna)
513 Maple Ave. West
Vienna, VA 22180
(703)281-1333
Fax: (703)242-1482

SCORE Office (Shenandoah Valley)
301 W. Main St.
Waynesboro, VA 22980
(540)949-8203
Fax: (540)949-7740
E-mail: score427@intelos.net

SCORE Office (Williamsburg)
201 Penniman Rd.
Williamsburg, VA 23185
(757)229-6511
E-mail: wacc@williamsburgcc.com

SCORE Office (Northern Virginia)
1360 S. Pleasant Valley Rd.
Winchester, VA 22601
(540)662-4118

Washington

SCORE Office (Gray's Harbor)
506 Duffy St.
Aberdeen, WA 98520
(360)532-1924
Fax: (360)533-7945

SCORE Office (Bellingham)
101 E. Holly St.
Bellingham, WA 98225
(360)676-3307

SCORE Office (Everett)
2702 Hoyt Ave.
Everett, WA 98201-3556
(206)259-8000

SCORE Office (Gig Harbor)
3125 Judson St.
Gig Harbor, WA 98335
(206)851-6865

SCORE Office (Kennewick)
PO Box 6986
Kennewick, WA 99336
(509)736-0510

SCORE Office (Puyallup)
322 2nd St. SW
PO Box 1298
Puyallup, WA 98371
(206)845-6755
Fax: (206)848-6164

SCORE Office (Seattle)
1200 6th Ave., Ste. 1700
Seattle, WA 98101
(206)553-7320
Fax: (206)553-7044
E-mail: score55@aol.com
Website: http://www.scn.org/civic/score-
online/index55.html

SCORE Office (Spokane)
801 W. Riverside Ave., No. 240
Spokane, WA 99201
(509)353-2820
Fax: (509)353-2600
E-mail: score@dmi.net
Website: http://www.dmi.net/score/

SCORE Office (Clover Park)
PO Box 1933
Tacoma, WA 98401-1933
(206)627-2175

SCORE Office (Tacoma)
1101 Pacific Ave.
Tacoma, WA 98402
(253)274-1288
Fax: (253)274-1289

SCORE Office (Fort Vancouver)
1701 Broadway, S-1
Vancouver, WA 98663
(360)699-1079

SCORE Office (Walla Walla)
500 Tausick Way
Walla Walla, WA 99362
(509)527-4681

SCORE Office (Mid-Columbia)
1113 S. 14th Ave.
Yakima, WA 98907
(509)574-4944
Fax: (509)574-2943
Website: http://www.ellensburg.com/
~score/

West Virginia

SCORE Office (Charleston)
1116 Smith St.
Charleston, WV 25301
(304)347-5463
E-mail: score256@juno.com

SCORE Office (Virginia Street)
1116 Smith St., Ste. 302
Charleston, WV 25301
(304)347-5463

SCORE Office (Marion County)
PO Box 208
Fairmont, WV 26555-0208
(304)363-0486

SCORE Office (Upper Monongahela Valley)
1000 Technology Dr., Ste. 1111
Fairmont, WV 26555
(304)363-0486
E-mail: score537@hotmail.com

SCORE Office (Huntington)
1101 6th Ave., Ste. 220
Huntington, WV 25701-2309
(304)523-4092

SCORE Office (Wheeling)
1310 Market St.
Wheeling, WV 26003
(304)233-2575
Fax: (304)233-1320

Wisconsin

SCORE Office (Fox Cities)
227 S. Walnut St.
Appleton, WI 54913
(920)734-7101
Fax: (920)734-7161

SCORE Office (Beloit)
136 W. Grand Ave., Ste. 100
PO Box 717
Beloit, WI 53511
(608)365-8835
Fax: (608)365-9170

SCORE Office (Eau Claire)
Federal Bldg., Rm. B11
510 S. Barstow St.
Eau Claire, WI 54701
(715)834-1573
E-mail: score@ecol.net
Website: http://www.ecol.net/~score/

SCORE Office (Fond du Lac)
207 N. Main St.
Fond du Lac, WI 54935
(414)921-9500
Fax: (414)921-9559

SCORE Office (Green Bay)
835 Potts Ave.
Green Bay, WI 54304
(414)496-8930
Fax: (414)496-6009

SCORE Office (Janesville)
20 S. Main St., Ste. 11
PO Box 8008
Janesville, WI 53547
(608)757-3160
Fax: (608)757-3170

SCORE Office (La Crosse)
712 Main St.
La Crosse, WI 54602-0219
(608)784-4880

SCORE Office (Madison)
505 S. Rosa Rd.
Madison, WI 53719
(608)441-2820

SCORE Office (Manitowoc)
1515 Memorial Dr.
PO Box 903
Manitowoc, WI 54221-0903
(414)684-5575
Fax: (414)684-1915

SCORE Office (Milwaukee)
310 W. Wisconsin Ave., Ste. 425
Milwaukee, WI 53203
(414)297-3942
Fax: (414)297-1377

SCORE Office (Central Wisconsin)
1224 Lindbergh Ave.
Stevens Point, WI 54481
(715)344-7729

SCORE Office (Superior)
Superior Business Center Inc.
1423 N. 8th St.
Superior, WI 54880
(715)394-7388
Fax: (715)393-7414

SCORE Office (Waukesha)
223 Wisconsin Ave.
Waukesha, WI 53186-4926
(414)542-4249

SCORE Office (Wausau)
300 3rd St., Ste. 200
Wausau, WI 54402-6190
(715)845-6231

SCORE Office (Wisconsin Rapids)
2240 Kingston Rd.
Wisconsin Rapids, WI 54494
(715)423-1830

Wyoming

SCORE Office (Casper)
Federal Bldg., No. 2215
100 East B St.

Casper, WY 82602
(307)261-6529
Fax: (307)261-6530

Venture capital & financing companies

This section contains a listing of financing and loan companies in the United States and Canada. These listing are arranged alphabetically by country, then by state or province, then by city, then by organization name.

Canada

Alberta

Launchworks Inc.
1902J 11th St., S.E.
Calgary, AB, Canada T2G 3G2
(403)269-1119
Fax: (403)269-1141
Website: http://www.launchworks.com

Native Venture Capital Company, Inc.
21 Artist View Point, Box 7
Site 25, RR 12
Calgary, AB, Canada T3E 6W3
(903)208-5380

Miralta Capital Inc.
4445 Calgary Trail South
888 Terrace Plaza Alberta
Edmonton, AB, Canada T6H 5R7
(780)438-3535
Fax: (780)438-3129

Vencap Equities Alberta Ltd.
10180-101st St., Ste. 1980
Edmonton, AB, Canada T5J 3S4
(403)420-1171
Fax: (403)429-2541

British Columbia

Discovery Capital
5th Fl., 1199 West Hastings
Vancouver, BC, Canada V6E 3T5
(604)683-3000
Fax: (604)662-3457
E-mail: info@discoverycapital.com
Website: http://www.discoverycapital.com

Greenstone Venture Partners
1177 West Hastings St.
Ste. 400
Vancouver, BC, Canada V6E 2K3
(604)717-1977
Fax: (604)717-1976
Website: http://www.greenstonevc.com

Growthworks Capital
2600-1055 West Georgia St.
Box 11170 Royal Centre
Vancouver, BC, Canada V6E 3R5
(604)895-7259
Fax: (604)669-7605
Website: http://www.wofund.com

MDS Discovery Venture Management, Inc.
555 W. Eighth Ave., Ste. 305
Vancouver, BC, Canada V5Z 1C6
(604)872-8464
Fax: (604)872-2977
E-mail: info@mds-ventures.com

Ventures West Management Inc.
1285 W. Pender St., Ste. 280
Vancouver, BC, Canada V6E 4B1
(604)688-9495
Fax: (604)687-2145
Website: http://www.ventureswest.com

Nova Scotia

ACF Equity Atlantic Inc.
Purdy's Wharf Tower II
Ste. 2106
Halifax, NS, Canada B3J 3R7
(902)421-1965
Fax: (902)421-1808

Montgomerie, Huck & Co.
146 Bluenose Dr.
PO Box 538
Lunenburg, NS, Canada B0J 2C0
(902)634-7125
Fax: (902)634-7130

Ontario

IPS Industrial Promotion Services Ltd.
60 Columbia Way, Ste. 720
Markham, ON, Canada L3R 0C9
(905)475-9400
Fax: (905)475-5003

Betwin Investments Inc.
Box 23110
Sault Ste. Marie, ON, Canada P6A 6W6
(705)253-0744
Fax: (705)253-0744

Bailey & Company, Inc.
594 Spadina Ave.
Toronto, ON, Canada M5S 2H4
(416)921-6930
Fax: (416)925-4670

BCE Capital
200 Bay St.

South Tower, Ste. 3120
Toronto, ON, Canada M5J 2J2
(416)815-0078
Fax: (416)941-1073
Website: http://www.bcecapital.com

Castlehill Ventures
55 University Ave., Ste. 500
Toronto, ON, Canada M5J 2H7
(416)862-8574
Fax: (416)862-8875

CCFL Mezzanine Partners of Canada
70 University Ave.
Ste. 1450
Toronto, ON, Canada M5J 2M4
(416)977-1450
Fax: (416)977-6764
E-mail: info@ccfl.com
Website: http://www.ccfl.com

Celtic House International
100 Simcoe St., Ste. 100
Toronto, ON, Canada M5H 3G2
(416)542-2436
Fax: (416)542-2435
Website: http://www.celtic-house.com

Clairvest Group Inc.
22 St. Clair Ave. East
Ste. 1700
Toronto, ON, Canada M4T 2S3
(416)925-9270
Fax: (416)925-5753

Crosbie & Co., Inc.
One First Canadian Place
9th Fl.
PO Box 116
Toronto, ON, Canada M5X 1A4
(416)362-7726
Fax: (416)362-3447
E-mail: info@crosbieco.com
Website: http://www.crosbieco.com

Drug Royalty Corp.
Eight King St. East
Ste. 202
Toronto, ON, Canada M5C 1B5
(416)863-1865
Fax: (416)863-5161

Grieve, Horner, Brown & Asculai
8 King St. E, Ste. 1704
Toronto, ON, Canada M5C 1B5
(416)362-7668
Fax: (416)362-7660

Jefferson Partners
77 King St. West
Ste. 4010

PO Box 136
Toronto, ON, Canada M5K 1H1
(416)367-1533
Fax: (416)367-5827
Website: http://www.jefferson.com

J.L. Albright Venture Partners
Canada Trust Tower, 161 Bay St.
Ste. 4440
PO Box 215
Toronto, ON, Canada M5J 2S1
(416)367-2440
Fax: (416)367-4604
Website: http://www.jlaventures.com

McLean Watson Capital Inc.
One First Canadian Place
Ste. 1410
PO Box 129
Toronto, ON, Canada M5X 1A4
(416)363-2000
Fax: (416)363-2010
Website: http://www.mcleanwatson.com

Middlefield Capital Fund
One First Canadian Place
85th Fl.
PO Box 192
Toronto, ON, Canada M5X 1A6
(416)362-0714
Fax: (416)362-7925
Website: http://www.middlefield.com

Mosaic Venture Partners
24 Duncan St.
Ste. 300
Toronto, ON, Canada M5V 3M6
(416)597-8889
Fax: (416)597-2345

Onex Corp.
161 Bay St.
PO Box 700
Toronto, ON, Canada M5J 2S1
(416)362-7711
Fax: (416)362-5765

Penfund Partners Inc.
145 King St. West
Ste. 1920
Toronto, ON, Canada M5H 1J8
(416)865-0300
Fax: (416)364-6912
Website: http://www.penfund.com

Primaxis Technology Ventures Inc.
1 Richmond St. West, 8th Fl.
Toronto, ON, Canada M5H 3W4
(416)313-5210
Fax: (416)313-5218
Website: http://www.primaxis.com

Priveq Capital Funds
240 Duncan Mill Rd., Ste. 602
Toronto, ON, Canada M3B 3P1
(416)447-3330
Fax: (416)447-3331
E-mail: priveq@sympatico.ca

Roynat Ventures
40 King St. West, 26th Fl.
Toronto, ON, Canada M5H 1H1
(416)933-2667
Fax: (416)933-2783
Website: http://www.roynatcapital.com

Tera Capital Corp.
366 Adelaide St. East, Ste. 337
Toronto, ON, Canada M5A 3X9
(416)368-1024
Fax: (416)368-1427

Working Ventures Canadian Fund Inc.
250 Bloor St. East, Ste. 1600
Toronto, ON, Canada M4W 1E6
(416)934-7718
Fax: (416)929-0901
Website: http://www.workingventures.ca

Quebec

Altamira Capital Corp.
202 University
Niveau de Maisoneuve, Bur. 201
Montreal, QC, Canada H3A 2A5
(514)499-1656
Fax: (514)499-9570

Federal Business Development Bank
Venture Capital Division
Five Place Ville Marie, Ste. 600
Montreal, QC, Canada H3B 5E7
(514)283-1896
Fax: (514)283-5455

Hydro-Quebec Capitech Inc.
75 Boul, Rene Levesque Quest
Montreal, QC, Canada H2Z 1A4
(514)289-4783
Fax: (514)289-5420
Website: http://www.hqcapitech.com

Investissement Desjardins
2 complexe Desjardins
C.P. 760
Montreal, QC, Canada H5B 1B8
(514)281-7131
Fax: (514)281-7808
Website: http://www.desjardins.com/id

Marleau Lemire Inc.
One Place Ville-Marie, Ste. 3601
Montreal, QC, Canada H3B 3P2

(514)877-3800
Fax: (514)875-6415

Speirs Consultants Inc.
365 Stanstead
Montreal, QC, Canada H3R 1X5
(514)342-3858
Fax: (514)342-1977

Tecnocap Inc.
4028 Marlowe
Montreal, QC, Canada H4A 3M2
(514)483-6009
Fax: (514)483-6045
Website: http://www.technocap.com

Telsoft Ventures
1000, Rue de la Gauchetiere
Quest, 25eme Etage
Montreal, QC, Canada H3B 4W5
(514)397-8450
Fax: (514)397-8451

Saskatchewan

Saskatchewan Government Growth Fund
1801 Hamilton St., Ste. 1210
Canada Trust Tower
Regina, SK, Canada S4P 4B4
(306)787-2994
Fax: (306)787-2086

United states

Alabama

FHL Capital Corp.
600 20th Street North
Suite 350
Birmingham, AL 35203
(205)328-3098
Fax: (205)323-0001

Harbert Management Corp.
One Riverchase Pkwy. South
Birmingham, AL 35244
(205)987-5500
Fax: (205)987-5707
Website: http://www.harbert.net

Jefferson Capital Fund
PO Box 13129
Birmingham, AL 35213
(205)324-7709

Private Capital Corp.
100 Brookwood Pl., 4th Fl.
Birmingham, AL 35209
(205)879-2722
Fax: (205)879-5121

21st Century Health Ventures
One Health South Pkwy.
Birmingham, AL 35243
(256)268-6250
Fax: (256)970-8928

FJC Growth Capital Corp.
200 W. Side Sq., Ste. 340
Huntsville, AL 35801
(256)922-2918
Fax: (256)922-2909

Hickory Venture Capital Corp.
301 Washington St. NW
Suite 301
Huntsville, AL 35801
(256)539-1931
Fax: (256)539-5130
E-mail: hvcc@hvcc.com
Website: http://www.hvcc.com

Southeastern Technology Fund
7910 South Memorial Pkwy., Ste. F
Huntsville, AL 35802
(256)883-8711
Fax: (256)883-8558

Cordova Ventures
4121 Carmichael Rd., Ste. 301
Montgomery, AL 36106
(334)271-6011
Fax: (334)260-0120
Website: http://www.cordova
ventures.com

**Small Business Clinic of Alabama/AG
Bartholomew & Associates**
PO Box 231074
Montgomery, AL 36123-1074
(334)284-3640

Arizona

Miller Capital Corp.
4909 E. McDowell Rd.
Phoenix, AZ 85008
(602)225-0504
Fax: (602)225-9024
Website: http://www.themiller
group.com

The Columbine Venture Funds
9449 North 90th St., Ste. 200
Scottsdale, AZ 85258
(602)661-9222
Fax: (602)661-6262

Koch Ventures
17767 N. Perimeter Dr., Ste. 101
Scottsdale, AZ 85255
(480)419-3600

Fax: (480)419-3606
Website: http://www.kochventures.com

McKee & Co.
7702 E. Doubletree Ranch Rd.
Suite 230
Scottsdale, AZ 85258
(480)368-0333
Fax: (480)607-7446

Merita Capital Ltd.
7350 E. Stetson Dr., Ste. 108-A
Scottsdale, AZ 85251
(480)947-8700
Fax: (480)947-8766

Valley Ventures / Arizona Growth Partners L.P.
6720 N. Scottsdale Rd., Ste. 208
Scottsdale, AZ 85253
(480)661-6600
Fax: (480)661-6262

Estreetcapital.com
660 South Mill Ave., Ste. 315
Tempe, AZ 85281
(480)968-8400
Fax: (480)968-8480
Website: http://www.estreetcapital.com

Coronado Venture Fund
PO Box 65420
Tucson, AZ 85728-5420
(520)577-3764
Fax: (520)299-8491

Arkansas

Arkansas Capital Corp.
225 South Pulaski St.
Little Rock, AR 72201
(501)374-9247
Fax: (501)374-9425
Website: http://www.arcapital.com

California

Sundance Venture Partners, L.P.
100 Clocktower Place, Ste. 130
Carmel, CA 93923
(831)625-6500
Fax: (831)625-6590

Westar Capital (Costa Mesa)
949 South Coast Dr., Ste. 650
Costa Mesa, CA 92626
(714)481-5160
Fax: (714)481-5166
E-mail: mailbox@westarcapital.com
Website: http://www.westarcapital.com

Alpine Technology Ventures
20300 Stevens Creek Boulevard, Ste. 495
Cupertino, CA 95014
(408)725-1810
Fax: (408)725-1207
Website: http://www.alpineventures.com

Bay Partners
10600 N. De Anza Blvd.
Cupertino, CA 95014-2031
(408)725-2444
Fax: (408)446-4502
Website: http://www.baypartners.com

Novus Ventures
20111 Stevens Creek Blvd., Ste. 130
Cupertino, CA 95014
(408)252-3900
Fax: (408)252-1713
Website: http://www.novusventures.com

Triune Capital
19925 Stevens Creek Blvd., Ste. 200
Cupertino, CA 95014
(310)284-6800
Fax: (310)284-3290

Acorn Ventures
268 Bush St., Ste. 2829
Daly City, CA 94014
(650)994-7801
Fax: (650)994-3305
Website: http://www.acornventures.com

Digital Media Campus
2221 Park Place
El Segundo, CA 90245
(310)426-8000
Fax: (310)426-8010
E-mail: info@thecampus.com
Website: http://www.digital
mediacampus.com

BankAmerica Ventures / BA Venture Partners
950 Tower Ln., Ste. 700
Foster City, CA 94404
(650)378-6000
Fax: (650)378-6040
Website: http://
www.baventurepartners.com

Starting Point Partners
666 Portofino Lane
Foster City, CA 94404
(650)722-1035
Website: http://www.startingpoint
partners.com

Opportunity Capital Partners
2201 Walnut Ave., Ste. 210

Fremont, CA 94538
(510)795-7000
Fax: (510)494-5439
Website: http://www.ocpcapital.com

Imperial Ventures Inc.
9920 S. La Cienega Boulevar, 14th Fl.
Inglewood, CA 90301
(310)417-5409
Fax: (310)338-6115

Ventana Global (Irvine)
18881 Von Karman Ave., Ste. 1150
Irvine, CA 92612
(949)476-2204
Fax: (949)752-0223
Website: http://www.ventanaglobal.com

Integrated Consortium Inc.
50 Ridgecrest Rd.
Kentfield, CA 94904
(415)925-0386
Fax: (415)461-2726

Enterprise Partners
979 Ivanhoe Ave., Ste. 550
La Jolla, CA 92037
(858)454-8833
Fax: (858)454-2489
Website: http://www.epvc.com

Domain Associates
28202 Cabot Rd., Ste. 200
Laguna Niguel, CA 92677
(949)347-2446
Fax: (949)347-9720
Website: http://www.domainvc.com

Cascade Communications Ventures
60 E. Sir Francis Drake Blvd., Ste. 300
Larkspur, CA 94939
(415)925-6500
Fax: (415)925-6501

Allegis Capital
One First St., Ste. Two
Los Altos, CA 94022
(650)917-5900
Fax: (650)917-5901
Website: http://www.allegiscapital.com

Aspen Ventures
1000 Fremont Ave., Ste. 200
Los Altos, CA 94024
(650)917-5670
Fax: (650)917-5677
Website: http://www.aspenventures.com

AVI Capital L.P.
1 First St., Ste. 2
Los Altos, CA 94022

(650)949-9862
Fax: (650)949-8510
Website: http://www.avicapital.com

Bastion Capital Corp.
1999 Avenue of the Stars, Ste. 2960
Los Angeles, CA 90067
(310)788-5700
Fax: (310)277-7582
E-mail: ga@bastioncapital.com
Website: http://www.bastioncapital.com

Davis Group
PO Box 69953
Los Angeles, CA 90069-0953
(310)659-6327
Fax: (310)659-6337

Developers Equity Corp.
1880 Century Park East, Ste. 211
Los Angeles, CA 90067
(213)277-0300

Far East Capital Corp.
350 S. Grand Ave., Ste. 4100
Los Angeles, CA 90071
(213)687-1361
Fax: (213)617-7939
E-mail: free@fareastnationalbank.com

Kline Hawkes & Co.
11726 San Vicente Blvd., Ste. 300
Los Angeles, CA 90049
(310)442-4700
Fax: (310)442-4707
Website: http://www.klinehawkes.com

Lawrence Financial Group
701 Teakwood
PO Box 491773
Los Angeles, CA 90049
(310)471-4060
Fax: (310)472-3155

Riordan Lewis & Haden
300 S. Grand Ave., 29th Fl.
Los Angeles, CA 90071
(213)229-8500
Fax: (213)229-8597

Union Venture Corp.
445 S. Figueroa St., 9th Fl.
Los Angeles, CA 90071
(213)236-4092
Fax: (213)236-6329

Wedbush Capital Partners
1000 Wilshire Blvd.
Los Angeles, CA 90017
(213)688-4545
Fax: (213)688-6642
Website: http://www.wedbush.com

Advent International Corp.
2180 Sand Hill Rd., Ste. 420
Menlo Park, CA 94025
(650)233-7500
Fax: (650)233-7515
Website: http://www.adventinternational.com

Altos Ventures
2882 Sand Hill Rd., Ste. 100
Menlo Park, CA 94025
(650)234-9771
Fax: (650)233-9821
Website: http://www.altosvc.com

Applied Technology
1010 El Camino Real, Ste. 300
Menlo Park, CA 94025
(415)326-8622
Fax: (415)326-8163

APV Technology Partners
535 Middlefield, Ste. 150
Menlo Park, CA 94025
(650)327-7871
Fax: (650)327-7631
Website: http://www.apvtp.com

August Capital Management
2480 Sand Hill Rd., Ste. 101
Menlo Park, CA 94025
(650)234-9900
Fax: (650)234-9910
Website: http://www.augustcap.com

Baccharis Capital Inc.
2420 Sand Hill Rd., Ste. 100
Menlo Park, CA 94025
(650)324-6844
Fax: (650)854-3025

Benchmark Capital
2480 Sand Hill Rd., Ste. 200
Menlo Park, CA 94025
(650)854-8180
Fax: (650)854-8183
E-mail: info@benchmark.com
Website: http://www.benchmark.com

Bessemer Venture Partners (Menlo Park)
535 Middlefield Rd., Ste. 245
Menlo Park, CA 94025
(650)853-7000
Fax: (650)853-7001
Website: http://www.bvp.com

The Cambria Group
1600 El Camino Real Rd., Ste. 155
Menlo Park, CA 94025
(650)329-8600

Fax: (650)329-8601
Website: http://www.cambriagroup.com

Canaan Partners
2884 Sand Hill Rd., Ste. 115
Menlo Park, CA 94025
(650)854-8092
Fax: (650)854-8127
Website: http://www.canaan.com

Capstone Ventures
3000 Sand Hill Rd., Bldg. One, Ste. 290
Menlo Park, CA 94025
(650)854-2523
Fax: (650)854-9010
Website: http://www.capstonevc.com

Comdisco Venture Group (Silicon Valley)
3000 Sand Hill Rd., Bldg. 1, Ste. 155
Menlo Park, CA 94025
(650)854-9484
Fax: (650)854-4026

Commtech International
535 Middlefield Rd., Ste. 200
Menlo Park, CA 94025
(650)328-0190
Fax: (650)328-6442

Compass Technology Partners
1550 El Camino Real, Ste. 275
Menlo Park, CA 94025-4111
(650)322-7595
Fax: (650)322-0588
Website: http://www.compasstechpartners.com

Convergence Partners
3000 Sand Hill Rd., Ste. 235
Menlo Park, CA 94025
(650)854-3010
Fax: (650)854-3015
Website: http://www.convergencepartners.com

The Dakota Group
PO Box 1025
Menlo Park, CA 94025
(650)853-0600
Fax: (650)851-4899
E-mail: info@dakota.com

Delphi Ventures
3000 Sand Hill Rd.
Bldg. One, Ste. 135
Menlo Park, CA 94025
(650)854-9650
Fax: (650)854-2961
Website: http://www.delphiventures.com

El Dorado Ventures
2884 Sand Hill Rd., Ste. 121
Menlo Park, CA 94025
(650)854-1200
Fax: (650)854-1202
Website: http://www.eldorado
ventures.com

Glynn Ventures
3000 Sand Hill Rd., Bldg. 4, Ste. 235
Menlo Park, CA 94025
(650)854-2215

Indosuez Ventures
2180 Sand Hill Rd., Ste. 450
Menlo Park, CA 94025
(650)854-0587
Fax: (650)323-5561
Website: http://www.indosuez
ventures.com

Institutional Venture Partners
3000 Sand Hill Rd., Bldg. 2, Ste. 290
Menlo Park, CA 94025
(650)854-0132
Fax: (650)854-5762
Website: http://www.ivp.com

Interwest Partners (Menlo Park)
3000 Sand Hill Rd., Bldg. 3, Ste. 255
Menlo Park, CA 94025-7112
(650)854-8585
Fax: (650)854-4706
Website: http://www.interwest.com

**Kleiner Perkins Caufield & Byers
(Menlo Park)**
2750 Sand Hill Rd.
Menlo Park, CA 94025
(650)233-2750
Fax: (650)233-0300
Website: http://www.kpcb.com

Magic Venture Capital LLC
1010 El Camino Real, Ste. 300
Menlo Park, CA 94025
(650)325-4149

Matrix Partners
2500 Sand Hill Rd., Ste. 113
Menlo Park, CA 94025
(650)854-3131
Fax: (650)854-3296
Website: http://www.matrixpartners.com

Mayfield Fund
2800 Sand Hill Rd.
Menlo Park, CA 94025
(650)854-5560
Fax: (650)854-5712
Website: http://www.mayfield.com

**McCown De Leeuw and Co. (Menlo
Park)**
3000 Sand Hill Rd., Bldg. 3, Ste. 290
Menlo Park, CA 94025-7111
(650)854-6000
Fax: (650)854-0853
Website: http://www.mdcpartners.com

Menlo Ventures
3000 Sand Hill Rd., Bldg. 4, Ste. 100
Menlo Park, CA 94025
(650)854-8540
Fax: (650)854-7059
Website: http://www.menloventures.com

Merrill Pickard Anderson & Eyre
2480 Sand Hill Rd., Ste. 200
Menlo Park, CA 94025
(650)854-8600
Fax: (650)854-0345

**New Enterprise Associates (Menlo
Park)**
2490 Sand Hill Rd.
Menlo Park, CA 94025
(650)854-9499
Fax: (650)854-9397
Website: http://www.nea.com

Onset Ventures
2400 Sand Hill Rd., Ste. 150
Menlo Park, CA 94025
(650)529-0700
Fax: (650)529-0777
Website: http://www.onset.com

Paragon Venture Partners
3000 Sand Hill Rd., Bldg. 1, Ste. 275
Menlo Park, CA 94025
(650)854-8000
Fax: (650)854-7260

**Pathfinder Venture Capital Funds
(Menlo Park)**
3000 Sand Hill Rd., Bldg. 3, Ste. 255
Menlo Park, CA 94025
(650)854-0650
Fax: (650)854-4706

Rocket Ventures
3000 Sandhill Rd., Bldg. 1, Ste. 170
Menlo Park, CA 94025
(650)561-9100
Fax: (650)561-9183
Website: http://www.rocketventures.com

Sequoia Capital
3000 Sand Hill Rd., Bldg. 4, Ste. 280
Menlo Park, CA 94025
(650)854-3927
Fax: (650)854-2977

E-mail: sequoia@sequioacap.com
Website: http://www.sequoiacap.com

Sierra Ventures
3000 Sand Hill Rd., Bldg. 4, Ste. 210
Menlo Park, CA 94025
(650)854-1000
Fax: (650)854-5593
Website: http://www.sierraventures.com

Sigma Partners
2884 Sand Hill Rd., Ste. 121
Menlo Park, CA 94025-7022
(650)853-1700
Fax: (650)853-1717
E-mail: info@sigmapartners.com
Website: http://www.sigmapartners.com

Sprout Group (Menlo Park)
3000 Sand Hill Rd.
Bldg. 3, Ste. 170
Menlo Park, CA 94025
(650)234-2700
Fax: (650)234-2779
Website: http://www.sproutgroup.com

TA Associates (Menlo Park)
70 Willow Rd., Ste. 100
Menlo Park, CA 94025
(650)328-1210
Fax: (650)326-4933
Website: http://www.ta.com

Thompson Clive & Partners Ltd.
3000 Sand Hill Rd., Bldg. 1, Ste. 185
Menlo Park, CA 94025-7102
(650)854-0314
Fax: (650)854-0670
E-mail: mail@tcvc.com
Website: http://www.tcvc.com

Trinity Ventures Ltd.
3000 Sand Hill Rd., Bldg. 1, Ste. 240
Menlo Park, CA 94025
(650)854-9500
Fax: (650)854-9501
Website: http://www.trinityventures.com

U.S. Venture Partners
2180 Sand Hill Rd., Ste. 300
Menlo Park, CA 94025
(650)854-9080
Fax: (650)854-3018
Website: http://www.usvp.com

USVP-Schlein Marketing Fund
2180 Sand Hill Rd., Ste. 300
Menlo Park, CA 94025
(415)854-9080
Fax: (415)854-3018
Website: http://www.usvp.com

Venrock Associates
2494 Sand Hill Rd., Ste. 200
Menlo Park, CA 94025
(650)561-9580
Fax: (650)561-9180
Website: http://www.venrock.com

Brad Peery Capital Inc.
145 Chapel Pkwy.
Mill Valley, CA 94941
(415)389-0625
Fax: (415)389-1336

Dot Edu Ventures
650 Castro St., Ste. 270
Mountain View, CA 94041
(650)575-5638
Fax: (650)325-5247
Website: http://www.dotedu
ventures.com

Forrest, Binkley & Brown
840 Newport Ctr. Dr., Ste. 480
Newport Beach, CA 92660
(949)729-3222
Fax: (949)729-3226
Website: http://www.fbbvc.com

Marwit Capital LLC
180 Newport Center Dr., Ste. 200
Newport Beach, CA 92660
(949)640-6234
Fax: (949)720-8077
Website: http://www.marwit.com

Kaiser Permanente / National Venture Development
1800 Harrison St., 22nd Fl.
Oakland, CA 94612
(510)267-4010
Fax: (510)267-4036
Website: http://www.kpventures.com

Nu Capital Access Group, Ltd.
7677 Oakport St., Ste. 105
Oakland, CA 94621
(510)635-7345
Fax: (510)635-7068

Inman and Bowman
4 Orinda Way, Bldg. D, Ste. 150
Orinda, CA 94563
(510)253-1611
Fax: (510)253-9037

Accel Partners (San Francisco)
428 University Ave.
Palo Alto, CA 94301
(650)614-4800
Fax: (650)614-4880
Website: http://www.accel.com

Advanced Technology Ventures
485 Ramona St., Ste. 200
Palo Alto, CA 94301
(650)321-8601
Fax: (650)321-0934
Website: http://www.atvcapital.com

Anila Fund
400 Channing Ave.
Palo Alto, CA 94301
(650)833-5790
Fax: (650)833-0590
Website: http://www.anila.com

Asset Management Company Venture Capital
2275 E. Bayshore, Ste. 150
Palo Alto, CA 94303
(650)494-7400
Fax: (650)856-1826
E-mail: postmaster@assetman.com
Website: http://www.assetman.com

BancBoston Capital / BancBoston Ventures
435 Tasso St., Ste. 250
Palo Alto, CA 94305
(650)470-4100
Fax: (650)853-1425
Website: http://www.bancboston
capital.com

Charter Ventures
525 University Ave., Ste. 1400
Palo Alto, CA 94301
(650)325-6953
Fax: (650)325-4762
Website: http://www.charterventures.com

Communications Ventures
505 Hamilton Avenue, Ste. 305
Palo Alto, CA 94301
(650)325-9600
Fax: (650)325-9608
Website: http://www.comven.com

HMS Group
2468 Embarcadero Way
Palo Alto, CA 94303-3313
(650)856-9862
Fax: (650)856-9864

Jafco America Ventures, Inc.
505 Hamilton Ste. 310
Palto Alto, CA 94301
(650)463-8800
Fax: (650)463-8801
Website: http://www.jafco.com

New Vista Capital
540 Cowper St., Ste. 200

Palo Alto, CA 94301
(650)329-9333
Fax: (650)328-9434
E-mail: fgreene@nvcap.com
Website: http://www.nvcap.com

Norwest Equity Partners (Palo Alto)
245 Lytton Ave., Ste. 250
Palo Alto, CA 94301-1426
(650)321-8000
Fax: (650)321-8010
Website: http://www.norwestvp.com

Oak Investment Partners
525 University Ave., Ste. 1300
Palo Alto, CA 94301
(650)614-3700
Fax: (650)328-6345
Website: http://www.oakinv.com

Patricof & Co. Ventures, Inc. (Palo Alto)
2100 Geng Rd., Ste. 150
Palo Alto, CA 94303
(650)494-9944
Fax: (650)494-6751
Website: http://www.patricof.com

RWI Group
835 Page Mill Rd.
Palo Alto, CA 94304
(650)251-1800
Fax: (650)213-8660
Website: http://www.rwigroup.com

Summit Partners (Palo Alto)
499 Hamilton Ave., Ste. 200
Palo Alto, CA 94301
(650)321-1166
Fax: (650)321-1188
Website: http://www.summit
partners.com

Sutter Hill Ventures
755 Page Mill Rd., Ste. A-200
Palo Alto, CA 94304
(650)493-5600
Fax: (650)858-1854
E-mail: shv@shv.com

Vanguard Venture Partners
525 University Ave., Ste. 600
Palo Alto, CA 94301
(650)321-2900
Fax: (650)321-2902
Website: http://www.vanguard
ventures.com

Venture Growth Associates
2479 East Bayshore St., Ste. 710
Palo Alto, CA 94303

(650)855-9100
Fax: (650)855-9104

Worldview Technology Partners
435 Tasso St., Ste. 120
Palo Alto, CA 94301
(650)322-3800
Fax: (650)322-3880
Website: http://www.worldview.com

Draper, Fisher, Jurvetson / Draper Associates
400 Seaport Ct., Ste.250
Redwood City, CA 94063
(415)599-9000
Fax: (415)599-9726
Website: http://www.dfj.com

Gabriel Venture Partners
350 Marine Pkwy., Ste. 200
Redwood Shores, CA 94065
(650)551-5000
Fax: (650)551-5001
Website: http://www.gabrielvp.com

Hallador Venture Partners, L.L.C.
740 University Ave., Ste. 110
Sacramento, CA 95825-6710
(916)920-0191
Fax: (916)920-5188
E-mail: chris@hallador.com

Emerald Venture Group
12396 World Trade Dr., Ste. 116
San Diego, CA 92128
(858)451-1001
Fax: (858)451-1003
Website: http://www.emerald
venture.com

Forward Ventures
9255 Towne Centre Dr.
San Diego, CA 92121
(858)677-6077
Fax: (858)452-8799
E-mail: info@forwardventure.com
Website: http://www.forward
venture.com

Idanta Partners Ltd.
4660 La Jolla Village Dr., Ste. 850
San Diego, CA 92122
(619)452-9690
Fax: (619)452-2013
Website: http://www.idanta.com

Kingsbury Associates
3655 Nobel Dr., Ste. 490
San Diego, CA 92122
(858)677-0600
Fax: (858)677-0800

Kyocera International Inc.
Corporate Development
8611 Balboa Ave.
San Diego, CA 92123
(858)576-2600
Fax: (858)492-1456

Sorrento Associates, Inc.
4370 LaJolla Village Dr., Ste. 1040
San Diego, CA 92122
(619)452-3100
Fax: (619)452-7607
Website: http://www.sorrento
ventures.com

Western States Investment Group
9191 Towne Ctr. Dr., Ste. 310
San Diego, CA 92122
(619)678-0800
Fax: (619)678-0900

Aberdare Ventures
One Embarcadero Center, Ste. 4000
San Francisco, CA 94111
(415)392-7442
Fax: (415)392-4264
Website: http://www.aberdare.com

Acacia Venture Partners
101 California St., Ste. 3160
San Francisco, CA 94111
(415)433-4200
Fax: (415)433-4250
Website: http://www.acaciavp.com

Access Venture Partners
319 Laidley St.
San Francisco, CA 94131
(415)586-0132
Fax: (415)392-6310
Website: http://www.access
venturepartners.com

Alta Partners
One Embarcadero Center, Ste. 4050
San Francisco, CA 94111
(415)362-4022
Fax: (415)362-6178
E-mail: alta@altapartners.com
Website: http://www.altapartners.com

Bangert Dawes Reade Davis & Thom
220 Montgomery St., Ste. 424
San Francisco, CA 94104
(415)954-9900
Fax: (415)954-9901
E-mail: bdrdt@pacbell.net

Berkeley International Capital Corp.
650 California St., Ste. 2800
San Francisco, CA 94108-2609

(415)249-0450
Fax: (415)392-3929
Website: http://www.berkeleyvc.com

Blueprint Ventures LLC
456 Montgomery St., 22nd Fl.
San Francisco, CA 94104
(415)901-4000
Fax: (415)901-4035
Website: http://www.blue
printventures.com

Blumberg Capital Ventures
580 Howard St., Ste. 401
San Francisco, CA 94105
(415)905-5007
Fax: (415)357-5027
Website: http://www.blumberg-
capital.com

Burr, Egan, Deleage, and Co. (San Francisco)
1 Embarcadero Center, Ste. 4050
San Francisco, CA 94111
(415)362-4022
Fax: (415)362-6178

Burrill & Company
120 Montgomery St., Ste. 1370
San Francisco, CA 94104
(415)743-3160
Fax: (415)743-3161
Website: http://www.burrillandco.com

CMEA Ventures
235 Montgomery St., Ste. 920
San Francisco, CA 94401
(415)352-1520
Fax: (415)352-1524
Website: http://www.cmeaventures.com

Crocker Capital
1 Post St., Ste. 2500
San Francisco, CA 94101
(415)956-5250
Fax: (415)959-5710

Dominion Ventures, Inc.
44 Montgomery St., Ste. 4200
San Francisco, CA 94104
(415)362-4890
Fax: (415)394-9245

Dorset Capital
Pier 1
Bay 2
San Francisco, CA 94111
(415)398-7101
Fax: (415)398-7141
Website: http://www.dorsetcapital.com

Gatx Capital
Four Embarcadero Center, Ste. 2200
San Francisco, CA 94904
(415)955-3200
Fax: (415)955-3449

IMinds
135 Main St., Ste. 1350
San Francisco, CA 94105
(415)547-0000
Fax: (415)227-0300
Website: http://www.iminds.com

LF International Inc.
360 Post St., Ste. 705
San Francisco, CA 94108
(415)399-0110
Fax: (415)399-9222
Website: http://www.lfvc.com

Newbury Ventures
535 Pacific Ave., 2nd Fl.
San Francisco, CA 94133
(415)296-7408
Fax: (415)296-7416
Website: http://www.newburyven.com

Quest Ventures (San Francisco)
333 Bush St., Ste. 1750
San Francisco, CA 94104
(415)782-1414
Fax: (415)782-1415

Robertson-Stephens Co.
555 California St., Ste. 2600
San Francisco, CA 94104
(415)781-9700
Fax: (415)781-2556
Website: http://www.omegaad
ventures.com

Rosewood Capital, L.P.
One Maritime Plaza, Ste. 1330
San Francisco, CA 94111-3503
(415)362-5526
Fax: (415)362-1192
Website: http://www.rosewoodvc.com

Ticonderoga Capital Inc.
555 California St., No. 4950
San Francisco, CA 94104
(415)296-7900
Fax: (415)296-8956

21st Century Internet Venture Partners
Two South Park
2nd Floor
San Francisco, CA 94107
(415)512-1221
Fax: (415)512-2650
Website: http://www.21vc.com

VK Ventures
600 California St., Ste.1700
San Francisco, CA 94111
(415)391-5600
Fax: (415)397-2744

Walden Group of Venture Capital Funds
750 Battery St., Seventh Floor
San Francisco, CA 94111
(415)391-7225
Fax: (415)391-7262

Acer Technology Ventures
2641 Orchard Pkwy.
San Jose, CA 95134
(408)433-4945
Fax: (408)433-5230

Authosis
226 Airport Pkwy., Ste. 405
San Jose, CA 95110
(650)814-3603
Website: http://www.authosis.com

Western Technology Investment
2010 N. First St., Ste. 310
San Jose, CA 95131
(408)436-8577
Fax: (408)436-8625
E-mail: mktg@westerntech.com

Drysdale Enterprises
177 Bovet Rd., Ste. 600
San Mateo, CA 94402
(650)341-6336
Fax: (650)341-1329
E-mail: drysdale@aol.com

Greylock
2929 Campus Dr., Ste. 400
San Mateo, CA 94401
(650)493-5525
Fax: (650)493-5575
Website: http://www.greylock.com

Technology Funding
2000 Alameda de las Pulgas, Ste. 250
San Mateo, CA 94403
(415)345-2200
Fax: (415)345-1797

2M Invest Inc.
1875 S. Grant St.
Suite 750
San Mateo, CA 94402
(650)655-3765
Fax: (650)372-9107
E-mail: 2minfo@2minvest.com
Website: http://www.2minvest.com

Phoenix Growth Capital Corp.
2401 Kerner Blvd.
San Rafael, CA 94901
(415)485-4569
Fax: (415)485-4663

NextGen Partners LLC
1705 East Valley Rd.
Santa Barbara, CA 93108
(805)969-8540
Fax: (805)969-8542
Website: http://www.nextgen
partners.com

Denali Venture Capital
1925 Woodland Ave.
Santa Clara, CA 95050
(408)690-4838
Fax: (408)247-6979
E-mail: wael@denaliventurecapital.com
Website: http://www.denali
venturecapital.com

Dotcom Ventures LP
3945 Freedom Circle, Ste. 740
Santa Clara, CA 95045
(408)919-9855
Fax: (408)919-9857
Website: http://www.dotcom
venturesatl.com

Silicon Valley Bank
3003 Tasman
Santa Clara, CA 95054
(408)654-7400
Fax: (408)727-8728

Al Shugart International
920 41st Ave.
Santa Cruz, CA 95062
(831)479-7852
Fax: (831)479-7852
Website: http://www.alshugart.com

Leonard Mautner Associates
1434 Sixth St.
Santa Monica, CA 90401
(213)393-9788
Fax: (310)459-9918

Palomar Ventures
100 Wilshire Blvd., Ste. 450
Santa Monica, CA 90401
(310)260-6050
Fax: (310)656-4150
Website: http://www.palomar
ventures.com

Medicus Venture Partners
12930 Saratoga Ave., Ste. D8
Saratoga, CA 95070

(408)447-8600
Fax: (408)447-8599
Website: http://www.medicusvc.com

Redleaf Venture Management
14395 Saratoga Ave., Ste. 130
Saratoga, CA 95070
(408)868-0800
Fax: (408)868-0810
E-mail: nancy@redleaf.com
Website: http://www.redleaf.com

Artemis Ventures
207 Second St., Ste. E
3rd Fl.
Sausalito, CA 94965
(415)289-2500
Fax: (415)289-1789
Website: http://www.artemisventures.com

Deucalion Venture Partners
19501 Brooklime
Sonoma, CA 95476
(707)938-4974
Fax: (707)938-8921

Windward Ventures
PO Box 7688
Thousand Oaks, CA 91359-7688
(805)497-3332
Fax: (805)497-9331

National Investment Management, Inc.
2601 Airport Dr., Ste.210
Torrance, CA 90505
(310)784-7600
Fax: (310)784-7605

Southern California Ventures
406 Amapola Ave. Ste. 125
Torrance, CA 90501
(310)787-4381
Fax: (310)787-4382

Sandton Financial Group
21550 Oxnard St., Ste. 300
Woodland Hills, CA 91367
(818)702-9283

Woodside Fund
850 Woodside Dr.
Woodside, CA 94062
(650)368-5545
Fax: (650)368-2416
Website: http://www.woodsidefund.com

Colorado

Colorado Venture Management
Ste. 300
Boulder, CO 80301

(303)440-4055
Fax: (303)440-4636

Dean & Associates
4362 Apple Way
Boulder, CO 80301
Fax: (303)473-9900

Roser Ventures LLC
1105 Spruce St.
Boulder, CO 80302
(303)443-6436
Fax: (303)443-1885
Website: http://www.roserventures.com

Sequel Venture Partners
4430 Arapahoe Ave., Ste. 220
Boulder, CO 80303
(303)546-0400
Fax: (303)546-9728
E-mail: tom@sequelvc.com
Website: http://www.sequelvc.com

New Venture Resources
445C E. Cheyenne Mtn. Blvd.
Colorado Springs, CO 80906-4570
(719)598-9272
Fax: (719)598-9272

The Centennial Funds
1428 15th St.
Denver, CO 80202-1318
(303)405-7500
Fax: (303)405-7575
Website: http://www.centennial.com

Rocky Mountain Capital Partners
1125 17th St., Ste. 2260
Denver, CO 80202
(303)291-5200
Fax: (303)291-5327

Sandlot Capital LLC
600 South Cherry St., Ste. 525
Denver, CO 80246
(303)893-3400
Fax: (303)893-3403
Website: http://www.sandlotcapital.com

Wolf Ventures
50 South Steele St., Ste. 777
Denver, CO 80209
(303)321-4800
Fax: (303)321-4848
E-mail: businessplan@wolf
ventures.com
Website: http://www.wolfventures.com

The Columbine Venture Funds
5460 S. Quebec St., Ste. 270
Englewood, CO 80111

(303)694-3222
Fax: (303)694-9007

Investment Securities of Colorado, Inc.
4605 Denice Dr.
Englewood, CO 80111
(303)796-9192

Kinship Partners
6300 S. Syracuse Way, Ste. 484
Englewood, CO 80111
(303)694-0268
Fax: (303)694-1707
E-mail: block@vailsys.com

Boranco Management, L.L.C.
1528 Hillside Dr.
Fort Collins, CO 80524-1969
(970)221-2297
Fax: (970)221-4787

Aweida Ventures
890 West Cherry St., Ste. 220
Louisville, CO 80027
(303)664-9520
Fax: (303)664-9530
Website: http://www.aweida.com

Access Venture Partners
8787 Turnpike Dr., Ste. 260
Westminster, CO 80030
(303)426-8899
Fax: (303)426-8828

Medmax Ventures LP
1 Northwestern Dr., Ste. 203
Bloomfield, CT 06002
(860)286-2960
Fax: (860)286-9960

James B. Kobak & Co.
Four Mansfield Place
Darien, CT 06820
(203)656-3471
Fax: (203)655-2905

Orien Ventures
1 Post Rd.
Fairfield, CT 06430
(203)259-9933
Fax: (203)259-5288

ABP Acquisition Corporation
115 Maple Ave.
Greenwich, CT 06830
(203)625-8287
Fax: (203)447-6187

Catterton Partners
9 Greenwich Office Park
Greenwich, CT 06830
(203)629-4901

Fax: (203)629-4903
Website: http://www.cpequity.com

Consumer Venture Partners
3 Pickwick Plz.
Greenwich, CT 06830
(203)629-8800
Fax: (203)629-2019

Insurance Venture Partners
31 Brookside Dr., Ste. 211
Greenwich, CT 06830
(203)861-0030
Fax: (203)861-2745

The NTC Group
Three Pickwick Plaza
Ste. 200
Greenwich, CT 06830
(203)862-2800
Fax: (203)622-6538

Regulus International Capital Co., Inc.
140 Greenwich Ave.
Greenwich, CT 06830
(203)625-9700
Fax: (203)625-9706

Axiom Venture Partners
City Place II
185 Asylum St., 17th Fl.
Hartford, CT 06103
(860)548-7799
Fax: (860)548-7797
Website: http://www.axiomventures.com

Conning Capital Partners
City Place II
185 Asylum St.
Hartford, CT 06103-4105
(860)520-1289
Fax: (860)520-1299
E-mail: pe@conning.com
Website: http://www.conning.com

First New England Capital L.P.
100 Pearl St.
Hartford, CT 06103
(860)293-3333
Fax: (860)293-3338
E-mail: info@firstnewenglandcapital.com
Website: http://www.firstnewengland capital.com

Northeast Ventures
One State St., Ste. 1720
Hartford, CT 06103
(860)547-1414
Fax: (860)246-8755

Windward Holdings
38 Sylvan Rd.
Madison, CT 06443
(203)245-6870
Fax: (203)245-6865

Advanced Materials Partners, Inc.
45 Pine St.
PO Box 1022
New Canaan, CT 06840
(203)966-6415
Fax: (203)966-8448
E-mail: wkb@amplink.com

RFE Investment Partners
36 Grove St.
New Canaan, CT 06840
(203)966-2800
Fax: (203)966-3109
Website: http://www.rfeip.com

Connecticut Innovations, Inc.
999 West St.
Rocky Hill, CT 06067
(860)563-5851
Fax: (860)563-4877
E-mail: pamela.hartley@ctin novations.com
Website: http://www.ctinnovations.com

Canaan Partners
105 Rowayton Ave.
Rowayton, CT 06853
(203)855-0400
Fax: (203)854-9117
Website: http://www.canaan.com

Landmark Partners, Inc.
10 Mill Pond Ln.
Simsbury, CT 06070
(860)651-9760
Fax: (860)651-8890
Website: http:// www.landmarkpartners.com

Sweeney & Company
PO Box 567
Southport, CT 06490
(203)255-0220
Fax: (203)255-0220
E-mail: sweeney@connix.com

Baxter Associates, Inc.
PO Box 1333
Stamford, CT 06904
(203)323-3143
Fax: (203)348-0622

Beacon Partners Inc.
6 Landmark Sq., 4th Fl.
Stamford, CT 06901-2792

(203)359-5776
Fax: (203)359-5876

Collinson, Howe, and Lennox, LLC
1055 Washington Blvd., 5th Fl.
Stamford, CT 06901
(203)324-7700
Fax: (203)324-3636
E-mail: info@chlmedical.com
Website: http://www.chlmedical.com

Prime Capital Management Co.
550 West Ave.
Stamford, CT 06902
(203)964-0642
Fax: (203)964-0862

Saugatuck Capital Co.
1 Canterbury Green
Stamford, CT 06901
(203)348-6669
Fax: (203)324-6995
Website: http://www.sauga tuckcapital.com

Soundview Financial Group Inc.
22 Gatehouse Rd.
Stamford, CT 06902
(203)462-7200
Fax: (203)462-7350
Website: http://www.sndv.com

TSG Ventures, L.L.C.
177 Broad St., 12th Fl.
Stamford, CT 06901
(203)406-1500
Fax: (203)406-1590

Whitney & Company
177 Broad St.
Stamford, CT 06901
(203)973-1400
Fax: (203)973-1422
Website: http://www.jhwhitney.com

Cullinane & Donnelly Venture Partners L.P.
970 Farmington Ave.
West Hartford, CT 06107
(860)521-7811

The Crestview Investment and Financial Group
431 Post Rd. E, Ste. 1
Westport, CT 06880-4403
(203)222-0333
Fax: (203)222-0000

Marketcorp Venture Associates, L.P. (MCV)
274 Riverside Ave.
Westport, CT 06880

(203)222-3030
Fax: (203)222-3033

Oak Investment Partners (Westport)
1 Gorham Island
Westport, CT 06880
(203)226-8346
Fax: (203)227-0372
Website: http://www.oakinv.com

Oxford Bioscience Partners
315 Post Rd. W
Westport, CT 06880-5200
(203)341-3300
Fax: (203)341-3309
Website: http://www.oxbio.com

Prince Ventures (Westport)
25 Ford Rd.
Westport, CT 06880
(203)227-8332
Fax: (203)226-5302

LTI Venture Leasing Corp.
221 Danbury Rd.
Wilton, CT 06897
(203)563-1100
Fax: (203)563-1111
Website: http://www.ltileasing.com

Delaware

Blue Rock Capital
5803 Kennett Pike, Ste. A
Wilmington, DE 19807
(302)426-0981
Fax: (302)426-0982
Website: http://www.bluerockcapital.com

District of Columbia

Allied Capital Corp.
1919 Pennsylvania Ave. NW
Washington, DC 20006-3434
(202)331-2444
Fax: (202)659-2053
Website: http://www.alliedcapital.com

Atlantic Coastal Ventures, L.P.
3101 South St. NW
Washington, DC 20007
(202)293-1166
Fax: (202)293-1181
Website: http://www.atlanticcv.com

Columbia Capital Group, Inc.
1660 L St. NW, Ste. 308
Washington, DC 20036
(202)775-8815
Fax: (202)223-0544

Core Capital Partners
901 15th St., NW
9th Fl.
Washington, DC 20005
(202)589-0090
Fax: (202)589-0091
Website: http://www.core-capital.com

Next Point Partners
701 Pennsylvania Ave. NW, Ste. 900
Washington, DC 20004
(202)661-8703
Fax: (202)434-7400
E-mail: mf@nextpoint.vc
Website: http://www.nextpointvc.com

Telecommunications Development Fund
2020 K. St. NW
Ste. 375
Washington, DC 20006
(202)293-8840
Fax: (202)293-8850
Website: http://www.tdfund.com

Wachtel & Co., Inc.
1101 4th St. NW
Washington, DC 20005-5680
(202)898-1144

Winslow Partners LLC
1300 Connecticut Ave. NW
Washington, DC 20036-1703
(202)530-5000
Fax: (202)530-5010
E-mail: winslow@winslowpartners.com

Women's Growth Capital Fund
1054 31st St., NW
Ste. 110
Washington, DC 20007
(202)342-1431
Fax: (202)341-1203
Website: http://www.wgcf.com

Sigma Capital Corp.
22668 Caravelle Circle
Boca Raton, FL 33433
(561)368-9783

North American Business Development Co., L.L.C.
111 East Las Olas Blvd.
Ft. Lauderdale, FL 33301
(305)463-0681
Fax: (305)527-0904
Website: http://
www.northamericanfund.com

Chartwell Capital Management Co. Inc.
1 Independent Dr., Ste. 3120

Jacksonville, FL 32202
(904)355-3519
Fax: (904)353-5833
E-mail: info@chartwellcap.com

CEO Advisors
1061 Maitland Center Commons
Ste. 209
Maitland, FL 32751
(407)660-9327
Fax: (407)660-2109

Henry & Co.
8201 Peters Rd., Ste. 1000
Plantation, FL 33324
(954)797-7400

Avery Business Development Services
2506 St. Michel Ct.
Ponte Vedra, FL 32082
(904)285-6033

New South Ventures
5053 Ocean Blvd.
Sarasota, FL 34242
(941)358-6000
Fax: (941)358-6078
Website: http://www.newsouth
ventures.com

Venture Capital Management Corp.
PO Box 2626
Satellite Beach, FL 32937
(407)777-1969

Florida Capital Venture Ltd.
325 Florida Bank Plaza
100 W. Kennedy Blvd.
Tampa, FL 33602
(813)229-2294
Fax: (813)229-2028

Quantum Capital Partners
339 South Plant Ave.
Tampa, FL 33606
(813)250-1999
Fax: (813)250-1998
Website: http://www.quantum
capitalpartners.com

South Atlantic Venture Fund
614 W. Bay St.
Tampa, FL 33606-2704
(813)253-2500
Fax: (813)253-2360
E-mail: venture@southatlantic.com
Website: http://www.southatlantic.com

LM Capital Corp.
120 S. Olive, Ste. 400
West Palm Beach, FL 33401

(561)833-9700
Fax: (561)655-6587
Website: http://www.lmcapital
securities.com

Georgia

Venture First Associates
4811 Thornwood Dr.
Acworth, GA 30102
(770)928-3733
Fax: (770)928-6455

Alliance Technology Ventures
8995 Westside Pkwy., Ste. 200
Alpharetta, GA 30004
(678)336-2000
Fax: (678)336-2001
E-mail: info@atv.com
Website: http://www.atv.com

Cordova Ventures
2500 North Winds Pkwy., Ste. 475
Alpharetta, GA 30004
(678)942-0300
Fax: (678)942-0301
Website: http://www.cordovaventures.
com

Advanced Technology Development Fund
1000 Abernathy, Ste. 1420
Atlanta, GA 30328-5614
(404)668-2333
Fax: (404)668-2333

CGW Southeast Partners
12 Piedmont Center, Ste. 210
Atlanta, GA 30305
(404)816-3255
Fax: (404)816-3258
Website: http://www.cgwlp.com

Cyberstarts
1900 Emery St., NW
3rd Fl.
Atlanta, GA 30318
(404)267-5000
Fax: (404)267-5200
Website: http://www.cyberstarts.com

EGL Holdings, Inc.
10 Piedmont Center, Ste. 412
Atlanta, GA 30305
(404)949-8300
Fax: (404)949-8311

Equity South
1790 The Lenox Bldg.
3399 Peachtree Rd. NE
Atlanta, GA 30326

(404)237-6222
Fax: (404)261-1578

Five Paces
3400 Peachtree Rd., Ste. 200
Atlanta, GA 30326
(404)439-8300
Fax: (404)439-8301
Website: http://www.fivepaces.com

Frontline Capital, Inc.
3475 Lenox Rd., Ste. 400
Atlanta, GA 30326
(404)240-7280
Fax: (404)240-7281

Fuqua Ventures LLC
1201 W. Peachtree St. NW, Ste. 5000
Atlanta, GA 30309
(404)815-4500
Fax: (404)815-4528
Website: http://www.fuquaventures.com

Noro-Moseley Partners
4200 Northside Pkwy., Bldg. 9
Atlanta, GA 30327
(404)233-1966
Fax: (404)239-9280
Website: http://www.noro-moseley.com

Renaissance Capital Corp.
34 Peachtree St. NW, Ste. 2230
Atlanta, GA 30303
(404)658-9061
Fax: (404)658-9064

River Capital, Inc.
Two Midtown Plaza
1360 Peachtree St. NE, Ste. 1430
Atlanta, GA 30309
(404)873-2166
Fax: (404)873-2158

State Street Bank & Trust Co.
3414 Peachtree Rd. NE, Ste. 1010
Atlanta, GA 30326
(404)364-9500
Fax: (404)261-4469

UPS Strategic Enterprise Fund
55 Glenlake Pkwy. NE
Atlanta, GA 30328
(404)828-8814
Fax: (404)828-8088
E-mail: jcacyce@ups.com
Website: http://www.ups.com/sef/
sef_home

Wachovia
191 Peachtree St. NE, 26th Fl.
Atlanta, GA 30303

(404)332-1000
Fax: (404)332-1392
Website: http://www.wachovia.com/wca

Brainworks Ventures
4243 Dunwoody Club Dr.
Chamblee, GA 30341
(770)239-7447

First Growth Capital Inc.
Best Western Plaza, Ste. 105
PO Box 815
Forsyth, GA 31029
(912)781-7131

Financial Capital Resources, Inc.
21 Eastbrook Bend, Ste. 116
Peachtree City, GA 30269
(404)487-6650

Hawaii

HMS Hawaii Management Partners
Davies Pacific Center
841 Bishop St., Ste. 860
Honolulu, HI 96813
(808)545-3755
Fax: (808)531-2611

Idaho

Sun Valley Ventures
160 Second St.
Ketchum, ID 83340
(208)726-5005
Fax: (208)726-5094

Illinois

Open Prairie Ventures
115 N. Neil St., Ste. 209
Champaign, IL 61820
(217)351-7000
Fax: (217)351-7051
E-mail: inquire@openprairie.com
Website: http://www.openprairie.com

ABN AMRO Private Equity
208 S. La Salle St., 10th Fl.
Chicago, IL 60604
(312)855-7079
Fax: (312)553-6648
Website: http://www.abnequity.com

Alpha Capital Partners, Ltd.
122 S. Michigan Ave., Ste. 1700
Chicago, IL 60603
(312)322-9800
Fax: (312)322-9808
E-mail: acp@alphacapital.com

Ameritech Development Corp.
30 S. Wacker Dr., 37th Fl.
Chicago, IL 60606
(312)750-5083
Fax: (312)609-0244

Apex Investment Partners
225 W. Washington, Ste. 1450
Chicago, IL 60606
(312)857-2800
Fax: (312)857-1800
E-mail: apex@apexvc.com
Website: http://www.apexvc.com

Arch Venture Partners
8725 W. Higgins Rd., Ste. 290
Chicago, IL 60631
(773)380-6600
Fax: (773)380-6606
Website: http://www.archventure.com

The Bank Funds
208 South LaSalle St., Ste. 1680
Chicago, IL 60604
(312)855-6020
Fax: (312)855-8910

Batterson Venture Partners
303 W. Madison St., Ste. 1110
Chicago, IL 60606-3309
(312)269-0300
Fax: (312)269-0021
Website: http://www.battersonvp.com

William Blair Capital Partners, L.L.C.
222 W. Adams St., Ste. 1300
Chicago, IL 60606
(312)364-8250
Fax: (312)236-1042
E-mail: privateequity@wmblair.com
Website: http://www.wmblair.com

Bluestar Ventures
208 South LaSalle St., Ste. 1020
Chicago, IL 60604
(312)384-5000
Fax: (312)384-5005
Website: http://www.bluestarventures.com

The Capital Strategy Management Co.
233 S. Wacker Dr.
Box 06334
Chicago, IL 60606
(312)444-1170

DN Partners
77 West Wacker Dr., Ste. 4550
Chicago, IL 60601
(312)332-7960
Fax: (312)332-7979

Dresner Capital Inc.
29 South LaSalle St., Ste. 310
Chicago, IL 60603
(312)726-3600
Fax: (312)726-7448

Eblast Ventures LLC
11 South LaSalle St., 5th Fl.
Chicago, IL 60603
(312)372-2600
Fax: (312)372-5621
Website: http://www.eblastventures.com

Essex Woodlands Health Ventures, L.P.
190 S. LaSalle St., Ste. 2800
Chicago, IL 60603
(312)444-6040
Fax: (312)444-6034
Website: http://www.essexwood
lands.com

First Analysis Venture Capital
233 S. Wacker Dr., Ste. 9500
Chicago, IL 60606
(312)258-1400
Fax: (312)258-0334
Website: http://www.firstanalysis.com

Frontenac Co.
135 S. LaSalle St., Ste.3800
Chicago, IL 60603
(312)368-0044
Fax: (312)368-9520
Website: http://www.frontenac.com

GTCR Golder Rauner, LLC
6100 Sears Tower
Chicago, IL 60606
(312)382-2200
Fax: (312)382-2201
Website: http://www.gtcr.com

High Street Capital LLC
311 South Wacker Dr., Ste. 4550
Chicago, IL 60606
(312)697-4990
Fax: (312)697-4994
Website: http://www.highstr.com

IEG Venture Management, Inc.
70 West Madison
Chicago, IL 60602
(312)644-0890
Fax: (312)454-0369
Website: http://www.iegventure.com

JK&B Capital
180 North Stetson, Ste. 4500
Chicago, IL 60601
(312)946-1200
Fax: (312)946-1103

E-mail: gspencer@jkbcapital.com
Website: http://www.jkbcapital.com

Kettle Partners L.P.
350 W. Hubbard, Ste. 350
Chicago, IL 60610
(312)329-9300
Fax: (312)527-4519
Website: http://www.kettlevc.com

Lake Shore Capital Partners
20 N. Wacker Dr., Ste. 2807
Chicago, IL 60606
(312)803-3536
Fax: (312)803-3534

LaSalle Capital Group Inc.
70 W. Madison St., Ste. 5710
Chicago, IL 60602
(312)236-7041
Fax: (312)236-0720

Linc Capital, Inc.
303 E. Wacker Pkwy., Ste. 1000
Chicago, IL 60601
(312)946-2670
Fax: (312)938-4290
E-mail: bdemars@linccap.com

Madison Dearborn Partners, Inc.
3 First National Plz., Ste. 3800
Chicago, IL 60602
(312)895-1000
Fax: (312)895-1001
E-mail: invest@mdcp.com
Website: http://www.mdcp.com

Mesirow Private Equity Investments Inc.
350 N. Clark St.
Chicago, IL 60610
(312)595-6950
Fax: (312)595-6211
Website: http://www.meisrow
financial.com

Mosaix Ventures LLC
1822 North Mohawk
Chicago, IL 60614
(312)274-0988
Fax: (312)274-0989
Website: http://www.mosaix
ventures.com

Nesbitt Burns
111 West Monroe St.
Chicago, IL 60603
(312)416-3855
Fax: (312)765-8000
Website: http://www.harrisbank.com

Polestar Capital, Inc.
180 N. Michigan Ave., Ste. 1905
Chicago, IL 60601
(312)984-9090
Fax: (312)984-9877
E-mail: wl@polestarvc.com
Website: http://www.polestarvc.com

Prince Ventures (Chicago)
10 S. Wacker Dr., Ste. 2575
Chicago, IL 60606-7407
(312)454-1408
Fax: (312)454-9125

Prism Capital
444 N. Michigan Ave.
Chicago, IL 60611
(312)464-7900
Fax: (312)464-7915
Website: http://www.prismfund.com

Third Coast Capital
900 N. Franklin St., Ste. 700
Chicago, IL 60610
(312)337-3303
Fax: (312)337-2567
E-mail: manic@earthlink.com
Website: http://www.third
coastcapital.com

Thoma Cressey Equity Partners
4460 Sears Tower, 92nd Fl.
233 S. Wacker Dr.
Chicago, IL 60606
(312)777-4444
Fax: (312)777-4445
Website: http://www.thomacressey.com

Tribune Ventures
435 N. Michigan Ave., Ste. 600
Chicago, IL 60611
(312)527-8797
Fax: (312)222-5993
Website: http://www.tribuneventures.com

Wind Point Partners (Chicago)
676 N. Michigan Ave., Ste. 330
Chicago, IL 60611
(312)649-4000
Website: http://www.wppartners.com

Marquette Venture Partners
520 Lake Cook Rd., Ste. 450
Deerfield, IL 60015
(847)940-1700
Fax: (847)940-1724
Website: http://www.marquette
ventures.com

Duchossois Investments Limited, LLC
845 Larch Ave.
Elmhurst, IL 60126

(630)530-6105
Fax: (630)993-8644
Website: http://www.duchtec.com

Evanston Business Investment Corp.
1840 Oak Ave.
Evanston, IL 60201
(847)866-1840
Fax: (847)866-1808
E-mail: t-parkinson@nwu.com
Website: http://www.ebic.com

Inroads Capital Partners L.P.
1603 Orrington Ave., Ste. 2050
Evanston, IL 60201-3841
(847)864-2000
Fax: (847)864-9692

The Cerulean Fund/WGC Enterprises
1701 E. Lake Ave., Ste. 170
Glenview, IL 60025
(847)657-8002
Fax: (847)657-8168

Ventana Financial Resources, Inc.
249 Market Sq.
Lake Forest, IL 60045
(847)234-3434

Beecken, Petty & Co.
901 Warrenville Rd., Ste. 205
Lisle, IL 60532
(630)435-0300
Fax: (630)435-0370
E-mail: hep@bpcompany.com
Website: http://www.bpcompany.com

Allstate Private Equity
3075 Sanders Rd., Ste. G5D
Northbrook, IL 60062-7127
(847)402-8247
Fax: (847)402-0880

KB Partners
1101 Skokie Blvd., Ste. 260
Northbrook, IL 60062-2856
(847)714-0444
Fax: (847)714-0445
E-mail: keith@kbpartners.com
Website: http://www.kbpartners.com

Transcap Associates Inc.
900 Skokie Blvd., Ste. 210
Northbrook, IL 60062
(847)753-9600
Fax: (847)753-9090

**Graystone Venture Partners, L.L.C. /
Portage Venture Partners**
One Northfield Plaza, Ste. 530
Northfield, IL 60093

(847)446-9460
Fax: (847)446-9470
Website: http://www.portage
ventures.com

Motorola Inc.
1303 E. Algonquin Rd.
Schaumburg, IL 60196-1065
(847)576-4929
Fax: (847)538-2250
Website: http://www.mot.com/mne

Indiana

Irwin Ventures LLC
500 Washington St.
Columbus, IN 47202
(812)373-1434
Fax: (812)376-1709
Website: http://www.irwinventures.com

Cambridge Venture Partners
4181 East 96th St., Ste. 200
Indianapolis, IN 46240
(317)814-6192
Fax: (317)944-9815

CID Equity Partners
One American Square, Ste. 2850
Box 82074
Indianapolis, IN 46282
(317)269-2350
Fax: (317)269-2355
Website: http://www.cidequity.com

Gazelle Techventures
6325 Digital Way, Ste. 460
Indianapolis, IN 46278
(317)275-6800
Fax: (317)275-1101
Website: http://www.gazellevc.com

Monument Advisors Inc.
Bank One Center/Circle
111 Monument Circle, Ste. 600
Indianapolis, IN 46204-5172
(317)656-5065
Fax: (317)656-5060
Website: http://www.monumentadv.com

MWV Capital Partners
201 N. Illinois St., Ste. 300
Indianapolis, IN 46204
(317)237-2323
Fax: (317)237-2325
Website: http://www.mwvcapital.com

First Source Capital Corp.
100 North Michigan St.
PO Box 1602
South Bend, IN 46601

(219)235-2180
Fax: (219)235-2227

Iowa

Allsop Venture Partners
118 Third Ave. SE, Ste. 837
Cedar Rapids, IA 52401
(319)368-6675
Fax: (319)363-9515

InvestAmerica Investment Advisors, Inc.
101 2nd St. SE, Ste. 800
Cedar Rapids, IA 52401
(319)363-8249
Fax: (319)363-9683

Pappajohn Capital Resources
2116 Financial Center
Des Moines, IA 50309
(515)244-5746
Fax: (515)244-2346
Website: http://www.pappajohn.com

Berthel Fisher & Company Planning Inc.
701 Tama St.
PO Box 609
Marion, IA 52302
(319)497-5700
Fax: (319)497-4244

Kansas

Enterprise Merchant Bank
7400 West 110th St., Ste. 560
Overland Park, KS 66210
(913)327-8500
Fax: (913)327-8505

Kansas Venture Capital, Inc. (Overland Park)
6700 Antioch Plz., Ste. 460
Overland Park, KS 66204
(913)262-7117
Fax: (913)262-3509
E-mail: jdalton@kvci.com

Child Health Investment Corp.
6803 W. 64th St., Ste. 208
Shawnee Mission, KS 66202
(913)262-1436
Fax: (913)262-1575
Website: http://www.chca.com

Kansas Technology Enterprise Corp.
214 SW 6th, 1st Fl.
Topeka, KS 66603-3719
(785)296-5272
Fax: (785)296-1160

E-mail: ktec@ktec.com
Website: http://www.ktec.com

Kentucky

Kentucky Highlands Investment Corp.
362 Old Whitley Rd.
London, KY 40741
(606)864-5175
Fax: (606)864-5194
Website: http://www.khic.org

Chrysalis Ventures, L.L.C.
1850 National City Tower
Louisville, KY 40202
(502)583-7644
Fax: (502)583-7648
E-mail: bobsany@chrysalisventures.com
Website: http://www.chrysalis
ventures.com

Humana Venture Capital
500 West Main St.
Louisville, KY 40202
(502)580-3922
Fax: (502)580-2051
E-mail: gemont@humana.com
George Emont, Director

Summit Capital Group, Inc.
6510 Glenridge Park Pl., Ste. 8
Louisville, KY 40222
(502)332-2700

Louisiana

Bank One Equity Investors, Inc.
451 Florida St.
Baton Rouge, LA 70801
(504)332-4421
Fax: (504)332-7377

Advantage Capital Partners
LLE Tower
909 Poydras St., Ste. 2230
New Orleans, LA 70112
(504)522-4850
Fax: (504)522-4950
Website: http://www.advantagecap.com

Maine

CEI Ventures / Coastal Ventures LP
2 Portland Fish Pier, Ste. 201
Portland, ME 04101
(207)772-5356
Fax: (207)772-5503
Website: http://www.ceiventures.com

Commwealth Bioventures, Inc.
4 Milk St.
Portland, ME 04101

(207)780-0904
Fax: (207)780-0913

Maryland

Annapolis Ventures LLC
151 West St., Ste. 302
Annapolis, MD 21401
(443)482-9555
Fax: (443)482-9565
Website: http://www.annapolis
ventures.com

Delmag Ventures
220 Wardour Dr.
Annapolis, MD 21401
(410)267-8196
Fax: (410)267-8017
Website: http://www.delmag
ventures.com

Abell Venture Fund
111 S. Calvert St., Ste. 2300
Baltimore, MD 21202
(410)547-1300
Fax: (410)539-6579
Website: http://www.abell.org

ABS Ventures (Baltimore)
1 South St., Ste. 2150
Baltimore, MD 21202
(410)895-3895
Fax: (410)895-3899
Website: http://www.absventures.com

Anthem Capital, L.P.
16 S. Calvert St., Ste. 800
Baltimore, MD 21202-1305
(410)625-1510
Fax: (410)625-1735
Website: http://www.anthemcapital.com

Catalyst Ventures
1119 St. Paul St.
Baltimore, MD 21202
(410)244-0123
Fax: (410)752-7721

Maryland Venture Capital Trust
217 E. Redwood St., Ste. 2200
Baltimore, MD 21202
(410)767-6361
Fax: (410)333-6931

New Enterprise Associates (Baltimore)
1119 St. Paul St.
Baltimore, MD 21202
(410)244-0115
Fax: (410)752-7721
Website: http://www.nea.com

T. Rowe Price Threshold Partnerships
100 E. Pratt St., 8th Fl.
Baltimore, MD 21202
(410)345-2000
Fax: (410)345-2800

Spring Capital Partners
16 W. Madison St.
Baltimore, MD 21201
(410)685-8000
Fax: (410)727-1436
E-mail: mailbox@springcap.com

Arete Corporation
3 Bethesda Metro Ctr., Ste. 770
Bethesda, MD 20814
(301)657-6268
Fax: (301)657-6254
Website: http://www.arete-
microgen.com

Embryon Capital
7903 Sleaford Place
Bethesda, MD 20814
(301)656-6837
Fax: (301)656-8056

Potomac Ventures
7920 Norfolk Ave., Ste. 1100
Bethesda, MD 20814
(301)215-9240
Website: http://www.potomac
ventures.com

Toucan Capital Corp.
3 Bethesda Metro Center, Ste. 700
Bethesda, MD 20814
(301)961-1970
Fax: (301)961-1969
Website: http://www.toucancapital.com

Kinetic Ventures LLC
2 Wisconsin Cir., Ste. 620
Chevy Chase, MD 20815
(301)652-8066
Fax: (301)652-8310
Website: http://www.kineticventures.com

Boulder Ventures Ltd.
4750 Owings Mills Blvd.
Owings Mills, MD 21117
(410)998-3114
Fax: (410)356-5492
Website: http://www.boulderventures.com

Grotech Capital Group
9690 Deereco Rd., Ste. 800
Timonium, MD 21093
(410)560-2000
Fax: (410)560-1910
Website: http://www.grotech.com

Massachusetts

Adams, Harkness & Hill, Inc.
60 State St.
Boston, MA 02109
(617)371-3900

Advent International
75 State St., 29th Fl.
Boston, MA 02109
(617)951-9400
Fax: (617)951-0566
Website: http://www.adventiner
national.com

American Research and Development
30 Federal St.
Boston, MA 02110-2508
(617)423-7500
Fax: (617)423-9655

Ascent Venture Partners
255 State St., 5th Fl.
Boston, MA 02109
(617)270-9400
Fax: (617)270-9401
E-mail: info@ascentvp.com
Website: http://www.ascentvp.com

Atlas Venture
222 Berkeley St.
Boston, MA 02116
(617)488-2200
Fax: (617)859-9292
Website: http://www.atlasventure.com

Axxon Capital
28 State St., 37th Fl.
Boston, MA 02109
(617)722-0980
Fax: (617)557-6014
Website: http://www.axxoncapital.com

BancBoston Capital/BancBoston Ventures
175 Federal St., 10th Fl.
Boston, MA 02110
(617)434-2509
Fax: (617)434-6175
Website: http://
www.bancbostoncapital.com

Boston Capital Ventures
Old City Hall
45 School St.
Boston, MA 02108
(617)227-6550
Fax: (617)227-3847
E-mail: info@bcv.com
Website: http://www.bcv.com

Boston Financial & Equity Corp.
20 Overland St.
PO Box 15071
Boston, MA 02215
(617)267-2900
Fax: (617)437-7601
E-mail: debbie@bfec.com

Boston Millennia Partners
30 Rowes Wharf
Boston, MA 02110
(617)428-5150
Fax: (617)428-5160
Website: http://www.millennia
partners.com

Bristol Investment Trust
842A Beacon St.
Boston, MA 02215-3199
(617)566-5212
Fax: (617)267-0932

Brook Venture Management LLC
50 Federal St., 5th Fl.
Boston, MA 02110
(617)451-8989
Fax: (617)451-2369
Website: http://www.brookventure.com

Burr, Egan, Deleage, and Co. (Boston)
200 Clarendon St., Ste. 3800
Boston, MA 02116
(617)262-7770
Fax: (617)262-9779

Cambridge/Samsung Partners
One Exeter Plaza
Ninth Fl.
Boston, MA 02116
(617)262-4440
Fax: (617)262-5562

Chestnut Street Partners, Inc.
75 State St., Ste. 2500
Boston, MA 02109
(617)345-7220
Fax: (617)345-7201
E-mail: chestnut@chestnutp.com

Claflin Capital Management, Inc.
10 Liberty Sq., Ste. 300
Boston, MA 02109
(617)426-6505
Fax: (617)482-0016
Website: http://www.claflincapital.com

Copley Venture Partners
99 Summer St., Ste. 1720
Boston, MA 02110
(617)737-1253
Fax: (617)439-0699

Corning Capital / Corning Technology Ventures
121 High Street, Ste. 400
Boston, MA 02110
(617)338-2656
Fax: (617)261-3864
Website: http://www.corningventures.com

Downer & Co.
211 Congress St.
Boston, MA 02110
(617)482-6200
Fax: (617)482-6201
E-mail: cdowner@downer.com
Website: http://www.downer.com

Fidelity Ventures
82 Devonshire St.
Boston, MA 02109
(617)563-6370
Fax: (617)476-9023
Website: http://www.fidelityventures.com

Greylock Management Corp. (Boston)
1 Federal St.
Boston, MA 02110-2065
(617)423-5525
Fax: (617)482-0059

Gryphon Ventures
222 Berkeley St., Ste.1600
Boston, MA 02116
(617)267-9191
Fax: (617)267-4293
E-mail: all@gryphoninc.com

Halpern, Denny & Co.
500 Boylston St.
Boston, MA 02116
(617)536-6602
Fax: (617)536-8535

Harbourvest Partners, LLC
1 Financial Center, 44th Fl.
Boston, MA 02111
(617)348-3707
Fax: (617)350-0305
Website: http://www.hvpllc.com

Highland Capital Partners
2 International Pl.
Boston, MA 02110
(617)981-1500
Fax: (617)531-1550
E-mail: info@hcp.com
Website: http://www.hcp.com

Lee Munder Venture Partners
John Hancock Tower T-53
200 Clarendon St.
Boston, MA 02103

(617)380-5600
Fax: (617)380-5601
Website: http://www.leemunder.com

M/C Venture Partners
75 State St., Ste. 2500
Boston, MA 02109
(617)345-7200
Fax: (617)345-7201
Website: http://www.mcventure
partners.com

Massachusetts Capital Resources Co.
420 Boylston St.
Boston, MA 02116
(617)536-3900
Fax: (617)536-7930

Massachusetts Technology Development Corp. (MTDC)
148 State St.
Boston, MA 02109
(617)723-4920
Fax: (617)723-5983
E-mail: jhodgman@mtdc.com
Website: http://www.mtdc.com

New England Partners
One Boston Place, Ste. 2100
Boston, MA 02108
(617)624-8400
Fax: (617)624-8999
Website: http://www.nepartners.com

North Hill Ventures
Ten Post Office Square
11th Fl.
Boston, MA 02109
(617)788-2112
Fax: (617)788-2152
Website: http://www.northhill
ventures.com

OneLiberty Ventures
150 Cambridge Park Dr.
Boston, MA 02140
(617)492-7280
Fax: (617)492-7290
Website: http://www.oneliberty.com

Schroder Ventures
Life Sciences
60 State St., Ste. 3650
Boston, MA 02109
(617)367-8100
Fax: (617)367-1590
Website: http://www.shroderventures.com

Shawmut Capital Partners
75 Federal St., 18th Fl.
Boston, MA 02110

(617)368-4900
Fax: (617)368-4910
Website: http://www.shawmutcapital.com

Solstice Capital LLC
15 Broad St., 3rd Fl.
Boston, MA 02109
(617)523-7733
Fax: (617)523-5827
E-mail: solticecapital@solcap.com

Spectrum Equity Investors
One International Pl., 29th Fl.
Boston, MA 02110
(617)464-4600
Fax: (617)464-4601
Website: http://www.spectrumequity.com

Spray Venture Partners
One Walnut St.
Boston, MA 02108
(617)305-4140
Fax: (617)305-4144
Website: http://www.sprayventure.com

The Still River Fund
100 Federal St., 29th Fl.
Boston, MA 02110
(617)348-2327
Fax: (617)348-2371
Website: http://www.stillriverfund.com

Summit Partners
600 Atlantic Ave., Ste. 2800
Boston, MA 02210-2227
(617)824-1000
Fax: (617)824-1159
Website: http://www.summitpartners.com

TA Associates, Inc. (Boston)
High Street Tower
125 High St., Ste. 2500
Boston, MA 02110
(617)574-6700
Fax: (617)574-6728
Website: http://www.ta.com

TVM Techno Venture Management
101 Arch St., Ste. 1950
Boston, MA 02110
(617)345-9320
Fax: (617)345-9377
E-mail: info@tvmvc.com
Website: http://www.tvmvc.com

UNC Ventures
64 Burough St.
Boston, MA 02130-4017
(617)482-7070
Fax: (617)522-2176

Venture Investment Management Company (VIMAC)
177 Milk St.
Boston, MA 02190-3410
(617)292-3300
Fax: (617)292-7979
E-mail: bzeisig@vimac.com
Website: http://www.vimac.com

MDT Advisers, Inc.
125 Cambridge Park Dr.
Cambridge, MA 02140-2314
(617)234-2200
Fax: (617)234-2210
Website: http://www.mdtai.com

TTC Ventures
One Main St., 6th Fl.
Cambridge, MA 02142
(617)528-3137
Fax: (617)577-1715
E-mail: info@ttcventures.com

Zero Stage Capital Co. Inc.
101 Main St., 17th Fl.
Cambridge, MA 02142
(617)876-5355
Fax: (617)876-1248
Website: http://www.zerostage.com

Atlantic Capital
164 Cushing Hwy.
Cohasset, MA 02025
(617)383-9449
Fax: (617)383-6040
E-mail: info@atlanticcap.com
Website: http://www.atlanticcap.com

Seacoast Capital Partners
55 Ferncroft Rd.
Danvers, MA 01923
(978)750-1300
Fax: (978)750-1301
E-mail: gdeli@seacoastcapital.com
Website: http://www.seacoast
capital.com

Sage Management Group
44 South Street
PO Box 2026
East Dennis, MA 02641
(508)385-7172
Fax: (508)385-7272
E-mail: sagemgt@capecod.net

Applied Technology
1 Cranberry Hill
Lexington, MA 02421-7397
(617)862-8622
Fax: (617)862-8367

Royalty Capital Management
5 Downing Rd.
Lexington, MA 02421-6918
(781)861-8490

Argo Global Capital
210 Broadway, Ste. 101
Lynnfield, MA 01940
(781)592-5250
Fax: (781)592-5230
Website: http://www.gsmcapital.com

Industry Ventures
6 Bayne Lane
Newburyport, MA 01950
(978)499-7606
Fax: (978)499-0686
Website: http://
www.industryventures.com

Softbank Capital Partners
10 Langley Rd., Ste. 202
Newton Center, MA 02459
(617)928-9300
Fax: (617)928-9305
E-mail: clax@bvc.com

Advanced Technology Ventures (Boston)
281 Winter St., Ste. 350
Waltham, MA 02451
(781)290-0707
Fax: (781)684-0045
E-mail: info@atvcapital.com
Website: http://www.atvcapital.com

Castile Ventures
890 Winter St., Ste. 140
Waltham, MA 02451
(781)890-0060
Fax: (781)890-0065
Website: http://www.castileventures.com

Charles River Ventures
1000 Winter St., Ste. 3300
Waltham, MA 02451
(781)487-7060
Fax: (781)487-7065
Website: http://www.crv.com

Comdisco Venture Group (Waltham)
Totton Pond Office Center
400-1 Totten Pond Rd.
Waltham, MA 02451
(617)672-0250
Fax: (617)398-8099

Marconi Ventures
890 Winter St., Ste. 310
Waltham, MA 02451
(781)839-7177

Fax: (781)522-7477
Website: http://www.marconi.com

Matrix Partners
Bay Colony Corporate Center
1000 Winter St., Ste.4500
Waltham, MA 02451
(781)890-2244
Fax: (781)890-2288
Website: http://www.matrix
partners.com

North Bridge Venture Partners
950 Winter St. Ste. 4600
Waltham, MA 02451
(781)290-0004
Fax: (781)290-0999
E-mail: eta@nbvp.com

Polaris Venture Partners
Bay Colony Corporate Ctr.
1000 Winter St., Ste. 3500
Waltham, MA 02451
(781)290-0770
Fax: (781)290-0880
E-mail: partners@polarisventures.com
Website: http://www.polar
isventures.com

Seaflower Ventures
Bay Colony Corporate Ctr.
1000 Winter St. Ste. 1000
Waltham, MA 02451
(781)466-9552
Fax: (781)466-9553
E-mail: moot@seaflower.com
Website: http://www.seaflower.com

Ampersand Ventures
55 William St., Ste. 240
Wellesley, MA 02481
(617)239-0700
Fax: (617)239-0824
E-mail: info@ampersandventures.com
Website: http://www.ampersand
ventures.com

Battery Ventures (Boston)
20 William St., Ste. 200
Wellesley, MA 02481
(781)577-1000
Fax: (781)577-1001
Website: http://www.battery.com

Commonwealth Capital Ventures, L.P.
20 William St., Ste.225
Wellesley, MA 02481
(781)237-7373
Fax: (781)235-8627
Website: http://www.ccvlp.com

Fowler, Anthony & Company
20 Walnut St.
Wellesley, MA 02481
(781)237-4201
Fax: (781)237-7718

Gemini Investors
20 William St.
Wellesley, MA 02481
(781)237-7001
Fax: (781)237-7233

Grove Street Advisors Inc.
20 William St., Ste. 230
Wellesley, MA 02481
(781)263-6100
Fax: (781)263-6101
Website: http://www.groves
treetadvisors.com

Mees Pierson Investeringsmaat B.V.
20 William St., Ste. 210
Wellesley, MA 02482
(781)239-7600
Fax: (781)239-0377

Norwest Equity Partners
40 William St., Ste. 305
Wellesley, MA 02481-3902
(781)237-5870
Fax: (781)237-6270
Website: http://www.norwestvp.com

Bessemer Venture Partners (Wellesley Hills)
83 Walnut St.
Wellesley Hills, MA 02481
(781)237-6050
Fax: (781)235-7576
E-mail: travis@bvpny.com
Website: http://www.bvp.com

Venture Capital Fund of New England
20 Walnut St., Ste. 120
Wellesley Hills, MA 02481-2175
(781)239-8262
Fax: (781)239-8263

Prism Venture Partners
100 Lowder Brook Dr., Ste. 2500
Westwood, MA 02090
(781)302-4000
Fax: (781)302-4040
E-mail: dwbaum@prismventure.com

Palmer Partners LP
200 Unicorn Park Dr.
Woburn, MA 01801
(781)933-5445
Fax: (781)933-0698

Michigan

Arbor Partners, L.L.C.
130 South First St.
Ann Arbor, MI 48104
(734)668-9000
Fax: (734)669-4195
Website: http://www.arborpartners.com

EDF Ventures
425 N. Main St.
Ann Arbor, MI 48104
(734)663-3213
Fax: (734)663-7358
E-mail: edf@edfvc.com
Website: http://www.edfvc.com

White Pines Management, L.L.C.
2401 Plymouth Rd., Ste. B
Ann Arbor, MI 48105
(734)747-9401
Fax: (734)747-9704
E-mail: ibund@whitepines.com
Website: http://www.whitepines.com

Wellmax, Inc.
3541 Bendway Blvd., Ste. 100
Bloomfield Hills, MI 48301
(248)646-3554
Fax: (248)646-6220

Venture Funding, Ltd.
Fisher Bldg.
3011 West Grand Blvd., Ste. 321
Detroit, MI 48202
(313)871-3606
Fax: (313)873-4935

Investcare Partners L.P. / GMA Capital LLC
32330 W. Twelve Mile Rd.
Farmington Hills, MI 48334
(248)489-9000
Fax: (248)489-8819
E-mail: gma@gmacapital.com
Website: http://www.gmacapital.com

Liberty Bidco Investment Corp.
30833 Northwestern Highway, Ste. 211
Farmington Hills, MI 48334
(248)626-6070
Fax: (248)626-6072

Seaflower Ventures
5170 Nicholson Rd.
PO Box 474
Fowlerville, MI 48836
(517)223-3335
Fax: (517)223-3337
E-mail: gibbons@seaflower.com
Website: http://www.seaflower.com

Ralph Wilson Equity Fund LLC
15400 E. Jefferson Ave.
Gross Pointe Park, MI 48230
(313)821-9122
Fax: (313)821-9101
Website: http://www.Ralph
WilsonEquityFund.com
J. Skip Simms, President

Minnesota

Development Corp. of Austin
1900 Eighth Ave., NW
Austin, MN 55912
(507)433-0346
Fax: (507)433-0361
E-mail: dca@smig.net
Website: http://www.spamtownusa.com

Northeast Ventures Corp.
802 Alworth Bldg.
Duluth, MN 55802
(218)722-9915
Fax: (218)722-9871

Medical Innovation Partners, Inc.
6450 City West Pkwy.
Eden Prairie, MN 55344-3245
(612)828-9616
Fax: (612)828-9596

St. Paul Venture Capital, Inc.
10400 Vicking Dr., Ste. 550
Eden Prairie, MN 55344
(612)995-7474
Fax: (612)995-7475
Website: http://www.stpaulvc.com

Cherry Tree Investments, Inc.
7601 France Ave. S, Ste. 150
Edina, MN 55435
(612)893-9012
Fax: (612)893-9036
Website: http://www.cherrytree.com

Shared Ventures, Inc.
6550 York Ave. S
Edina, MN 55435
(612)925-3411

Sherpa Partners LLC
5050 Lincoln Dr., Ste. 490
Edina, MN 55436
(952)942-1070
Fax: (952)942-1071
Website: http://www.sherpapartners.com

Affinity Capital Management
901 Marquette Ave., Ste. 1810
Minneapolis, MN 55402
(612)252-9900

Fax: (612)252-9911
Website: http://www.affinitycapital.com

Artesian Capital
1700 Foshay Tower
821 Marquette Ave.
Minneapolis, MN 55402
(612)334-5600
Fax: (612)334-5601
E-mail: artesian@artesian.com

Coral Ventures
60 S. 6th St., Ste. 3510
Minneapolis, MN 55402
(612)335-8666
Fax: (612)335-8668
Website: http://www.coralventures.com

Crescendo Venture Management, L.L.C.
800 LaSalle Ave., Ste. 2250
Minneapolis, MN 55402
(612)607-2800
Fax: (612)607-2801
Website: http://www.crescendo
ventures.com

Gideon Hixon Venture
1900 Foshay Tower
821 Marquette Ave.
Minneapolis, MN 55402
(612)904-2314
Fax: (612)204-0913

Norwest Equity Partners
3600 IDS Center
80 S. 8th St.
Minneapolis, MN 55402
(612)215-1600
Fax: (612)215-1601
Website: http://www.norwestvp.com

Oak Investment Partners (Minneapolis)
4550 Norwest Center
90 S. 7th St.
Minneapolis, MN 55402
(612)339-9322
Fax: (612)337-8017
Website: http://www.oakinv.com

Pathfinder Venture Capital Funds (Minneapolis)
7300 Metro Blvd., Ste. 585
Minneapolis, MN 55439
(612)835-1121
Fax: (612)835-8389
E-mail: jahrens620@aol.com

U.S. Bancorp Piper Jaffray Ventures, Inc.
800 Nicollet Mall, Ste. 800
Minneapolis, MN 55402

(612)303-5686
Fax: (612)303-1350
Website: http://www.paperjaffrey
ventures.com

The Food Fund, Ltd. Partnership
5720 Smatana Dr., Ste. 300
Minnetonka, MN 55343
(612)939-3950
Fax: (612)939-8106

Mayo Medical Ventures
200 First St. SW
Rochester, MN 55905
(507)266-4586
Fax: (507)284-5410
Website: http://www.mayo.edu

Missouri

Bankers Capital Corp.
3100 Gillham Rd.
Kansas City, MO 64109
(816)531-1600
Fax: (816)531-1334

Capital for Business, Inc. (Kansas City)
1000 Walnut St., 18th Fl.
Kansas City, MO 64106
(816)234-2357
Fax: (816)234-2952
Website: http://
www.capitalforbusiness.com

De Vries & Co. Inc.
800 West 47th St.
Kansas City, MO 64112
(816)756-0055
Fax: (816)756-0061

InvestAmerica Venture Group Inc. (Kansas City)
Commerce Tower
911 Main St., Ste. 2424
Kansas City, MO 64105
(816)842-0114
Fax: (816)471-7339

Kansas City Equity Partners
233 W. 47th St.
Kansas City, MO 64112
(816)960-1771
Fax: (816)960-1777
Website: http://www.kcep.com

Bome Investors, Inc.
8000 Maryland Ave., Ste. 1190
St. Louis, MO 63105
(314)721-5707
Fax: (314)721-5135

Website: http://www.gateway
ventures.com

Capital for Business, Inc. (St. Louis)
11 S. Meramac St., Ste. 1430
St. Louis, MO 63105
(314)746-7427
Fax: (314)746-8739
Website: http://www.capitalfor
business.com

Crown Capital Corp.
540 Maryville Centre Dr., Ste. 120
Saint Louis, MO 63141
(314)576-1201
Fax: (314)576-1525
Website: http://www.crown-
cap.com

Gateway Associates L.P.
8000 Maryland Ave., Ste. 1190
St. Louis, MO 63105
(314)721-5707
Fax: (314)721-5135

Harbison Corp.
8112 Maryland Ave., Ste. 250
Saint Louis, MO 63105
(314)727-8200
Fax: (314)727-0249

Heartland Capital Fund, Ltd.
PO Box 642117
Omaha, NE 68154
(402)778-5124
Fax: (402)445-2370
Website: http://www.heartland
capitalfund.com

Odin Capital Group
1625 Farnam St., Ste. 700
Omaha, NE 68102
(402)346-6200
Fax: (402)342-9311
Website: http://www.odincapital.com

Nevada

Edge Capital Investment Co. LLC
1350 E. Flamingo Rd., Ste. 3000
Las Vegas, NV 89119
(702)438-3343
E-mail: info@edgecapital.net
Website: http://www.edgecapital.net

The Benefit Capital Companies Inc.
PO Box 542
Logandale, NV 89021
(702)398-3222
Fax: (702)398-3700

Millennium Three Venture Group LLC
6880 South McCarran Blvd., Ste. A-11
Reno, NV 89509
(775)954-2020
Fax: (775)954-2023
Website: http://www.m3vg.com

New Jersey

Alan I. Goldman & Associates
497 Ridgewood Ave.
Glen Ridge, NJ 07028
(973)857-5680
Fax: (973)509-8856

CS Capital Partners LLC
328 Second St., Ste. 200
Lakewood, NJ 08701
(732)901-1111
Fax: (212)202-5071
Website: http://www.cs-capital.com

Edison Venture Fund
1009 Lenox Dr., Ste. 4
Lawrenceville, NJ 08648
(609)896-1900
Fax: (609)896-0066
E-mail: info@edisonventure.com
Website: http://www.edisonventure.com

Tappan Zee Capital Corp. (New Jersey)
201 Lower Notch Rd.
PO Box 416
Little Falls, NJ 07424
(973)256-8280
Fax: (973)256-2841

The CIT Group/Venture Capital, Inc.
650 CIT Dr.
Livingston, NJ 07039
(973)740-5429
Fax: (973)740-5555
Website: http://www.cit.com

Capital Express, L.L.C.
1100 Valleybrook Ave.
Lyndhurst, NJ 07071
(201)438-8228
Fax: (201)438-5131
E-mail: niles@capitalexpress.com
Website: http://www.capitalexpress.com

Westford Technology Ventures, L.P.
17 Academy St.
Newark, NJ 07102
(973)624-2131
Fax: (973)624-2008

Accel Partners
1 Palmer Sq.
Princeton, NJ 08542

(609)683-4500
Fax: (609)683-4880
Website: http://www.accel.com

Cardinal Partners
221 Nassau St.
Princeton, NJ 08542
(609)924-6452
Fax: (609)683-0174
Website: http://www.cardinal
healthpartners.com

Domain Associates L.L.C.
One Palmer Sq., Ste. 515
Princeton, NJ 08542
(609)683-5656
Fax: (609)683-9789
Website: http://www.domainvc.com

Johnston Associates, Inc.
181 Cherry Valley Rd.
Princeton, NJ 08540
(609)924-3131
Fax: (609)683-7524
E-mail: jaincorp@aol.com

Kemper Ventures
Princeton Forrestal Village
155 Village Blvd.
Princeton, NJ 08540
(609)936-3035
Fax: (609)936-3051

Penny Lane Parnters
One Palmer Sq., Ste. 309
Princeton, NJ 08542
(609)497-4646
Fax: (609)497-0611

Early Stage Enterprises L.P.
995 Route 518
Skillman, NJ 08558
(609)921-8896
Fax: (609)921-8703
Website: http://www.esevc.com

MBW Management Inc.
1 Springfield Ave.
Summit, NJ 07901
(908)273-4060
Fax: (908)273-4430

BCI Advisors, Inc.
Glenpointe Center W.
Teaneck, NJ 07666
(201)836-3900
Fax: (201)836-6368
E-mail: info@bciadvisors.com
Website: http://www.bci
partners.com

Demuth, Folger & Wetherill / DFW Capital Partners
Glenpointe Center E., 5th Fl.
300 Frank W. Burr Blvd.
Teaneck, NJ 07666
(201)836-2233
Fax: (201)836-5666
Website: http://www.dfwcapital.com

First Princeton Capital Corp.
189 Berdan Ave., No. 131
Wayne, NJ 07470-3233
(973)278-3233
Fax: (973)278-4290
Website: http://www.lytellcatt.net

Edelson Technology Partners
300 Tice Blvd.
Woodcliff Lake, NJ 07675
(201)930-9898
Fax: (201)930-8899
Website: http://www.edelsontech.com

New Mexico

Bruce F. Glaspell & Associates
10400 Academy Rd. NE, Ste. 313
Albuquerque, NM 87111
(505)292-4505
Fax: (505)292-4258

High Desert Ventures, Inc.
6101 Imparata St. NE, Ste. 1721
Albuquerque, NM 87111
(505)797-3330
Fax: (505)338-5147

New Business Capital Fund, Ltd.
5805 Torreon NE
Albuquerque, NM 87109
(505)822-8445

SBC Ventures
10400 Academy Rd. NE, Ste. 313
Albuquerque, NM 87111
(505)292-4505
Fax: (505)292-4528

Technology Ventures Corp.
1155 University Blvd. SE
Albuquerque, NM 87106
(505)246-2882
Fax: (505)246-2891

New York

New York State Science & Technology Foundation
Small Business Technology Investment Fund
99 Washington Ave., Ste. 1731
Albany, NY 12210

(518)473-9741
Fax: (518)473-6876

Rand Capital Corp.
2200 Rand Bldg.
Buffalo, NY 14203
(716)853-0802
Fax: (716)854-8480
Website: http://www.randcapital.com

Seed Capital Partners
620 Main St.
Buffalo, NY 14202
(716)845-7520
Fax: (716)845-7539
Website: http://www.seedcp.com

Coleman Venture Group
5909 Northern Blvd.
PO Box 224
East Norwich, NY 11732
(516)626-3642
Fax: (516)626-9722

Vega Capital Corp.
45 Knollwood Rd.
Elmsford, NY 10523
(914)345-9500
Fax: (914)345-9505

Herbert Young Securities, Inc.
98 Cuttermill Rd.
Great Neck, NY 11021
(516)487-8300
Fax: (516)487-8319

Sterling/Carl Marks Capital, Inc.
175 Great Neck Rd., Ste. 408
Great Neck, NY 11021
(516)482-7374
Fax: (516)487-0781
E-mail: stercrlmar@aol.com
Website: http://www.serling
carlmarks.com

Impex Venture Management Co.
PO Box 1570
Green Island, NY 12183
(518)271-8008
Fax: (518)271-9101

Corporate Venture Partners L.P.
200 Sunset Park
Ithaca, NY 14850
(607)257-6323
Fax: (607)257-6128

Arthur P. Gould & Co.
One Wilshire Dr.
Lake Success, NY 11020
(516)773-3000
Fax: (516)773-3289

Dauphin Capital Partners
108 Forest Ave.
Locust Valley, NY 11560
(516)759-3339
Fax: (516)759-3322
Website: http://www.dauphincapital.com

550 Digital Media Ventures
555 Madison Ave., 10th Fl.
New York, NY 10022
Website: http://www.550dmv.com

Aberlyn Capital Management Co., Inc.
500 Fifth Ave.
New York, NY 10110
(212)391-7750
Fax: (212)391-7762

Adler & Company
342 Madison Ave., Ste. 807
New York, NY 10173
(212)599-2535
Fax: (212)599-2526

Alimansky Capital Group, Inc.
605 Madison Ave., Ste. 300
New York, NY 10022-1901
(212)832-7300
Fax: (212)832-7338

Allegra Partners
515 Madison Ave., 29th Fl.
New York, NY 10022
(212)826-9080
Fax: (212)759-2561

The Argentum Group
The Chyrsler Bldg.
405 Lexington Ave.
New York, NY 10174
(212)949-6262
Fax: (212)949-8294
Website: http://www.argentum
group.com

Axavision Inc.
14 Wall St., 26th Fl.
New York, NY 10005
(212)619-4000
Fax: (212)619-7202

Bedford Capital Corp.
18 East 48th St., Ste. 1800
New York, NY 10017
(212)688-5700
Fax: (212)754-4699
E-mail: info@bedfordnyc.com
Website: http://www.bedfordnyc.com

Bloom & Co.
950 Third Ave.

New York, NY 10022
(212)838-1858
Fax: (212)838-1843

Bristol Capital Management
300 Park Ave., 17th Fl.
New York, NY 10022
(212)572-6306
Fax: (212)705-4292

Citicorp Venture Capital Ltd. (New York City)
399 Park Ave., 14th Fl.
Zone 4
New York, NY 10043
(212)559-1127
Fax: (212)888-2940

CM Equity Partners
135 E. 57th St.
New York, NY 10022
(212)909-8428
Fax: (212)980-2630

Cohen & Co., L.L.C.
800 Third Ave.
New York, NY 10022
(212)317-2250
Fax: (212)317-2255
E-mail: nlcohen@aol.com

Cornerstone Equity Investors, L.L.C.
717 5th Ave., Ste. 1100
New York, NY 10022
(212)753-0901
Fax: (212)826-6798
Website: http://www.cornerstone-equity.com

CW Group, Inc.
1041 3rd Ave., 2nd fl.
New York, NY 10021
(212)308-5266
Fax: (212)644-0354
Website: http://www.cwventures.com

DH Blair Investment Banking Corp.
44 Wall St., 2nd Fl.
New York, NY 10005
(212)495-5000
Fax: (212)269-1438

Dresdner Kleinwort Capital
75 Wall St.
New York, NY 10005
(212)429-3131
Fax: (212)429-3139
Website: http://www.dresdnerkb.com

East River Ventures, L.P.
645 Madison Ave., 22nd Fl.

New York, NY 10022
(212)644-2322
Fax: (212)644-5498

Easton Hunt Capital Partners
641 Lexington Ave., 21st Fl.
New York, NY 10017
(212)702-0950
Fax: (212)702-0952
Website: http://www.eastoncapital.com

Elk Associates Funding Corp.
747 3rd Ave., Ste. 4C
New York, NY 10017
(212)355-2449
Fax: (212)759-3338

EOS Partners, L.P.
320 Park Ave., 22nd Fl.
New York, NY 10022
(212)832-5800
Fax: (212)832-5815
E-mail: mfirst@eospartners.com
Website: http://www.eospartners.com

Euclid Partners
45 Rockefeller Plaza, Ste. 3240
New York, NY 10111
(212)218-6880
Fax: (212)218-6877
E-mail: graham@euclidpartners.com
Website: http://www.euclidpartners.com

Evergreen Capital Partners, Inc.
150 East 58th St.
New York, NY 10155
(212)813-0758
Fax: (212)813-0754

Exeter Capital L.P.
10 E. 53rd St.
New York, NY 10022
(212)872-1172
Fax: (212)872-1198
E-mail: exeter@usa.net

Financial Technology Research Corp.
518 Broadway
Penthouse
New York, NY 10012
(212)625-9100
Fax: (212)431-0300
E-mail: fintek@financier.com

4C Ventures
237 Park Ave., Ste. 801
New York, NY 10017
(212)692-3680
Fax: (212)692-3685
Website: http://www.4cventures.com

Fusient Ventures
99 Park Ave., 20th Fl.
New York, NY 10016
(212)972-8999
Fax: (212)972-9876
E-mail: info@fusient.com
Website: http://www.fusient.com

Generation Capital Partners
551 Fifth Ave., Ste. 3100
New York, NY 10176
(212)450-8507
Fax: (212)450-8550
Website: http://www.genpartners.com

Golub Associates, Inc.
555 Madison Ave.
New York, NY 10022
(212)750-6060
Fax: (212)750-5505

Hambro America Biosciences Inc.
650 Madison Ave., 21st Floor
New York, NY 10022
(212)223-7400
Fax: (212)223-0305

Hanover Capital Corp.
505 Park Ave., 15th Fl.
New York, NY 10022
(212)755-1222
Fax: (212)935-1787

Harvest Partners, Inc.
280 Park Ave, 33rd Fl.
New York, NY 10017
(212)559-6300
Fax: (212)812-0100
Website: http://www.harvpart.com

Holding Capital Group, Inc.
10 E. 53rd St., 30th Fl.
New York, NY 10022
(212)486-6670
Fax: (212)486-0843

Hudson Venture Partners
660 Madison Ave., 14th Fl.
New York, NY 10021-8405
(212)644-9797
Fax: (212)644-7430
Website: http://www.hudsonptr.com

IBJS Capital Corp.
1 State St., 9th Fl.
New York, NY 10004
(212)858-2018
Fax: (212)858-2768

InterEquity Capital Partners, L.P.
220 5th Ave.
New York, NY 10001

(212)779-2022
Fax: (212)779-2103
Website: http://www.interequity-capital.com

The Jordan Edmiston Group Inc.
150 East 52nd St., 18th Fl.
New York, NY 10022
(212)754-0710
Fax: (212)754-0337

Josephberg, Grosz and Co., Inc.
633 3rd Ave., 13th Fl.
New York, NY 10017
(212)974-9926
Fax: (212)397-5832

J.P. Morgan Capital Corp.
60 Wall St.
New York, NY 10260-0060
(212)648-9000
Fax: (212)648-5002
Website: http://www.jpmorgan.com

The Lambda Funds
380 Lexington Ave., 54th Fl.
New York, NY 10168
(212)682-3454
Fax: (212)682-9231

Lepercq Capital Management Inc.
1675 Broadway
New York, NY 10019
(212)698-0795
Fax: (212)262-0155

Loeb Partners Corp.
61 Broadway, Ste. 2400
New York, NY 10006
(212)483-7000
Fax: (212)574-2001

Madison Investment Partners
660 Madison Ave.
New York, NY 10021
(212)223-2600
Fax: (212)223-8208

MC Capital Inc.
520 Madison Ave., 16th Fl.
New York, NY 10022
(212)644-0841
Fax: (212)644-2926

McCown, De Leeuw and Co. (New York)
65 E. 55th St., 36th Fl.
New York, NY 10022
(212)355-5500
Fax: (212)355-6283
Website: http://www.mdcpartners.com

Morgan Stanley Venture Partners
1221 Avenue of the Americas, 33rd Fl.
New York, NY 10020
(212)762-7900
Fax: (212)762-8424
E-mail: msventures@ms.com
Website: http://www.msvp.com

Nazem and Co.
645 Madison Ave., 12th Fl.
New York, NY 10022
(212)371-7900
Fax: (212)371-2150

Needham Capital Management, L.L.C.
445 Park Ave.
New York, NY 10022
(212)371-8300
Fax: (212)705-0299
Website: http://www.needhamco.com

Norwood Venture Corp.
1430 Broadway, Ste. 1607
New York, NY 10018
(212)869-5075
Fax: (212)869-5331
E-mail: nvc@mail.idt.net
Website: http://www.norven.com

Noveltek Venture Corp.
521 Fifth Ave., Ste. 1700
New York, NY 10175
(212)286-1963

Paribas Principal, Inc.
787 7th Ave.
New York, NY 10019
(212)841-2005
Fax: (212)841-3558

Patricof & Co. Ventures, Inc. (New York)
445 Park Ave.
New York, NY 10022
(212)753-6300
Fax: (212)319-6155
Website: http://www.patricof.com

The Platinum Group, Inc.
350 Fifth Ave, Ste. 7113
New York, NY 10118
(212)736-4300
Fax: (212)736-6086
Website: http://www.platinumgroup.com

Pomona Capital
780 Third Ave., 28th Fl.
New York, NY 10017
(212)593-3639
Fax: (212)593-3987
Website: http://www.pomonacapital.com

Prospect Street Ventures
10 East 40th St., 44th Fl.
New York, NY 10016
(212)448-0702
Fax: (212)448-9652
E-mail: wkohler@prospectstreet.com
Website: http://www.prospectstreet.com

Regent Capital Management
505 Park Ave., Ste. 1700
New York, NY 10022
(212)735-9900
Fax: (212)735-9908

Rothschild Ventures, Inc.
1251 Avenue of the Americas, 51st Fl.
New York, NY 10020
(212)403-3500
Fax: (212)403-3652
Website: http://www.nmrothschild.com

Sandler Capital Management
767 Fifth Ave., 45th Fl.
New York, NY 10153
(212)754-8100
Fax: (212)826-0280

Siguler Guff & Company
630 Fifth Ave., 16th Fl.
New York, NY 10111
(212)332-5100
Fax: (212)332-5120

Spencer Trask Ventures Inc.
535 Madison Ave.
New York, NY 10022
(212)355-5565
Fax: (212)751-3362
Website: http://www.spencertrask.com

Sprout Group (New York City)
277 Park Ave.
New York, NY 10172
(212)892-3600
Fax: (212)892-3444
E-mail: info@sproutgroup.com
Website: http://www.sproutgroup.com

US Trust Private Equity
114 W.47th St.
New York, NY 10036
(212)852-3949
Fax: (212)852-3759
Website: http://www.ustrust.com/privateequity

Vencon Management Inc.
301 West 53rd St., Ste. 10F
New York, NY 10019
(212)581-8787
Fax: (212)397-4126
Website: http://www.venconinc.com

Venrock Associates
30 Rockefeller Plaza, Ste. 5508
New York, NY 10112
(212)649-5600
Fax: (212)649-5788
Website: http://www.venrock.com

Venture Capital Fund of America, Inc.
509 Madison Ave., Ste. 812
New York, NY 10022
(212)838-5577
Fax: (212)838-7614
E-mail: mail@vcfa.com
Website: http://www.vcfa.com

Venture Opportunities Corp.
150 E. 58th St.
New York, NY 10155
(212)832-3737
Fax: (212)980-6603

Warburg Pincus Ventures, Inc.
466 Lexington Ave., 11th Fl.
New York, NY 10017
(212)878-9309
Fax: (212)878-9200
Website: http://www.warburgpincus.com

Wasserstein, Perella & Co. Inc.
31 W. 52nd St., 27th Fl.
New York, NY 10019
(212)702-5691
Fax: (212)969-7879

Welsh, Carson, Anderson, & Stowe
320 Park Ave., Ste. 2500
New York, NY 10022-6815
(212)893-9500
Fax: (212)893-9575

Whitney and Co. (New York)
630 Fifth Ave. Ste. 3225
New York, NY 10111
(212)332-2400
Fax: (212)332-2422
Website: http://www.jhwitney.com

Winthrop Ventures
74 Trinity Place, Ste. 600
New York, NY 10006
(212)422-0100

The Pittsford Group
8 Lodge Pole Rd.
Pittsford, NY 14534
(716)223-3523

Genesee Funding
70 Linden Oaks, 3rd Fl.
Rochester, NY 14625
(716)383-5550
Fax: (716)383-5305

Gabelli Multimedia Partners
One Corporate Center
Rye, NY 10580
(914)921-5395
Fax: (914)921-5031

Stamford Financial
108 Main St.
Stamford, NY 12167
(607)652-3311
Fax: (607)652-6301
Website: http://www.stamford
financial.com

Northwood Ventures LLC
485 Underhill Blvd., Ste. 205
Syosset, NY 11791
(516)364-5544
Fax: (516)364-0879
E-mail: northwood@northwood.com
Website: http://www.north
woodventures.com

Exponential Business Development Co.
216 Walton St.
Syracuse, NY 13202-1227
(315)474-4500
Fax: (315)474-4682
E-mail: dirksonn@aol.com
Website: http://www.exponential-ny.com

Onondaga Venture Capital Fund Inc.
714 State Tower Bldg.
Syracuse, NY 13202
(315)478-0157
Fax: (315)478-0158

Bessemer Venture Partners (Westbury)
1400 Old Country Rd., Ste. 109
Westbury, NY 11590
(516)997-2300
Fax: (516)997-2371
E-mail: bob@bvpny.com
Website: http://www.bvp.com

Ovation Capital Partners
120 Bloomingdale Rd., 4th Fl.
White Plains, NY 10605
(914)258-0011
Fax: (914)684-0848
Website: http://www.ovation
capital.com

North Carolina

Carolinas Capital Investment Corp.
1408 Biltmore Dr.
Charlotte, NC 28207
(704)375-3888
Fax: (704)375-6226

First Union Capital Partners
1st Union Center, 12th Fl.
301 S. College St.
Charlotte, NC 28288-0732
(704)383-0000
Fax: (704)374-6711
Website: http://www.fucp.com

Frontier Capital LLC
525 North Tryon St., Ste. 1700
Charlotte, NC 28202
(704)414-2880
Fax: (704)414-2881
Website: http://www.frontierfunds.com

Kitty Hawk Capital
2700 Coltsgate Rd., Ste. 202
Charlotte, NC 28211
(704)362-3909
Fax: (704)362-2774
Website: http://www.kittyhawk
capital.com

Piedmont Venture Partners
One Morrocroft Centre
6805 Morisson Blvd., Ste. 380
Charlotte, NC 28211
(704)731-5200
Fax: (704)365-9733
Website: http://www.piedmontvp.com

Ruddick Investment Co.
1800 Two First Union Center
Charlotte, NC 28282
(704)372-5404
Fax: (704)372-6409

The Shelton Companies Inc.
3600 One First Union Center
301 S. College St.
Charlotte, NC 28202
(704)348-2200
Fax: (704)348-2260

Wakefield Group
1110 E. Morehead St.
PO Box 36329
Charlotte, NC 28236
(704)372-0355
Fax: (704)372-8216
Website: http://www.wakefiel
dgroup.com

Aurora Funds, Inc.
2525 Meridian Pkwy., Ste. 220
Durham, NC 27713
(919)484-0400
Fax: (919)484-0444
Website: http://www.aurora
funds.com

Intersouth Partners
3211 Shannon Rd., Ste. 610
Durham, NC 27707
(919)493-6640
Fax: (919)493-6649
E-mail: info@intersouth.com
Website: http://www.intersouth.com

Geneva Merchant Banking Partners
PO Box 21962
Greensboro, NC 27420
(336)275-7002
Fax: (336)275-9155
Website: http://www.geneva
merchantbank.com

The North Carolina Enterprise Fund, L.P.
3600 Glenwood Ave., Ste. 107
Raleigh, NC 27612
(919)781-2691
Fax: (919)783-9195
Website: http://www.ncef.com

Ohio

Senmend Medical Ventures
4445 Lake Forest Dr., Ste. 600
Cincinnati, OH 45242
(513)563-3264
Fax: (513)563-3261

The Walnut Group
312 Walnut St., Ste. 1151
Cincinnati, OH 45202
(513)651-3300
Fax: (513)929-4441
Website: http://www.thewal
nutgroup.com

Brantley Venture Partners
20600 Chagrin Blvd., Ste. 1150
Cleveland, OH 44122
(216)283-4800
Fax: (216)283-5324

Clarion Capital Corp.
1801 E. 9th St., Ste. 1120
Cleveland, OH 44114
(216)687-1096
Fax: (216)694-3545

Crystal Internet Venture Fund, L.P.
1120 Chester Ave., Ste. 418
Cleveland, OH 44114
(216)263-5515
Fax: (216)263-5518
E-mail: jf@crystalventure.com
Website: http://www.crystal
venture.com

Key Equity Capital Corp.
127 Public Sq., 28th Fl.
Cleveland, OH 44114
(216)689-3000
Fax: (216)689-3204
Website: http://www.keybank.com

Morgenthaler Ventures
Terminal Tower
50 Public Square, Ste. 2700
Cleveland, OH 44113
(216)416-7500
Fax: (216)416-7501
Website: http://www.morgenthaler.com

National City Equity Partners Inc.
1965 E. 6th St.
Cleveland, OH 44114
(216)575-2491
Fax: (216)575-9965
E-mail: nccap@aol.com
Website: http://www.nccapital.com

Primus Venture Partners, Inc.
5900 LanderBrook Dr., Ste. 2000
Cleveland, OH 44124-4020
(440)684-7300
Fax: (440)684-7342
E-mail: info@primusventure.com
Website: http://www.primusventure.com

Banc One Capital Partners (Columbus)
150 East Gay St., 24th Fl.
Columbus, OH 43215
(614)217-1100
Fax: (614)217-1217

Battelle Venture Partners
505 King Ave.
Columbus, OH 43201
(614)424-7005
Fax: (614)424-4874

Ohio Partners
62 E. Board St., 3rd Fl.
Columbus, OH 43215
(614)621-1210
Fax: (614)621-1240

Capital Technology Group, L.L.C.
400 Metro Place North, Ste. 300
Dublin, OH 43017
(614)792-6066
Fax: (614)792-6036
E-mail: info@capitaltech.com
Website: http://www.capitaltech.com

Northwest Ohio Venture Fund
4159 Holland-Sylvania R., Ste. 202
Toledo, OH 43623
(419)824-8144

Fax: (419)882-2035
E-mail: bwalsh@novf.com

Oklahoma

Moore & Associates
1000 W. Wilshire Blvd., Ste. 370
Oklahoma City, OK 73116
(405)842-3660
Fax: (405)842-3763

Chisholm Private Capital Partners
100 West 5th St., Ste. 805
Tulsa, OK 74103
(918)584-0440
Fax: (918)584-0441
Website: http://www.chisholmvc.com

Davis, Tuttle Venture Partners (Tulsa)
320 S. Boston, Ste. 1000
Tulsa, OK 74103-3703
(918)584-7272
Fax: (918)582-3404
Website: http://www.davistuttle.com

RBC Ventures
2627 E. 21st St.
Tulsa, OK 74114
(918)744-5607
Fax: (918)743-8630

Oregon

Utah Ventures II LP
10700 SW Beaverton-Hillsdale Hwy.,
Ste. 548
Beaverton, OR 97005
(503)574-4125
E-mail: adishlip@uven.com
Website: http://www.uven.com

Orien Ventures
14523 SW Westlake Dr.
Lake Oswego, OR 97035
(503)699-1680
Fax: (503)699-1681

OVP Venture Partners (Lake Oswego)
340 Oswego Pointe Dr., Ste. 200
Lake Oswego, OR 97034
(503)697-8766
Fax: (503)697-8863
E-mail: info@ovp.com
Website: http://www.ovp.com

Oregon Resource and Technology Development Fund
4370 NE Halsey St., Ste. 233
Portland, OR 97213-1566
(503)282-4462
Fax: (503)282-2976

Shaw Venture Partners
400 SW 6th Ave., Ste. 1100
Portland, OR 97204-1636
(503)228-4884
Fax: (503)227-2471
Website: http://www.shawventures.com

Pennsylvania

Mid-Atlantic Venture Funds
125 Goodman Dr.
Bethlehem, PA 18015
(610)865-6550
Fax: (610)865-6427
Website: http://www.mavf.com

Newspring Ventures
100 W. Elm St., Ste. 101
Conshohocken, PA 19428
(610)567-2380
Fax: (610)567-2388
Website: http://www.news
printventures.com

Patricof & Co. Ventures, Inc.
455 S. Gulph Rd., Ste. 410
King of Prussia, PA 19406
(610)265-0286
Fax: (610)265-4959
Website: http://www.patricof.com

Loyalhanna Venture Fund
527 Cedar Way, Ste. 104
Oakmont, PA 15139
(412)820-7035
Fax: (412)820-7036

Innovest Group Inc.
2000 Market St., Ste. 1400
Philadelphia, PA 19103
(215)564-3960
Fax: (215)569-3272

Keystone Venture Capital Management Co.
1601 Market St., Ste. 2500
Philadelphia, PA 19103
(215)241-1200
Fax: (215)241-1211
Website: http://www.keystonevc.com

Liberty Venture Partners
2005 Market St., Ste. 200
Philadelphia, PA 19103
(215)282-4484
Fax: (215)282-4485
E-mail: info@libertyvp.com
Website: http://www.libertyvp.com

Penn Janney Fund, Inc.
1801 Market St., 11th Fl.
Philadelphia, PA 19103

Organizations, Agencies, & Consultants

(215)665-4447
Fax: (215)557-0820

Philadelphia Ventures, Inc.
The Bellevue
200 S. Broad St.
Philadelphia, PA 19102
(215)732-4445
Fax: (215)732-4644

Birchmere Ventures Inc.
2000 Technology Dr.
Pittsburgh, PA 15219-3109
(412)803-8000
Fax: (412)687-8139
Website: http://www.birchmerevc.com

CEO Venture Fund
2000 Technology Dr., Ste. 160
Pittsburgh, PA 15219-3109
(412)687-3451
Fax: (412)687-8139
E-mail: ceofund@aol.com
Website: http://www.ceoventure
fund.com

Innovation Works Inc.
2000 Technology Dr., Ste. 250
Pittsburgh, PA 15219
(412)681-1520
Fax: (412)681-2625
Website: http://www.innovation
works.org

Keystone Minority Capital Fund L.P.
1801 Centre Ave., Ste. 201
Williams Sq.
Pittsburgh, PA 15219
(412)338-2230
Fax: (412)338-2224

Mellon Ventures, Inc.
One Mellon Bank Ctr., Rm. 3500
Pittsburgh, PA 15258
(412)236-3594
Fax: (412)236-3593
Website: http://www.mellon
ventures.com

Pennsylvania Growth Fund
5850 Ellsworth Ave., Ste. 303
Pittsburgh, PA 15232
(412)661-1000
Fax: (412)361-0676

Point Venture Partners
The Century Bldg.
130 Seventh St., 7th Fl.
Pittsburgh, PA 15222
(412)261-1966
Fax: (412)261-1718

Cross Atlantic Capital Partners
5 Radnor Corporate Center, Ste. 555
Radnor, PA 19087
(610)995-2650
Fax: (610)971-2062
Website: http://www.xacp.com

Meridian Venture Partners (Radnor)
The Radnor Court Bldg., Ste. 140
259 Radnor-Chester Rd.
Radnor, PA 19087
(610)254-2999
Fax: (610)254-2996
E-mail: mvpart@ix.netcom.com

TDH
919 Conestoga Rd., Bldg. 1, Ste. 301
Rosemont, PA 19010
(610)526-9970
Fax: (610)526-9971

Adams Capital Management
500 Blackburn Ave.
Sewickley, PA 15143
(412)749-9454
Fax: (412)749-9459
Website: http://www.acm.com

S.R. One, Ltd.
Four Tower Bridge
200 Barr Harbor Dr., Ste. 250
W. Conshohocken, PA 19428
(610)567-1000
Fax: (610)567-1039

Greater Philadelphia Venture Capital Corp.
351 East Conestoga Rd.
Wayne, PA 19087
(610)688-6829
Fax: (610)254-8958

PA Early Stage
435 Devon Park Dr., Bldg. 500, Ste. 510
Wayne, PA 19087
(610)293-4075
Fax: (610)254-4240
Website: http://www.paearlystage.com

The Sandhurst Venture Fund, L.P.
351 E. Constoga Rd.
Wayne, PA 19087
(610)254-8900
Fax: (610)254-8958

TL Ventures
700 Bldg.
435 Devon Park Dr.
Wayne, PA 19087-1990
(610)975-3765
Fax: (610)254-4210
Website: http://www.tlventures.com

Rockhill Ventures, Inc.
100 Front St., Ste. 1350
West Conshohocken, PA 19428
(610)940-0300
Fax: (610)940-0301

Puerto Rico

Advent-Morro Equity Partners
Banco Popular Bldg.
206 Tetuan St., Ste. 903
San Juan, PR 00902
(787)725-5285
Fax: (787)721-1735

North America Investment Corp.
Mercantil Plaza, Ste. 813
PO Box 191831
San Juan, PR 00919
(787)754-6178
Fax: (787)754-6181

Rhode Island

Manchester Humphreys, Inc.
40 Westminster St., Ste. 900
Providence, RI 02903
(401)454-0400
Fax: (401)454-0403

Navis Partners
50 Kennedy Plaza, 12th Fl.
Providence, RI 02903
(401)278-6770
Fax: (401)278-6387
Website: http://www.navis
partners.com

South Carolina

Capital Insights, L.L.C.
PO Box 27162
Greenville, SC 29616-2162
(864)242-6832
Fax: (864)242-6755
E-mail: jwarner@capitalinsights.com
Website: http://www.capitalin
sights.com

Transamerica Mezzanine Financing
7 N. Laurens St., Ste. 603
Greenville, SC 29601
(864)232-6198
Fax: (864)241-4444

Tennessee

Valley Capital Corp.
Krystal Bldg.
100 W. Martin Luther King Blvd.,
Ste. 212

Chattanooga, TN 37402
(423)265-1557
Fax: (423)265-1588

Coleman Swenson Booth Inc.
237 2nd Ave. S
Franklin, TN 37064-2649
(615)791-9462
Fax: (615)791-9636
Website: http://
www.colemanswenson.com

Capital Services & Resources, Inc.
5159 Wheelis Dr., Ste. 106
Memphis, TN 38117
(901)761-2156
Fax: (907)767-0060

Paradigm Capital Partners LLC
6410 Poplar Ave., Ste. 395
Memphis, TN 38119
(901)682-6060
Fax: (901)328-3061

SSM Ventures
845 Crossover Ln., Ste. 140
Memphis, TN 38117
(901)767-1131
Fax: (901)767-1135
Website: http://www.ssm
ventures.com

Capital Across America L.P.
501 Union St., Ste. 201
Nashville, TN 37219
(615)254-1414
Fax: (615)254-1856
Website: http://
www.capitalacrossamerica.com

Equitas L.P.
2000 Glen Echo Rd., Ste. 101
PO Box 158838
Nashville, TN 37215-8838
(615)383-8673
Fax: (615)383-8693

Massey Burch Capital Corp.
One Burton Hills Blvd., Ste. 350
Nashville, TN 37215
(615)665-3221
Fax: (615)665-3240
E-mail: tcalton@masseyburch.com
Website: http://www.masseyburch.com

Nelson Capital Corp.
3401 West End Ave., Ste. 300
Nashville, TN 37203
(615)292-8787
Fax: (615)385-3150

Texas

Phillips-Smith Specialty Retail Group
5080 Spectrum Dr., Ste. 805 W
Addison, TX 75001
(972)387-0725
Fax: (972)458-2560
E-mail: pssrg@aol.com
Website: http://www.phillips-smith.com

Austin Ventures, L.P.
701 Brazos St., Ste. 1400
Austin, TX 78701
(512)485-1900
Fax: (512)476-3952
E-mail: info@ausven.com
Website: http://www.austinventures.com

The Capital Network
3925 West Braker Lane, Ste. 406
Austin, TX 78759-5321
(512)305-0826
Fax: (512)305-0836

Techxas Ventures LLC
5000 Plaza on the Lake
Austin, TX 78746
(512)343-0118
Fax: (512)343-1879
E-mail: bruce@techxas.com
Website: http://www.techxas.com

Alliance Financial of Houston
218 Heather Ln.
Conroe, TX 77385-9013
(936)447-3300
Fax: (936)447-4222

Amerimark Capital Corp.
1111 W. Mockingbird, Ste. 1111
Dallas, TX 75247
(214)638-7878
Fax: (214)638-7612
E-mail: amerimark@amcapital.com
Website: http://www.amcapital.com

AMT Venture Partners / AMT Capital Ltd.
5220 Spring Valley Rd., Ste. 600
Dallas, TX 75240
(214)905-9757
Fax: (214)905-9761
Website: http://www.amtcapital.com

Arkoma Venture Partners
5950 Berkshire Lane, Ste. 1400
Dallas, TX 75225
(214)739-3515
Fax: (214)739-3572
E-mail: joelf@arkomavp.com

Capital Southwest Corp.
12900 Preston Rd., Ste. 700
Dallas, TX 75230
(972)233-8242
Fax: (972)233-7362
Website: http://
www.capitalsouthwest.com

Dali, Hook Partners
One Lincoln Center, Ste. 1550
5400 LBJ Freeway
Dallas, TX 75240
(972)991-5457
Fax: (972)991-5458
E-mail: dhook@hookpartners.com
Website: http://www.hookpartners.com

HO2 Partners
Two Galleria Tower
13455 Noel Rd., Ste. 1670
Dallas, TX 75240
(972)702-1144
Fax: (972)702-8234
Website: http://www.ho2.com

Interwest Partners (Dallas)
2 Galleria Tower
13455 Noel Rd., Ste. 1670
Dallas, TX 75240
(972)392-7279
Fax: (972)490-6348
Website: http://www.interwest.com

Kahala Investments, Inc.
8214 Westchester Dr., Ste. 715
Dallas, TX 75225
(214)987-0077
Fax: (214)987-2332

MESBIC Ventures Holding Co.
2435 North Central Expressway, Ste. 200
Dallas, TX 75080
(972)991-1597
Fax: (972)991-4770
Website: http://www.mvhc.com

North Texas MESBIC, Inc.
9500 Forest Lane, Ste. 430
Dallas, TX 75243
(214)221-3565
Fax: (214)221-3566

Richard Jaffe & Company, Inc,
7318 Royal Cir.
Dallas, TX 75230
(214)265-9397
Fax: (214)739-1845

Sevin Rosen Management Co.
13455 Noel Rd., Ste. 1670
Dallas, TX 75240

(972)702-1100
Fax: (972)702-1103
E-mail: info@srfunds.com
Website: http://www.srfunds.com

Stratford Capital Partners, L.P.
300 Crescent Ct., Ste. 500
Dallas, TX 75201
(214)740-7377
Fax: (214)720-7393
E-mail: stratcap@hmtf.com

Sunwestern Investment Group
12221 Merit Dr., Ste. 935
Dallas, TX 75251
(972)239-5650
Fax: (972)701-0024

Wingate Partners
750 N. St. Paul St., Ste. 1200
Dallas, TX 75201
(214)720-1313
Fax: (214)871-8799

Buena Venture Associates
201 Main St., 32nd Fl.
Fort Worth, TX 76102
(817)339-7400
Fax: (817)390-8408
Website: http://www.buenaventure.com

The Catalyst Group
3 Riverway, Ste. 770
Houston, TX 77056
(713)623-8133
Fax: (713)623-0473
E-mail: herman@thecatalystgroup.net
Website: http://www.thecatalyst
group.net

Cureton & Co., Inc.
1100 Louisiana, Ste. 3250
Houston, TX 77002
(713)658-9806
Fax: (713)658-0476

Davis, Tuttle Venture Partners (Dallas)
8 Greenway Plaza, Ste. 1020
Houston, TX 77046
(713)993-0440
Fax: (713)621-2297
Website: http://www.davistuttle.com

Houston Partners
401 Louisiana, 8th Fl.
Houston, TX 77002
(713)222-8600
Fax: (713)222-8932

Southwest Venture Group
10878 Westheimer, Ste. 178

Houston, TX 77042
(713)827-8947
(713)461-1470

AM Fund
4600 Post Oak Place, Ste. 100
Houston, TX 77027
(713)627-9111
Fax: (713)627-9119

Ventex Management, Inc.
3417 Milam St.
Houston, TX 77002-9531
(713)659-7870
Fax: (713)659-7855

MBA Venture Group
1004 Olde Town Rd., Ste. 102
Irving, TX 75061
(972)986-6703

First Capital Group Management Co.
750 East Mulberry St., Ste. 305
PO Box 15616
San Antonio, TX 78212
(210)736-4233
Fax: (210)736-5449

The Southwest Venture Partnerships
16414 San Pedro, Ste. 345
San Antonio, TX 78232
(210)402-1200
Fax: (210)402-1221
E-mail: swvp@aol.com

Medtech International Inc.
1742 Carriageway
Sugarland, TX 77478
(713)980-8474
Fax: (713)980-6343

Utah

First Security Business Investment Corp.
15 East 100 South, Ste. 100
Salt Lake City, UT 84111
(801)246-5737
Fax: (801)246-5740

Utah Ventures II, L.P.
423 Wakara Way, Ste. 206
Salt Lake City, UT 84108
(801)583-5922
Fax: (801)583-4105
Website: http://www.uven.com

Wasatch Venture Corp.
1 S. Main St., Ste. 1400
Salt Lake City, UT 84133
(801)524-8939

Fax: (801)524-8941
E-mail: mail@wasatchvc.com

Vermont

North Atlantic Capital Corp.
76 Saint Paul St., Ste. 600
Burlington, VT 05401
(802)658-7820
Fax: (802)658-5757
Website: http://www.north
atlanticcapital.com

Green Mountain Advisors Inc.
PO Box 1230
Quechee, VT 05059
(802)296-7800
Fax: (802)296-6012
Website: http://www.gmtcap.com

Virginia

Oxford Financial Services Corp.
Alexandria, VA 22314
(703)519-4900
Fax: (703)519-4910
E-mail: oxford133@aol.com

Continental SBIC
4141 N. Henderson Rd.
Arlington, VA 22203
(703)527-5200
Fax: (703)527-3700

Novak Biddle Venture Partners
1750 Tysons Blvd., Ste. 1190
McLean, VA 22102
(703)847-3770
Fax: (703)847-3771
E-mail: roger@novakbiddle.com
Website: http://www.novakbiddle.com

Spacevest
11911 Freedom Dr., Ste. 500
Reston, VA 20190
(703)904-9800
Fax: (703)904-0571
E-mail: spacevest@spacevest.com
Website: http://www.spacevest.com

Virginia Capital
1801 Libbie Ave., Ste. 201
Richmond, VA 23226
(804)648-4802
Fax: (804)648-4809
E-mail: webmaster@vacapital.com
Website: http://www.vacapital.com

Calvert Social Venture Partners
402 Maple Ave. W
Vienna, VA 22180

(703)255-4930
Fax: (703)255-4931
E-mail: calven2000@aol.com

Fairfax Partners
8000 Towers Crescent Dr., Ste. 940
Vienna, VA 22182
(703)847-9486
Fax: (703)847-0911

Global Internet Ventures
8150 Leesburg Pike, Ste. 1210
Vienna, VA 22182
(703)442-3300
Fax: (703)442-3388
Website: http://www.givinc.com

Walnut Capital Corp. (Vienna)
8000 Towers Crescent Dr., Ste. 1070
Vienna, VA 22182
(703)448-3771
Fax: (703)448-7751

Washington

Encompass Ventures
777 108th Ave. NE, Ste. 2300
Bellevue, WA 98004
(425)486-3900
Fax: (425)486-3901
E-mail: info@evpartners.com
Website: http://www.encom
passventures.com

Fluke Venture Partners
11400 SE Sixth St., Ste. 230
Bellevue, WA 98004
(425)453-4590
Fax: (425)453-4675
E-mail: gabelein@flukeventures.com
Website: http://www.flukeventures.com

Pacific Northwest Partners SBIC, L.P.
15352 SE 53rd St.
Bellevue, WA 98006
(425)455-9967
Fax: (425)455-9404

Materia Venture Associates, L.P.
3435 Carillon Pointe
Kirkland, WA 98033-7354
(425)822-4100
Fax: (425)827-4086

OVP Venture Partners (Kirkland)
2420 Carillon Pt.
Kirkland, WA 98033
(425)889-9192
Fax: (425)889-0152
E-mail: info@ovp.com
Website: http://www.ovp.com

Digital Partners
999 3rd Ave., Ste. 1610
Seattle, WA 98104
(206)405-3607
Fax: (206)405-3617
Website: http://www.digitalpartners.com

Frazier & Company
601 Union St., Ste. 3300
Seattle, WA 98101
(206)621-7200
Fax: (206)621-1848
E-mail: jon@frazierco.com

Kirlan Venture Capital, Inc.
221 First Ave. W, Ste. 108
Seattle, WA 98119-4223
(206)281-8610
Fax: (206)285-3451
Website: http://www.kirlanventure.com

Phoenix Partners
1000 2nd Ave., Ste. 3600
Seattle, WA 98104
(206)624-8968
Fax: (206)624-1907

Voyager Capital
800 5th St., Ste. 4100
Seattle, WA 98103
(206)470-1180
Fax: (206)470-1185
E-mail: info@voyagercap.com
Website: http://www.voyagercap.com

Northwest Venture Associates
221 N. Wall St., Ste. 628
Spokane, WA 99201
(509)747-0728
Fax: (509)747-0758
Website: http://www.nwva.com

Wisconsin

Venture Investors Management, L.L.C.
University Research Park
505 S. Rosa Rd.
Madison, WI 53719
(608)441-2700
Fax: (608)441-2727
E-mail: roger@ventureinvestors.com
Website: http://www.venture
investers.com

Capital Investments, Inc.
1009 West Glen Oaks Lane, Ste. 103
Mequon, WI 53092
(414)241-0303
Fax: (414)241-8451
Website: http://
www.capitalinvestmentsinc.com

Future Value Venture, Inc.
2745 N. Martin Luther King
Dr., Ste. 204
Milwaukee, WI 53212-2300
(414)264-2252
Fax: (414)264-2253
E-mail: fvventures@aol.com
William Beckett, President

Lubar and Co., Inc.
700 N. Water St., Ste. 1200
Milwaukee, WI 53202
(414)291-9000
Fax: (414)291-9061

GCI
20875 Crossroads Cir., Ste. 100
Waukesha, WI 53186
(262)798-5080
Fax: (262)798-5087

Glossary of Small Business Terms

Absolute liability
Liability that is incurred due to product defects or negligent actions. Manufacturers or retail establishments are held responsible, even though the defect or action may not have been intentional or negligent.

ACE
See Active Corps of Executives

Accident and health benefits
Benefits offered to employees and their families in order to offset the costs associated with accidental death, accidental injury, or sickness.

Account statement
A record of transactions, including payments, new debt, and deposits, incurred during a defined period of time.

Accounting system
System capturing the costs of all employees and/or machinery included in business expenses.

Accounts payable
See Trade credit

Accounts receivable
Unpaid accounts which arise from unsettled claims and transactions from the sale of a company's products or services to its customers.

Active Corps of Executives (ACE)
A group of volunteers for a management assistance program of the U.S. Small Business Administration; volunteers provide one-on-one counseling and teach workshops and seminars for small firms.

ADA
See Americans with Disabilities Act

Adaptation
The process whereby an invention is modified to meet the needs of users.

Adaptive engineering
The process whereby an invention is modified to meet the manufacturing and commercial requirements of a targeted market.

Adverse selection
The tendency for higher-risk individuals to purchase health care and more comprehensive plans, resulting in increased costs.

Advertising
A marketing tool used to capture public attention and influence purchasing decisions for a product or service. Utilizes various forms of media to generate consumer response, such as flyers, magazines, newspapers, radio, and television.

Age discrimination
The denial of the rights and privileges of employment based solely on the age of an individual.

Agency costs
Costs incurred to insure that the lender or investor maintains control over assets while allowing the borrower or entrepreneur to use them. Monitoring and information costs are the two major types of agency costs.

Agribusiness
The production and sale of commodities and products from the commercial farming industry.

America Online
An online service which is accessible by computer modem. The service features Internet access, bulletin boards, online periodicals, electronic mail, and other services for subscribers.

Americans with Disabilities Act (ADA)
Law designed to ensure equal access and opportunity to handicapped persons.

Annual report
Yearly financial report prepared by a business that adheres to the requirements set forth by the Securities and Exchange Commission (SEC).

Antitrust immunity
Exemption from prosecution under antitrust laws. In the transportation industry, firms with antitrust immunity are permitted under certain conditions to set schedules and sometimes prices for the public benefit.

Applied research
Scientific study targeted for use in a product or process.

Asians
A minority category used by the U.S. Bureau of the Census to represent a diverse group that includes Aleuts, Eskimos, American Indians, Asian Indians, Chinese, Japanese, Koreans, Vietnamese, Filipinos, Hawaiians, and other Pacific Islanders.

Assets
Anything of value owned by a company.

Audit
The verification of accounting records and business procedures conducted by an outside accounting service.

Average cost
Total production costs divided by the quantity produced.

Balance Sheet
A financial statement listing the total assets and liabilities of a company at a given time.

Bankruptcy
The condition in which a business cannot meet its debt obligations and petitions a federal district court either for reorganization of its debts (Chapter 11) or for liquidation of its assets (Chapter 7).

Basic research
Theoretical scientific exploration not targeted to application.

Basket clause
A provision specifying the amount of public pension funds that may be placed in investments not included on a state's legal list (see separate citation).

BBS
See Bulletin Board Service

BDC
See Business development corporation

Benefit
Various services, such as health care, flextime, day care, insurance, and vacation, offered to employees as part of a hiring package. Typically subsidized in whole or in part by the business.

BIDCO
See Business and industrial development company

Billing cycle
A system designed to evenly distribute customer billing throughout the month, preventing clerical backlogs.

Birth
See Business birth

Blue chip security
A low-risk, low-yield security representing an interest in a very stable company.

Blue sky laws
A general term that denotes various states' laws regulating securities.

Bond
A written instrument executed by a bidder or contractor (the principal) and a second party (the surety or sureties) to assure fulfillment of the principal's obligations to a third party (the obligee or government) identified in the bond. If the principal's obligations are not met, the bond assures payment to the extent stipulated of any loss sustained by the obligee.

Bonding requirements
Terms contained in a bond (see separate citation).

Bonus
An amount of money paid to an employee as a reward for achieving certain business goals or objectives.

Brainstorming
A group session where employees contribute their ideas for solving a problem or meeting a company objective without fear of retribution or ridicule.

Brand name
The part of a brand, trademark, or service mark that can be spoken. It can be a word, letter, or group of words or letters.

Bridge financing
A short-term loan made in expectation of intermediateterm or long-term financing. Can be used when a company plans to go public in the near future.

Broker
One who matches resources available for innovation with those who need them.

Budget
An estimate of the spending necessary to complete a project or offer a service in comparison to cash-on-hand and expected earnings for the coming year, with an emphasis on cost control.

Bulletin Board Service (BBS)
An online service enabling users to communicate with each other about specific topics.

Business and industrial development company (BIDCO)
A private, for-profit financing corporation chartered by the state to provide both equity and long-term debt capital to small business owners (see separate citations for equity and debt capital).

Business birth
The formation of a new establishment or enterprise. The appearance of a new establishment or enterprise in the Small Business Data Base (see separate citation).

Business conditions
Outside factors that can affect the financial performance of a business.

Business contractions
The number of establishments that have decreased in employment during a specified time.

Business cycle
A period of economic recession and recovery. These cycles vary in duration.

Business death
The voluntary or involuntary closure of a firm or establishment. The disappearance of an establishment or enterprise from the Small Business Data Base (see separate citation).

Business development corporation (BDC)
A business financing agency, usually composed of the financial institutions in an area or state, organized to assist in financing businesses unable to obtain assistance through normal channels; the risk is spread among various members of the business development corporation, and interest rates may vary somewhat from those charged by member institutions. A venture capital firm in which shares of ownership are publicly held and to which the Investment Act of 1940 applies.

Business dissolution
For enumeration purposes, the absence of a business that was present in the prior time period from any current record.

Business entry
See Business birth

Business ethics
Moral values and principles espoused by members of the business community as a guide to fair and honest business practices.

Business exit
See Business death

Business expansions
The number of establishments that added employees during a specified time.

Business failure
Closure of a business causing a loss to at least one creditor.

Business format franchising
The purchase of the name, trademark, and an ongoing business plan of the parent corporation or franchisor by the franchisee.

Business license
A legal authorization issued by municipal and state governments and required for business operations.

Business name
Enterprises must register their business names with local governments usually on a "doing business as" (DBA) form. (This name is sometimes referred to as a "fictional name.") The procedure is part of the business licensing process and prevents any other business from using that same name for a similar business in the same locality.

Business norms
See Financial ratios

Business permit
See Business license

Business plan
A document that spells out a company's expected course of action for a specified period, usually including a detailed listing and analysis of risks and uncertainties. For the small business, it should examine the proposed products, the market, the industry, the management policies, the marketing policies, production needs, and financial needs. Frequently, it is used as a prospectus for potential investors and lenders.

Business proposal
See Business plan

Business service firm
An establishment primarily engaged in rendering services to other business organizations on a fee or contract basis.

Business start
For enumeration purposes, a business with a name or similar designation that did not exist in a prior time period.

Cafeteria plan
See Flexible benefit plan

Capacity
Level of a firm's, industry's, or nation's output corresponding to full practical utilization of available resources.

Capital
Assets less liabilities, representing the ownership interest in a business. A stock of accumulated goods, especially at a specified time and in contrast to income received during a specified time period. Accumulated goods devoted to production. Accumulated possessions calculated to bring income.

Capital expenditure
Expenses incurred by a business for improvements that will depreciate over time.

Capital gain
The monetary difference between the purchase price and the selling price of capital. Capital gains are taxed at a rate of 28% by the federal government.

Capital intensity
The relative importance of capital in the production process, usually expressed as the ratio of capital to labor but also sometimes as the ratio of capital to output.

Capital resource
The equipment, facilities and labor used to create products and services.

Caribbean Basin Initiative
An interdisciplinary program to support commerce among the businesses in the nations of the Caribbean Basin and the United States. Agencies involved include: the Agency for International Development, the U.S. Small Business Administration, the International Trade Administration of the U.S. Department of Commerce, and various private sector groups.

Catastrophic care
Medical and other services for acute and long-term illnesses that cost more than insurance coverage limits or that cost the amount most families may be expected to pay with their own resources.

CDC
See Certified development corporation

CD-ROM
Compact disc with read-only memory used to store large amounts of digitized data.

Certified development corporation (CDC)
A local area or statewide corporation or authority (for profit or nonprofit) that packages U.S. Small Business Administration (SBA), bank, state, and/or private money into financial assistance for existing business capital improvements. The SBA holds the second lien on its maximum share of 40 percent involvement. Each state has at least one certified development corporation. This program is called the SBA 504 Program.

Certified lenders
Banks that participate in the SBA guaranteed loan program (see separate citation). Such banks must have a good track record with the U.S. Small Business Administration (SBA) and must agree to certain conditions set forth by the agency. In return, the SBA agrees to process any guaranteed loan application within three business days.

Champion
An advocate for the development of an innovation.

Channel of distribution
The means used to transport merchandise from the manufacturer to the consumer.

Chapter 7 of the 1978 Bankruptcy Act
Provides for a court-appointed trustee who is responsible for liquidating a company's assets in order to settle outstanding debts.

Chapter 11 of the 1978 Bankruptcy Act
Allows the business owners to retain control of the company while working with their creditors to reorganize their finances and establish better business practices to prevent liquidation of assets.

Closely held corporation
A corporation in which the shares are held by a few persons, usually officers, employees, or others close to the management; these shares are rarely offered to the public.

Code of Federal Regulations
Codification of general and permanent rules of the federal government published in the Federal Register.

Code sharing
See Computer code sharing

Coinsurance
Upon meeting the deductible payment, health insurance participants may be required to make additional health care cost-sharing payments. Coinsurance is a payment of a fixed percentage of the cost of each service; copayment is usually a fixed amount to be paid with each service.

Collateral
Securities, evidence of deposit, or other property pledged by a borrower to secure repayment of a loan.

Collective ratemaking
The establishment of uniform charges for services by a group of businesses in the same industry.

Commercial insurance plan
See Underwriting

Commercial loans
Short-term renewable loans used to finance specific capital needs of a business.

Commercialization
The final stage of the innovation process, including production and distribution.

Common stock
The most frequently used instrument for purchasing ownership in private or public companies. Common stock generally carries the right to vote on certain corporate actions and may pay dividends, although it rarely does in venture investments. In liquidation, common stockholders are the last to share in the proceeds from the sale of a corporation's assets; bondholders and preferred shareholders have priority. Common stock is often used in firstround start-up financing.

Community development corporation
A corporation established to develop economic programs for a community and, in most cases, to provide financial support for such development.

Competitor
A business whose product or service is marketed for the same purpose/use and to the same consumer group as the product or service of another.

Computer code sharing
An arrangement whereby flights of a regional airline are identified by the two-letter code of a major carrier in the computer reservation system to help direct passengers to new regional carriers.

Consignment
A merchandising agreement, usually referring to secondhand shops, where the dealer pays the owner of an item a percentage of the profit when the item is sold.

Consortium
A coalition of organizations such as banks and corporations for ventures requiring large capital resources.

Consultant
An individual that is paid by a business to provide advice and expertise in a particular area.

Consumer price index
A measure of the fluctuation in prices between two points in time.

Consumer research
Research conducted by a business to obtain information about existing or potential consumer markets.

Continuation coverage
Health coverage offered for a specified period of time to employees who leave their jobs and to their widows, divorced spouses, or dependents.

Contractions
See Business contractions

Convertible preferred stock
A class of stock that pays a reasonable dividend and is convertible into common stock (see separate citation). Generally the convertible feature may only be exercised after being held for a stated period of time. This arrangement is usually considered second-round financing when a company needs equity to maintain its cash flow.

Convertible securities
A feature of certain bonds, debentures, or preferred stocks that allows them to be exchanged by the owner for another class of securities at a future date and in accordance with any other terms of the issue.

Copayment
See Coinsurance

Copyright
A legal form of protection available to creators and authors to safeguard their works from unlawful use or claim of ownership by others. Copyrights may be acquired for works of art, sculpture, music, and published or unpublished manuscripts. All copyrights should be registered at the Copyright Office of the Library of Congress.

Corporate financial ratios
The relationship between key figures found in a company's financial statement expressed as a numeric value. Used to evaluate risk and company performance. Also known as Financial averages, Operating ratios, and Business ratios.

Corporation
A legal entity, chartered by a state or the federal government, recognized as a separate entity having its own rights, privileges, and liabilities distinct from those of its members.

Cost containment
Actions taken by employers and insurers to curtail rising health care costs; for example, increasing

employee cost sharing (see separate citation), requiring second opinions, or preadmission screening.

Cost sharing
The requirement that health care consumers contribute to their own medical care costs through deductibles and coinsurance (see separate citations). Cost sharing does not include the amounts paid in premiums. It is used to control utilization of services; for example, requiring a fixed amount to be paid with each health care service.

Cottage industry
Businesses based in the home in which the family members are the labor force and family-owned equipment is used to process the goods.

Credit Rating
A letter or number calculated by an organization (such as Dun & Bradstreet) to represent the ability and disposition of a business to meet its financial obligations.

Customer service
Various techniques used to ensure the satisfaction of a customer.

Cyclical peak
The upper turning point in a business cycle.

Cyclical trough
The lower turning point in a business cycle.

DBA
See Business name

Death
See Business death

Debenture
A certificate given as acknowledgment of a debt (see separate citation) secured by the general credit of the issuing corporation. A bond, usually without security, issued by a corporation and sometimes convertible to common stock.

Debt
Something owed by one person to another. Financing in which a company receives capital that must be repaid; no ownership is transferred.

Debt capital
Business financing that normally requires periodic interest payments and repayment of the principal within a specified time.

Debt financing
See Debt capital

Debt securities
Loans such as bonds and notes that provide a specified rate of return for a specified period of time.

Deductible
A set amount that an individual must pay before any benefits are received.

Demand shock absorbers
A term used to describe the role that some small firms play by expanding their output levels to accommodate a transient surge in demand.

Demographics
Statistics on various markets, including age, income, and education, used to target specific products or services to appropriate consumer groups.

Demonstration
Showing that a product or process has been modified sufficiently to meet the needs of users.

Deregulation
The lifting of government restrictions; for example, the lifting of government restrictions on the entry of new businesses, the expansion of services, and the setting of prices in particular industries.

Desktop Publishing
Using personal computers and specialized software to produce camera-ready copy for publications.

Disaster loans
Various types of physical and economic assistance available to individuals and businesses through the U.S. Small Business Administration (SBA). This is the only SBA loan program available for residential purposes.

Discrimination
The denial of the rights and privileges of employment based on factors such as age, race, religion, or gender.

Diseconomies of scale
The condition in which the costs of production increase faster than the volume of production.

Dissolution
See Business dissolution

Distribution
Delivering a product or process to the user.

Distributor
One who delivers merchandise to the user.

Diversified company
A company whose products and services are used by several different markets.

Doing business as (DBA)
See Business name

Dow Jones
An information services company that publishes the Wall Street Journal and other sources of financial information.

Dow Jones Industrial Average
An indicator of stock market performance.

Earned income
A tax term that refers to wages and salaries earned by the recipient, as opposed to monies earned through interest and dividends.

Economic efficiency
The use of productive resources to the fullest practical extent in the provision of the set of goods and services that is most preferred by purchasers in the economy.

Economic indicators
Statistics used to express the state of the economy. These include the length of the average work week, the rate of unemployment, and stock prices.

Economically disadvantaged
See Socially and economically disadvantaged

Economies of scale
See Scale economies

EEOC
See Equal Employment Opportunity Commission

8(a) Program
A program authorized by the Small Business Act that directs federal contracts to small businesses owned and

operated by socially and economically disadvantaged individuals.

Electronic mail (e-mail)
The electronic transmission of mail via phone lines.

E-mail
See Electronic mail

Employee leasing
A contract by which employers arrange to have their workers hired by a leasing company and then leased back to them for a management fee. The leasing company typically assumes the administrative burden of payroll and provides a benefit package to the workers.

Employee tenure
The length of time an employee works for a particular employer.

Employer identification number
The business equivalent of a social security number. Assigned by the U.S. Internal Revenue Service.

Enterprise
An aggregation of all establishments owned by a parent company. An enterprise may consist of a single, independent establishment or include subsidiaries and other branches under the same ownership and control.

Enterprise zone
A designated area, usually found in inner cities and other areas with significant unemployment, where businesses receive tax credits and other incentives to entice them to establish operations there.

Entrepreneur
A person who takes the risk of organizing and operating a new business venture.

Entry
See Business entry

Equal Employment Opportunity Commission (EEOC)
A federal agency that ensures nondiscrimination in the hiring and firing practices of a business.

Equal opportunity employer
An employer who adheres to the standards set by the Equal Employment Opportunity Commission (see separate citation).

Equity
The ownership interest. Financing in which partial or total ownership of a company is surrendered in exchange for capital. An investor's financial return comes from dividend payments and from growth in the net worth of the business.

Equity capital
See Equity; Equity midrisk venture capital

Equity financing
See Equity; Equity midrisk venture capital

Equity midrisk venture capital
An unsecured investment in a company. Usually a purchase of ownership interest in a company that occurs in the later stages of a company's development.

Equity partnership
A limited partnership arrangement for providing start-up and seed capital to businesses.

Equity securities
See Equity

Equity-type
Debt financing subordinated to conventional debt.

Establishment
A single-location business unit that may be independent (a single-establishment enterprise) or owned by a parent enterprise.

Establishment and Enterprise Microdata File
See U.S. Establishment and Enterprise Microdata File

Establishment birth
See Business birth

Establishment Longitudinal Microdata File
See U.S. Establishment Longitudinal Microdata File

Ethics
See Business ethics

Evaluation
Determining the potential success of translating an invention into a product or process.

Exit
See Business exit

Experience rating
See Underwriting

Export
A product sold outside of the country.

Export license
A general or specific license granted by the U.S. Department of Commerce required of anyone wishing to export goods. Some restricted articles need approval from the U.S. Departments of State, Defense, or Energy.

Failure
See Business failure

Fair share agreement
An agreement reached between a franchisor and a minority business organization to extend business ownership to minorities by either reducing the amount of capital required or by setting aside certain marketing areas for minority business owners.

Feasibility study
A study to determine the likelihood that a proposed product or development will fulfill the objectives of a particular investor.

Federal Trade Commission (FTC)
Federal agency that promotes free enterprise and competition within the U.S.

Federal Trade Mark Act of 1946
See Lanham Act

Fictional name
See Business name

Fiduciary
An individual or group that hold assets in trust for a beneficiary.

Financial analysis
The techniques used to determine money needs in a business. Techniques include ratio analysis, calculation of return on investment, guides for measuring profitability, and break-even analysis to determine ultimate success.

Financial intermediary
A financial institution that acts as the intermediary between borrowers and lenders. Banks, savings and loan associations, finance companies, and venture capital companies are major financial intermediaries in the United States.

Financial ratios
See Corporate financial ratios; Industry financial ratios

Financial statement
A written record of business finances, including balance sheets and profit and loss statements.

Financing
See First-stage financing; Second-stage financing; Thirdstage financing

First-stage financing
Financing provided to companies that have expended their initial capital, and require funds to start full-scale manufacturing and sales. Also known as First-round financing.

Fiscal year
Any twelve-month period used by businesses for accounting purposes.

504 Program
See Certified development corporation

Flexible benefit plan
A plan that offers a choice among cash and/or qualified benefits such as group term life insurance, accident and health insurance, group legal services, dependent care assistance, and vacations.

FOB
See Free on board

Format franchising
See Business format franchising; Franchising

401(k) plan
A financial plan where employees contribute a percentage of their earnings to a fund that is invested in stocks, bonds, or money markets for the purpose of saving money for retirement.

Four Ps
Marketing terms referring to Product, Price, Place, and Promotion.

Franchising
A form of licensing by which the owner-the franchisor- distributes or markets a product, method, or service through affiliated dealers called franchisees. The product, method, or service being marketed is identified by a brand name, and the franchisor

maintains control over the marketing methods employed. The franchisee is often given exclusive access to a defined geographic area.

Free on board (FOB)
A pricing term indicating that the quoted price includes the cost of loading goods into transport vessels at a specified place.

Frictional unemployment
See Unemployment

FTC
See Federal Trade Commission

Fulfillment
The systems necessary for accurate delivery of an ordered item, including subscriptions and direct marketing.

Full-time workers
Generally, those who work a regular schedule of more than 35 hours per week.

Garment registration number
A number that must appear on every garment sold in the U.S. to indicate the manufacturer of the garment, which may or may not be the same as the label under which the garment is sold. The U.S. Federal Trade Commission assigns and regulates garment registration numbers.

Gatekeeper
A key contact point for entry into a network.

GDP
See Gross domestic product

General obligation bond
A municipal bond secured by the taxing power of the municipality. The Tax Reform Act of 1986 limits the purposes for which such bonds may be issued and establishes volume limits on the extent of their issuance.

GNP
See Gross national product

Good Housekeeping Seal
Seal appearing on products that signifies the fulfillment of the standards set by the Good Housekeeping Institute to protect consumer interests.

Goods sector
All businesses producing tangible goods, including agriculture, mining, construction, and manufacturing businesses.

GPO
See Gross product originating

Gross domestic product (GDP)
The part of the nation's gross national product (see separate citation) generated by private business using resources from within the country.

Gross national product (GNP)
The most comprehensive single measure of aggregate economic output. Represents the market value of the total output of goods and services produced by a nation's economy.

Gross product originating (GPO)
A measure of business output estimated from the income or production side using employee compensation, profit income, net interest, capital consumption, and indirect business taxes.

HAL
See Handicapped assistance loan program

Handicapped assistance loan program (HAL)
Low-interest direct loan program through the U.S. Small Business Administration (SBA) for handicapped persons. The SBA requires that these persons demonstrate that their disability is such that it is impossible for them to secure employment, thus making it necessary to go into their own business to make a living.

Health maintenance organization (HMO)
Organization of physicians and other health care professionals that provides health services to subscribers and their dependents on a prepaid basis.

Health provider
An individual or institution that gives medical care. Under Medicare, an institutional provider is a hospital, skilled nursing facility, home health agency, or provider of certain physical therapy services.

Hispanic
A person of Cuban, Mexican, Puerto Rican, Latin American (Central or South American), European Spanish, or other Spanish-speaking origin or ancestry.

HMO
See Health maintenance organization

Home-based business
A business with an operating address that is also a residential address (usually the residential address of the proprietor).

Hub-and-spoke system
A system in which flights of an airline from many different cities (the spokes) converge at a single airport (the hub). After allowing passengers sufficient time to make connections, planes then depart for different cities.

Human Resources Management
A business program designed to oversee recruiting, pay, benefits, and other issues related to the company's work force, including planning to determine the optimal use of labor to increase production, thereby increasing profit.

Idea
An original concept for a new product or process.

Import
Products produced outside the country in which they are consumed.

Income
Money or its equivalent, earned or accrued, resulting from the sale of goods and services.

Income statement
A financial statement that lists the profits and losses of a company at a given time.

Incorporation
The filing of a certificate of incorporation with a state's secretary of state, thereby limiting the business owner's liability.

Incubator
A facility designed to encourage entrepreneurship and minimize obstacles to new business formation and growth, particularly for high-technology firms, by housing a number of fledgling enterprises that share an array of services, such as meeting areas, secretarial services, accounting, research library, on-site financial and management counseling, and word processing facilities.

Independent contractor
An individual considered self-employed (see separate citation) and responsible for paying Social Security taxes and income taxes on earnings.

Indirect health coverage
Health insurance obtained through another individual's health care plan; for example, a spouse's employersponsored plan.

Industrial development authority
The financial arm of a state or other political subdivision established for the purpose of financing economic development in an area, usually through loans to nonprofit organizations, which in turn provide facilities for manufacturing and other industrial operations.

Industry financial ratios
Corporate financial ratios averaged for a specified industry. These are used for comparison purposes and reveal industry trends and identify differences between the performance of a specific company and the performance of its industry. Also known as Industrial averages, Industry ratios, Financial averages, and Business or Industrial norms.

Inflation
Increases in volume of currency and credit, generally resulting in a sharp and continuing rise in price levels.

Informal capital
Financing from informal, unorganized sources; includes informal debt capital such as trade credit or loans from friends and relatives and equity capital from informal investors.

Initial public offering (IPO)
A corporation's first offering of stock to the public.

Innovation
The introduction of a new idea into the marketplace in the form of a new product or service or an improvement in organization or process.

Intellectual property
Any idea or work that can be considered proprietary in nature and is thus protected from infringement by others.

Internal capital
Debt or equity financing obtained from the owner or through retained business earnings.

Internet
A government-designed computer network that contains large amounts of information and is accessible through various vendors for a fee.

Intrapreneurship
The state of employing entrepreneurial principles to nonentrepreneurial situations.

Invention
The tangible form of a technological idea, which could include a laboratory prototype, drawings, formulas, etc.

IPO
See Initial public offering

Job description
The duties and responsibilities required in a particular position.

Job tenure
A period of time during which an individual is continuously employed in the same job.

Joint marketing agreements
Agreements between regional and major airlines, often involving the coordination of flight schedules, fares, and baggage transfer. These agreements help regional carriers operate at lower cost.

Joint venture
Venture in which two or more people combine efforts in a particular business enterprise, usually a single transaction or a limited activity, and agree to share the profits and losses jointly or in proportion to their contributions.

Keogh plan
Designed for self-employed persons and unincorporated businesses as a tax-deferred pension account.

Labor force
Civilians considered eligible for employment who are also willing and able to work.

Labor force participation rate
The civilian labor force as a percentage of the civilian population.

Labor intensity
The relative importance of labor in the production process, usually measured as the capital-labor ratio; i.e., the ratio of units of capital (typically, dollars of tangible assets) to the number of employees. The higher the capital-labor ratio exhibited by a firm or industry, the lower the capital intensity of that firm or industry is said to be.

Labor surplus area
An area in which there exists a high unemployment rate. In procurement (see separate citation), extra points are given to firms in counties that are designated a labor surplus area; this information is requested on procurement bid sheets.

Labor union
An organization of similarly-skilled workers who collectively bargain with management over the conditions of employment.

Laboratory prototype
See Prototype

LAN
See Local Area Network

Lanham Act
Refers to the Federal Trade Mark Act of 1946. Protects registered trademarks, trade names, and other service marks used in commerce.

Large business-dominated industry
Industry in which a minimum of 60 percent of employment or sales is in firms with more than 500 workers.

LBO
See Leveraged buy-out

Leader pricing
A reduction in the price of a good or service in order to generate more sales of that good or service.

Legal list
A list of securities selected by a state in which certain institutions and fiduciaries (such as pension funds, insurance companies, and banks) may invest. Securities not on the list are not eligible for investment. Legal lists typically restrict investments to high quality securities meeting certain specifications. Generally, investment is

limited to U.S. securities and investment-grade blue chip securities (see separate citation).

Leveraged buy-out (LBO)
The purchase of a business or a division of a corporation through a highly leveraged financing package.

Liability
An obligation or duty to perform a service or an act. Also defined as money owed.

License
A legal agreement granting to another the right to use a technological innovation.

Limited partnerships
See Venture capital limited partnerships

Liquidity
The ability to convert a security into cash promptly.

Loans
See Commercial loans; Disaster loans; SBA direct loans; SBA guaranteed loans; SBA special lending institution categories Local Area Network (LAN) Computer networks contained within a single building or small area; used to facilitate the sharing of information.

Local development corporation
An organization, usually made up of local citizens of a community, designed to improve the economy of the area by inducing business and industry to locate and expand there. A local development corporation establishes a capability to finance local growth.

Long-haul rates
Rates charged by a transporter in which the distance traveled is more than 800 miles.

Long-term debt
An obligation that matures in a period that exceeds five years.

Low-grade bond
A corporate bond that is rated below investment grade by the major rating agencies (Standard and Poor's, Moody's).

Macro-efficiency
Efficiency as it pertains to the operation of markets and market systems.

Managed care
A cost-effective health care program initiated by employers whereby low-cost health care is made available to the employees in return for exclusive patronage to program doctors.

Management Assistance Programs
See SBA Management Assistance Programs

Management and technical assistance
A term used by many programs to mean business (as opposed to technological) assistance.

Mandated benefits
Specific treatments, providers, or individuals required by law to be included in commercial health plans.

Market evaluation
The use of market information to determine the sales potential of a specific product or process.

Market failure
The situation in which the workings of a competitive market do not produce the best results from the point of view of the entire society.

Market information
Data of any type that can be used for market evaluation, which could include demographic data, technology forecasting, regulatory changes, etc.

Market research
A systematic collection, analysis, and reporting of data about the market and its preferences, opinions, trends, and plans; used for corporate decision-making.

Market share
In a particular market, the percentage of sales of a specific product.

Marketing
Promotion of goods or services through various media.

Master Establishment List (MEL)
A list of firms in the United States developed by the U.S. Small Business Administration; firms can be selected by industry, region, state, standard metropolitan statistical area (see separate citation), county, and zip code.

Maturity
The date upon which the principal or stated value of a bond or other indebtedness becomes due and payable.

Medicaid (Title XIX)
A federally aided, state-operated and administered program that provides medical benefits for certain low income persons in need of health and medical care who are eligible for one of the government's welfare cash payment programs, including the aged, the blind, the disabled, and members of families with dependent children where one parent is absent, incapacitated, or unemployed.

Medicare (Title XVIII)
A nationwide health insurance program for disabled and aged persons. Health insurance is available to insured persons without regard to income. Monies from payroll taxes cover hospital insurance and monies from general revenues and beneficiary premiums pay for supplementary medical insurance.

MEL
See Master Establishment List

MESBIC
See Minority enterprise small business investment corporation

MET
See Multiple employer trust

Metropolitan statistical area (MSA)
A means used by the government to define large population centers that may transverse different governmental jurisdictions. For example, the Washington, D.C. MSA includes the District of Columbia and contiguous parts of Maryland and Virginia because all of these geopolitical areas comprise one population and economic operating unit.

Mezzanine financing
See Third-stage financing

Micro-efficiency
Efficiency as it pertains to the operation of individual firms.

Microdata
Information on the characteristics of an individual business firm.

Mid-term debt
An obligation that matures within one to five years.

Midrisk venture capital
See Equity midrisk venture capital

Minimum premium plan
A combination approach to funding an insurance plan aimed primarily at premium tax savings. The employer self-funds a fixed percentage of estimated monthly claims and the insurance company insures the excess.

Minimum wage
The lowest hourly wage allowed by the federal government.

Minority Business Development Agency
Contracts with private firms throughout the nation to sponsor Minority Business Development Centers which provide minority firms with advice and technical assistance on a fee basis.

Minority Enterprise Small Business Investment Corporation (MESBIC)
A federally funded private venture capital firm licensed by the U.S. Small Business Administration to provide capital to minority-owned businesses (see separate citation).

Minority-owned business
Businesses owned by those who are socially or economically disadvantaged (see separate citation).

Mom and Pop business
A small store or enterprise having limited capital, principally employing family members.

Moonlighter
A wage-and-salary worker with a side business.

MSA
See Metropolitan statistical area

Multi-employer plan
A health plan to which more than one employer is required to contribute and that may be maintained through a collective bargaining agreement and required to meet standards prescribed by the U.S. Department of Labor.

Multi-level marketing
A system of selling in which you sign up other people to assist you and they, in turn, recruit others to help them. Some entrepreneurs have built successful

companies on this concept because the main focus of their activities is their product and product sales.

Multimedia
The use of several types of media to promote a product or service. Also, refers to the use of several different types of media (sight, sound, pictures, text) in a CD-ROM (see separate citation) product.

Multiple employer trust (MET)
A self-funded benefit plan generally geared toward small employers sharing a common interest.

NAFTA
See North American Free Trade Agreement

NASDAQ
See National Association of Securities Dealers Automated Quotations

National Association of Securities Dealers Automated Quotations
Provides price quotes on over-the-counter securities as well as securities listed on the New York Stock Exchange.

National income
Aggregate earnings of labor and property arising from the production of goods and services in a nation's economy.

Net assets
See Net worth

Net income
The amount remaining from earnings and profits after all expenses and costs have been met or deducted. Also known as Net earnings.

Net profit
Money earned after production and overhead expenses (see separate citations) have been deducted.

Net worth
The difference between a company's total assets and its total liabilities.

Network
A chain of interconnected individuals or organizations sharing information and/or services.

New York Stock Exchange (NYSE)
The oldest stock exchange in the U.S. Allows for trading in stocks, bonds, warrants, options, and rights that meet listing requirements.

Niche
A career or business for which a person is well-suited. Also, a product which fulfills one need of a particular market segment, often with little or no competition.

Nodes
One workstation in a network, either local area or wide area (see separate citations).

Nonbank bank
A bank that either accepts deposits or makes loans, but not both. Used to create many new branch banks.

Noncompetitive awards
A method of contracting whereby the federal government negotiates with only one contractor to supply a product or service.

Nonmember bank
A state-regulated bank that does not belong to the federal bank system.

Nonprofit
An organization that has no shareholders, does not distribute profits, and is without federal and state tax liabilities.

Norms
See Financial ratios

North American Free Trade Agreement (NAFTA)
Passed in 1993, NAFTA eliminates trade barriers among businesses in the U.S., Canada, and Mexico.

NYSE
See New York Stock Exchange

Occupational Safety & Health Administration (OSHA)
Federal agency that regulates health and safety standards within the workplace.

Optimal firm size
The business size at which the production cost per unit of output (average cost) is, in the long run, at its minimum.

Glossary

Organizational chart
A hierarchical chart tracking the chain of command within an organization.

OSHA
See Occupational Safety & Health Administration

Overhead
Expenses, such as employee benefits and building utilities, incurred by a business that are unrelated to the actual product or service sold.

Owner's capital
Debt or equity funds provided by the owner(s) of a business; sources of owner's capital are personal savings, sales of assets, or loans from financial institutions.

P & L
See Profit and loss statement

Part-time workers
Normally, those who work less than 35 hours per week. The Tax Reform Act indicated that part-time workers who work less than 17.5 hours per week may be excluded from health plans for purposes of complying with federal nondiscrimination rules.

Part-year workers
Those who work less than 50 weeks per year.

Partnership
Two or more parties who enter into a legal relationship to conduct business for profit. Defined by the U.S. Internal Revenue Code as joint ventures, syndicates, groups, pools, and other associations of two or more persons organized for profit that are not specifically classified in the IRS code as corporations or proprietorships.

Patent
A grant made by the government assuring an inventor the sole right to make, use, and sell an invention for a period of 17 years.

PC
See Professional corporation

Peak
See Cyclical peak

Pension
A series of payments made monthly, semiannually, annually, or at other specified intervals during the lifetime of the pensioner for distribution upon retirement. The term is sometimes used to denote the portion of the retirement allowance financed by the employer's contributions.

Pension fund
A fund established to provide for the payment of pension benefits; the collective contributions made by all of the parties to the pension plan.

Performance appraisal
An established set of objective criteria, based on job description and requirements, that is used to evaluate the performance of an employee in a specific job.

Permit
See Business license

Plan
See Business plan

Pooling
An arrangement for employers to achieve efficiencies and lower health costs by joining together to purchase group health insurance or self-insurance.

PPO
See Preferred provider organization

Preferred lenders program
See SBA special lending institution categories

Preferred provider organization (PPO)
A contractual arrangement with a health care services organization that agrees to discount its health care rates in return for faster payment and/or a patient base.

Premiums
The amount of money paid to an insurer for health insurance under a policy. The premium is generally paid periodically (e.g., monthly), and often is split between the employer and the employee. Unlike deductibles and coinsurance or copayments, premiums are paid for coverage whether or not benefits are actually used.

Prime-age workers
Employees 25 to 54 years of age.

Prime contract
A contract awarded directly by the U.S. Federal Government.

Private company
See Closely held corporation

Private placement
A method of raising capital by offering for sale an investment or business to a small group of investors (generally avoiding registration with the Securities and Exchange Commission or state securities registration agencies). Also known as Private financing or Private offering.

Pro forma
The use of hypothetical figures in financial statements to represent future expenditures, debts, and other potential financial expenses.

Proactive
Taking the initiative to solve problems and anticipate future events before they happen, instead of reacting to an already existing problem or waiting for a difficult situation to occur.

Procurement
A contract from an agency of the federal government for goods or services from a small business.

Prodigy
An online service which is accessible by computer modem. The service features Internet access, bulletin boards, online periodicals, electronic mail, and other services for subscribers.

Product development
The stage of the innovation process where research is translated into a product or process through evaluation, adaptation, and demonstration.

Product franchising
An arrangement for a franchisee to use the name and to produce the product line of the franchisor or parent corporation.

Production
The manufacture of a product.

Production prototype
See Prototype

Productivity
A measurement of the number of goods produced during a specific amount of time.

Professional corporation (PC)
Organized by members of a profession such as medicine, dentistry, or law for the purpose of conducting their professional activities as a corporation. Liability of a member or shareholder is limited in the same manner as in a business corporation.

Profit and loss statement (P & L)
The summary of the incomes (total revenues) and costs of a company's operation during a specific period of time. Also known as Income and expense statement.

Proposal
See Business plan

Proprietorship
The most common legal form of business ownership; about 85 percent of all small businesses are proprietorships. The liability of the owner is unlimited in this form of ownership.

Prospective payment system
A cost-containment measure included in the Social Security Amendments of 1983 whereby Medicare payments to hospitals are based on established prices, rather than on cost reimbursement.

Prototype
A model that demonstrates the validity of the concept of an invention (laboratory prototype); a model that meets the needs of the manufacturing process and the user (production prototype).

Prudent investor rule or standard
A legal doctrine that requires fiduciaries to make investments using the prudence, diligence, and intelligence that would be used by a prudent person in making similar investments. Because fiduciaries make investments on behalf of third-party beneficiaries, the standard results in very conservative investments. Until recently, most state regulations required the fiduciary to apply this standard to each investment. Newer, more progressive regulations permit fiduciaries to apply this standard to the portfolio taken as a whole, thereby allowing a fiduciary to balance a portfolio with higher-yield, higher-risk investments. In states with more progressive regulations, practically every type of security is eligible for inclusion in the portfolio of investments made by a fiduciary, provided

that the portfolio investments, in their totality, are those of a prudent person.

Public equity markets
Organized markets for trading in equity shares such as common stocks, preferred stocks, and warrants. Includes markets for both regularly traded and nonregularly traded securities.

Public offering
General solicitation for participation in an investment opportunity. Interstate public offerings are supervised by the U.S. Securities and Exchange Commission (see separate citation).

Quality control
The process by which a product is checked and tested to ensure consistent standards of high quality.

Rate of return
The yield obtained on a security or other investment based on its purchase price or its current market price. The total rate of return is current income plus or minus capital appreciation or depreciation.

Real property
Includes the land and all that is contained on it.

Realignment
See Resource realignment

Recession
Contraction of economic activity occurring between the peak and trough (see separate citations) of a business cycle.

Regulated market
A market in which the government controls the forces of supply and demand, such as who may enter and what price may be charged.

Regulation D
A vehicle by which small businesses make small offerings and private placements of securities with limited disclosure requirements. It was designed to ease the burdens imposed on small businesses utilizing this method of capital formation.

Regulatory Flexibility Act
An act requiring federal agencies to evaluate the impact of their regulations on small businesses before

the regulations are issued and to consider less burdensome alternatives.

Research
The initial stage of the innovation process, which includes idea generation and invention.

Research and development financing
A tax-advantaged partnership set up to finance product development for start-ups as well as more mature companies.

Resource mobility
The ease with which labor and capital move from firm to firm or from industry to industry.

Resource realignment
The adjustment of productive resources to interindustry changes in demand.

Resources
The sources of support or help in the innovation process, including sources of financing, technical evaluation, market evaluation, management and business assistance, etc.

Retained business earnings
Business profits that are retained by the business rather than being distributed to the shareholders as dividends.

Revolving credit
An agreement with a lending institution for an amount of money, which cannot exceed a set maximum, over a specified period of time. Each time the borrower repays a portion of the loan, the amount of the repayment may be borrowed yet again.

Risk capital
See Venture capital

Risk management
The act of identifying potential sources of financial loss and taking action to minimize their negative impact.

Routing
The sequence of steps necessary to complete a product during production.

S corporations
See Sub chapter S corporations

SBA
See Small Business Administration

SBA direct loans
Loans made directly by the U.S. Small Business Administration (SBA); monies come from funds appropriated specifically for this purpose. In general, SBA direct loans carry interest rates slightly lower than those in the private financial markets and are available only to applicants unable to secure private financing or an SBA guaranteed loan.

SBA 504 Program
See Certified development corporation

SBA guaranteed loans
Loans made by lending institutions in which the U.S. Small Business Administration (SBA) will pay a prior agreed-upon percentage of the outstanding principal in the event the borrower of the loan defaults. The terms of the loan and the interest rate are negotiated between theborrower and the lending institution, within set parameters.

SBA loans
See Disaster loans; SBA direct loans; SBA guaranteed loans; SBA special lending institution categories

SBA Management Assistance Programs
Classes, workshops, counseling, and publications offered by the U.S. Small Business Administration.

SBA special lending institution categories
U.S. Small Business Administration (SBA) loan program in which the SBA promises certified banks a 72-hour turnaround period in giving its approval for a loan, and in which preferred lenders in a pilot program are allowed to write SBA loans without seeking prior SBA approval.

SBDB
See Small Business Data Base

SBDC
See Small business development centers

SBI
See Small business institutes program

SBIC
See Small business investment corporation

SBIR Program
See Small Business Innovation Development Act of 1982

Scale economies
The decline of the production cost per unit of output (average cost) as the volume of output increases.

Scale efficiency
The reduction in unit cost available to a firm when producing at a higher output volume.

SCORE
See Service Corps of Retired Executives

SEC
See Securities and Exchange Commission

SECA
See Self-Employment Contributions Act

Second-stage financing
Working capital for the initial expansion of a company that is producing, shipping, and has growing accounts receivable and inventories. Also known as Second-round financing.

Secondary market
A market established for the purchase and sale of outstanding securities following their initial distribution.

Secondary worker
Any worker in a family other than the person who is the primary source of income for the family.

Secondhand capital
Previously used and subsequently resold capital equipment (e.g., buildings and machinery).

Securities and Exchange Commission (SEC)
Federal agency charged with regulating the trade of securities to prevent unethical practices in the investor market.

Securitized debt
A marketing technique that converts long-term loans to marketable securities.

Seed capital
Venture financing provided in the early stages of the innovation process, usually during product development.

Glossary

Self-employed person
One who works for a profit or fees in his or her own business, profession, or trade, or who operates a farm.

Self-Employment Contributions Act (SECA)
Federal law that governs the self-employment tax (see separate citation).

Self-employment income
Income covered by Social Security if a business earns a net income of at least $400.00 during the year. Taxes are paid on earnings that exceed $400.00.

Self-employment retirement plan
See Keogh plan

Self-employment tax
Required tax imposed on self-employed individuals for the provision of Social Security and Medicare. The tax must be paid quarterly with estimated income tax statements.

Self-funding
A health benefit plan in which a firm uses its own funds to pay claims, rather than transferring the financial risks of paying claims to an outside insurer in exchange for premium payments.

Service Corps of Retired Executives (SCORE)
Volunteers for the SBA Management Assistance Program who provide one-on-one counseling and teach workshops and seminars for small firms.

Service firm
See Business service firm

Service sector
Broadly defined, all U.S. industries that produce intangibles, including the five major industry divisions of transportation, communications, and utilities; wholesale trade; retail trade; finance, insurance, and real estate; and services.

Set asides
See Small business set asides

Short-haul service
A type of transportation service in which the transporter supplies service between cities where the maximum distance is no more than 200 miles.

Short-term debt
An obligation that matures in one year.

SIC codes
See Standard Industrial Classification codes

Single-establishment enterprise
See Establishment

Small business
An enterprise that is independently owned and operated, is not dominant in its field, and employs fewer than 500 people. For SBA purposes, the U.S. Small Business Administration (SBA) considers various other factors (such as gross annual sales) in determining size of a business.

Small Business Administration (SBA)
An independent federal agency that provides assistance with loans, management, and advocating interests before other federal agencies.

Small Business Data Base
A collection of microdata (see separate citation) files on individual firms developed and maintained by the U.S. Small Business Administration.

Small business development centers (SBDC)
Centers that provide support services to small businesses, such as individual counseling, SBA advice, seminars and conferences, and other learning center activities. Most services are free of charge, or available at minimal cost.

Small business development corporation
See Certified development corporation

Small business-dominated industry
Industry in which a minimum of 60 percent of employment or sales is in firms with fewer than 500 employees.

Small Business Innovation Development Act of 1982
Federal statute requiring federal agencies with large extramural research and development budgets to allocate a certain percentage of these funds to small research and development firms. The program, called the Small Business Innovation Research (SBIR) Program, is designed to stimulate technological innovation and make greater use of small businesses in meeting national innovation needs.

Small business institutes (SBI) program
Cooperative arrangements made by U.S. Small Business Administration district offices and local colleges and

universities to provide small business firms with graduate students to counsel them without charge.

Small business investment corporation (SBIC)
A privately owned company licensed and funded through the U.S. Small Business Administration and private sector sources to provide equity or debt capital to small businesses.

Small business set asides
Procurement (see separate citation) opportunities required by law to be on all contracts under $10,000 or a certain percentage of an agency's total procurement expenditure.

Smaller firms
For U.S. Department of Commerce purposes, those firms not included in the Fortune 1000.

SMSA
See Metropolitan statistical area

Socially and economically disadvantaged
Individuals who have been subjected to racial or ethnic prejudice or cultural bias without regard to their qualities as individuals, and whose abilities to compete are impaired because of diminished opportunities to obtain capital and credit.

Sole proprietorship
An unincorporated, one-owner business, farm, or professional practice.

Special lending institution categories
See SBA special lending institution categories

Standard Industrial Classification (SIC) codes
Four-digit codes established by the U.S. Federal Government to categorize businesses by type of economic activity; the first two digits correspond to major groups such as construction and manufacturing, while the last two digits correspond to subgroups such as home construction or highway construction.

Standard metropolitan statistical area (SMSA)
See Metropolitan statistical area

Start-up
A new business, at the earliest stages of development and financing.

Start-up costs
Costs incurred before a business can commence operations.

Start-up financing
Financing provided to companies that have either completed product development and initial marketing or have been in business for less than one year but have not yet sold their product commercially.

Stock
A certificate of equity ownership in a business.

Stop-loss coverage
Insurance for a self-insured plan that reimburses the company for any losses it might incur in its health claims beyond a specified amount.

Strategic planning
Projected growth and development of a business to establish a guiding direction for the future. Also used to determine which market segments to explore for optimal sales of products or services.

Structural unemployment
See Unemployment

Sub chapter S corporations
Corporations that are considered noncorporate for tax purposes but legally remain corporations.

Subcontract
A contract between a prime contractor and a subcontractor, or between subcontractors, to furnish supplies or services for performance of a prime contract (see separate citation) or a subcontract.

Surety bonds
Bonds providing reimbursement to an individual, company, or the government if a firm fails to complete a contract. The U.S. Small Business Administration guarantees surety bonds in a program much like the SBA guaranteed loan program (see separate citation).

Swing loan
See Bridge financing

Target market
The clients or customers sought for a business' product or service.

Targeted Jobs Tax Credit
Federal legislation enacted in 1978 that provides a tax credit to an employer who hires structurally unemployed individuals.

Tax number
A number assigned to a business by a state revenue department that enables the business to buy goods without paying sales tax.

Taxable bonds
An interest-bearing certificate of public or private indebtedness. Bonds are issued by public agencies to finance economic development.

Technical assistance
See Management and technical assistance

Technical evaluation
Assessment of technological feasibility.

Technology
The method in which a firm combines and utilizes labor and capital resources to produce goods or services; the application of science for commercial or industrial purposes.

Technology transfer
The movement of information about a technology or intellectual property from one party to another for use.

Tenure
See Employee tenure

Term
The length of time for which a loan is made.

Terms of a note
The conditions or limits of a note; includes the interest rate per annum, the due date, and transferability and convertibility features, if any.

Third-party administrator
An outside company responsible for handling claims and performing administrative tasks associated with health insurance plan maintenance.

Third-stage financing
Financing provided for the major expansion of a company whose sales volume is increasing and that is breaking even or profitable. These funds are used for further plant expansion, marketing, working capital,

or development of an improved product. Also known as Third-round or Mezzanine financing.

Time deposit
A bank deposit that cannot be withdrawn before a specified future time.

Time management
Skills and scheduling techniques used to maximize productivity.

Trade credit
Credit extended by suppliers of raw materials or finished products. In an accounting statement, trade credit is referred to as "accounts payable."

Trade name
The name under which a company conducts business, or by which its business, goods, or services are identified. It may or may not be registered as a trademark.

Trade periodical
A publication with a specific focus on one or more aspects of business and industry.

Trade secret
Competitive advantage gained by a business through the use of a unique manufacturing process or formula.

Trade show
An exhibition of goods or services used in a particular industry. Typically held in exhibition centers where exhibitors rent space to display their merchandise.

Trademark
A graphic symbol, device, or slogan that identifies a business. A business has property rights to its trademark from the inception of its use, but it is still prudent to register all trademarks with the Trademark Office of the U.S. Department of Commerce.

Translation
See Product development

Treasury bills
Investment tender issued by the Federal Reserve Bank in amounts of $10,000 that mature in 91 to 182 days.

Treasury bonds
Long-term notes with maturity dates of not less than seven and not more than twenty-five years.

Treasury notes
Short-term notes maturing in less than seven years.

Trend
A statistical measurement used to track changes that occur over time.

Trough
See Cyclical trough

UCC
See Uniform Commercial Code

UL
See Underwriters Laboratories

Underwriters Laboratories (UL)
One of several private firms that tests products and processes to determine their safety. Although various firms can provide this kind of testing service, many local and insurance codes specify UL certification.

Underwriting
A process by which an insurer determines whether or not and on what basis it will accept an application for insurance. In an experience-rated plan, premiums are based on a firm's or group's past claims; factors other than prior claims are used for community-rated or manually rated plans.

Unfair competition
Refers to business practices, usually unethical, such as using unlicensed products, pirating merchandise, or misleading the public through false advertising, which give the offending business an unequitable advantage over others.

Unfunded accrued liability
The excess of total liabilities, both present and prospective, over present and prospective assets.

Unemployment
The joblessness of individuals who are willing to work, who are legally and physically able to work, and who are seeking work. Unemployment may represent the temporary joblessness of a worker between jobs (frictional unemployment) or the joblessness of a worker whose skills are not suitable for jobs available in the labor market (structural unemployment).

Uniform Commercial Code (UCC)
A code of laws governing commercial transactions across the U.S., except Louisiana. Their purpose is to bring uniformity to financial transactions.

Uniform product code (UPC symbol)
A computer-readable label comprised of ten digits and stripes that encodes what a product is and how much it costs. The first five digits are assigned by the Uniform Product Code Council, and the last five digits by the individual manufacturer.

Unit cost
See Average cost

UPC symbol
See Uniform product code

U.S. Establishment and Enterprise Microdata (USEEM) File
A cross-sectional database containing information on employment, sales, and location for individual enterprises and establishments with employees that have a Dun & Bradstreet credit rating.

U.S. Establishment Longitudinal Microdata (USELM) File
A database containing longitudinally linked sample microdata on establishments drawn from the U.S. Establishment and Enterprise Microdata file (see separate citation).

U.S. Small Business Administration 504 Program
See Certified development corporation

USEEM
See U.S. Establishment and Enterprise Microdata File

USELM
See U.S. Establishment Longitudinal Microdata File

VCN
See Venture capital network

Venture capital
Money used to support new or unusual business ventures that exhibit above-average growth rates, significant potential for market expansion, and are in need of additional financing to sustain growth or further research and development; equity or equity-type financing traditionally provided at the

commercialization stage, increasingly available prior to commercialization.

Venture capital company

A company organized to provide seed capital to a business in its formation stage, or in its first or second stage of expansion. Funding is obtained through public or private pension funds, commercial banks and bank holding companies, small business investment corporations licensed by the U.S. Small Business Administration, private venture capital firms, insurance companies, investment management companies, bank trust departments, industrial companies seeking to diversify their investment, and investment bankers acting as intermediaries for other investors or directly investing on their own behalf.

Venture capital limited partnerships

Designed for business development, these partnerships are an institutional mechanism for providing capital for young, technology-oriented businesses. The investors' money is pooled and invested in money market assets until venture investments have been selected. The general partners are experienced investment managers who select and invest the equity and debt securities of firms with high growth potential and the ability to go public in the near future.

Venture capital network (VCN)

A computer database that matches investors with entrepreneurs.

WAN

See Wide Area Network

Wide Area Network (WAN)

Computer networks linking systems throughout a state or around the world in order to facilitate the sharing of information.

Withholding

Federal, state, social security, and unemployment taxes withheld by the employer from employees' wages; employers are liable for these taxes and the corporate umbrella and bankruptcy will not exonerate an employer from paying back payroll withholding. Employers should escrow these funds in a separate account and disperse them quarterly to withholding authorities.

Workers' compensation

A state-mandated form of insurance covering workers injured in job-related accidents. In some states, the state is the insurer; in other states, insurance must be acquired from commercial insurance firms. Insurance rates are based on a number of factors, including salaries, firm history, and risk of occupation.

Working capital

Refers to a firm's short-term investment of current assets, including cash, short-term securities, accounts receivable, and inventories.

Yield

The rate of income returned on an investment, expressed as a percentage. Income yield is obtained by dividing the current dollar income by the current market price of the security. Net yield or yield to maturity is the current income yield minus any premium above par or plus any discount from par in purchase price, with the adjustment spread over the period from the date of purchase to the date of maturity.

Index

Listings in this index are arranged alphabetically by business plan type, then alphabetically by business plan name. Users are provided with the volume number in which the plan appears.

Index